Continued on next page

CLARENDON LAW SERIES

Law in Modern Society
DENIS GALLIGAN

Land Law
ELIZABETH COOKE

Philosophy of Private Law
WILLIAM LUCY

Policies and Perceptions of Insurance
Law in the Twenty-First Century
MALCOLM CLARKE

Civil Liberties
CONOR GEARTY

Intellectual Property
MICHAEL SPENCE

INTERNATIONAL LAW

VAUGHAN LOWE

Chichele Professor of Public International Law at the University of
Oxford, and Fellow of All Souls College

OXFORD
UNIVERSITY PRESS

OXFORD
UNIVERSITY PRESS

Great Clarendon Street, Oxford OX2 6DP

Oxford University Press is a department of the University of Oxford.
It furthers the University's objective of excellence in research, scholarship,
and education by publishing worldwide in

Oxford New York

Auckland Cape Town Dar es Salaam Hong Kong Karachi
Kuala Lumpur Madrid Melbourne Mexico City Nairobi
New Delhi Shanghai Taipei Toronto

With offices in

Argentina Austria Brazil Chile Czech Republic France Greece
Guatemala Hungary Italy Japan Poland Portugal Singapore
South Korea Switzerland Thailand Turkey Ukraine Vietnam

Oxford is a registered trade mark of Oxford University Press
in the UK and in certain other countries

Published in the United States
by Oxford University Press Inc., New York

British Library Cataloguing in Publication Data

Data available

Library of Congress Cataloging-in-Publication Data
Lowe, A. V. (Alan Vaughan)
International law / Vaughan Lowe.
p. cm.—(Clarendon law series)
Includes bibliographical references and index.
ISBN 978–0–19–923083–9 (hardback : alk. paper)
ISBN 978–0–19–926884–9 (pbk. : alk. paper)
1. International law—History. I. Title.
KZ1242.L69 2007
341.09—dc22   2007034282

Typeset by Newgen Imaging Systems (P) Ltd, Chennai, India
Printed in Great Britain on acid-free paper
by the MPG Books Group,
Bodmin and King's Lynn

ISBN 978–0–19–923083–9 (Hbk)
ISBN 978–0–19–926884–9 (Pbk)

5 7 9 10 8 6 4

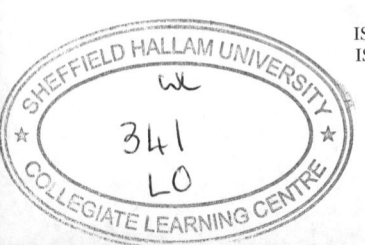

Preface

This book began its life as a successor to James Brierly's *Law of Nations*. That excellent book provided an introduction to international law of the kind that might be helpful for a student to read in the vacation before starting to study the subject, or for an interested lay reader. Largely shorn of footnotes and technical details, it offered an overview of the scope and principles of international law. I hope that this text does much the same.

I have largely eliminated footnote references that can be found quickly and easily with Google. More readers are likely to be within reach of the Internet than within reach of a good law library. In particular, I have excised the references to the scores of websites maintained by the various international organizations and treaty secretariats mentioned in this book. Those websites are, however, invaluable to the novice and the specialist alike for their gentle introductions to the relevant field and their up-to-date information.

I must thank John Louth of OUP for his support for this and a huge range of other international law publishing projects. The text has been read in whole or in part by Sally Lowe, Jenny Hassan, and Guy Goodwin-Gill. I am grateful to them for drawing my attention to the distinction between material that it is enjoyable to write and material that it is enjoyable to read. Above all I am grateful to Sally for pointing out that my treatment of the subject of comparative advantage appears to ignore the fact that efficiency in work and production is not the only, nor the best, index of human happiness.

AVL
All Souls College, Oxford
29 May 2007

Contents

Abbreviations

[The table includes only abbreviations used more than once. Other abbreviations are listed in the Index.]

BIT	Bilateral investment protection treaty
CCAMLR	Conservation of Antarctic Marine Living Resources
CFCs	chlorofluorocarbons
CITES	Convention on International Trade in Endangered Species of Wild Fauna and Flora
DSU	(WTO) Dispute Settlement Understanding
ECGD	Export Credit Guarantee Department
ECOSOC	(UN) Economic and Social Council
ECOWAS	Economic Community of West African States
ECSC	European Coal and Steel Community
EEC	European Economic Community
EEZ	Exclusive Economic Zone
EU	European Union
FAO	Food and Agriculture Organization
FCN	Friendship, Commerce and Navigation
GA	(UN) General Assembly
GATS	General Agreement on Trade in Services
GATT	General Agreement on Tariffs and Trade
IAEA	International Atomic Energy Agency
ICCPR	International Covenant on Civil and Political Rights
ICJ	International Court of Justice
ICSID	International Centre for the Settlement of Investment Disputes
ILC	International Law Commission
ILDC	International Law in Domestic Courts
ILM	International Legal Materials
ILO	International Labour Organization
ILR	International Law Reports
IMF	International Monetary Fund
IMO	International Maritime Organization
ITLOS	International Tribunal for the Law of the Sea
ITU	International Telecommunications Union

MFN	Most Favoured Nation
NAFTA	North American Free Trade Agreement
NATO	North Atlantic Treaty Organization
NGO	Non-governmental organization
PCIJ	Permanent Court of International Justice
SDR	(IMF) Special Drawing Rights
UN	United Nations
UNCED	UN Conference on Environment and Development
UNCLOS III	Third UN Conference on the Law of the Sea
UNCTAD	UN Conference on Trade and Development
UNEP	United Nations Environment Programme
UNRIAA	UN Reports of International Arbitral Awards
UNTS	UN Treaty Series
WHO	World Health Organization
WTO	World Trade Organization

Table of Cases

Table of International
Conventions and Treaties

UK legislation

US legislation

Introduction and Overview: The Ambit of International Law

I.I AIM OF THE BOOK

The world needs international law, because no State acting alone can achieve its aims. International co-operation is necessary; and international law is the framework within which international co-operation takes place. The point was well made by a former British Foreign Secretary, Douglas Hurd:

> [N]ation states are . . . incompetent. Not one of them, not even the United States as the single remaining super-power, can adequately provide for the needs that its citizens now articulate. The extent of that incompetence has become sharply clearer during this century. The inadequacies of national governments to provide security, prosperity or a decent environment has brought into being a huge array of international rules, conferences and institutions; the only answer to the puzzle of the immortal but incompetent nation state is effective co-operation between those states for all the purposes that lie beyond the reach of any one of them.[1]

That passage suggests some of the matters with which international law is concerned. The national security of each State depends upon an acceptance by other States of restrictions upon the right to use force to achieve their aims. Those restrictions are given their definitive expression in international law. National prosperity depends upon trade; and international trade is conducted within the rules that constitute the World Trade Organization (WTO) trading system and regional systems such as the North American Free Trade Agreement (NAFTA), the Southern Common Market (MERCOSUR), and the Common Market for Eastern and Southern Africa (COMESA). Factors that affect international competitiveness, such as national health and safety legislation and minimum employment standards, are also regulated as part of this broad scheme. Pollution of the land, sea, and air is the subject of a large and growing

---

[1] Douglas Hurd, *The Search for Peace* (London: Warner Books, 1997), p. 6.

network of global and regional treaties. Fundamental human rights are secured by multilateral treaty regimes in Africa, the Americas, and Europe, and are supplemented by increasing numbers of agreements on more specific matters such as the rights of children, minorities, and migrant workers. Plant and animal diseases, and drugs, and scientific research are the subject of international agreements. So, too, are transportation, banking, arms control, educational exchanges, and extradition: the list, and the scope of international law, is almost infinite. More will be said about these subjects in the following pages.

The reference to the 'huge array of international rules, conferences and institutions' suggests something of the processes by which the rules of international law are made. Take for example the question of the environment. No State can prevent global warming by acting alone. It may impose severe restrictions upon carbon dioxide emissions and engage in massive tree-planting programmes; but if no other State is doing so, its efforts will be practically pointless. Worse, the additional costs imposed on manufacturers and tax-payers as a result of those measures will tend to put that State's economy at a competitive disadvantage: the role of ecological custodian comes at a real cost. Unless 'greenness' can be sold as a consumer good (as many companies, making a virtue of necessity in the face of environmental legislation, now seek to do) whatever international influence the State has as a competitor will begin to dwindle as businesses abroad unencumbered by strict environmental constraints increase their market shares. Unilateral action is at best ineffective and may be positively counter-productive. In a perfect world, all States would impose the same environmental regulations, at a level just sufficient to achieve the desired safety of the environment. The environmental aims would be secured; and no State would be at a competitive disadvantage as a result.

Co-operation is necessary; and co-operation needs a framework. In order even to begin to attempt to co-operate, States must contact each other and know who is competent to give binding undertakings that will be respected by the government, the courts, and other public authorities of the other State. They need to know how to indicate that a particular agreement made by a State is formally binding, as a matter of legal obligation, and is not regarded simply as a matter of policy that can be varied or abandoned at will by the other State. These matters are governed by principles of diplomatic law and treaty law.

In order to negotiate an agreement on environmental controls, State representatives need to discuss the issue. States may already have established an international organization with competence in the field, under whose auspices negotiations can take place. If not, States will have to convene a conference. This is not easy. If a State representative visits, say, Brussels, he or she may be threatened with arrest or with being sued in respect of some wrong that was allegedly committed by the State that sent them. The work of State representatives is greatly helped if they are assured that they will not be subject to such distractions, and the advantages of such immunity are generally thought to outweigh the disadvantages of closing off that particular means of challenging the conduct of foreign States before courts of law. Hence, international law provides for the immunity of diplomats and other State representatives.

If an agreement on environmental controls is negotiated, it will be necessary to decide how far States may, or must, apply the controls to polluting activity. Certainly, States will be expected to apply it to everyone within their borders, whether or not the people concerned—car owners, factory owners, or whatever—are nationals of the State (and the determination both of borders and of nationality are themselves questions of international law). But what of, say, foreign subsidiaries of companies based in the State? May a company avoid pollution controls by shifting its manufacturing operations to another country, or may the State regulate its activities even when they take place abroad? And what if the country where the activities do take place has different rules for pollution control? These questions of the extent of a State's right to regulate conduct are questions governed by the principles of international law concerning jurisdiction.

Suppose that the foreign country where the subsidiary's operations are located introduces draconian environmental laws that render either the subsidiary's, or even the parent company's, operations commercially unviable—a question that turns partly upon the way in which accounts may or must be drawn up in the different countries and on the ways in which taxes are imposed and taxes paid abroad are taken into account. Would the subsidiary or the parent company have any remedy, and if so, how could it be obtained? And suppose that some States that have become parties to the environmental treaty impose lower environmental standards than those required by the treaty, or adopt a lax approach to the enforcement of standards, so as to help their domestic businesses: would other, more conscientious States Parties have any remedy against the resulting inequities in the regulatory burden and tilting of the competitive playing field?

The questions can be multiplied almost endlessly; and to almost all of them international law provides an answer.

It will be apparent from that example that international law is concerned with the actions and treatment of individuals, corporations, and international organizations, as well as States; and is the concern of lawyers advising all of them. Corporate lawyers, environmental campaigners, and governments alike will scrutinize the way in which national environmental laws are drafted and imposed and measure them against the State's international obligations—not only its obligations under environmental treaties but also obligations concerning conditions upon which international trade takes place, the treatment of foreign investments, non-discrimination, and other matters. Indeed, no lawyers now starting in practice are likely to avoid all contact with international law in their professional careers. Human rights obligations arising from international instruments are now a common ingredient of cases arising within the framework of administrative law and criminal law; family lawyers increasingly look to international treaties and the national legislation that implements them for assistance in matters such as child abduction and the collection of maintenance payments; labour lawyers invoke international standards in cases concerning working conditions; and commercial lawyers wade deep into the waters of international trade law in advising their clients. Though sometimes concealed by the overlay of municipal[2] legislation, international law flows throughout the whole of national law.

Little thought is given to the workings of international law until it ceases to operate satisfactorily. When international law malfunctions or disappoints the expectations of onlookers, trenchant questions are asked. Does it matter if international law is violated? Is international law anything more than a respectable cloak for the exercise of naked power, or an exercise in utopian idealism? Are there right and wrong answers in international law, or is it all a matter of interpretation? What can international law *do*?

I try to answer such questions in this short book. It is a book about international law, not a book *of* international law; and this is one reason why I have abandoned the lapidary prose traditional in legal textbooks in favour of a first-person narrative. I try to explain what international law does and how the international legal system operates, but not to set out a comprehensive or systematic account of what the rules of international law are. This approach was well described in the Preface to the first edition of the book that is, in the genealogy of Oxford publishing on international law, the ancestor of the present text, J.L. Brierly's *The Law of Nations*, where Brierly wrote that:

Any intelligent study of the problems of international relations must raise the question of the role, if any, to be assigned in them to law. Unfortunately current

---

[2] 'Municipal' and 'domestic' are terms used by international lawyers to signify something within the legal order of a single State, in contrast to something within the international, inter-State legal order: for example, domestic courts in contrast to international courts; municipal law, such as English or Scots or French law, in contrast to international law.

discussions of the matter too often assume that this question can be answered by *a priori* methods, to the neglect of any serious examination either of the part that law is actually playing in the relation of states today, or of the conditions upon which an effective legal order in any society depends.[3]

Brierly thought that some knowledge of the system as it is actually practised between States is necessary as a corrective both for exaggerated hopes and for cynical indifference, and he tried to show that international law 'is neither a chimera nor a panacea, but just one institution among others which we have at our disposal for the building up of a saner international order'. The need that Brierly identified is as urgent now as it was when he wrote, almost eighty years ago.

The rest of this chapter consists of a brief outline of the scope and nature of international law. The remaining pages of this book consist largely of a gentle tour of the main areas in which international law is currently active and of the principles upon which international law is built and the methods used to build it.

1.2 THE SCOPE AND NATURE OF INTERNATIONAL LAW

The central core of international law may be described as the body of rules and principles that determine the rights and duties of States, primarily in respect of their dealings with other States and the citizens of other States, and that determine what *is* a State—which political entities, such as Australia and Palestine and Quebec, count as States, and when and within what geographical territory they exist.

It may seem odd to describe the core of international law, rather than to define it. I have done so because definitions necessarily draw lines to distinguish one thing from another; and that approach is inappropriate in the case of international law. There is a penumbral area which can equally well be classified as international law or as some other branch of the law. Archetypal international law is concerned with the rights and duties of States towards one another; but the principles, materials and techniques of international law are applied much more widely.

For example, the powers and duties of international organizations are governed by international law. Thus, while the Member States of the European Union are bound by internal EU law in their dealings with one another and with organs of the EU (such as the European Commission),

---

[3] J.L. Brierly, *The Law of Nations. An Introduction to the International Law of Peace* (Oxford: Oxford University Press, 1928), p. v.

relations of other, non-member States with the EU are governed by international law. As a matter of EU law, competence over fisheries is a matter for the EU and not for Member States: it is the EU that makes fishery treaties under which EU vessels fish in the waters of non-Member States and *vice versa*; and those treaties are governed by international law in the same way as are treaties made between two States.

Similarly, human rights treaties and treaties providing for the protection of foreign investments limit the powers of States Parties in their dealings with individuals and companies; and many such treaties give individuals and companies the right to bring proceedings against a State that has violated the treaty terms. To that extent, international law also encompasses dealings with individuals. But one might equally well regard the right of an individual to bring a case against a State in, say, the European Court of Justice, as an extension of the individual's rights to sue that State in the State's own national courts, under some such process as judicial review. There is no absolute line that sets the boundaries between international law and national laws; and some bodies of law and legal procedures have characteristics of each.

What, then, are the particular characteristics of international law? There are obvious differences in the material sources. International lawyers are largely concerned with treaties and customary international law, while municipal lawyers are largely concerned with statutes and reports of court decisions. There are also differences of methodology. National courts, mindful of their duty not to usurp the role of the lawmakers in the legislature, tend to adopt relatively inflexible and literal interpretations of legislation: international tribunals tend to have a more flexible and pragmatic approach, bending the interpretation of the text to current conditions where circumstances seem to demand it. But these differences are relatively minor. They are no greater than the differences between common law systems based upon case-law and legislation, such as English Law, civil law systems based upon comprehensive Codes, such as French law, and customary law systems based upon the application of customary rules, such as the customary courts in Tanzania.

The crucial difference between international law and municipal laws is one of fundamental principle. National laws are invariably based upon some notion of sovereignty. National courts defer to national legislatures. If a national law says that the government or anyone else has the right to do a certain thing, the courts will not disagree. The legislature can do no wrong. Even where, as in the United States, statutes may be struck down because they are unconstitutional, the courts are still bound by the

Constitution, which is itself a national law. The fact that the exercise of a right under national law may violate international law will not entitle national courts to deny the existence of that right (unless national law itself directs the courts to apply international law in certain circumstances, as do the constitutions of Germany and The Netherlands for example).

This subordination of the courts to the legislature is at the heart of what is meant when people assert the sovereignty of national parliaments. It means that no-one can tell the State (or more accurately the rulers of the State) what to do. That principle of sovereignty underpins national legal systems: it answers the question, who's in charge here? It affirms the right of each State to be different, so that conduct that is lawful in one, such as smoking cannabis or stoning someone to death, may be punishable as a crime in another. National laws on matters such as credit, pornography, blasphemy, gun control, employment terms, marriage and divorce, abortion, drugs, taxation and social security, military service, and so on do much to define the nature of a State. They are a significant part of what makes the State, and the society within the State, different from its neighbours.

International law, on the other hand, proceeds from precisely the opposite premise. It is based upon the principle that all States, whether they like it or not, are subject to international law and must comply with it. It may appear to be in this respect the antithesis of national sovereignty. But that is an oversimplification. Far from suppressing national sovereignty, in the way in which EU law suppresses national sovereignty in certain defined fields in order to secure the goals of economic and social advancement, international law seeks to secure the conditions that allow sovereign States to co-exist, and to enable each State to choose what kind of society will exist within its borders.

International law does this by regulating relations between States. It is a little like a global equivalent of the laws that allocate certain powers to towns, counties, provinces, and other political subdivisions within a single State—with the crucial difference that in international law there is no equivalent of the central or federal government with rights to override the will of the local and provincial governments. In more abstract terms, we might say that international law governs the relationship between one particular level of distinct political communities (by which I mean simply social groups that are organized and impose rules made by the community upon the members of that community, and usually upon visitors sojourning within it). International law does not generally concern itself with relations between provinces or towns or whatever. It leaves those questions to the authorities within the State concerned. It concerns itself essentially with relations between States.

From the earliest recorded times when mankind was organized into distinct tribal or political groups there was a body of rules that regulated the conduct of affairs between different 'countries' and their sovereigns. We still have many of the clay tablets upon which treaties were written in Babylonia the best part of four thousand years ago. Extradition arrangements were in place between Egyptian pharaohs and Hittite kings. In ancient Greece and Rome and India, the exchange of envoys between nations followed well-established rules, the violation of which could be a justification for war. It seems likely that a form of international law arises whenever groups begin to identify themselves as distinct from their neighbours; that international law is as primitive and elemental a social institution as law itself. One wonders whether it is not hard-wired into human consciousness, a corollary of a view of the world which, linguistically, divides actions in the patterns of verbs that distinguish between *I*, *we*, and *they*. *I*, the individual; *we*, the tribe; *they*, the others. From these primitive distinctions, which seem to be universal (or near universal), emerge the basic legal conditions that characterize international law.

There is *us*; and there is *them*. We can be their friends, or their enemies. If they fight someone else, we can be for them, against them, or keep out of it altogether. We can, in international law terms, be at peace, at war, or neutral. To find out which, we need to send envoys, representatives. Our peace is sealed by treaties—the Latin word for allies, *foederati*, comes straight from the word for treaties, *foedera*. Our wars are bounded by rules. We fight because we have rights to uphold; and the morality that justifies the end also constrains the means that we use to achieve it. Our neutrality, which excuses us from involvement in the fights of our neighbours, similarly limits what we may and may not do without being considered to have taken sides. And when peace exists, and we trade with one another, we have rules that stipulate what rights and duties our traders have in each other's territory: how far they are subject to the criminal law and so on.

International law is not a unified, manufactured system, imposed upon the world of international or inter-communal relations. Nor, despite its deep roots in basic forms of social organization, is its scope determined *a priori*. The rules of international law cover whatever topics happen to have been regarded as appropriate for legal solution on the international plane. It is simply a formalized account of practices and principles which spring spontaneously and inevitably from the coexistence of distinct communities or which result from conscious efforts of States to co-operate in dealing with certain problems. From the earliest days those rules covered matters such as the making of war and peace and alliances, diplomatic exchanges, trade, and the return of fugitive offenders, and were initially evident simply as the customary practices, the 'way of doing things' in the field concerned.

Gradually these practices and principles were reduced to writing and systematized, and the principles of the Law of Nations (as international law used to be known) were set out in textbooks, often intermingled with discussions of the principles of domestic government and right behaviour in general. Some such texts are of great antiquity. Fragments are readily iden-tifiable in the Old Testament. In the Book of Deuteronomy, for example, there are clear rules on what armies are and are not permitted to do during the belligerent occupation of enemy territory—rules which (as I explain in Chapter 8) are very close to those which apply today in situations such as the occupation of Iraq by the United Kingdom and the United States and the Israeli occupation of the West Bank and Gaza. The *Arthashastra* of Kautilya, a magisterial treatise on statecraft written in India almost two thousand years ago, and the *Siyar* of the eighth-century Hanafite jurist, Shaybani, from what is now Iraq, are among the early classics.

It is often asserted that international law in its modern form dates from the Treaty of Westphalia in 1648, which is said to have 'created' the system of modern nation-States. It is far from clear that this is so. The primacy of territorial units as the basis of social organization was evident in the Peace of Augsburg in 1555, and the notion of sovereignty was developed by Jean Bodin a little later in the sixteenth century. Either could be taken as indi-cations of the emergence of a 'new' order of sovereign territorial States within the increasingly fragile chrysalis of the Holy Roman Empire.

But there is another, more important, objection to the fixation with Westphalia as the birth of international law. The 'Westphalia' thesis focuses on the wrong issue. The strength and continuity of international law flows not from its conceptual basis but from its routine incorporation within the daily life of governments. The forms—treaties, embassies, claims to jurisdiction or immunity, to territory and nationality, and so on—go back far beyond the Treaty of Westphalia; and it is in the forms and formulas of governmental intercourse that the lifeblood of inter-national law has always flowed. If one seeks a critical development to which the origins of modern international law might be attached, that development should probably be the routine recording of official dealings between different rulers or countries and the emergence of organized governmental archives, which occurred in Europe some time around the thirteenth century and many centuries earlier in Asia and the Middle East. One measure of this development is the consumption of the wax used to seal official documents. In the late 1220s, England's Royal Chancery used about 3½ pounds of sealing wax each week: by the late 1260s, this had risen to about 32 pounds each week.

In Europe, there were by the fourteenth or fifteenth century very well-established rules regulating the relations of States in times of war and of peace. Some of the rules find vivid expression in literature of the period. In England, the best-known examples arise a little later, in Shakespeare's histories. *Henry V*, in particular, gives a central dramatic role to the Laws of War, as Theodor Meron has shown in his entertaining and erudite studies of international law in Shakespeare's plays.[4] These rules were rehearsed in court decisions and in opinions drafted by the international lawyers of the day, and eventually set out in the classic European tracts on international law.

Those texts began to appear in the sixteenth century, centuries after the Middle Eastern and Asian texts. Their appearance coincided with the age of exploration and colonization by the European powers. While some of the earliest European texts, such as those by the great Spanish theologian-jurists Vitoria, Suarez and Ayala, addressed questions of the rights and duties of the European towards the peoples of the New World, most of the early European treatises dealt mainly with war, peace, diplomacy, and treaty-making—the traditional occupations of governments. That pattern continued for three centuries, and is reflected in the classic texts by Gentili, Grotius, Pufendorf, Vattel, and von Martens, albeit from a range of doctrinal perspectives. But by the later nineteenth century the scope of the texts was beginning to be considerably extended, so as to reflect the increasing range of topics upon which States were finding it useful to co-operate.

In the nineteenth century treaties regulating the waging of war, designed to limit unnecessary suffering, were adopted. International organizations were established, such as the Commissions regulating the uses of several of the great European rivers and, rather later, bodies such as the International Telegraphic Union, designed to facilitate international co-operation in the wake of technological developments. These moves, which began around two hundred years ago, heralded a period of extraordinary development in international law, propelled by the coincidence of the realization of the need for international co-operation to address problems insoluble by individual States acting alone and the greatly increased possibility of international communication through innovations in road, rail, sea and air transport, and telegraphy. Over that period major developments have occurred in

---

[4] Theodor Meron, *Henry's Wars and Shakespeare's Laws* (Oxford: Clarendon, 1993) and *Bloody Constraint: War and Chivalry in Shakespeare* (New York: OUP, 1998).

three areas: in the scope of international law, in the range of international organizations, and in the range of international actors.

1.3 THE CHANGING SCOPE OF INTERNATIONAL LAW

The first development is the massive expansion in the scope and sophistication of international law. The creation of the European Empires, and their gradual dismantlement from the time of the wars of independence in the Americas in the late eighteenth and early nineteenth century onwards, demanded explanations of the differences between the various kinds of States—Great Powers, colonies, protectorates and so on—and of how they emerge and how one replaces another. These are the now familiar questions of international personality and State succession. At what point, for example, did the conflict in Yugoslavia in the 1990s cease to be an internal Yugoslavian problem in which outside States should not intervene and become an international conflict between Bosnia, Serbia, and Croatia in which other States might ally themselves with one or other of those newly emerged States? In contexts such as this the traditional rules evolved and were refined.

A much more radical change occurred in the field of human rights. Classical international law was based on the supposition that it dealt with relations between States, and that each State could and should look after the interests of its own citizens. If a citizen was injured by a foreign State, it was for the citizen's own State to demand compensation from the foreign State—to make a diplomatic claim. But no State had any right to tell another how it should treat its own citizens. That supposition was shaken to the core during the twentieth century. Close attention was paid in the years after the Great War to the treatment of ethnic minorities within States; but the decisive development followed the discovery of the way in which Nazi Germany and the communist Soviet Union had treated their own citizens. States could no longer remain indifferent to the mass slaughter of human beings. If pure altruism was not a sufficient reason for their intervention, the desirability of avoiding becoming embroiled in international conflicts such as World War Two, with the immense cost in suffering and resources that it entailed, was. The treatment of people was pulled out of the sphere of the domestic jurisdiction of States—the sphere of internal affairs, in which no other State has the right to intervene—and Human Rights law was added to the canon of international law.

The making in 1948 of the Universal Declaration of Human Rights, along with the adoption of regional instruments such as the American

Declaration of the Rights of Man in 1948 and the European Convention on Human Rights in 1950, marked the inception of modern international human rights law. They were followed by instruments such as the 1981 African Charter on Human and People's Rights, and the 1994 Arab Charter on Human Rights. The emergence of human rights law is notable not only because it represented the acknowledgement that States had some *legal*, as opposed to purely political, interest in the way in which the internal affairs of other States were conducted, but also because the justification for this development lay not in existing legal principles but in moral imperatives lying outside the legal system. International law has, from the earliest times, had as close a relationship with moral principle as does criminal law within a State, although the moral principles applicable in relations between States are by no means the same as those applicable between individual human beings.

As the scope of State activity expanded, so did the scope of international law. Much of the development was incremental, with specific initiatives responding to the particular needs of the time; but there were larger scale movements. Two are particularly notable. The first, building on attempts in the late nineteenth and early twentieth centuries to deal with certain aspects of the international economy, is the creation of a near-comprehensive framework for international trade. Early agreements dealt with matters such as arrangements for international payments and exchange rates. The reconstruction of the international order that began after World War Two and centred upon the creation of the United Nations also saw the creation of the World Bank and the International Monetary Fund (IMF), the General Agreement on Tariffs and Trade (GATT), and later the World Trade Organization (WTO), as well as various agreements regulating trade in primary commodities such as coffee and tropical timber. Regional economic organizations of immense importance were formed, first in Europe, and later in Africa, in North America, and in Latin America. International economic law is, perhaps, the fastest moving area of international law at present.

A little later, international environmental law developed. International concern focused first on marine pollution, partly because that was one of the most visible forms of pollution and because its regulation intruded least upon the way that domestic and industrial life proceeded within States' borders, and partly because it had the great benefit of falling within the competences of one of the most vigorous and successful of all international organizations, the International Maritime Organization (IMO).

Economic law and environmental law have in common the characteristic that they bite deep into the internal order of a State. They touch detailed questions of financial and trade controls and of governmental regulation of business that are the stuff of party politics—issues on which elections are fought and won or lost. That is an indication both of the pervasive significance of international law in contemporary life and of the intensity of the pressure that drives governments to bind themselves to international policies in these fields as the only practical way of addressing some of the major problems that confront them.

The development of international law is, of course, a continuing process. Much attention is being paid, for example, to the regulation of the Internet; and it is notable that some of the private industry initiatives such as the procedure for resolving disputes over internet domain names, established by the Internet Corporation for Assigned Names and Numbers (ICANN), dovetail into procedures established by international organizations of the traditional inter-State type, such as the World Intellectual Property Organization (WIPO), a specialized UN agency.

1.4 THE EMERGENCE OF INTERNATIONAL ORGANIZATIONS

This great expansion in the scope of international law was accompanied by a second major development: the growth of international institutions. The existence in the early nineteenth century of administrative bodies such as the European River Commissions has already been noted. At the end of the nineteenth century, international judicial bodies appeared. The seminal episode, which signalled the possibility of the then Great Powers accepting judicial settlement of disputes between them, was the establishment in 1871 of the arbitration tribunal that settled the United States' claims against Britain for compensation for the damage inflicted upon the Union by the confederate warship *Alabama* during the American Civil War.[5] The *Alabama*, one of the most destructive warships in naval history, had been built in Birkenhead and delivered to the Confederacy in breach, so the United States argued, successfully, of Britain's obligations as a neutral in the Civil War.

The advantages of third-party involvement in the peaceful settlement of international disputes was underlined in 1902. An attack on British fishing vessels in the North Sea by the Russian Navy brought Britain to the brink of intervention on the side of Japan in the Russo-Japanese War; but again the matter was settled peacefully and swiftly, this time by a quasi-judicial Commission of Inquiry. The path to international adjudication was

[5] See T. Bingham, 'The Alabama Claims Arbitration' (2005) 54 *ICLQ* pp. 1–25.

clear. It led to the establishment of the Permanent Court of International Justice (PCIJ) under the League of Nations, and its successor, the International Court of Justice (ICJ), under the United Nations. At first little used, in the 1990s the International Court became extremely busy, handling cases referred to it by States from all around the world. It is, however, only one among many international tribunals. International courts and tribunals are multiplying fast. Among the most notable are the dispute panels established by the World Trade Organization (WTO), the International Tribunal for the Law of the Sea (ITLOS), and the large number of *ad hoc* arbitration tribunals that have adjudicated upon investment disputes under the auspices of the International Centre for the Settlement of Investment Disputes (ICSID), the North American Free Trade Agreement (NAFTA), and some of the 2,000 or so bilateral investment protection treaties that now exist.

International institutions also arose in the legislative field. International rule-making began in the late nineteenth century with the establishment of bodies such as the International Telecommunications Union (ITU), as it is now known. It grew from the perception that in areas of international activity, where goods or services or activities cross national borders, it is more efficient to agree upon regulations internationally than it is to leave it to each State to adopt its own, possibly idiosyncratic, measures. Today, there are scores of such bodies, in all areas of human activity.

Many international organizations have competences that extend well beyond adjudication and rule-making, and which include the monitoring of compliance with the law and the formulation of policy. The United Nations is the pre-eminent global example; but developments within bodies such as the Organization for Security and Co-operation in Europe (OSCE), and the Economic Community of West African States (ECOWAS), indicate a recognition on the part of States that wide-ranging international co-operation is today a practical necessity, because few, if any, States have the capacity by themselves to deal with *every* problem that they may face.

1.5 THE EMERGENCE OF NEW INTERNATIONAL ACTORS

A third development in the international legal system was more radical. In the nineteenth century international law was primarily the concern of independent States, several of them colonial powers, in their dealings with one another. They applied their own imperial legal systems to dealing with their colonies and dependencies; but even those imperial systems mirrored the basic mechanisms and institutions of international law. At that time, however, international law could still properly be described as the body of rules that States applied in their dealings with one another. Sovereign States were, one might say, the only actors entitled to appear on the stage of international law.

As international organizations became more familiar features of the international scene, and particularly after the establishment of the League of Nations in 1920, the question of their legal status arose. Unlike companies and corporations in domestic law, they were not the creatures or possessions of any single State, but there was a reluctance to accept that anything other than a State could truly claim a right to a place on the international stage. Nonetheless, practical necessities such as the making of agreements governing relations between the headquarters of international organizations and the State 'hosting' them led slowly to the acceptance that they should be recognized as having an independent status and the capacity to make international agreements in their own name. Just as companies make contracts in the same way as people do in domestic legal systems, and are therefore 'persons' recognized by those systems, so too are international organizations recognized as persons within the international legal system. Their capacities differ greatly. Some have very narrow remits and correspondingly narrow powers. Others, notably the European Union, have very extensive powers. Indeed, in certain fields of international activity, such as fisheries management and trade regulation, the EU has formally supplanted its Member States, the Union alone having the legal competence to negotiate international agreements with non-EU States.

International organizations are not the only persons to share the stage of contemporary international law with States. States have long been held responsible under international law for the mistreatment of nationals of other States—'aliens' as they are often termed—but the traditional mechanism for invoking that responsibility was for the national State of the injured alien to take up the matter with the allegedly wrongdoing State. Indeed, that pattern is still followed on occasion. For example, in 1998 Paraguay brought a claim in the International Court of Justice against the United States in respect of a Paraguayan national threatened with the death sentence without, Paraguay said, having had the benefit of access to the Paraguayan consul when he was arrested, as required by the Vienna Convention on Consular Relations. Similar cases were subsequently brought against the United States by Germany in 1999 and by Mexico in 2003.

The involvement of the State in the formal steps of preparing an international claim is, however, a time-consuming and expensive business which most governments usually consider to be an undesirable alternative to persisting with attempts to find a negotiated settlement. Moreover, where the injured person is not an individual but a company, the company may be better placed than its national government to pursue its claim. A large company will have the resources, the time, and the uncomplicated interest in pursuing the company's particular interests against the foreign State, none of which may exist in the foreign ministry of the company's home State. Indeed, companies have long negotiated with the governments of foreign States to conclude long-term concession contracts, for the building and operation of railways, mines, oil wells and refineries, and other large industrial projects. Those concessions, as might be expected of agreements between a State and foreign companies who are not its citizens and not entirely subject to its jurisdiction, have many of the characteristics of international agreements concluded between States. In their form, language and content they are a cross between a complex commercial contract and a treaty. It was a natural extension of the activity of companies in making these agreements with foreign States that the companies should be given the right themselves to make formal legal claims in cases where they considered that the agreement or their basic rights under international law had been violated. Thus, from the first half of the twentieth century onwards companies began to edge their way on to the international stage, making concession agreements with States and litigating against States as if they were their equals. Their place is now secured by the provision made for such actions by companies in the hundreds of bilateral investment treaties that protect their interests, and in multilateral agreements such as the 1965 Convention on the Settlement of Investment Disputes Between States and Nationals of Other States (the ICSID Convention), the NAFTA, and the Energy Charter Treaty.

Concurrently, in the mid twentieth century, a parallel development occurred in the field of human rights. The protection of human rights could have been left to States. The enforcement mechanism could have required that one State Party to a human rights convention should institute proceedings against another State Party if it considered that the other had violated the convention. This is, indeed, one of the mechanisms that still exists for the enforcement of human rights. But it was and is regarded as a mechanism of limited value. Effective constraints upon the abuse of government power are more likely to result from the internalization of human rights obligations into the everyday life of the State; and one way of ensuring this, and maximizing vigilance over the actions of States, is to give the individuals directly affected the right to institute proceedings in their own name. This right of individual petition, as it is known, was introduced in the 1950 European

Convention on Human Rights, at first as an optional matter, individuals being entitled to initiate proceedings only against States that had chosen to accept the right of individual petition. It is now compulsory, binding on all the forty-four States currently Parties to the Convention; and around 14,000 individual petitions are lodged each year. Individuals, too, are in this field prominent actors on the international stage.

Sometimes individuals are unable to pursue their rights effectively. They may be held in prison; the victims of government purges may be unknown; villages in remote areas may lack the facilities for communication with the relevant international bodies. In recognition of this some conventions, such as the 1978 American Convention on Human Rights, permit applications to be made by representative organizations. In this way Non-Governmental Organizations (NGOs) have secured an acknowledged place within the international legal system. They also have another, less formally acknowledged, role. Particular NGOs have been enormously influential in promoting international agreements upon specific topics, especially in the fields of human rights and environmental law. Indeed, it is not uncommon to see NGO representatives occupying positions on the delegations of some, particularly very small, States at international conferences. The expertise and energy contributed by such NGO activity is of great value; but there are significant unresolved issues as to the principles that should govern the participation of unelected single-issue campaigning organizations in international legal processes.

States, international organizations, individuals, and companies are by no means the only entities with which international law is concerned. Alongside the concern for human rights there has developed a concern for the rights of human groups as such. Indeed, the development of international mechanisms for the protection of human rights developed rather earlier in the context of group rights than it did for individual rights. Concern for minority groups was a prominent feature of the Versailles settlement in 1919, at the end of the Great War, thirty years before the Universal Declaration and the European Convention on Human Rights brought the defence of individual rights to the fore. In its most significant contemporary incarnation, the concern for group rights is evident in the recognition given by international law to the rights of 'peoples'—a development reflected in the title of the 1981 African Charter of Human and Peoples' Rights. The rights of peoples have also been promoted in agreements on national minorities and minority languages, and less directly, by the development of areas of the law which are of particular importance when the rights of peoples and minority groups are under threat, such as refugee and humanitarian law.

In principle, then, international law governs all activities of States that involve a foreign element: that is to say, all dealings by public authorities with foreign States or foreign citizens or with matters outside the borders of the State. The high tide of government regulation may have passed at some point in the late twentieth century: but governments still regulate so many aspects of life that barely any field of human activity escapes their attention, and with it the relevance of international law. Moreover, when international organizations and companies (and to a lesser extent individuals) come on to the international stage and deal with States as juridical equals, they adopt the forms and methods of international law. The character of international law will doubtless change with the mutation of the sovereign nation-State, but it will certainly not lose its importance.

I have mentioned three broad areas of regulation: human rights, trade, and the environment. These are examined in more detail later, after the more fundamental principles of international law concerning the rights and duties of States have been considered. These principles are like the skeleton, the framework on which the flesh of international co-operation is built; and it is necessary to consider them first. But before I do so, I must complete these introductory remarks by saying something about the reasons for the high level of compliance with international law, and the manner in which international law is made, invoked, and applied.

1.6 WHY DO PEOPLE COMPLY WITH INTERNATIONAL LAW?

I have said that the crucial difference between international law and municipal law is that in municipal law the State is sovereign. It has what may be called internal sovereignty, which means that its courts and its government are subject to the laws of that State, but only to the laws of that State. No superior governmental authority is recognized. I also noted that international law has no legislature. Nor is there an international police force, or even a compulsory system of courts before which States can be compelled to appear. Nevertheless, most States comply with most of the rules of international law most of the time. In the light of these characteristics, some people have asked why States do in fact obey international law.

In fact, there are two questions that arise here: why *do* States comply with international law and why *should* States comply with international law?

The first question, which asks why States *do* comply with international law, is largely empirical. We could ask those who decide on the actions that a State takes—or, to put it more precisely, those whose actions count as actions of the State—what role they give to international law in deciding upon courses of action and, to the extent that they are guided by it, why they are guided by it and what circumstances they regard as warranting action inconsistent with international law. International lawyers are not very good at making empirical inquiries of this kind, and the evidence is patchy, in large measure anecdotal and based upon the experience of those at the fringes of political power. Some points are, however, clear beyond dispute.

The first point is that international law is not imposed on States against their will by an external legislature. Rules of international law mostly arise either from treaties or from customary international law. Treaties are like contracts, in as much as they are agreed and reciprocal commitments, which States are free to enter into or not as they please but which are binding once made. If a State considers that a particular treaty will confer on it more benefit than harm, knowing that every treaty involves some give and take between the parties, it may decide to become a party to the treaty. If the treaty seems likely to do more harm than good, it will not become a party. Treaties are, therefore, commitments that States have already decided that it is in their interest to comply with. It is scarcely surprising, therefore, that all States do generally comply with their treaty obligations.

The position is broadly similar with regard to customary international law. Rules of customary law are not so much made as discerned. International relations, like all social relations, fall into certain patterns. For as long as there have been formal dealings between States, envoys and ambassadors have been sent from one to another. Perhaps somewhere in unrecorded history there was a time when envoys were regarded as disposable, and killed or captured once they had delivered their message. But for all recorded history they have been regarded as entitled to a degree of immunity and inviolability. Officials of a State did not have to consider each time a new envoy appeared how they should treat him. It was well known what the 'right' or 'proper' way to treat an envoy was; and it was understood that this was more than a matter of convention or convenience. It was an obligation. Rules of customary international law are, in essence, simply those international rules that are discerned as having this obligatory force. And again, because the customary practices are rooted in what States habitually do, it is no surprise that States should habitually comply with customary international law. Indeed, it is almost tautologous to make the point.

One powerful reason why States do, and always have, complied with international law is, therefore, that they make the rules to suit them. International law constrains errant States, which seek to break away from established patterns of behaviour or to abandon treaty commitments that they have made. But by definition, international law is a constraint that sits very lightly on the shoulders of those who conform to it. While that inevitably gives international law, like all law, a conservative character, it also means that States can in general predict how other States will react in certain circumstances. States can reasonably suppose that their neighbours will, in general, act within the confines of the law. This aspect of State behaviour has been extensively analysed in terms of game theory, which analyses the ways in which actors in multi-player situations where the reactions of other players are not certainly known in advance can best maximize their gains or minimize their losses. While the simple models of game theory[6] seem to me ill-suited to the analysis of governmental decision-making, spread between different departments and subject to trade-offs across the whole range of governmental activity, the techniques offer some interesting insights into how compliance with the law might be analysed if government were a rational process.

Perhaps because some violations of international law are so dramatic, there is a tendency to suppose that States only obey it when they choose, and that the hard calculations of *realpolitik* give little weight to the law. That view, particularly widespread among those whose vision is unsullied by any knowledge or experience of the matter, is hopelessly wrong. If it were possible to quantify breaches of the law, giving points to each transgression of speed limits or parking offence, each technical assault in a crowded commuter train, each theft of office paper clips and pencils and computer time, each slander in home or school, and so on—not to mention the murders, rapes, burglaries, and woundings that are the stock in trade of every local newspaper, one might have a useful index against which the score for international law-breaking could be measured. But the fact is that, while wars and unarrested international villains are quite properly given much prominence, they no more indicate global lawlessness than riots, unlawful strikes, and unarrested national villains indicate domestic lawlessness. My guess is that the extent of compliance with international law is in fact significantly higher than the extent of compliance with many, perhaps most, national legal systems.

Why? One reason has been given. International law is made by States to serve their interests, so it is likely that it will be in their interest to comply with it. A second powerful reason for compliance is caution. We speak of States acting. States do not, of course, act: people act for them. Most of the time the people acting for States are not tyrants or charismatic leaders: they

---

[6] Among which the Prisoner's Dilemma, and the minimax method devised for card players by James Waldegrave in 1713, are perhaps the best known.

are ordinary men and women holding down jobs in the civil service and hoping to be promoted, or at least not to be sacked. Complying with international law is almost always a safe option. It is a good answer, when anyone asks why a particular policy or action was implemented, to say that international law required it. Occasionally a bold step unjustified by the law may succeed and be applauded; but few are tempted to take the risk. As anyone who has any familiarity with the great machines of government will know, the functionaries who crave power are far fewer than those who crave immunity and a quiet life.

There is an interesting field of inquiry here. Moral philosophy subjects human behaviour to searching scrutiny, pressing hard the analysis of motives and reasons and of intended and unintended consequences. On rare occasions, individuals consciously deliberate upon the actions that they should take, or are called upon to justify their actions. But moral behaviour is never taught in such a systematic manner. All parents will know that young children are taught, by the use of various incarnations of the stick and the carrot, that there are acceptable and unacceptable ways of doing things, and that there comes a point when the painful drilling of a child's demand to know 'why?' is met with a blank 'because'. Irrational and perhaps unjustifiable as such edicts may be, they form the bedrock of behavioural norms, the foundation upon which individual choice is built. So it is with States. The new intern or desk officer in a Foreign Ministry rapidly absorbs the culture, and knows how things are and are not done. And because bureaucracies are run by those who have been promoted for their skills at playing by the rules, there is an immense inertial attraction in all government departments to playing by the rules.

There is another point embedded in the one just made. States are governed by elites. I make no particular political point here. I am not saying that international law is necessarily a weapon of class oppression or anything of that kind. States must be governed; government can only be carried on by a small minority of the population (otherwise there is no-one left to be governed); and the commitments into which the State enters will inevitably reflect what that small minority thinks is best. Whether what is 'best' is determined by referendum, representative democracy and accountable government, corruption, or self-interest, depends upon how the State is organized. But the point is important because it underlies another reason for what is in many respects the extraordinary cohesiveness and effectiveness of international law.

States themselves differ widely in their characteristics. There are States with massive industrial and commercial bases, able to defend themselves economically and militarily against practically all conceivable threats;

States where the life expectancy is under forty years, and governments lack the money and the infrastructure to provide basic governance and social welfare to populations regularly decimated by starvation and disease; States run by corrupt and brutal governments or dynasties, practically indistinguishable from criminal gangs. Yet all of them can, and usually will, have their well-dressed representatives smoothly making the circuit of diplomatic receptions in New York or Geneva. All can, and often do, sit down in international conferences and hammer out treaty after treaty by negotiations in which national interests may appear to be no more diverse than those in a gathering where representatives of a drug cartel (whether wanted international criminals or decorated captains of industry) negotiate over the terms of supply. Why?

Observation suggests that one reason is simply that those who govern States have much more in common with each other than they have with many, perhaps most, of the people whom they govern. This is particularly true of the officials or foreign ministries, who conduct a large part of the international dealings of the State, and above all of the lawyers who serve in those ministries. They undergo a *déformation professionnelle*. They are trained in the lawyer's and diplomat's arts, often in one of a handful of universities in Europe or North America; dispatched to international conferences and organizations, where they meet others who have read the same books, the same law reports and treaties and are perhaps alumni of the same university; set to the drafting of diplomatic notes, treaties, and reports, according to a style so homogenous as to delight the drafter of a medieval book of court forms. To a significant degree they think alike and act alike. And international law is their *lingua franca*, the vehicle for their discussions, and the optic through which they view the world. Little surprise that officials the world over should align themselves with the view that international law, their professional calling and livelihood, should be taken seriously. I exaggerate, perhaps: but not much.

A further reason for the general observance of international law is the nature of the interest of governments in it. Their interests are long term; and they are varied. Governments are repeat players in international relations. Each decision they take must make sense not only in isolation, in the short term, but also in the long term. A government-run 'buy locally' campaign may have the short-term advantage of assisting domestic industry and agriculture. If, however, the consequence is that some months or years later trading partners whose exports to the State dried up because of the campaign retaliate by prohibiting imports of manufactured goods from the State, the advantage is likely to be outweighed by adverse effects—as it may if other States are encouraged by the campaign to put aside their international trading obligations and discourage imports from all States. Again, a government that is strenuously defending claims that it has in some way mistreated a foreign investor will be mindful of the fact that there may soon be a claim by one of its companies against a foreign government, and that the language of its defence may be quoted against that company.

Consistency of behaviour is highly prized; and because of the way in which international law is formed, the balance of advantage for a State is likely to lie in consistently complying with it. While it is often said that politicians rarely look more than four or five years ahead, their horizons being bounded by the date of the next election, that is not true of the civil servants who run the day-to-day business of international relations. Their view of the interests of the State is usually close to that of the immortals. They know that a breach of international law today may well be cited against them in months or years to come.

Similarly, the variety of a government's interests weighs in favour of compliance with international law. If restrictions on imports from a particular State make it less likely that the restricted State will permit use of its ports and airports for the replenishment of military vessels and aircraft in some future conflict, that is an important argument against imposing the restrictions. Any government contemplating a violation of its international legal obligations needs to consider the long-term impact upon its relations with all States across the whole range of international relations. There is likely to be a price to be paid for violations; and it is not easy to foresee when and where that price will be exacted. In most cases it is preferable to obey the law and sleep soundly.

This point is often made by referring to the inter-dependence of States in the modern world. No State is so completely self-reliant that it can afford to offend, and invite retaliatory action from, other States by acting in disregard of its international commitments—though in particular circumstances it may decide that the advantages of non-compliance justify the risk of adverse consequences. The point is obvious, and applies to the social rules that hold any society together. The point does, however, have its limits.

What has been said is true of governments as players in international relations, and also of international organizations. But earlier in this chapter I made the point that international law was now the concern also of companies and individuals. Most companies tend to have a much narrower range of interests than most States (there are no doubt exceptions, if multinational conglomerates are compared with tiny States dependent upon a handful of export products). Ultimately, companies are interested primarily in money. Individuals tend to have neither the breadth of interest nor the long-term views of States. There is, accordingly, much less of a restraint upon the manner in which companies and individuals pursue their interests in international law. For example, a company claiming compensation for the violation of its rights under an investment protection treaty has every reason to pitch its claim at the highest level. It has no fear that its words will later be cited against it, because it can never find itself in a position where it is called to account for the treatment of foreign investors. This asymmetry in certain branches of international law, which results from the fact that companies and individuals litigate against States on a footing of juridical equality, will, I suspect, distort the development of international law. It will remove a natural brake on the development of legal doctrine, permitting tribunals to develop the law rapidly in certain areas, with the possible consequence that States may rein in the rights of individuals and companies to litigate against them.

1.7 WHY SHOULD PEOPLE COMPLY WITH INTERNATIONAL LAW?

I have left hanging the question, why *should* States (or more exactly, the people who run them) comply with international law? This is not a question that matters much to States. As I explained above, there are good explanations of why States operate in accordance with the normal rules of international intercourse, and those explanations do not depend upon a fundamental basis of obligation that renders rules of international law 'binding'. The question seems to have arisen only for the sake of symmetry. People ask, particularly during civil wars and coups, why government decrees or parliamentary laws should be obeyed. The answer is always given in terms that seek to legitimize those in power: you should obey me not simply because if you do not I will tell the police to arrest you or the army to kill you, but because lawful authority is vested in me. Asked how I came by that lawful authority, I may say that I had a mandate from the people, or from God, or from the previous monarch. The history of the answers to the question makes up a large part of the history of political philosophy.

The situation is similar in the case of international law. In the distant past, and indeed up to the Middle Ages in Europe, international law was widely regarded as in some way ordained by God. Kings were God's anointed; an attack on the King's representative was tantamount to an attack on the King himself; hence representatives were inviolable. There we have the seeds of the legal doctrine of diplomatic immunity. Treaties were commonly sworn before God, and their observance was accordingly a matter of religious obligation; hence the legal duty to observe treaties. Many examples could be taken.

This essentially theological view of the rules applicable between rulers, and later between States, persisted in Europe into the sixteenth century. The tradition, rooted in a combination of Roman law and the theologies of Augustine and Aquinas, is most evident in the works of the Spanish writers such as Vitoria and Suarez. As the secular powers waxed and began to eclipse ecclesiastical powers, writers such as Hugo Grotius began to shift to a more secular idea of natural law, a necessary order of society that was inherent in the natural order of the world. If the early writers might be said to answer the question, 'why should rulers obey the Law of Nations?' by saying that God has ordained it, those who adopted this increasingly secular view would say, because the natural order of the world demands it. This development was coupled with a growing prominence given to treaties and the customary law of nations, by writers such as Alberico Gentili and Richard Zouche. Alongside the principles derived from the natural order of things, the commitments that States freely made in the form of treaty and customary law also defined the rights and duties of States. International lawyers up until the end of the eighteenth century tended to position themselves on a spectrum according to the relative importance that they accorded to the law of nature on the one hand and to customary international law and treaties on the other.

Changes in perspectives and modes of thought are characteristic of ages rather than of particular dates. Perspectives emerge slowly, and they never entirely disappear, no matter how faint their echoes may be. The critical change from the earlier traditions came with the rejection of the idea that there was a natural order, whether ordained by God or otherwise, that entitled rulers to rule and obliged their subjects to submit. That rejection, epitomized in the famous words of Thomas Rainsborough in the Putney Debates during the English Civil War that 'every man that is to live under a government ought first by his own consent to put himself under that government', was clearly evident in the seventeenth century challenges to the divine right of kings. It reached its apotheosis in the late eighteenth century in the American and French revolutions, and the idea of consent as the basis of the authority of government became firmly rooted.

The parallel development in international law shifted the explanation of its binding force onto the notion that States had consented to be bound by international law, through participation in the making of customary international law or treaty law. That notion was refined throughout the nineteenth century, under the influence of the curious notion of the 'will' of the State. By the end of that century the idea was firmly established that the authority of international law derived from the fact that States had—or were to be treated as if they had—consented to be bound by its rules, and not from any external source such as the 'will of God' or 'the natural order'. That perspective, often described as the 'positivist' approach to international law, was by no means revolutionary. It was a descendant of much earlier views that gave prominence to the role of custom and treaties in the Law of Nations. But it was important because it slackened the bonds that held international law and theology or natural law theory close together.

This change, like all doctrinal changes, was of course a conscious shift in political perspective. It was not that international lawyers came to realize that they had been mistaken as to the theoretical basis of obligation. Rather, they rejected the idea that those claiming the right to exercise power and authority could rest their claims upon appeals to the will of God or to the natural order of things, which the powerful have always had little difficulty in discerning. The shift in perspective was made in order to effect a shift in political power. Priests and divinely appointed kings, out: professional politicians and civil servants, in.

International law in the twentieth century was understood and developed largely on the basis of this positivist outlook. States made new laws by agreement. States that had plainly not consented to be bound by certain rules, such as newly independent States emerging during the period of decolonization, asserted the right to decide whether or not they would subscribe to them. Treaty regimes, such as that which created the European Community, were regarded as matters for Member States only, so that non-Members could not be obliged to recognize the organization or regime created by the treaty. Yet throughout the twentieth century the natural law tradition remained as a *basso continuo* underlying international law. It came to the fore in developments such as the Nuremburg war crimes tribunals and the notion of human rights law, and also in the resurrected idea that there are some rules in international law (the rules of *jus cogens* or peremptory rules of international law, as they are known), that are binding on all States regardless of whether or not the States have consented to be bound by them.

In essence, positivists say that a State is bound by rules of international law because it has signed up to them, either literally in the case of treaty rules or metaphorically by the State's participation in the making of customary law. That has been the dominant ideology of international law throughout the last century. The practical significance of this ideology upon the day-to-day operation of international law is not entirely negligible, as will be seen when I explain the role of consent in the making of international law; but it is small. The most important characteristic of twentieth century international law was its bureaucratization and the pervasive colouring of inter-governmental dealings by the concepts and vocabulary of international law: the nature of international governmental dealings is, as they say, subdued to what it works in, like the dyer's hand. Those who actually engage in international lawyering are troubled seldom and little by the question of the theoretical basis of obligation. James Brierly, who devoted one of his more substantial articles to the question of the basis of obligation in international law, wisely observed that 'we are all of us obliged to act as if we were convinced of the reality of an objective order, both physical and moral, if we are to go on living and acting at all'.[7] Quite what the theoretical basis of that objective order might be is a matter that can in practice usually remain a mystery.

Indeed, it is unhelpful to start from the question, what gives international law its binding force? This way of asking the question often signals a misconception as to what international law is. It suggests that international law is something outside States, an external body of rules imposed upon States against their will. This is not a helpful perspective for anyone wishing to understand how international law works. It makes much more sense to say that international law consists of that body of rules that States have decided are binding.

Let me explain that point. All social life runs on the basis of regularities of behaviour and response. We expect drivers in the United Kingdom to keep to the left-hand side of the road; we do not expect that if we say 'how are you' we will be met with a punch in the mouth; we expect that the deliberately scratching of someone's car will be met with an emphatic protest; if we agree to meet someone for coffee at a certain time and place, we expect them to turn up as agreed; some of us still expect people to queue for buses in an orderly manner. Knowing the likely behaviour and responses of other people allows us to function effectively as a society; and understanding the rules and the consequences of breaking them allows us to plan our lives. Breaches of some of the rules may elicit a frown or a rebuke from others; breaches of other rules may result in a slap or a punch; and breaches of some rules may result in a visit from the police and a fine or spell in prison. We know that some rules are more important than others—or at least, that violations of different rules are likely to lead to different results. (It is not, however, the case that the rules of criminal law are always the most serious: we may regard the seduction of a spouse as

---

[7] 'The Basis of Obligation in International Law', in H. Lauterpacht and C.H.M. Waldock, *The Basis of Obligation in International Law* (Oxford: Clarendon Press, 1959).

a matter of greater importance than a parking offence, even though the latter is a crime and the former is not.) There are, then, many regularities in social behaviour that map out our expectations of the way that we and our neighbours should behave. And we, as a society, regard some of those regularities as so important that compliance with them should not be a matter of individual choice, or even a matter to be settled exclusively by the wrongdoer and his neighbours, but as matters sufficiently important to warrant the punishment of infractions by invoking the apparatus of the Law and the repressive power of the State.

If we adopt the same perspective on international law, we can say that the rules of international law are those regularities in international behaviour that are regarded by the community of States as being so important that they do not accept that each State is entitled to decide freely for itself whether or not to comply with the rule. Thus, we should not ask, what makes international law binding? Rather, we should say that international law consists of those rules that are treated as legally binding.

The practical significance of the basis of obligation for the daily practice of international law is limited, but its significance for the broad development of international law is immense. During the twentieth century the general assumption was that States are equal and independent and entitled to be free from foreign intervention in their internal affairs. That assumption is fast eroding. In the late twentieth century, and particularly since the fall of communism in eastern Europe in the 1990s, the idea of a *pax Americana* began to gain hold—not least because the idea was implemented in a policy of intervention in various States that were regarded by the United States as having strayed intolerably from the straight and narrow. The interventions, sometimes involving uses of force as, for example, in Grenada, Panama, Afghanistan, Kosovo, and Iraq, had a variety of motivations and justifications, and should not be regarded as uniform instances of a single view. But there is underlying them a uniform view: that the United States has, in its own eyes, the right and the responsibility to impose the law in certain circumstances, and to do so unilaterally if necessary. The era of the independent sovereign State is drawing to a close. If this idea finds a coherent theoretical basis and is applied in the practice of States, it will produce a very significant shift in the nature of international law.

1.8 HOW INTERNATIONAL LAW IS INVOKED AND APPLIED

I have said something about the scope of international law, and about the main ways in which it is made and the reasons for the widespread compliance with it. I turn next to the question of the manner in which it is invoked and applied.

The application of the law proceeds in a way that is more subtle than is often assumed. As I observed above, government lawyers, and also lawyers in corporations and other organizations that operate internationally, tend to share a common intellectual background and to look at the world in much the same way. They see the world as made up of sovereign States, in principle co-equal before the law, with boundaries fixed and jurisdiction circumscribed by the law; they see links of nationality and territory as significant markers of the extent of States' legitimate interests, and so on. Thus, the international legal system and its principles and concepts become the framework for thinking about and practising international diplomacy.

Given this shared view of the world, and shared understanding of international legal principles, the invocation of the law can be a gentle and allusive process, even in the midst of crisis. It usually proceeds in practice by a process known in the field of linguistics as illocution: that is, approximately, the implicit meaning that the speaker intends to communicate when saying something. This can be illustrated by a domestic analogy.

I.9 THE DOMESTIC ANALOGY

Suppose that I, as a university professor, lend a book to a student. The book is not returned, and I ask for it back. If it is still not returned, despite increasingly urgent informal requests, I might write to the student on University notepaper. By doing so I can imply, or may expressly state, that within the University I am a Faculty member and the borrower is a student, bound by University regulations on good conduct and so on. My request—what I want the student to do—remains the same; but shifting it into the University context by means of such signals has the effect of suggesting that I regard the University as in some sense party to the argument, and on my side. If that fails I may turn the ratchet further, and invoke formal University disciplinary procedures. This will force the University to take a stand; and if I am right in thinking that the regulations are on my side, the University will take my part in the argument. That, in turn, may lead bystanders to shy away from taking the part of the student. They may believe that a community needs rules, and that rules should be obeyed; or they may themselves have lent the student books and fear for their return; or they may simply fear being branded by the University authorities as collaborators with the student. In these ways, the shift into the University context increases my power as against that of the student.

Moreover, the context of the dispute is redefined. The student may previously have argued that he needed the book for an essay, whereas I had no urgent need for it, or perhaps had a second copy. Such moral arguments are powerful in the straight request/refusal context; but they lose much force, and may be regarded as relevant (if at all) only to the mitigation of any punishment in the disciplinary context.

If these steps fail, I may hint at the possibility of civil legal action, or of turning the matter over to the police as a case of theft. This, too, may be done by the use of language. The mere use of a term such as 'court' or 'theft' in exchanges with the student is enough to indicate the change of context. If police or court action is taken, the new context again alters the position. The moral arguments become totally irrelevant to the question of guilt on a theft charge. Support from bystanders is likely to ebb still further when the police become involved. And my power is greatly increased by having the police and the courts on side.

There are a number of points to note. First, all of these shifts in the context of the dispute, in the factors and types of argument that are relevant, and the relative power of me and of the student, have been effected through the use of language. Indeed, all of the stages described above could have been traversed in the course of a single oral conversation. There is no need actually to have the police or the University proctors turn up at the scene: it is enough to allude to their existence and possible involvement. The power of the system, and power within the system, is a function of how the systems are structured and organized, and not immediately dependent upon actual exercises of power. There are of course limits to this. If the power in question is rarely or never exercised that will naturally diminish the force of the threat. If the student believes that the police are likely to tell me that they have better things to do than chase after the books of socially dysfunctional professors, my threat to involve them will carry little weight. Nonetheless, it is by no means the case that the persuasive power of the law depends upon the immediate availability of some means of enforcement.

Second, the shifts in context were a matter of choice. There is no reason why I must make the dispute a matter of University discipline or of criminal law: that choice is mine. Moreover, the rational choice in almost every context is to handle a dispute at the informal, 'social' level, rather than translating it into a legal context. The choice is, however, one that can be made unilaterally. If I choose to try to involve the police, the student cannot insist that the dispute be handled without involving the authorities.

There is a further lesson to be drawn from the domestic analogy. If the detention of the book does go before a University tribunal or a court, then whatever the outcome of the proceedings the authority of the tribunal or court is likely to be enhanced. Similarly, whatever rules are applied by the tribunal or court, the authority of those rules is also likely to be enhanced. The mere fact that the tribunal and the rule are used gives them greater prominence, and makes their existence more of a factor in the calculations of members of the community.

This analogy broadly holds good on the international plane; and the 1990 Kuwait crisis offers an example. On 1 August 1990 Iraq invaded Kuwait, and the matter was quickly taken up by the UN Security Council. Many statements were made in the Security Council concerning the invasion. Typical examples include the following, all drawn from Security Council debates on the Kuwait crisis during August 1990:

Mr Fortier (Canada) There can be no question that the brutal Iraqi aggression against Kuwait is totally unacceptable and represents a flagrant violation of the Charter of the United Nations as well as international law.
. . .

Mr Redzuan (Malaysia) . . . Malaysia considers the principles embodied in the Charter of the United Nations as sacrosanct in the conduct of relations between sovereign States.
. . .

Mr Blanc (France) The magnitude of these measures is justified, in the view of my Government, because of the unacceptable nature of Iraq's military aggression, which is a major violation of international law and a serious threat to international peace and security.
. . .

Mr Rasi (Finland) The acquisition of the territory of another State by the use of force contradicts one of the most basic and firm principles of international law.
. . .

Mr Al-Anbari (Iraq) . . . The Iraqi Revolutionary Command Council stated that the former colonizers had not left our region without first having undertaken certain tasks.

In the past, the Arab nation was one and indivisible. After independence was gained by the Arab States the many countries of the region were the result of foreign colonizers carving up the territory of the region. The colonizers re-drew the geopolitical map of the region in order to weaken the Arab States. That did indeed split the Arab nation and made it difficult for it to speak with a single voice. . . .

In that way a part of the region cherished by Iraq—Kuwait—was separated from Iraq. This was our country's area of strategic access. The colonizers did not hesitate to do in Iraq what they did in other countries of the region.

That is why the Iraqi Revolutionary Command Council decided to restore to our country the portion taken away from it, thus re-establishing the eternal, indestructible unity of our country.

The pattern of the argument is clear. The States opposed to Iraq cited international law in support of their case. Iraq defended its actions on the basis of political and historical arguments, rather than on the basis of international law. Each side sought to locate the debate in the normative framework that best supported its case, and within which it had the greatest power.

Notice that this explanation has not had to call upon any element of coercion in order to explain why the law is useful or why it is obeyed. In my domestic analogy, the law was brought to bear solely by the use of language in a face-to-face discussion. There is, however, one significant difference between the national and international legal orders. In national law it is generally true that individuals ultimately have the right, and accordingly the power, to insist upon the involvement of the authorities—the police, the courts, and so on—in their disputes. No international tribunal has compulsory jurisdiction. Even the discussion of an international dispute (let alone the taking of action to resolve it) by an organization such as the United Nations or NATO is a discretionary matter. States need to lobby and persuade in order to have the matter taken up. While the co-operation of the other party is not needed to shift the context, the co-operation of the members of the organization is. And if it is desired to refer the matter for judicial settlement in an international tribunal, that reference can only be made with the agreement, in some form or other, of both disputing States.

This weakens the analogy, but not seriously. Most law—domestic and international—is complied with as a matter of choice, not through fear of sanctions. International law does, however, have a range of sanctions, many of which do not depend upon action through international courts and organizations. States may respond to violations of international law by imposing economic or other sanctions on the wrongdoer, which may have much greater impact than any judgment that a court might hand down. If international opinion turns against a State, it may pay a heavy price. Credit becomes more difficult to obtain; trade links and concessions may be withdrawn; the State may be diplomatically isolated, and its attempts to use international organizations may be opposed. And in extreme cases, where a wrongdoer threatens to attack another State, the right to use force against it in self defence exists.

It might be said that such measures allow strong States to deter wrong-doing on the part of weak States but that no such measures can constrain strong States. That is not so. There are no States so strong that they are wholly immune to all of the pressures that may be brought to bear upon them. The military power of the United States cannot entirely insulate it from the economic power of OPEC or the European Union, for example;

and there have been several intense trade disputes between the blocs. International and domestic political pressure may require that a government act legitimately within the limits of international law.

Ultimately, a State set on disregarding the law may decide that the risks and potential sanctions are outweighed by the probable benefits, and choose to violate the law, just as an individual may choose to violate domestic law. That does not invalidate the law. All societies tolerate a certain level of law-breaking, which is the result of the balance between the resources that the society is prepared to put into preventing the crimes and the social costs of the crimes themselves. If every citizen were accompanied everywhere by three police officers, crime statistics would no doubt fall, but not in proportion to the increase in the cost of policing. What matters is that on the overwhelming majority of occasions the overwhelming majority of people obey the law. The law is not an end in itself. It is an instrument for achieving certain social goals. There is no particular merit inherent in complete compliance with the law. The law succeeds if it secures enough compliance to enable civilized social life to proceed and if its enforcement is sufficiently effective, impartial, and non-discriminatory to satisfy the basic demands of justice. That is as true internationally as it is within any national society.

FURTHER READING

There are many good introductory texts on international law. Among them are Antonio Cassese, *International Law* (Oxford: Oxford University Press, 2001), and Rosalyn Higgins, *Problems and Process: International Law and How We Use It* (Oxford: Oxford University Press, 1995), and Peter Malanczuk, *Akehurst's Modern Introduction to International Law* (7th revised edn., London: Routledge, 1997). More substantial introductions can be found in works such as Malcolm Shaw, *International Law* (5th edn., Cambridge: Cambridge University Press, 2003), and Malcolm Evans, *International Law* (2nd edn., Oxford: Oxford University Press, 2006).

2

How International Law is Made

I have explained in a general way how the rules of international law arise, but need to discuss the process in more detail in order that its potential and its limitations as a tool of social organization be understood. The three sections of this chapter describe how international law is made through the formation of customary international law and the making of treaties, and how tribunals apply other sources of law such as 'general principles' of law and 'soft law' principles derived from resolutions of international organizations. The chapter may contain more detail than many readers would wish, and they can skim through or skip over it.

The making of international law gives rise to a number of issues. One is the question, who has the power to make international law? Obviously, States are bound by treaties to which they have become parties, but are they bound to comply with provisions in treaties to which they are not parties? Are they bound by rules of customary international law that emerged before the State came into existence, for example before the State acquired its independence from a colonial power? The latter question illustrates another aspect of the issue. It may be important to determine *when* a rule of international law came into existence, and when it became binding upon a particular State. Similarly, some rules of international law are essentially local or regional, and questions may arise as to *where* they apply, and which States they apply to. The range of issues of this kind will become apparent as the processes of creating international law are considered.

In Chapter 1, I referred to the changing doctrinal basis of international law and the explanations of why international law is binding upon States. In the early days of the subject, those explanations acknowledged three main sources of obligations; treaties, customary international law, and the principles of natural law or theology. The shift to a positivist conception of international law largely excluded the appeal to the natural order as a source of legal obligation, although vestiges of it survive in the references to moral principles that have motivated some more recent legal developments. But in explaining what international law is, international lawyers have never confined themselves to these three sources of law. The early European texts, for instance, deployed arguments based on analogies with the rules and principles of the major municipal legal systems.

All of these sources are reflected in Article 38 of the Statute of the International Court of Justice (ICJ), which directs that Court to decide cases before it on the basis of:

a. international conventions, whether general or particular, establishing rules expressly recognized by the contesting states;

b. international custom, as evidence of a general practice accepted as law;

c. the general principles of law recognized by civilized nations.

That direction is specific to the ICJ, and in principle other international tribunals could be directed to apply other bodies of rules—as the European Court of Justice applies EU law, for instance. But Article 38 is generally regarded as an authoritative statement of the sources to which any tribunal may resort when it is directed to apply 'international law', and references to other sources such as Security Council resolutions are regarded as permissible only to the extent that such references are required or permitted by an applicable rule of treaty or customary law. That, at least, is the orthodox view, and is my starting point. But, as I shall explain when I turn to consider other candidates for inclusion in the catalogue of sources, tribunals have a tendency to be more flexible than this might suggest.

It makes good sense to begin this account by considering customary international law.

2.1 CUSTOMARY INTERNATIONAL LAW

2.1.1 THE COMPONENT ELEMENTS OF CUSTOMARY INTERNATIONAL LAW

2.1.1.1 A General Practice

The purpose of all rules of law is to introduce an element of predictability into the behaviour of other people. We wish to be able to act on the basis that others will behave in conformity with the law. In customary law systems, this means that people should behave in accordance with legal rules that are expressed in established practices. It is the same in international law. Hence Article 38 of the ICJ Statute refers to 'international custom, as evidence of a general practice accepted as law'. It should more properly refer to 'a general practice as evidence of an international custom accepted as law'; but everyone understands what Article 38 is getting at. For a rule of customary international law to exist, it must be manifested in the general practice of States.

The development of the legal concept of the continental shelf offers a good illustration. In 1945 the United States, which had realized during World War Two that a State's dependence upon imported energy was a major strategic vulnerability, sought to maximize its control over oil resources. Extensive oil fields existed in the shallow waters of the Gulf of Mexico, but mostly more than three miles from the coast. At that time international law allowed States to control only a narrow belt of coastal waters, known as the territorial sea. The United States claimed a three-mile territorial sea, beyond which waters had the status of high seas. No State could have exclusive rights over the resources of waters or the seabed of the high seas. In order to bring the more distant seabed oilfields under US control, President Truman issued a proclamation stating that:

the Government of the United States regards the natural resources of the subsoil and sea bed of the continental shelf beneath the high seas but contiguous to the coasts of the United States as appertaining to the United States, subject to its jurisdiction and control.

On its face that proclamation asserted a right for which there was no basis in international law. If, for example, the United States Coastguard had in 1945 arrested a foreign ship drilling for oil off the US coast, the arrest could have been challenged as a violation of international law. But far from objecting to the US assertion of rights over the continental shelf, other States followed its example. In the late 1940s and 1950s, State after State enacted legislation asserting its own exclusive rights over the resources of the continental shelf. By the mid 1950s many, but not all, States had made claims of the same kind as that in the Truman Proclamation. That was enough to amount to a 'general practice'.

There is no set proportion of the States in the world that must conform to a pattern of behaviour in order for it to be a 'general practice': even less is there any need for every State in the world to conform. It is, however, necessary that those States whose interests are particularly affected by the rule should participate in the practice. A rule concerning, say, the use of outer space could not be made without the participation of the States active in space exploration. Subject to that point, it is necessary only that the general practice be discernible, and that is a matter of judgement. Furthermore, if the putative rule is to have universal force it is necessary that participation in the practice should be broadly representative of all the States in the world and not confined to States in a particular region or political grouping.

It is said, perhaps apocryphally, that when one of the new universities was built, instead of laying down footpaths the campus was covered in loose gravel. At the end of the first year someone went up a tower block and looked down. There was a clearly discernible network of pathways made by the feet of the students over the preceding year. Some pathways had been beaten by many feet—the paths to the library and the bars, perhaps. Others were made by far fewer, if heavier, feet—the path to the rugby changing rooms, perhaps. But, narrow or wide, the paths could clearly be seen. What mattered was that the course of the path was identifiable, in a way that it would not be if the course were obscured by other footprints following random routes or a number of routes so varied that no one route could be identified as 'the' path between two points. No doubt in some areas there were lonely footprints charting unusual routes: but they would not count as paths. The metaphor works well for customary international law. Some practices are followed by many States, great and small. The practices concerning diplomats are examples, because every State has at least some diplomatic dealings. Other practices are followed by few States. Practices concerning outer space are an example, because few States have the capacity to engage in space exploration. But if the few States having that capacity follow a consistent practice, not obscured by a host of different practices, there will be enough to form the basis of a rule of customary international law.

To return to the continental shelf, the consistency of national claims that followed the Truman Proclamation, coupled with the absence of any significant challenges to or variations in those claims, constituted a 'general practice' for the purposes of generating a rule of international law.

I have spoken so far about practices forming the basis for rules of customary international law, rather than actually forming the rules themselves.
That is because not all consistent practices generate rules of law.

2.1.2 *OPINIO JURIS*: ACCEPTANCE OF A PRACTICE AS LAW

There are all sorts of consistent practices in international relations. Heads
of State are consistently treated as immune from arrest and prosecution
when they visit foreign States, no matter how bestial the offences they
have directed in their home States. The practice of according immunity
from arrest and prosecution to visiting Heads of State is long established
and has generated a rule of customary international law, so that States are
legally obliged to accord such immunity. A visiting Head of State also
expects that on official visits he will have a red carpet rolled out to the steps
of his aircraft. That is also a well-established practice. But if he were to be
greeted by the sight of a roll of the highly patterned carpeting much
favoured in 1960s Birmingham, he would not think that a violation of
international law had occurred. There are well-established patterns of
behaviour and expectations that, despite their consistency and clarity, are
not regarded as manifestations of rules of law. One function of the doctrine of sources is to distinguish those social conventions that are legally
binding from those that are not. That distinction is important because
breaches of legally binding rules entitle States to take various kinds of
corrective action that they could not properly take if the rules were not
legally binding. So, how is the distinction drawn?

The answer is almost a circular argument. International law requires, in
the words of Article 38 of the ICJ Statute, that the general practice be
'accepted as law'. The States engaged in the practice must regard their
practice as an expression of a rule of international law. Claims to immunity
or decisions to accord immunity to Heads of State are made in the knowledge that the matter is regulated by international law and that the action
is in conformity with it. The Truman Proclamation was made in the knowledge that the claim dealt with a matter regulated by international law and
impliedly asserted that the claim to a continental shelf was consistent with
international law. This belief in the conformity of the practice with international law is known as the *opinio juris*. A general practice of States and
opinio juris are the two essential components that together generate rules
of customary international law. The body of State practice is sometimes
referred to as the material element, and *opinio juris* as the psychological
element.

It is easy to see how practice that is consistent with a pre-existing rule
can be thought to be consistent with that rule, but less easy to see how that

can be the case where the practice asserts a new rule, as in the case of the Truman Proclamation.

This question is relevant to the process by which customary international law changes. If the practice of States had to be accompanied by the belief that the practice was in accordance with existing international law, international law could never change. But it must, and does, change in order to accommodate changing social circumstances. A State wishing to change the law makes, in effect, an 'offer' to States at large. It is as if the United States said in the Truman Proclamation, 'how about this for a new way of dealing with ownership of seabed resources?' If States agreed with the United States' proposal they would acquiesce in it, and perhaps make their own claims to the continental shelf. The new practice would be coupled with *opinio juris* in the sense that the States concerned would act with the belief that their practice related to a matter governed by international law and that their practice was consistent with what they believed that international law should be. This is what is sometimes called a proleptic approach, anticipating a future development and treating the practice and *opinio juris* as if there were already a rule of law corresponding to the rule implicit in the practice.

This may sound unnecessarily complicated. We need, however, some way of distinguishing between those innovative actions that are intended to propel the development of international law by starting the process of creating a new rule, and those that are not. For example, in 1967 the British Government was faced with the prospect of massive pollution of its coastline as a result of the grounding of a Liberian oil tanker, the *Torrey Canyon*, on the Seven Stones reef in the high seas off Cornwall. International law as it then stood provided no basis for the assertion of control by the coastal State over foreign ships on the high seas, but the British Government nonetheless bombed the tanker in an attempt to set fire to the oil and minimize pollution. It stated that 'the overriding concern of the Government throughout has been to preserve the coasts from oil pollution and to adopt the course most likely to achieve this end. Neither legal nor financial considerations inhibited Government action at any stage.' That is a good example of an innovative practice which one could not properly assume was accompanied by *opinio juris*—though paradoxically international approval for the United Kingdom's action was so general (even Liberia made no protest against it) that the right to take such action against shipping casualties on the high seas was established, a treaty concluded at a multilateral conference in 1969, and passed rapidly into customary law.

States do not usually assert explicitly that their actions are (or are not) consistent with international law: explicit statements of *opinio juris* are rare. Even the Truman Proclamation was not based on any express assertion that the American claim was lawful, but only that it was 'reasonable and just'. In some cases, however, it is so obvious that the conduct in question relates to a matter that is regulated by law that it may be presumed that a State's conduct is accompanied by *opinio juris*. Everyone understood that the question of the rights of a State over the resources of the high seas was a matter of international law, for example. There could be no doubt that the United States was taking a step that had legal significance; and the presumption is that States act in accordance with what they believe to be the law. Hence, it was proper to presume the existence of *opinio juris* in the case of the Truman Proclamation; but the presumption was rebutted by the government statement in the *Torrey Canyon* incident.

Where actions are not accompanied by any explanation, the practice is to assume that the State regarded itself as acting lawfully: but that would be consistent with the State either believing that it had a legal right or duty to do what it did but was acting in conformity with it, or believing that the matter is not regulated by law at all but is a matter of policy or expediency. In the case of the Truman Proclamation the position was clear, because a claim to exclusive rights could only have a legal basis. Debt relief is an example of a practice where the position is less clear. The government debts of the world's poorest countries have repeatedly been rescheduled or cancelled when they have been unable to service the debt. Debt relief is a partially institutionalized process operating through the Paris Club, whose Member States have developed principles and standard terms applicable to debtor States. Does this mean that debtor States have a right to debt relief? Is it a matter of legal rights and duties, or a matter of expediency or of policy unregulated by law?

This question is resolved in practice by approaching it from the point of view of the burden of proof. It is a general principle of international law that anyone who asserts a proposition has the burden of proving it. If someone asserts that a particular practice has crystallized into a rule of customary international law, they must prove it by demonstrating that the necessary general practice, coupled with *opinio juris*, exists. In the absence of proof of such *opinio juris* the practice would remain without legally binding force, no matter how consistently it is followed. And in the case of debt relief, it is not possible to show that there is the necessary *opinio juris*. Whatever moral, political or economic imperatives may drive it, as a matter of international law debt relief is a privilege and not a right.

The need to distinguish between conduct that is regarded as an expression of an underlying legal rule (even though the motives for undertaking the action may be rooted in non-legal policy considerations) and conduct that is not so regarded is particularly acute in the case of prohibitive rules. Here the conduct consists of inaction. Diplomatic immunity has already been mentioned. If a serving diplomat appears to have committed an offence, customary international law requires that the State in which he is serving should not prosecute him. Compliance with that rule requires precisely that the State should do nothing. But States often do nothing, and for a wide range of reasons. For example, so far as I know no State prosecutes people within its borders for having smoked cannabis in some foreign country where its consumption is legal. Does that pattern of conduct generate a rule of customary international law stipulating that States must not prosecute people in such circumstances? And if not, how is that pattern of inactivity to be distinguished from the inactivity underlying diplomatic immunity? The test is one of legal relevance. Is the conduct in question in principle regulated by international law, and is the inactivity an expression of the conviction that international law requires States to refrain from acting? It is a matter of *opinio juris*.

2.1.3 THE TIME ELEMENT

Before leaving the topic of the components of customary international law, I should say something about the temporal element, the duration of a particular practice. Customary law systems generally suppose that the rules that they apply are long-established, whatever that may mean within the particular system. The reason for the concern with time is a matter of authority. It is necessary to show that a putative rule is rooted in the community, and not an ephemeral reflection of the views or aspirations of particular litigants or lawyers. Proof that a practice has long been followed is good evidence that the rule evidenced by the practice is firmly established. But it may also be possible to provide that evidence in another way.

Space law offers a good example. International law is made in response to the actual concerns of the international community and rarely addresses hypothetical problems. When the first man-made satellite was launched in 1957, there was no international law of outer space. There was not (and is still not) even a settled definition of the upper limit of a State's jurisdiction over the airspace above its territory. In the absence of any rules it could perhaps have been argued that each State was entitled to that part of the universe that extends above its territory. The significance of man's first expedition beyond the planet was not lost on the United Nations, however, and the matter was debated in the General Assembly, which adopted a number of resolutions on the subject. Those resolutions, and notably the 1963 Declaration of Legal Principles Governing the Activities of States in the Exploration and Use of Outer Space, purported to set out the basic legal principles governing outer space, such as the principle that neither the moon nor other 'celestial bodies' (as they are known in the picturesque vocabulary of the UN) may be appropriated by any State.

Those resolutions were adopted without dissent, and evidenced an international consensus as to what the legal principles governing outer space should be. Since the basis of the binding force of customary international law is said to be the freely given consent of States to be bound by it, it was widely argued that these resolutions effectively created 'instant' customary international law. Though the resolutions were succeeded by several treaties on various aspects of outer space, this view of their effect is largely unchallenged. In the *North Sea Continental Shelf* cases in 1969 the ICJ expressly accepted the possibility that a widespread and representative practice could generate a rule of customary international law even without the passage of any considerable period of time. This means of creating customary international law is particularly appropriate where the rules in question are prohibitive. It makes little sense to wait for a long period to elapse during which States refrain from making claims to sovereignty over the moon, for example, if there is explicit agreement that no such claims would be lawful.

2.1.4 WHAT COUNTS AS STATE PRACTICE

I have spoken of the practice of States without so far explaining what that practice consists of or how it is identified.

We often speak of States as if they have a real existence and can themselves act. They have, of course, no material existence and must act through human agents. The question is, therefore, whose acts count as the acts of the State? In principle, anyone acting in an official capacity may be said to be acting on behalf of the State: the legislature, judiciary, and the executive government; the civil service and armed forces; police, immigration officers, tax inspectors, and so on. But it is necessary to bear in mind the context of the question. The question is, what is the practice of, say, the United Kingdom in relation to this or that matter? In effect, we are asking whether the United Kingdom should be regarded as having signed up to a particular rule of customary international law. It is therefore natural to seek State practice that evidences what one might call an 'official' and 'considered' view of the State concerned.

If the junior officers at the immigration desks of a State's airports consistently single out people of certain ethnic backgrounds for detailed questioning, allowing others to pass through unmolested, that does not necessarily mean that the State considers that as a matter of international law it is entitled to discriminate in this way. It may be that the government of the State abhors the practice and would discipline the officers concerned, and would reject the idea that international law permitted such discriminatory action. If a complaint were made about the action, the State could not disown it, because the practice was that of a person exercising official State functions and acting for the State. The State is, as a matter of international law, responsible for it. But the State could, while accepting that the practice was imputable to it, take the view that the practice was not an expression of its policy towards international law. Certainly, the higher the level of government at which a particular practice operates the more reasonable it is to regard it as the practice of the State.

That said, any official acts may count as State practice. When the United Kingdom Parliament enacted Part 12 of the Anti-terrorism, Crime and Security Act 2001 it made British citizens liable to prosecution for bribery and corruption even if committed abroad. The enactment of that law was a piece of British State practice evidencing a claim to exercise extraterritorial jurisdiction over the acts of its nationals in the circumstances set out in the statute. So, too, would be the prosecution of a person for a breach of that Act, as would the conviction of the person. The acts of the legislature, the police and the courts each evidence the underlying jurisdictional claim.

There is a need for some caution in interpreting practice, and in particular, statutes. The (UK) Theft Act, for example, makes it an offence to steal. It is not expressly said to apply only within the United Kingdom, or only to British citizens. The ordinary meaning of its language is wide enough to apply to Chinese pickpockets in Beijing. But the law has never been applied in that way and almost certainly will never be applied in that way. It is interpreted in accordance with the established canons of interpretation in English law as applying only within the borders of the United Kingdom. It would be incorrect to suppose that the statute asserts universal jurisdiction over all thieves. Statutes, and other items of State practice, must be interpreted carefully, in accordance with the principles of interpretation of the legal system in question.

Difficulties arise with State practice around the margins. Some functions that are widely considered to be typical of the State may in fact be undertaken by bodies that are not technically part of the State government. For instance, in many countries religious courts adjudicate upon a wide range of offences. Do the acts of such courts count as the practice of the State, for example if they convict and order the punishment of a person for an act committed abroad? Private institutions are licensed or acknowledged by government in many States to regulate commercial sectors, such as the securities and insurance industries. Should a requirement by such an institution—the Stock Exchange, or the Bank of England, for instance—that a foreign company report upon its overseas activities, or conduct its operations in a foreign country in a particular way, be counted as a practice of the State?

At the heart of this problem is the question of what a State *is*. There are different ways of organizing a State, and different ways of conceiving what the State is. Governments have controlled the prices of goods and services and labour, and mandated or forbidden compliance with certain religious prescriptions, and traded in commodities and goods on international markets. In other States and at other times governments have, by design or through impotence, exercised only the most minimal control over daily life. The provision of education and healthcare, and even the organization of policing, has been taken on by non-governmental organizations in order to fulfil public needs. In yet other States private organizations operate in parallel to the government. Prices may be regulated both by the government and by lawful private cartels; the security of persons and property may be protected by the regular police force, and by private security firms or bodyguards or criminal gangs. Which of these should we count as acting for 'the State'?

One cannot say that only governmental agencies should be counted, because that begs the question of what is governmental. The concepts of 'State' and 'government' have little in the way of necessary or natural content, and certainly not enough to provide a workable criterion.

There is another problem in identifying what is State practice. Take, for instance, the law on expropriation. Customary international law permits States to expropriate foreign property for public purposes on certain conditions, one of which is that the expropriation must not be discriminatory. That leaves open the question whether, say, a nationalization of all foreign-owned farms without discrimination, but of no farms owned by resident citizens, would be regarded as discriminatory or not. Suppose that in this context there had been many claims by companies of many different nationalities in which they had consistently argued that it was discriminatory, and suppose that those claims had been brought against, say, half a dozen States. If the claims were in this respect conceded by the States, could the companies' claims be counted in together with the State practice, so as to establish a much more widespread pattern of behaviour than would be possible if the States alone were taken into consideration? Or suppose (as is much more likely) that the States consistently reject the claims and assert that it is only discrimination among foreigners and not discrimination against foreigners that is forbidden. If there were a significant number of States engaged in this practice, there might appear to be enough of a consistent pattern to be discerned from their practice to establish a rule of customary international law. But can the claims of the companies be taken into account in order to contradict that practice, so that it cannot be said to be unchallenged?

This question is important and of great political significance, and there is much that could be said on it. It determines whether the power to make and change international law lies exclusively with States, as Article 38 of the ICJ Statute suggests, or whether it is to be shared with other organizations such as companies. It is a question that arises out of the changing nature of international law; and in broad terms there are two approaches that might be taken—or, more likely, a combination of the two. First, international law may accommodate non-State actors and accept their practice as one of the contributory sources of developments within the international legal system. That approach would be something like the approach to law in the Middle Ages, in which there existed a body of Law Merchant developed from a fusion of the common law and of customs of traders, and applied through a recognized system of tribunals more or less integrated into the national legal system. The alternative possibility is that international law will remain the preserve of States and governments, and that non-State actors are likely to seek to secure their interests either by the use of particular contractual arrangements or by persuading States to adopt sympathetic laws and policies.

It is difficult to offer a coherent theoretical explanation of the present position regarding the actors whose practice counts towards the formation of international law, but much easier to describe the present practice. International lawyers and international tribunals still look primarily, if not exclusively, to the practice of States, and the practice of States is implicitly regarded as being the practice that is recorded in official publications, such as law reports, statutes, records of parliamentary proceedings, and statements issued by the departments of central government. The solution is in practice found, in other words, not so much by focusing on the question of the authority of the actor as by focusing on the authority of the sources that record the practice.

I have spoken of the 'acts' or 'practice' of a State; but inaction is often equally important. If, say, a State expropriates only foreign-owned farms and no other State makes any protest, that is significant. At least in the case of States whose nationals had property taken, and which are aware of the expropriations, the silence will amount to acquiescence, because a State that is directly affected by a violation of international law is expected to protest. The expectation, imposed by a rule of international law, goes back to the question of predictability. It is undesirable as a matter of policy that an activity should be tolerated over a period of time, but later condemned as unlawful. Those engaged in the activity would not know where they stood. That policy is applied in all the main legal systems, forbidding a change of position once a certain practice or state of affairs has been acquiesced in. The same is true in international law. Evidence of acquiescence is in effect taken as evidence that the acquiescing State regards the activity or state of affairs as consistent with international law. The acquiescing State may be counted as a supporter of the rule in question along with any States whose positive actions have contributed to the 'general practice accepted as law'.

Protests against breaches of international law are particularly significant. As the ICJ recognized in the *Nicaragua (Merits)* case in 1986, if one State violates the law and others protest, the protests implicitly affirm the rule in question. Thus, breaches of international law may, paradoxically, strengthen the law rather than weaken it, if the offending State is condemned and isolated. Conversely, as I shall explain shortly, if other States remain silent in the face of an apparent violation of the law, it may be that the first steps towards a change in the law are being taken.

2.1.5 COLLECTIONS OF STATE PRACTICE

Unearthing evidence of State practice can be an enormously time-consuming and tedious process. Tunnelling through *Hansard*, Parliamentary Papers, official publications, law reports, newspaper reports, and so on in order to gather evidence of the practice of one State is a counsel of perfection: to do so in order to determine the practice of all of the 180 or so States in the world is beyond the limits of practicality.

Two devices are adopted to cope with this problem. The first is the compilation of digests of State practice. Some States, most of them the Old World States of Europe and North America and the larger States elsewhere, publish annual surveys of their practice on points of international law. Sometimes this is done officially, as in the *Digests* of United States practice in international law prepared by the State Department. Sometimes it is done unofficially, as in the section on United Kingdom Materials in International Law that has appeared at the end of each volume of the *British Yearbook of International Law* since 1978. (Many *Yearbooks* in other States also contain such sections.) With the material arranged topic by topic it is relatively easy to glean whatever practice there might have been on a particular point by consulting these collections.

The second device is to ignore the problem. In practice, both tribunals and writers are satisfied with very little in the way of State practice. It is rare for the practice of more than a couple of dozen States to be cited on a point of customary law; and not uncommon for far fewer States to be cited. One of the most dramatic decisions of an English court on customary international law was the 1977 *Trendtex* case, in which the Court of Appeal's decision that a new rule of international law on sovereign immunity had arisen was supported by the citation of the practice of a mere handful of (western) States. Of course, on some matters by no means all States will have relevant practice. Afghanistan's practice on the Law of the Sea, for example, is probably sparse. But on other matters practice is widespread. There is in principle no reason for neglecting the practice of any State; but international law as it is practised is a real-time activity. Practitioners do the best that they can within the time available; but that time rarely permits more than a limited scrutiny of material.

This plainly gives a disproportionate influence to the practice of those States whose practice is most easily accessible, and that depends largely on the language in which the material is written and the manner in which it is published, if it is published at all. A glance at the textbooks and articles written during the twentieth century confirms this. Evidence cited in support of propositions concerning customary international law rarely extends beyond material in European languages; and even within that category the well published and well publicized United States' digests exercised an exceptional influence. That position is slowly changing as the practice of more and more States is published. But the linguistic limitation of international lawyers is a much less tractable problem.

2.1.6 HOW RULES ARE DISCERNED

I have explained that rules of customary international law are formed by a general practice accepted as law. The relationship between the rule and the practice needs to be understood. It is not that by an exhaustive examination of State practice we could eventually discern all of the rules of international law, rather as a tropical botanist might eventually identify all of the species of plant in a rain forest. The practice does not push forward ready-formed rules, there for the seeing. Rather, lawyers think for some reason that there ought to be a rule on a particular point and then search to see if their hypothesis is supported by the practice. When one considers the circumstances in which rules of law are put in question one can see that this must be so.

Suppose, for example, that the United Kingdom wishes to complain against a foreign State that has refused to allow a British ship carrying nuclear materials to sail through its waters. The foreign State asserts that the ship has no right of passage. The United Kingdom does not wish to request permission for the ship to pass because it believes that passage is a right and not something that the foreign State may decide whether or not to permit. The United Kingdom accordingly will wish to show that there is a rule of international law allowing that passage. Unless the matter is settled by a treaty between the foreign State and the United Kingdom, it will be necessary to see if customary international law has a rule dealing with the matter. The foreign State, of course, will wish to find a rule of customary international law supporting its claimed right to refuse to permit the passage.

The search for the rule of customary international law is not as simple as might at first appear. It is unlikely that there are numerous instances on record of States explicitly acknowledging or denying a right of passage to ships carrying nuclear materials. There are relatively few voyages transporting nuclear cargoes, and coastal States may be unaware that those ships are passing through their waters, or unaware of their cargoes. If they are aware of the ship and its cargo they may prefer to preserve a diplomatic silence rather than object and precipitate a conflict of views from which neither State is likely to back down and from which the coastal State may have little to gain. And State practice may be inconsistent. While some States may object to passage, some may have expressly announced that such ships have a right of passage, and yet others may have decided to allow such ships to pass through their waters without comment. It may, therefore, be very difficult indeed to find a clear pattern evident in State practice that is precisely on the point. That is not, however, the end of the matter.

No legal system has rules that specifically cover all possible cases that might arise. A local bye-law may prohibit the taking of dogs into parks but say nothing about taking in pumas; but the omission is unlikely to confound a police constable intent on excluding from a park someone walking a puma on a rope. In cases such as this we extrapolate, we seek the general rationale behind the rule and extend it. We ask whether a particular interpretation of the law does or does not fit with the basic purpose behind the law. So, in the case of the disputed right of passage, it may be possible to point to practice concerning the passage of other dangerous cargoes, and to practice concerning the carriage of nuclear and other dangerous materials by road and by air, and practice concerning the passage of nuclear powered ships. If the result of that examination is that it appears that the rationale behind rules in this area is, as common sense would suggest, the balancing of the interests of carriers against the need of States to avert accidents involving hazardous materials, and if it appears that in the case of air and road transport nuclear materials are treated in broadly the same manner as other hazardous materials, it will seem reasonable to suppose that the same approach should be taken to the carriage of nuclear materials at sea. If there is in addition some small amount of State practice supporting this view, and no great body of practice contradicting it, it may be concluded that this approach is correct: there is a good basis for saying that there is a rule of customary international law that stipulates, say, that there is a right of passage for ships carrying nuclear cargoes subject to the compliance with reasonable regulations imposed by the coastal State in order to safeguard its waters and its land territory.

The same approach is adopted to a closely related methodological problem: that of determining what is the scope, the precise ambit, of a rule that is inferred from State practice. For example, there is a good deal of State practice evidencing a belief that States may enforce their customs and fisheries laws in the territorial sea around their coasts. Customs inspectors or police launches regularly visit and search foreign ships in the territorial sea; statutes prescribe rules that the ships must obey, and authorize the interception and prosecution of offenders; States acquiesce in the arrest of their ships by coastal authorities; and so on. The same is true of the enforcement of criminal laws in respect of serious crimes, and laws on certain other matters such as marine pollution. If we were to consider all of this practice and try to infer a rule or rules of customary international law from it, we would certainly be justified in inferring recognition of the rights of States to exercise jurisdiction in their territorial seas in respect of each of these topics. But under international law, coastal States enjoy sovereignty over their territorial seas: that is, they have the same plenary jurisdictional rights over the territorial sea as they have over their land territory, subject to certain limitations flowing from the existence of a right of passage for foreign ships through the territorial sea.

This is a conundrum. How could evidence of the acceptance of jurisdiction in respect of a range of specific matters ever warrant the inference of plenary jurisdiction in respect of all matters? As a matter of strict logic, it could never do so. The solution to the conundrum lies in the nature of legal reasoning. For all that Law is, in the nineteenth century nomenclature still used in most universities, a social science, the discerning of rules by inferring them from State practice is more of an art than a science. Questions of the 'fit' of putative rules with established rules and principles are approached in a manner that has more in common with aesthetic judgement than it has with calculation, computation, or rigorous logic. Consonance, symmetry, and economy are qualities admired in the structure of a legal regime made up of individual rules. Above all, lawyers look for an accord between the outcomes yielded in particular cases by the rules, and the dictates of common sense and common morality: if the application of international law to a particular case leads to an astonishing conclusion, the analysis is probably wrong.

In the case of maritime jurisdiction, sovereignty over the territorial sea was propounded long ago as a doctrine, and was claimed by States. States have sovereignty over the airspace above their territory and over deeply indented bays and estuaries that are, as it were, contained within the jaws of the land. Sovereignty over the territorial sea is consonant with these principles and mirrors them; and assimilation of the territorial sea to the land territory over which the State has sovereignty is an elegant and economical solution because it obviates the need for the creation of a novel legal regime for this part of the seas.

The dominant conceptual move that characterizes legal thought here, and everywhere else, is the 'as if' move. A particular state of affairs is treated 'as if' it were some other, simpler state of affairs. Complex business relationships are treated as if the relationship were defined by the rights and duties set out in a contract; an assertion of jurisdiction is treated as if it were the same as an earlier exercise of jurisdiction which had been regarded as lawful; and so on. The core characteristics of a situation are discerned, and the simplified structures of reality represented by legal rules are mapped on to them, to yield a legal characterization of the situation. This is particularly noticeable in the case of customary international law, where the two-way relationship between rule and reality is particularly evident. Simple, clear rules are inferred from the untidy mass of State practice; and the rule is then reapplied to new, perhaps equally untidy, situations. The new situation is treated as if it were another example of the practice that generated the rule. The new situation in turn is added to the store of examples of the customary law rule, expanding the catalogue of instances—instantiations—of the rule with which some future set of circumstances may be compared. This is reasoning by metaphor; and that is precisely how Law operates. The crucial step is finding the right metaphor.

2.1.7 SOME ASPECTS OF *OPINIO JURIS*

Let me now delve a little deeper into some aspects of customary international law.

2.1.7.1 Proving *Opinio Juris*

Opinio juris—the conviction on the part of a State that a particular practice is in conformity with international law—may appear to be a mysterious concept. As the ICJ remarked in the *North Sea Continental Shelf* cases in 1969, it is extremely difficult to find clear evidence on the question of *opinio juris*. Described as a 'component' of customary international law, it is easy to assume that it is like an ingredient in a recipe. In fact, it would be more accurately likened to a way of cooking the ingredients of State practice.

States, of course, do not have convictions. We speak as if States have minds of their own, about France opposing this policy and Russia proposing that action. But States do not have intentions, interests, aspirations, or any other of the anthropomorphic characteristics conventionally ascribed to them; the State's interests and actions are invariably and inevitably decided by those who control the State. There is more to this than the trite point that States must act through individuals, who do of course have intentions and interests. In practice, States very rarely act through an individual. Usually they act through committees that propose, select, refine, and implement agreed policies and courses of action. Whose state of mind is relevant? What if some members believe that an action is lawful and others disagree? How is the state of mind of any of them to be determined? Even to pose these questions is to point towards an unavoidable answer. It is wholly impractical to rest *opinio juris* upon any real conviction or belief; and to try to analyse State behaviour in accordance with models of rationality that may be serviceable in analysing individual behaviour is deeply problematic. There must be another approach.

The key lies in the process of checking to see if the practice of a particular State should count towards the generation of a rule of customary international law. The determination of the existence of *opinio juris* is in essence the process of characterizing the practice of the State. The characterization proceeds by means of presumptions. If a State does something, the State is regarded as acting with the belief that it is entitled so to act, that its action conforms with international law. *Opinio juris* is presumed to exist. That presumption may be rebutted by pointing to some statement, such as the British Government's statement over the *Torrey Canyon*, that plainly indicates that the action was not considered to be supported by international law or was even considered to be contrary to international law. If the presumption is not rebutted, it stands.

If the rule in question is not one that confers a right, but rather one that imposes a duty, this approach is inadequate because there may be many reasons why a State chooses to act in a manner mandated by the law. It may do so as a matter of expediency or policy, with no-one in the State believing that the law requires the State so to act. In such a case some additional evidence must be adduced. There may be an express statement asserting that the State was acting under legal constraints. For example, when

France and the United Kingdom built the Channel Tunnel each of them made a public statement to the effect that international law rights of passage and overflight through the Channel would not be affected. The subsequent toleration of such passages by France and the United Kingdom can therefore be read together with that statement to warrant the inference that the toleration is motivated by the belief that international law requires the two States to allow the passages.

In the absence of an express statement, there is another way of handling the matter, which a domestic analogy may help to make clear. As a matter on municipal contract law, agreements are only legally binding contracts if the agreement was made by the parties with the intention of creating legal relations between them. In general, if I buy a bottle of wine, I make a contract with the wine store; if I agree to meet someone for coffee, I do not enter into a binding legal contract with them. I can be sued if I do not pay for the wine, but not if I do not show up for the coffee, even though there were clear agreements in each case. This approach works in domestic law. But I have never, as yet, announced to the assistants in a shop that I wish to enter into legal relations with them and only rarely have I turned my mind silently to that issue. The 'intention' is simply presumed by virtue of the context in which the transaction takes place. The law presumes that all consumer purchases are concluded with the intention of creating a binding legal relationship, and that no social arrangements are concluded with that intention. If the parties intend otherwise, they must make that intention known. The contexts that do and the contexts that do not carry the presumption depend upon social conventions. These are not laid down by law but simply understood and applied by judges as part of the store of what is often regarded as the 'obvious common-sense' matrix of knowledge within which all legal analysis takes place. In fact, such extra-legal considerations are a powerful driving force for reform in the law—for example, when a relationship previously viewed as informal comes to be regarded as having a legal basis (the rights of unmarried co-habitees are a domestic law example).

A very similar process operates in international law. It is generally understood by international lawyers that certain matters are regulated by law and others are not. Diplomatic immunity, for example, is undoubtedly regulated by law. If a State abstains from prosecuting a diplomat who is known to have broken the law, it is presumed that the State 'knows' that international law requires that abstention, and that the State's abstention is motivated by the legal obligation. *Opinio juris* is presumed to exist. If a practice, such as the giving of foreign aid, is generally acknowledged to fall outside the scope of legal regulation and to be a matter of policy lying within the discretion of each State, *opinio juris* will be presumed not to exist. It will always be possible to find borderline cases, where opinion is divided as to whether or not the matter is regulated by law. In such cases, as in comparable circumstances in municipal law, each side will argue its case as best it can. State practice, international law textbooks and articles, resolutions of international organizations, and any other evidence supporting the proposition may be cited. If the matter is not resolved, the two sides may refer the question to an international tribunal; but in the great majority of cases they do not. They simply maintain their different views and get on with the business of negotiating over the various links that bind them together.

I noted earlier that it was possible to have 'instant' rules of customary international law in circumstances where there is an evident global consensus upon the rules in question. Little or nothing in the way of lapse of time or proof of State practice is required. The implication is that State practice is not essential as a component of customary international law. This is indeed the conclusion that reflection on the fundamental nature of international law would suggest. If the rules derive their authority from the fact that States have consented to be bound by them, proof of that consent should be enough to establish that they are bound. What, then, is the role of State practice?

State practice is important for two main reasons. First, States rarely make abstract declarations of acceptance of rules of law. The outer space resolutions are exceptions to the usual practice. How, then, are we to know if a State has accepted a rule? As I explained above, if the matter is acknowledged to be one regulated by international law, and the State has acted in conformity with the supposed rule of international law, *opinio juris* will be presumed. Evidence that many other States accept the rule in question supports that presumption. It is reasonable to presume that a State accepts a putative rule of international law if all or most other States have accepted it. The second reason is that international law is pragmatic. Many of its rules and principles are crafted so as to ensure that the law does not depart markedly from the realities of international life. There would be little point in 'accepting' a rule verbally if States in fact acted inconsistently with it. Hence, it is said to be necessary to show that the rule is evidenced in the practice of States. Both of those reasons give to State practice an essentially evidential role. The theoretical source of the binding nature of the rule rests in the *opinio juris*.

2.1.8 LOCAL AND REGIONAL CUSTOM

That central role of *opinio juris* has important implications. If two States can both be shown to have accepted a particular rule as a rule of international law, they should in theory be bound to observe it. It would be a bilateral rule of customary international law, a local custom. The possibility of local custom was admitted by the ICJ in the *Right of Passage* case in 1960. Portugal claimed that there was a right of passage over Indian territory between the Portuguese colonial enclaves of Dadrá and Nagar-Aveli and Damaõ in India. There is no general right to pass over the territory of a foreign State, but Portugal argued that such a right had in the past been asserted by Portugal and accepted by the authorities of what was at the time British India. The Court found that a long-established practice between two States, accepted by them as regulating their relations, had generated a local custom binding upon them, permitting civilian (but not military) transports between the enclaves.

Other local or regional customs have been found to exist. In the *Asylum* case in 1951 the ICJ accepted that there was a body of regional customary law in Latin America concerning diplomatic relations. There was also quite clearly a Latin American Law of the Sea during a good part of the late twentieth century, as I shall explain shortly. One of the most developed regional systems in the twentieth century was the body of Socialist international law, expounded by jurists in the former Soviet bloc. That contained a number of specific rules that were distinct from the general rules of international law. For example, a principle of socialist proletarian internationalism permitted one State to render 'assistance' to another if socialism in that other State was under fundamental attack. This principle, known in its broader political formulation as the Brezhnev doctrine, offered a (retrospective) legal justification of Soviet invasion of Czechoslovakia in 1968. The doctrine runs directly counter to the principle of non-intervention in the domestic affairs of foreign States, which is one of the fundamental principles of international law. While it is often regarded as no more than a cynical rationalization of Soviet dominance (despite its symmetry with the practice of the United States and its western allies), the Brezhnev doctrine was rooted in a distinctive and well-established conception of the international law applicable between socialist States. That is not to say that the analysis was correct as a matter of international law: but there is a legal argument to be considered and not simply dismissed.

There are other regional orders. The most highly developed is EU law. Though the detailed rules and regulations of EU law are based upon treaty provisions, there are more fundamental legal principles applicable to the Member States, concerning their relationship to each other and to the organs of the EU. The Commonwealth is another example. States within the British Commonwealth treat each other somewhat differently from non-Commonwealth States, which is why the United Kingdom has a Foreign and Commonwealth Office (Commonwealth States not being technically 'foreign'), why Commonwealth States have High Commissioners rather than Ambassadors, and why some Commonwealth States exclude disputes with other Commonwealth States from the category of disputes which they are prepared to refer to the ICJ. A case could be made out for other regional orders, such as that applicable between Islamic States; but enough has been said to make it clear that it is wrong to regard international law as a monolithic system. It is a complex system within which local and regional variations are accommodated.

2.1.9 PERSISTENT OBJECTION

The *Right of Passage* case might be said to have established that the consent of two States to be bound by a particular rule is sufficient to bind those States to comply with the rule. The correlative proposition, that the consent of a State is *necessary* for the State to be bound by a rule, is also supported by the case-law of the ICJ. In the *Anglo-Norwegian Fisheries* case in 1952 one question concerned the validity of Norwegian claims to measure its fishing zone from a notional straight baseline connecting the headlands of certain fjords, rather than from the low-water mark which is the normal baseline. The United Kingdom, whose fishing vessels had been excluded from large areas of the sea by Norway in reliance upon these straight baselines, tried to prove that State practice established a rule that no straight baseline could be more than ten miles long. That would have invalidated several Norwegian lines, some of which were more than thirty miles long. The United Kingdom failed to adduce enough evidence of State practice to persuade the Court that there was any such ten-mile rule. The significant point, however, is that the Court said that 'in any event the 10-mile rule would appear to be inapplicable against Norway inasmuch as she has always opposed any attempt to apply it to the Norwegian coast.'

That passage reflects what is known as the 'persistent objector' principle: that is, the principle that any State that has from the outset of a course of State practice made known that it does not consent to be bound by the rule, will not be bound by that rule. The principle is a natural consequence of the view that international law is based upon the consent of States. The objection must be persistent, and be raised before the practice hardens into a rule of law: States have no right to opt out of rules that have already become binding upon them. If they were to have such a right, no rule of international law would in practice have any binding force, and that would make a nonsense of the international legal system.

In practice, very few States persistently object, and to very few rules of law. The Norwegian objection to the ten-mile limit on straight baselines is one example; the objections by the United Kingdom and the United States to claims to maritime jurisdiction in excess of three nautical miles, maintained up to the 1970s and 1980s, is another. In the latter case the United Kingdom was in the habit of writing formally to any State laying claim to maritime jurisdiction extending further than three miles to say that 'Her Majesty's Government are obliged to place firmly on record . . . that they do not recognize territorial jurisdiction over waters outside the limit of three miles from the coast; nor will they regard British vessels engaged in their lawful pursuits on the high seas as being subject, without the consent of Her Majesty's Government, to any measures which the [coastal State] Government may see fit to promulgate.' That is a good example of an international protest, of the kind upon which persistent objection depends.

Persistent objectors face considerable pressures. Take, for example, the United States' insistence upon observance of the three-mile limit of the territorial sea, and of rights of innocent passage through the territorial sea for all ships. Its main concern was to preserve its navigation rights in the seas. If it had done nothing in practice to oppose claims by States that were inconsistent with those rights, it would have risked fatally undermining its policy of objection. A tribunal, faced with the question of the legality of the more extensive claims, might have regarded inaction as a sign that the United States accepted the claims in fact even though its rhetoric denied their validity: tribunals always tend to prefer to rely on facts rather than rhetoric. It was therefore necessary for the United States to demonstrate its rejection of the claims. That was done through the prolonged 'Freedom of the Seas' programme, in which the United States Navy deliberately asserted passage rights through foreign waters in defiance of the claims that it refused to accept. Those assertions of passage rights entailed substantial costs. Apart from the considerable cost of sending naval units anywhere, in some cases the coastal State sought physically to enforce its claims. In the Black Sea, for example, there were instances of Russian (then Soviet) warships 'bumping' US warships in an attempt to force them out of the twelve-mile territorial sea claimed by the then USSR. Bumped warships, like bumped cars, need to be repaired. That too costs money, and ties up naval units that may be required on operations elsewhere. Then there is the political cost. By the late 1970s almost all other States had accepted the validity of claims to twelve-mile territorial seas. For United States' delegates to turn up at international conferences and repeatedly oppose measures premised upon a twelve-mile territorial sea was at best tedious and at worst a damaging diversion from more fruitful co-operation. And the active assertion of United States opposition to these claims would inevitably be seized upon by those wishing to represent the United States as a self-interested State prepared to use military force in order to have its way. Such factors have to be weighed in the balance when asking—as governments must—if persistent opposition to the particular rule of international law is worthwhile. And of course those States whose claims are resisted will also have to make similar calculations. Those who run States generally appreciate a quiet life as much as anyone else: the pressure for compromise is evident.

There is another reason why persistent objectors are few. As is, I hope, now clear the processes for creating customary international law favour rules that are likely to be broadly acceptable to other States. If a particular practice were widely opposed, it would be unlikely to have gathered the weight of State practice and *opinio juris* necessary to translate it into a rule of customary international law, and so no question of persistent objection would arise. Where practices fail to take hold as emergent rules of customary international law the States advancing them may recast the practice. The invasion of Iraq in 2003 furnished a good example. Having failed to attract any support for the ill-conceived and barely coherent argument that States have a right to intervene in other States where the UN Security Council is prevented from directing matters by an 'unreasonable' use of the veto, the United Kingdom and United States fell back on other arguments in support of the invasion.

Shifts in argument are not necessarily duplicitous. The decision to intervene in another State, like all other decisions taken on behalf of a State, always has a non-legal, political motive. Even where a State refrains from taking some action that is forbidden by a rule of international law that is expressly discussed in policy-making meetings, its (in)action has extra-legal, political motives. But international law is concerned with the reasons for acting, not the motives for acting; and if a State can find a coherent and persuasive justification for its action, well and good. It is, accordingly, natural that States should seek the most persuasive justification from a range of justifications that may be open to them, abandoning or not raising less persuasive arguments. Sometimes a State will retreat more or less entirely from a legal claim. In the 1990s Chile advanced the concept of the 'presential sea', an area of the high seas beyond the limits of Chile's natural jurisdiction in which it claimed certain preferential rights over the exploitation of marine resources. That claim met with widespread rejection. It was not abandoned by Chile; but it did mutate into an essentially political and moral, rather than a legal, claim, in which Chile

sought to advance its special interests in those seas within the framework
of the existing law.

These are instances of the ways in which States avoid pressing claims
that they know will be strenuously opposed. It is because of the avoidance
of opposition that there are so few cases of persistent opposition. And even
where some States begin as persistent objectors, the costs of holding out
may be so high that in practice they seek an acceptable compromise and
come into line. The abandonment in the 1980s by the United States of its
opposition to maritime claims in excess of three miles, in the wake of a new
consensus that preserved passage rights through the wider maritime
zones, is a good example.

Some writers have doubted the validity of the principle of persistent
objection, regarding it as an anachronistic survival of the nineteenth-
century consensualist view of international law. But once the limited
scope of the principle, and its extremely limited invocation in practice, are
understood, it is hard to see why such doubts persist. It is plainly right that
a State should not be bound by obligations set out in a treaty to which it
is not a Party. Why, then, should other States be able to bind the State
by claiming that their practice has generated a rule of customary international law, if (and only if) the State has persistently made known its
objection to the rule? The question is not purely rhetorical. If international law is to be a coherent system, it needs to explain the bases upon
which obligations arise. This brings us to the topic of *jus cogens*.

2.1.10 *JUS COGENS*

In two sets of circumstances, however, there are reasons for imposing rules
of customary international law upon dissentient States that are theoretic-
ally persuasive and, more importantly, accord with the practice of States.
In each case the rule is binding for reasons that dispense with the need to
refer to *opinio juris*.

First, there are some rules or principles that are logically necessary. The
customary law rule that States are bound by their treaty obligations (*pacta
sunt servanda*) is one such rule. Without that rule, international law simply
could not operate as a legal system: States would be free to disregard treaty
commitments at will; States could not make truly binding commitments.
No State, therefore, could be allowed to persistently object to the rule that
it is bound by its treaty obligations, without destroying the basis of the
legal system. This is not strictly an exception to the requirement of
consent, because logically necessary rules do not 'arise': they have always
been necessarily implicit in the system, and so no State could have the
opportunity to object to them from the outset of their emergence.

There is a true exception in the case of certain rules that embody what are regarded as uncompromisable moral principles. One example is the rule prohibiting genocide. If two States make an agreement—a bilateral treaty—of military co-operation which provides for joint participation in an operation to liquidate members of a particular ethnic group in a neighbouring State, and one of the States subsequently seeks to enforce the treaty against the other, it is inconceivable that any modern international tribunal would uphold the treaty. It would not matter if the States had consistently objected to the emergence into customary international law of the prohibition on genocide. I think it is a practical certainty that those sitting on the tribunal would refuse to uphold the treaty even if no specific rule of law required them to do so, because it is incompatible with the most basic moral imperatives to order the upholding of such an agreement. Some moral principles are so clear-cut, and so strong, that exceptions to them cannot be tolerated in any civilized legal system.

There is also a category of rules or principles of customary international law that admit of no derogation: that is to say, States may not escape their binding force either by persistent objection or by making agreements to disregard the rule. These are the 'peremptory rules of international law', also known as rules of *jus cogens*. Quite what those rules are, precisely, is not easy to say. There are generally accepted examples: the prohibitions of the waging of aggressive war, and of genocide, and of slavery, and of piracy (the latter a curious historical anomaly, elevating armed robbery and attacks at sea above the level of the general run of crimes of violence). There are other, more controversial candidates: the prohibition on racial discrimination (at least in the form of *apartheid*), the principles of self-determination of peoples and of permanent sovereignty over natural resources, and perhaps also the prohibitions on the acquisition of sovereignty over the high seas and outer space. The difficulty lies in knowing how to resolve disputed cases.

Article 53 of the Vienna Convention on the Law of Treaties defines a rule of *jus cogens* as 'a norm accepted and recognized by the international community of States as a whole as a norm from which no derogation is permitted and which can be modified only by a subsequent norm of general international law having the same character'. That leaves the judgement in the hands of 'the international community of States as a whole', a concept that is not defined, although disputes over questions of the effect of *jus cogens* on treaties may ultimately be referred to the ICJ for decision. But this does not entirely remove the problem. If it is necessary that *all* States accept that a rule is a rule of *jus cogens*, no problem could arise, because there would be no dissentients. If it is enough that most

States regard a rule as a rule of *jus cogens* (and this is much the better interpretation), some writers have said that there is a paradox. If the rules start off life as 'ordinary' rules of public international law, and then achieve the 'super-normativity' of *jus cogens*, how can it be that a State that was never bound by the rule as an ordinary rule suddenly becomes bound by it as a rule of *jus cogens*? One possible answer is apparent if it is supposed that the category of *jus cogens* contains only rules that are either logically or morally necessary, in the senses that I outlined above. States become bound by the rules, whether or not they consent, because international law cannot admit that they are not bound by them if it is to retain its coherence and even a minimal moral authority. Those who argue for a wider category of norms of *jus cogens* must find another answer.

2.1.11 INSTITUTIONS

Though there is no established legal doctrine to this effect I think that there is another category of 'unavoidable' norms, sitting alongside the rules of *jus cogens*. These are the norms that are bound up in what we might refer to as legal 'institutions'.

International law entitles States to do certain things that are tantamount to establishing institutions (in the sense that we say that the church or the crown is an institution). For instance, States are entitled, but not bound, to claim a 200-mile Exclusive Economic Zone (EEZ) off their coasts, in which they enjoy certain rights in respect of marine resources and the marine environment; and States are entitled, but not bound, to accept the jurisdiction of the ICJ over legal disputes to which they are parties. If a State chooses to exercise the right in question I think that it must, as it were, sign up to the entitlement on the terms on which international law offers it. A State may not claim the rights in an EEZ but refuse to accept the concomitant obligations, such as the obligation to allow freedom of navigation through the EEZ to ships of other States. If the State expressly claims an EEZ it impliedly accepts all the rights and obligations that attach to the legal institution of the EEZ as a matter of customary international law. Nor may it accept the jurisdiction of the ICJ but refuse to accept the right of the Court to exercise its incidental jurisdiction by prescribing provisional measures, for example. In other words, there are some rights that come 'bundled' with other rights and duties, and from which they are inseparable. A State must claim the whole bundle, or none of it.

A State may, however, decide not to exercise all of the rights that come bundled in the institution. A curious instance of the latter phenomenon exists in the Aegean, where Greece maintains a six-mile territorial sea claim over the sea and seabed but a ten-mile claim in respect of the superjacent airspace—a position perhaps best understood as a ten-mile territorial sea claim in which Greece chooses, because of political tensions with Turkey over maritime claims in the Aegean, to forego its rights over the sea and seabed in the outer four miles.

2.1.12 HOW CUSTOMARY LAW CHANGES

The account of customary international law that I have given contains within it an explanation of how that law changes. Take, for example, the claim to control over the resources of the seas. At the beginning of the twentieth century most States claimed jurisdiction over a belt of sea stretching three miles from the coast, though a few claimed six or twelve miles. There were no claims to fisheries zones of more than twelve miles. In the late 1940s a number of Latin American States, observing the ease with which the United States had arrogated to itself the continental shelf resources off its coasts by issuing the 1945 Truman Proclamation, made their own claims to extended maritime jurisdiction. Those on the west coast, where the Andes plunge steeply into the sea leaving only a very narrow belt of continental shelf, benefited little from a claim to seabed resources. Their economies rested heavily upon fishing. Some of them decided that if it was acceptable for the United States to assert its jurisdiction over the resources off its coasts that it was able to exploit, it should be acceptable for them to do the same and to assert jurisdiction over the fish resources off their coasts. They made claims to 200-mile maritime zones in which they had the right to control access to the resources, including the fisheries. For instance, Chile, Ecuador, and Peru made 200-mile claims, and joined in the 1952 Declaration of Santiago to assert the right of all States to such maritime zones. Other States outside Latin America refused to accept the validity of the 200-mile claims which, unlike the United States claim over seabed resources, were thought to threaten important high seas freedoms.

In legal terms, there was by the early 1950s a special custom among the Latin American claimants (then including most States in South America) to 200-mile zones; and on the other hand there was persistent objection on the part of many other States, notably major maritime States such as the United States, the USSR, and the United Kingdom. Had, say, Chile arrested a Peruvian vessel fishing 180 miles off the coast of Chile, Peru could not have objected without abandoning its own claim. Having made a similar claim itself, Peru could not object that Chile's claim to extended fisheries jurisdiction violated international law. If, however, Chile had arrested a British vessel in the same place, the position would have been different. The United Kingdom had persistently objected to these claims: I quoted from one of the protests above. There was plainly no 'general practice accepted as law' supporting the claims: they were a Latin American aberration. Had the United Kingdom taken the issue to an international tribunal, the tribunal would have said that the arrest violated international law. Similarly, if a State—say, Egypt—that had neither expressly accepted nor expressly rejected the 200-mile claim were to have had one of its ships arrested, a tribunal would have held that the arrest was unlawful, because the 'general' practice was not to recognize the claims.

It is convenient to refer to this situation as a local or regional custom, but there is no need for the States bound by it to be in the same geographical region. If an African State had made a 200-mile claim at the time (which did not in fact happen), and if one of its ships had been arrested by Chile, the position would have been the same as in the case of an arrest of a Peruvian ship. The African flag State having itself made a 200-mile claim, it could not deny the validity of Chile's claim without abandoning its own claim.

At that point there were at least two rules of customary international law in effect concerning the extent of jurisdiction over fisheries: one applicable among the Latin American 200-milers, and another applicable to the rest of the world.

In the late 1960s attention again focused on fisheries, this time because of the overfishing of many commercial stocks, blamed on industrialized distant-water fishing fleets. Many States, particularly those that had not been independent when international law established the freedom of fishing on the high seas, resented the right of distant-water fleets to plunder the fisheries off their coasts and sought to persuade the UN Conference on the Law of the Sea, which met throughout the 1970s, to accept the right of States to 200-mile exclusive fishery zones. By the mid 1970s it was clear that there would be a broad consensus in favour of this, so long as passage right and certain other rights of foreign States were safeguarded. More States accordingly began to make unilateral claims to 200-mile zones. Each new claim put one more State in the 200-mile camp, and took one out of the opposing camp. By the early 1980s the balance between the two camps had wholly changed. Most coastal States claimed or had accepted the legality of 200-mile zones. There was a new 'general practice', so that any State that could not show that it had persistently objected would have been bound to accept the validity of the zones.

In that way a 'new' rule of customary international law had come into existence. More precisely, the balance between the two camps had shifted, so that the old 'special custom' in Latin America became the general practice and the general rule of customary international law. Apart from a few persistent objectors, the adherents of the old 'general' rule defected so that it withered away. That is how rules of customary international law can change. (No doubt some readers will wonder what the position was where the two camps were of roughly equal size. If a tribunal had been obliged to decide the issue at that State, in a dispute brought by a State that had neither expressly objected to the new rule nor expressly accepted it, the tribunal would no doubt have tried to determine which way the tide was flowing and to decide in accordance with the rule that it considered the rule of the future. In practice, however, it must be admitted that much would have turned on the views of the particular judges. For that very reason States tend to avoid litigating at such times, preferring to wait until the legal position and the probable outcome of the litigation becomes clearer.)

It should be evident that it is a mistake to think of international law as a monolithic body of law. The presence of local, regional, and special customs, and of the rare cases of persistent objection, mean that we can never properly speak of 'the' rule of international law, but only of the rule applicable to the particular States in question. In practice, however, the divergences from the rules that are (in a descriptive, but not a prescriptive sense) generally applicable are minor. Most rules are accepted by almost all States in the world. That is why textbooks on international law present the law as if it were a universally applicable system.

I should turn now to the second major source of international rules: treaties.

2.2 TREATIES

An international agreement may be called a Treaty, a Convention, an Exchange of Notes, a Memorandum of Understanding, a Covenant, a Charter, or any other suitable name. It is merely a matter of style, with the more august titles being given to the more important agreements. But all are subsumed under the broad heading of 'treaties'; and the Law of Treaties (as largely codified in the 1969 Vienna Convention on the Law of Treaties) applies to all such agreements. Treaties rank first in Article 38 of the ICJ Statute, and for good reason. Customary international law is in essence the body of law that applies by default; and within the limits set by the doctrine of *jus cogens*, to which I return below, States are free to vary its rules by agreement. It is in this respect similar to the body of tort law or the law of obligations, which individuals are free to vary by contract. Thus, treaties supersede customary international law: if States have made an agreement, the rights and duties of the parties are determined by the treaty, not by customary international law. Treaties are therefore the first place to look in order to determine a State's rights and duties. Hence their priority in Article 38 of the International Court's Statute.

That priority accords with political reality. If a State concludes a treaty, it makes a solemn commitment. States are expected to fulfil their commitments. If they were free to renege upon them or disregard them, it would be impossible for secure international arrangements to be made, and the consequent unpredictability would preclude all but the most rudimentary and short-term international dealings. That is reflected in the almost mystical significance that has been given to promises, contracts, and treaties throughout history.

Treaties—international agreements—are one of the two most elementary forms in which obligations are expressed, commands being the other. In the Koran and the Jewish and Christian scriptures God begins by issuing commandments to Adam, but makes covenants with Noah and Abraham. Both the commandments and the terms of the covenants are regarded as demanding compliance: that is their essence. But commands depend upon the existence of a superior who can issue them to an inferior, and outside the imperial context that relationship does not exist in international relations. For most of recorded history, much of the world has in fact been organized in one empire or another, and dealings between peoples have in many respects been conducted through the structures of empire. But, as far as we know, there has never been only one empire (a condition now meretriciously courted with the bombastic terminology of the 'unipolar world' and the 'single superpower'), and at least some 'international' dealings have been conducted between political units on terms of broad equality. Treaties have always been a feature of the land-scape. Jean Barbeyrac, an eighteenth-century French jurist who trans-lated several of the seminal early texts on international law, published in 1739 a collection of treaties reaching back into the second millennium BCE. There is, for example, a Sumerian treaty from around 2500 BCE on the Stele of Vultures, now held in the Louvre, which records the establish-ment of the boundary between the kingdoms of Lagash and Umma.

The earliest treaties appear to have been made in the context of reli-gious ceremonies, the parties calling upon the gods to witness the agree-ment and to sustain it, usually by visiting untold miseries upon anyone who violates the treaty. Ancient Greek treaties were also underwritten by the gods; and this may have been the case also for Roman treaties. (The tradition survives in Wagner's *Ring* cycle, in which all the treaties that Wotan must protect are engraved on the shaft of his spear.) Treaties were taken similarly seriously in Asia. The ancient Chinese practice was to make a sacrifice so that its blood, spilled into the earth and smeared onto the lips of the parties, would bear witness to the making of the treaty.

Now that the mystical trappings of treaty-making have all but disap-peared (though there seems still to be a belief that the more notable treaties must be signed with expensive pens at garlanded tables, and held in fine leather folders), the Law of Treaties may appear to be in large part 'lawyer's law'. That appearance is deceptive, because there are important political issues lying close to the surface.

2.2.1 MAKING TREATIES

All States may conclude treaties; but not only States may conclude treaties. In the nineteenth century, for example, Great Britain made many treaties with what the *Index of British Treaties 1101–1968* describes as 'African Tribes, etc'; and many Indian nations entered into treaties with the United States. Indeed, a significant part of the process of colonization was carried out, not by conquest or by the rarer fiction of treating lands as being empty and open to occupation by the colonial power, but rather by the making of agreements with the indigenous communities who put themselves into a relationship of subordination with the colonial power. Political entities that were not sovereign States continued to become par-ties to treaties throughout the nineteenth century.

Treaties are made on behalf of States by government officers within whose legal competence the subject-matter of the treaty falls. For instance, an agreement for the supply of natural gas might be made by the Minister of Energy, and an agreement for the use of military airfield facilities might be made by the Minister of Defence. Heads of State or Heads of Government, and Ministers for Foreign Affairs, are regarded as having plenary competence, able to enter into commitments on behalf of the State in any matter.

Other agents may be authorized to conclude treaties on behalf of a State, or have their actions subsequently ratified by the State. One of the most colourful examples is that of Philippe Bunau-Varilla, chief engineer to Ferdinand de Lesseps, the architect of the Panama Canal project. Obsessed with the desire to see the canal built and, it is said, his own name on the treaty under which the United States would build it across the central American isthmus, Bunau-Varilla paid $100,000 to the revolutionary Government in Panama to have himself made Panamanian Ambassador to the United States. Reading in the newspaper that government officials had been sent from Panama to the United States to negotiate the treaty that he was nurturing as his gift to posterity, Bunau-Varilla hastened to secure its conclusion. Sitting up all night to amend it, he struck out a draft provision which would have given the United States administrative control over the canal for one hundred years and replaced it with a provision which apparently gave the United States sovereign rights over the Canal Zone in perpetuity. Correctly guessing that this offer would prove irresistible to the United States, Bunau-Varilla managed to persuade US Secretary of State John Hay to sign what is known as the Hay-Bunau-Varilla treaty three hours before the train carrying the Panamanian officials arrived in Washington. Returning to Panama, he persuaded the deeply indebted revolutionary Government that it could not cope with its debts or with the displeasure of the United States, both of which problems would be solved by the prompt ratification of the treaty. Thus it was that the United States became, for three-quarters of a century, the possessor of sovereign rights over the Canal Zone that cut right across Panamanian territory.

Most governments are able to conduct their treaty-making in a more orderly manner, particularly in the case of multilateral treaties. Typically a delegation composed of officials from the various Ministries concerned with the subject matter of the treaty, now often accompanied by representatives of industry and of NGOs, will attend the drafting conference. After days spent debating drafts in the conference room and negotiating in smaller groups in the coffee lounges, the delegates will settle on the text that commands the highest level of acceptance. That text is then signed by the delegations. But signature merely authenticates the negotiated text: it usually does not bind the State to comply with the treaty. The position is determined in each case by what the parties intended: but multilateral treaties are usually intended to require ratification or 'acceptance' (i.e., confirmation of the acceptance of the Convention, even if the Convention is not subject to domestic processes of treaty ratification) by each State before it enters into force for that State. Bilateral treaties of limited import-ance, on the other hand, are often stipulated to enter into force on signature, without the need for ratification.

The process of ratification varies from State to State, according to the demands of their respective Constitutions. Practically all States will allow time for government ministries to consider the implications of acceptance (and of rejection) of the treaty. Beyond that, procedures differ widely. The United States, for example, requires the approval of the two-thirds of the Senate before a treaty can be ratified. The approval of the House of Representatives is not required; but the House can control budgetary appropriations and other matters that may be necessary for the imple-mentation of the treaty, so it is not without influence. Actual or anticipated opposition within the Senate has resulted in the United States not becom-ing a party to some important international treaties. For instance, Senate opposition prevented the United States ratification of the 1979 Strategic Arms Limitation Treaty (SALT II) after it had been negotiated and signed by President Jimmy Carter and President Leonid Brezhnev of the USSR. In an effort to avoid such Senate defeats, the Administration will sometimes involve Senators in the negotiations. Thus, in 1985 the Senate created a bipartisan Senate Observer Group which attended the arms control nego-tiations between the USA and the USSR that produced the 1987 Intermediate-Range Nuclear Forces Treaty.

In the United Kingdom, treaties do not require Parliamentary approval before they are ratified. Treaty-making is part of the prerogative of the Crown—that is to say, the Government. But the Government cannot use its prerogative powers to alter the rights and duties of persons subject to English law. That is the issue of principle over which the English Civil War was fought and won in the seventeenth century. Accordingly, if the imple-mentation of a treaty requires some modification in domestic law that modification will have to be effected by Parliament. This gives some indir-ect Parliamentary control over treaty-making. Even in cases where no amendment of domestic law is needed, however, the practice has arisen of laying the texts of treaties before both Houses of Parliament for twenty-one days prior to their ratification. This is the so-called 'Ponsonby Rule',[1]

---

[1] Named after Arthur Ponsonby, one of the unsung heroes of Parliamentary democracy. Ponsonby was a Liberal MP during the First World War, later becoming a Labour MP and subsequently leader of the House of Lords. He is credited with the line, 'When war is declared, truth is the first casualty', drawn from his study of black propaganda, *Falsehood in War-Time: Propaganda Lies of the First World War* (London: George Allen & Unwin, 1928).

adopted by the Government as a constitutional convention in 1924 and followed in most cases since that time. The practice was intended to ensure that 'secret Treaties and secret clauses of Treaties will be rendered impossible' (though it is hard to see how this would work if the Government decided to keep an agreement secret from Parliament), but its impact is wider. In principle, a debate can be held on a tabled treaty in either House; and if the treaty is strongly opposed the Government might be persuaded not to proceed to ratification. Not all treaties and similar instruments are subject to the rule. 'International conventions of a purely technical character' which are not subject to ratification are outside the rule; and some treaties, such as the 1939 Treaty of Mutual Assistance between France, Turkey, and the United Kingdom, and other instruments that create legal rights and duties, such as the United Kingdom declarations accepting the jurisdiction of the International Court of Justice, have also been adopted without following the Ponsonby procedure.

2.2.2 RESERVATIONS TO TREATIES

Treaties are bargains struck by those who negotiate them on behalf of the State. The pause between signature and ratification permits the government to decide if the bargain is good enough, if it wishes to proceed to ratification or prefers to leave the treaty unratified as a dead letter. The possibility of non-ratification is small in the case of bilateral treaties: the negotiators will know what their negotiating position is, and if they do not secure it they will not even conclude a signed text to submit for ratification. But in the case of multilateral treaties the possibility is much greater. The negotiators will do their best to achieve a consensus; but it is very unlikely that the text will be wholly acceptable to all of them.

At this point a policy choice arises. We might say that every State has the choice of accepting the treaty as negotiated or of leaving it. That approach would preserve the integrity of the treaty regime, every State Party being bound by exactly the same rules, but it might lead to many States choosing to stay outside the treaty. Alternatively, we might permit States to modify the treaty in so far as it applies to themselves, accepting some but not all of the provisions. The modification would be effected by ratifying the treaty subject to a 'reservation'—that is, a statement that excludes or modifies the legal effect of certain provisions of the treaty in their application to that State.

For example, the 1958 Continental Shelf Convention set out some basic rules concerning the rights of a coastal State over the resources of the continental shelf adjacent to its coast. It also contained, in Article 6, a provision concerning the delimitation of the continental shelves with those of neighbouring States. This stipulated that in the absence of agreement to the contrary, and unless another boundary line is justified by special circumstances, the boundary is to be the line of points that are equidistant from the nearest points on the coast of each of the neighbouring States. A State might agree with all of the provisions of the 1958 Convention concerning the basic legal regime of the continental shelf but find the Article 6 provision on delimitation unacceptable, perhaps because it fears the possible impact of the equidistance principle on its coastline and is not confident that its coastal configuration will be recognized as a 'special circumstance'. France, for example, did not wish the delimitation provisions to apply in the Western Approaches/Channel area, where British possession of the Scilly Islands and the Channel Islands would, under the equidistance principle, have pushed back France's entitlement to an unacceptable extent.[2] As it happened, the 1958 Convention specifically permitted reservations to the delimitation provision; and France ratified the Convention with a reservation stipulating that Article 6 did not apply in the Western Approaches/Channel area (though the reservation did not exclude its application to France's Mediterranean coast, and so Article 6 continued to apply to that coast).

The acceptance of reservations makes it easier for States to become Parties to the treaty and so expand its membership, but does so at the expense of the integrity of the treaty because not all States Parties would be bound by exactly the same rules. The choice is one between the maximizing the number of Parties and maximizing the integrity of the treaty regime. The question is, who decides? Sometimes treaties themselves specify that reservations are entirely forbidden, or are freely permitted, or (as in the 1958 Continental Shelf Convention), are permitted in respect of certain provisions only. But what is the position where the treaty is silent on the matter?

The classical view was that reservations could be made only with the agreement of all of the other States Parties to the treaty. A contrary view was adopted in the Pan American Union, which favoured reservations as a means of increasing the acceptance of multilateral conventions. The issue arose in the context of the 1948 Convention on the Prevention and Punishment of the Crime of Genocide (the Genocide Convention), for which the United Nations was the depository, responsible for keeping the list of States Parties and other data concerning the Convention, including the date of its entry into force. Multilateral treaties commonly provide that they shall enter into force after a certain number of States have ratified

---

[2] See the *Anglo-French Continental Shelf* case (1978) 54 *ILR* p. 6.

them—a device that ensures that States are not dissuaded from early ratification by the fear that they will find themselves among a handful of States bound by a treaty that most States reject. It is accordingly important to know whether a State may ratify a treaty and subject its ratification to a reservation in circumstances where the treaty does not expressly permit reservations, and, if a State does so, whether such a State is to be counted in the total of ratifying States. The 1948 Genocide Convention is one of many multilateral treaties that contain no provision dealing expressly with reservations. The International Court of Justice, giving an Advisory Opinion to the UN General Assembly, held that reservations can be made so long as they are compatible with the object and purpose of the treaty. It also held that other States Parties may accept or reject the reservation, and that a State rejecting the reservation may consider the reserving State not to be a Party to the treaty. In other words, the International Court adopted the 'Pan American' approach, although it emphasized that it was ruling on the matter in the specific context of the Genocide Convention, whose object and purpose implied that it was the intention that as many States as possible should 'participate', so that the exclusion of any (reserving) State 'would not only restrict the scope of its application, but would detract from the authority of the moral and humanitarian principles which are its basis'.[3]

The same approach was adopted in the Vienna Convention on the Law of Treaties. Reservations compatible with the object and purpose of the treaty may be made, unless it appears from the limited number of negotiating States and the object and purpose of the treaty that the application of the treaty in its entirety is an essential condition of the consent of each State to be bound by it. A regional disarmament treaty would be an example of such a treaty. If another State Party accepts the reservation, the treaty is modified in accordance with the reservation, but only in respect of the treaty relations between the reserving and the accepting State. The accepting State remains bound by the unmodified treaty in its relations with all other States Parties who have not made reservations.

If another State Party objects to the reservation (as the United Kingdom rejected the French reservation to the 1958 Continental Shelf Convention) then the reservation obviously cannot take effect to modify the treaty. But it is equally clear that the reserving State has not consented to be bound by the provisions to which the treaty relates. Accordingly, the Vienna Convention stipulates that in such circumstances the treaty provisions to which the reservation relates do not apply as between the reserving and the objecting Parties, to the extent of the reservation.

[3] *ICJ Reports 1951*, p. 15 at p. 24.

Thus, in the *Anglo-French Continental Shelf* case, the United Kingdom's rejection of the French reservation meant that Article 6 of the Continental Shelf Convention did not apply as between France and the United Kingdom in relation to the Western Approaches/Channel area, though Article 6 would have applied as between the two States if they had been neighbouring States in any other area of the world. As between the United Kingdom and France the 1958 Convention thus contained no provision on delimitation applicable to that area, and the question was therefore regulated by customary international law (which was more or less the same as the treaty rule, as it happened).

The Vienna Convention does provide another option: the objecting State may refuse to accept that the treaty enters into force at all between it and the reserving State. The presumption, however, is that objection to a reservation does not preclude the entry into force of the treaty: the objecting State must express its intention clearly if it does wish to preclude the entry into force of the treaty.

This approach makes sense if a treaty is regarded as an exchange of obligations between States and the reservation is regarded as a kind of counter-offer which would modify the applicable terms of the treaty and which other States Parties are free to accept or reject. It is a robust, consensualist, contractarian approach. But not all treaties are best viewed as contracts. Human rights treaties, for instance, have the form of agreements between States Parties, to which the consensualist approach could well be applied. But the *substance* of human rights treaties is at odds with their form. Their substance consists of a set of guarantees and rights adopted for the benefit of individuals who are not parties to the treaties, including in some cases the right for individuals to petition international bodies with claims that their treaty rights have been violated by a State Party. These treaties are more in the nature of pledges by States Parties than of contracts between them. This distinction has led some scholars to argue that the Vienna Convention regime is not suitable for application to human rights treaties.

That argument received powerful support from the UN Human Rights Committee, which monitors the implementation of certain human rights treaties including the International Covenant on Civil and Political Rights (ICCPR). In its 1994 General Comment 24 on Reservations to the ICCPR, the Human Rights Committee adopted an approach to reservations at variance with that in the Vienna Convention. It asserted that it had the right to decide which reservations were compatible with the object and purpose of the Covenant, thus denying the States Parties the right to make that judgement themselves by their acceptance or rejection of a reservation.

The Committee made clear that it would not accept either reservations to provisions that codify customary international law (e.g., the prohibitions on torture and slavery, and the affirmation of the right of all peoples to determine their own political status), or reservations incompatible with the object and purpose of the ICCPR (e.g., reservations to the duty to respect and ensure all rights on a non-discriminatory basis, or to the duty to report to the Committee on the implementation of rights). It also suggested that it would generally sever invalid reservations and treat the State that made them as bound by the Covenant as if the reservation had not been made. The robust approach of the Human Rights Committee provoked vigorous reactions from several States, including the United Kingdom and United States, which considered that the Vienna Convention rules should be applied and objected in particular to the suggestion that invalid reservations would simply be disregarded.

The question of the effect of reservations remains controversial, despite further study of the question by the International Law Commission (ILC). Many would share the view of the ILC that the record of States objecting to reservations is very poor and patchy and offers no real assurance of 'quality control'. Even reservations that eviscerate commitments to be bound by treaties (such as Saudi Arabia's reservation to the 1979 Convention on the Elimination of All Forms of Discrimination Against Women, which states that 'in case of contradiction between any term of the Convention and the norms of Islamic law, the Kingdom is not under obligation to observe the contradictory terms of the Convention') often go unchallenged by other States Parties. Few States are so confident of their own records on human rights, and so altruistic in the conduct of their foreign policy, that they are likely to challenge another State on the legality of its reservation to a human rights treaty. Bodies such as the Human Rights Committee are the best guardians of the treaties whose implementation they supervise. On the other hand, it is not surprising that States resist the seepage of power away from the States Parties and towards such bodies, which is the practical consequence of what may appear to be abstruse debates over highly technical rules of treaty law.

One final point should be made concerning reservations. Sometimes States do not make reservations, but what they call 'interpretative declarations'—that is, declarations of the meaning that the State considers some provision of the treaty to bear, and therefore of the manner in which the State intends to implement that provision. The distinction between interpretative declarations and reservations is fine. It depends essentially upon whether the State making the declaration insists that its interpretation be accepted whether or not it is the 'correct' interpretation of the treaty. If acceptance of the State's declaration is a condition of its consent to be bound by the treaty, it will constitute a reservation unless its interpretation is held to be correct. As the correctness of the interpretation cannot be known in advance of litigation on the question, any State that does not share the interpretation will be well advised to treat it as a reservation and object to it. If it does not, it risks being held to have accepted the reservation and therefore bound by it under Vienna Convention rules. If the interpretative declaration is not a condition of consent, so that the State making it is, as it were, prepared to be told that it was wrong in its interpretation and to accept the correct interpretation, the declaration will not be a reservation. Its only significance will be as a piece of practice lending support to one particular interpretation of the treaty, and as a statement of how the State intends, unless and until corrected, to interpret it.

2.2.3 TREATY INTERPRETATION

In any international dispute where there is a treaty bearing upon the subject-matter of the dispute, the parties will almost certainly have to address the question of the precise effect of the treaty. Its words may clearly support one party's case. If they do not, the party will probably argue that when 'properly interpreted' either the treaty does support its case, or the treaty does not apply to the particular circumstances of the dispute at all. Lawyers put much energy and imagination into treaty interpretation; courts respond by ruling on the submissions; and enough material emerges to fuel an entire field of legal analysis and scholarship. There are discussions concerning the relative merits of the teleological approach (which looks at the purpose that the treaty was designed to achieve) and the literal approach (which focuses on the text, as the only certain foothold in the shifting sands of interpretation). There are debates about the materials, such as the *travaux préparatoires* (preparatory works or negotiating history) that are admissible to support or to counter a particular interpretation; and there are debates over presumptions that might be applied in interpreting treaty texts. Indeed, there are debates over practically every step in the reasoning process that leads from a treaty text to the conclusion concerning its effects in a concrete case.

This analysis is largely detached from the reality of treaty interpretation in practice, for the fact is that courts do not rely upon nice distinctions or the rigid pursuit of particular approaches to interpretation. They are encouraged to adopt a robust approach by the Vienna Convention on the Law of Treaties, whose provisions on interpretation are frequently cited. Article 31 sets out the basic rule:

A treaty shall be interpreted in good faith in accordance with the ordinary meaning to be given to the terms of the treaty in their context and in the light of its object and purpose.

The Vienna Convention goes on to describe the categories of evidence that may be referred to in order to establish the 'context' (and presumably also the 'object and purpose') of the treaty, and to specify 'supplementary means of interpretation' including the *travaux préparatoires* that may be used to 'confirm' the ordinary meaning or resolve ambiguities left by a reading based on the ordinary meaning. In fact most courts—and particularly municipal courts—interpreting treaties do not draw fine distinctions as to the sequence and purpose for which interpretative aids are applied. Lawyers are even less restrained, and commonly present a wide range of material to tribunals as aids to interpretation: monographs and journal articles, commentaries and summaries produced by one party or another, implementing legislation—anything that will fit on a photocopier and will lend some support to the interpretation for which they contend.

If one were to try to distil a rule of interpretation from what tribunals actually do (rather than what they say they do), it would probably be something like 'interpret the treaty as reasonable parties would have interpreted it if they had faced the questions now before the court'. That is, of course, an oversimplification: for example, it does not help to settle questions that the parties could not have foreseen, such as the question whether a reference to disputes over 'territory' in an early twentieth-century treaty should be interpreted so as to include the continental shelf of a State—a legal concept that did not come into existence until the middle of that century. But treaty interpretation is an area in which the returns on abstract theorizing are low, and diminishing; and there are many other topics to discuss.

2.2.4 INVALID TREATIES

The rule that treaty commitments must be observed—*pacta sunt servanda*—is one of the most fundamental in international law, and is rooted in an even more fundamental principle that States must act in good faith. But no State could be required by the principle of good faith to adhere to a treaty that was procured by fraud or corruption, or as a result of a fundamental error, or as a result of coercion. As might be expected, the Vienna Convention provides that these are all grounds upon which the consent of a State to be bound by a treaty may be invalidated.

Instances are few, but not unknown. History records that the German ministers Goering and Ribbentrop physically harassed President Hacha of Czechoslovakia, and threatened the immediate bombardment of Prague, in order to coerce him into signing in the early hours of the morning the treaty that established a German protectorate over Bohemia and Moravia in 1939. That, clearly, is coercion. But what of situations where one State makes it known that unless the other State signs a treaty, it will lose all manner of economic and political benefits in the gift of the first State? Is that coercion? Or is that just how the world is?

And what of 'unequal treaties', made between a very powerful State and a weak State which may think that it has no option but to go along with the wishes of the stronger State? It has been said that treaties procured by the threat or use of force by imperialist powers during the period of colonization should be regarded as invalid. In practice, however, this idea has not taken root, and States have not sought to escape from large numbers of treaties by pleading coercion. The reasons are plain. What effect would the renunciation of the treaty have? What practical effects would have followed if China had purported to terminate the leases and the cession of the territories around Hong Kong? Would the United Kingdom have simply walked out of the territory? What would renunci-ation have done that China could not do by persuading the United Kingdom to negotiate its withdrawal? It was in the interest of both States to have an agreed termination of the treaty arrangements.

And sometimes it suits the weaker State to maintain the treaties in force. Guantanamo Bay is an example. It was leased as a coaling station to the United States in 1903 by a treaty that some might have expected the Government of Cuba to renounce as an anachronistic survival of American imperialism in the Caribbean, or more recently as an offence against human rights. But one suspects that Cuba (among others) relishes the international outrage over the holding facility for alleged terrorists, appar-ently beyond the reach of the law, which the United States established in Guantanamo. The sight of such discomfort on the part of the United States, as it approached the fourth decade of its economic embargo against Cuba, may have appeared to be a price well worth paying for the loss of a little piece of Cuban territory.

Sometimes treaties may be concluded in breach of the national law of a State Party, for example because the person negotiating the treaty exceeded his mandate or because the treaty was concluded without obtaining some necessary authorization from the Government. International law does not permit constraints under national law to invalidate treaties. This is another aspect of the principle that national law may not be raised as a defence to a breach of an obligation under international law—though not a logical consequence of it, because the question here is whether an international obligation was validly created in the first place. The Law of Treaties operates on the basis of ostensible authority. If the State representatives purporting to conclude the treaty appear to have authority to do so, the treaty will be validly concluded unless the other party is actually aware of some defect in the authority of the representatives. The one exception is where the defect in the authority of the representatives arises from a manifest violation of a rule of the internal law of the State that is of fundamental importance. The requirement for Senate approval of treaties in the United States would be an example. It is a very well-known rule, which everyone negotiating a treaty with the United States may be presumed to understand. Even there, however, the matter is not free of difficulty. Under US law it is only 'treaties' and not, for example, so-called 'executive agreements', that require Senate approval. One wonders what would happen if a US Administration assured a foreign State that it had the authority to conclude an agreement without the need for Senate approval.

The Vienna Convention also provides that a treaty is void if at the time that it is concluded it conflicts with a peremptory norm of general international law, i.e., a rule of customary international law that allows of no derogation (a rule of *jus cogens*). Put in that way the point is almost circular, because the obvious form that a 'derogation' from a rule of customary international law takes is a treaty which supplants the rule of customary law as between the parties. To say that a treaty is void if it conflicts with a rule of customary international law that cannot be modified by treaty casts little light on the principle. The difficulty is that while all States accept that a handful of fundamental moral principles (such as the prohibitions on aggressive war, genocide, and slavery) are to be counted among the peremptory norms of international law, there is no consensus on what other rules fall within the category. Because peremptory norms trump other rules of international law, the uncertainty concerning the content of this category of norms is a matter of much significance. It is, for instance, one of the main reasons for France's decision not to ratify the Vienna Convention on the Law of Treaties.

The concept of peremptory norms is an important element of the international legal system, playing a role that corresponds to the rules of public policy which operate in municipal law to invalidate certain contracts. International tribunals have relied upon the concept cautiously and rarely. For many years the International Court of Justice avoided the term, except in its Separate and Dissenting Opinions. More recently, in the *Armed Activities on the Territory of the Congo* and the *Application of the Convention on the Prevention and Punishment of the Crime of Genocide* cases the Court has dared to speak the word, affirming that 'the norm prohibiting genocide was assuredly a peremptory norm of international law (*jus cogens*)'. This caution no doubt reflects the continuing controversy over the concept on the international plane. Curiously, municipal courts appear to be more willing to base decisions at least partly upon the concept. It has, for example, been used by United Kingdom courts to explain the non-availability of State immunity in respect of international crimes.[4]

2.2.5 RELEASE FROM TREATY OBLIGATIONS

Treaties are binding, but only within reason. One circumstance in which a treaty ceases to bind follows naturally from the concept of peremptory norms. If a treaty, valid when made, conflicts with a peremptory norm that emerges after the treaty was made, it automatically becomes void and terminates. Examples are rare, but one may be found in the 1993 *Aloeboetoe* case, where the Inter-American Court of Human Rights indicated that it would strike down an eighteenth-century treaty between the Netherlands and the Saramaka tribe of Surinam under which the Saramakas agreed to capture and return escaped slaves to the Dutch. Peremptory norms (i.e., rules of *jus cogens*) thus have a potentially destabilizing effect upon treaty and other relations between States, which is one reason why they remain controversial.

The other grounds upon which States may be released from treaty obligations are less dramatic. First, a State Party may invoke a supervening impossibility of performance of the treaty as a ground for terminating a bilateral treaty or withdrawing from a multilateral treaty. Again, examples are rare; but the kind of circumstance that this provision (Article 61) of the Vienna Convention contemplates is the drying up of a river indispensable for the execution of the treaty concerning a hydroelectric project. Such impossibility may be contrasted with the right to terminate or withdraw from treaties where a 'fundamental change of circumstances' has occurred. This provision (Article 62 of the Vienna Convention) is now a free-standing doctrine, but used to be asserted on the basis that every treaty should be understood to have an implied term that the treaty would stand only so long as the conditions essential to the consent of the Parties to be bound by the treaty remained as they were when the treaty was made—the so-called *clausula rebus sic stantibus*. For the 'fundamental change' doctrine to operate the change must have been unforeseen. If the Parties foresaw it but nonetheless concluded the treaty there would be no ground for allowing termination or withdrawal. The change must affect an essential basis of the consent of the Parties to be bound; and the change must radically transform the extent of obligations still to be performed under the treaty. If one

---

[4] See, e.g., *R v Bow Street Magistrate, Ex p. Pinochet (No. 3)* [2000] 1 AC 147 at 275.

considers the example of a treaty between two States to construct a hydro-electric plant on a shared river, where the main flow of the river changes its course as a result of geological activity, one can see the weakness in this formulation. Building the dam would not be impossible, and the extent of obligations under the treaty would, literally, not be radically transformed. It would be possible, but pointless, to execute the treaty and build the dam. Yet few can doubt that in such circumstances it would make no sense to hold the Parties to their obligations under the treaty.

Perhaps surprisingly, the fundamental change doctrine is invoked only rarely. It has been used in cases in the ICJ, such as the *Fisheries Jurisdiction* case between the United Kingdom and Iceland, where it was suggested (unsuccessfully) that the increased threat to fish stocks from over-exploitation released Iceland from its treaty obligations to the United Kingdom, and in the *Gabcikovo-Nagymaros Dam* case between Hungary and Slovakia where it was argued (unsuccessfully) that changes in the profitability of a venture and technological developments cumulatively amounted to a fundamental change. Tribunals are plainly reluctant to rely on the doctrine.

A fundamental change of circumstances may be invoked as a ground for suspending, rather than terminating, the treaty; and this option is import-ant. There may be a fundamental but non-permanent change of circum-stances. Roads serving the site of the projected dam (to pursue the hypothetical example raised above) may have been severely damaged by an earthquake; but one or both of the States may prefer to repair the infra-structure and proceed with the project after a delay.

The Vienna Convention (Article 60) also permits the termination or suspension treaties in cases of a 'material breach' of the treaty. A breach is 'material' if it amounts to a repudiation of the treaty or the violation of a provision essential for the achievement its object or purpose. The right to terminate or suspend bilateral treaties for material breach is well estab-lished, and is one of the mechanisms by which miscreant States may be pressured into compliance with their obligations. An example arose in the *Air Services Agreement* dispute in 1979. France refused to allow the decanting of the few passengers flying to France on large planes from the west coast of America via London onto smaller planes for the London to Paris leg of their flight. Such a 'change of gauge', as the change in the size of aircraft is known, would have put French airlines at a commercial disadvantage, because the French airlines would naturally fly large aircraft all the way to and from Paris. The United States regarded the French action as a breach of the 1946 Air Services Agreement between the two States and responded by suspending landing rights for Air France flights to Los Angeles. The Tribunal which heard the dispute regarded the suspension of France's rights under the treaty as a proportionate counter-measure, justified by the prior French breach of the treaty.

The position regarding multilateral treaties is more complex. A breach by one State may have no real impact upon most other States Parties. For example, if one of the 150 or so States Parties to the 1982 Law of the Sea Convention unlawfully arrests a merchant ship belonging to another State Party on the high seas (where ships are in principle subject only to the jurisdiction of their flag States), the arrest directly affects only those two States. The Vienna Convention sets out, in Article 60(2), the rule that might be expected: a material breach of a multilateral treaty permits a State Party 'specially affected' by the breach to invoke it as a ground for suspending the treaty in its relations with the State in breach. (A single 'specially affected State' may not terminate the treaty, although termination may be effected by the unanimous agreement of all the States Parties other than the State in breach.) The 'suspending' State remains bound by the treaty in its relations with other States Parties.

Sometimes a material breach of a multilateral treaty affects all of the parties. Breach of a regional disarmament convention would be an example. If the effect of the material breach is radically to change the position of every other State Party, every State Party (other than the defaulting Party—no State may benefit from its own wrong) may suspend the treaty. Humanitarian provisions in treaties, however, may never be terminated or suspended on this ground: that rule, set out in Article 60(5) of the Vienna Convention, reflects the belief that the individuals protected by humanitarian provisions should never be deprived of that protection as a result of any unlawful conduct by a State Party.

I have not yet mentioned the most common way in which a State is released from its treaty obligations: that is, termination in accordance with the express or implied terms of the treaty. Many treaties provide that they are to last for a certain period, following which they may be renewed, or in some cases are automatically renewed unless notice of termination is given. If the treaty contains no such provision, it may still be terminated by the giving of notice (not less than twelve months, under Article 56 of the Vienna Convention), if it can be established that the Parties intended to allow denunciation or withdrawal. Treaties establishing borders are examples of treaties that will never be held to have an implied right of denunciation. A bilateral treaty of friendship and co-operation, on the other hand, may well be thought to be of a character that implies a right to terminate it on notice.

Before leaving the subject of the termination or suspension of treaties I should mention a doctrine that has a similar effect: the defence of necessity. The defence is not found in the Vienna Convention, no doubt because it is not classified as part of the Law of Treaties but as a part of the law of State responsibility. It operates to 'preclude the wrongfulness' of acts taken by a State that are the only means for the State to safeguard an essential interest against a grave and imminent peril, although the defence is available only as long as the act does not seriously impair an essential interest of a State towards which the obligation exists, or of the international community as a whole. A State may therefore plead that it was 'necessary' to act in breach of its treaty obligations, in a way comparable to the invocation of impossibility or of a fundamental change of circumstances as a ground for termination or suspension. There are significant differences. The necessity defence does not terminate or suspend the treaty (or particular parts of it, if the obligations are severable): it merely excuses non-performance. And of course the requirements for invoking the defence are different: necessity may be invoked in circumstances that fall short of literal impossibility of performance, and where there is no change in the extent of the obligations of the State under the treaty.

The necessity defence has been enshrined in the International Law Commission's 2001 Articles on State Responsibility, rather to the surprise of those who thought that many States would resist the inclusion of such a powerful and open-ended defence. It is uncertain how wide an interpretation the defence will be given, but its invocation by Argentina to excuse its failure to comply with treaty obligations towards foreign investors during its severe financial crisis of 2001–2002 has met with mixed success. The necessity defence was rejected on the facts (but acknowledged to exist in principle) in one case conducted under the auspices of ICSID, *CMS Gas Transmission Co. v Argentine Republic*, but accepted in another, *LG&E v Argentine Republic*. However the defence comes to be applied, it will not easily be made available to States.

2.2.6 AMENDING TREATIES

The circumstances in which treaties may be terminated or suspended under the Vienna Convention rules are far from covering the whole range of circumstances in which States may wish that they could escape from or modify some of their treaty obligations. International law has no principles that govern the renegotiation of treaties in circumstances where performance becomes onerous or intolerable or unacceptable for some other reason; but there are various mechanisms that play a similar role. Some treaties and other agreements may themselves provide for the renegotiation of particular provisions in such circumstances: many agreements between States and foreign investors giving rights to exploit mineral resources contain such provisions. Others provide more generally for the amendment of the treaty. Some of the most important international treaties have been concluded as 'framework' treaties, with basic provisions in the body of the treaty supplemented by detailed regulations set out in protocols which can be amended more easily than the main treaty. For example, some International Maritime Organization (IMO) treaties provide for a 'tacit amendment' procedure under which amendments to detailed technical provisions are adopted by a majority vote and the amendments then become binding upon all States Parties unless they positively reject the amendment. There have also been plans, as yet unrealized, to create internationally agreed mechanisms for the renegotiation of government debts in situations where States face a financial crisis.

In the absence of such express provisions the parties are left to their own devices. They may choose to renegotiate the treaty. They may denounce the treaty. They may decide to act in breach of the treaty, in which case the other parties may tolerate the breach and thereby effect a *de facto* amendment of the treaty, or object and seek some remedy for the breach. But whatever happens, the result will involve some renegotiation of the relationship between the Parties. This is an inevitable consequence of the primacy given to ensuring that States comply with the treaty obligations that they have assumed, but only with those obligations. While particular treaties and clauses may appropriately be made subject to renegotiation procedures, it is by no means the case that such procedures could be devised for all treaties, or that all treaties would benefit from them.

2.2.7 TREATIES AND CUSTOMARY INTERNATIONAL LAW

Treaties bind only the States parties to them. They cannot in principle create rights or obligations for third States without their consent—and consent amounts in essence to an extension of the treaty relationship. This principle is, however, subject to an important modification in respect of treaties which are intended to create rights for third States. Under the Vienna Convention (Article 36), if a third State gives its assent, it acquires the intended right; and the assent of third States is presumed. The Permanent Court of International Justice (the predecessor of the International Court of Justice) observed in the *Free Zones* case that 'it cannot lightly be presumed that stipulations favourable to a third State have been adopted with the object of creating an actual right in its favour'. It is necessary to establish that the Parties intended the third State to have a right, and not merely a benefit, under the treaty. Nonetheless, treaties bestowing rights on third States are not so very uncommon. The 1936 Treaty of Montreux, which recognizes and regulates rights of passage through the Dardanelles and the Bosphorus for ships of all States, whether or not sailing under the flag of one of the States Parties, is one example.

Where a right is given by treaty, and it is further established that it was intended that the right should not be revocable or be modified without the consent of the third State, the right cannot be revoked or modified by the Parties. That is, however, a very high threshold to cross. One of the few relatively common circumstances where such irrevocable rights could be established is the case of peace treaties after wars, where defeated States have often waived claims against certain States not signatories to the treaties.

The provision on third State rights applies only to rights given to States: it does not apply to 'rights' given to other persons, such as the 'rights' given to human beings under human rights treaties. This limitation makes sense within the traditional inter-State framework of international law, and is probably necessary on pragmatic grounds, too. A third State beneficiary can consent to the modification of a right; but who would express consent on behalf of human beneficiaries?

The rule that treaties cannot impose obligations on third States without their acceptance is more absolute; but even here there is an exception. It arose in the *Reparations* case in the International Court in 1949. Count Bernadotte, the UN mediator in Jerusalem and a Swedish national, was murdered by the 'Stern Gang', a terrorist group whose leaders included Yitzhak Shamir, later Prime Minister of Israel. The UN wished to know whether it could bring claims for injuries suffered by a UN agent in the course of his duties, or whether the agent's national State had to bring the claim, as was the normal rule in international law. At that time Israel, which might have been the Respondent State (if it had negligently failed to prevent Bernadotte's death), was not a member of the UN. The International Court held, however, that:

> . . . fifty States,[5] representing the vast majority of the members of the international community, had the power, in conformity with international law, to bring into being an entity possessing objective international personality and not merely personality recognised by them alone, together with the capacity to bring international claims . . .

This comes close to creating obligations for non-party States. The 'objective personality' of the UN meant that non-party States were obliged to recognize its existence and accept it as a person on the international stage, with the capacity to enter into a wide range of international transactions. It is at least arguable that this notion of the bringing into existence by treaty of an objective legal *status* could be applied elsewhere, for example

---

[5] i.e., the 50 States represented at the 1945 San Francisco conference which established the UN.

in the case of treaties that stipulate that certain areas (such as the moon, the deep seabed, and Antarctica) are not susceptible of appropriation by any State,[6] and of treaties establishing the permanent neutrality of certain areas such as the Panama Canal.[7]

The general limitation of the legally binding effect of treaties to States Parties does not mean that treaties can have no impact upon customary international law. This question was explored by the International Court of Justice in the *North Sea Continental Shelf* and *Nicaragua* cases, in both of which the Court was unable to apply a treaty provision that could have had a key role in the litigation.

In the *North Sea Continental Shelf* cases (Federal Republic of Germany/Denmark; Federal Republic of Germany/Netherlands) the provision was Article 6 of the 1958 Continental Shelf Convention, which stipulated that the equidistance line would apply in the absence of agreement or special circumstances. But Germany was not a Party to the 1958 Convention. The neighbouring States, Denmark, and the Netherlands, argued that the rule embodied in Article 6 was nonetheless binding on Germany as a matter of customary international law; and in that context the Court considered the relationship between treaty obligations and customary law. It identified three distinct ways in which a rule of law set out in a treaty text could be an accurate reflection of a rule of customary international law.

First, the treaty could have codified pre-existent international law. This was the case, for example, with the 1958 Geneva Convention on the High Seas, which asserted in its Preamble that it was concluded by the Parties 'desiring to codify the rules of international law relating to the high seas'.

Second, a treaty may crystallize an emergent rule of customary international law. This happened with many of the provisions of the 1982 UN Convention on the Law of the Sea, because of the particular manner in which that Convention was negotiated. Dissatisfaction with the rules that had been set out in four Conventions on the Law of the Sea concluded in Geneva in 1958 (which were seen as serving the interests of the former colonial powers and of the developed States in general) led to much

---

[6] See the 1967 Treaty on the Principles Governing the Activities of States in the Exploration and Use of Outer Space, including the Moon and Other Celestial Bodies. The treaty has 102 parties. And see the 1959 Antarctic Treaty, which has 46 parties. It might also be argued that the UN Law of the Sea Convention has this effect with regard to the seabed beyond the limits of national jurisdiction, although the better view is that this status arose as a matter of customary international law independently of the Convention.

[7] E.g., the 1977 Treaty Concerning the Permanent Neutrality and Operation of the Panama Canal.

pressure for change, particularly from the newly independent States. The proponents of change had an overwhelming numerical majority, but it was appreciated that there was little point in using that voting power to force through a text against the wishes of the more powerful developed States. Accordingly, the third UN Conference on the Law of the Sea (UNCLOS III) at which the 1982 Convention was drafted adopted a 'consensus' procedure, under which the chairman of each negotiating session would prepare a text which he thought represented the best chance of commanding general assent. Changes to these negotiating texts were made only when the chairman thought that they would substantially increase the chances of general acceptance of the final text. It was relatively easy to find consensus on the main lines of the legal regime, and it was apparent from an early stage, in the mid 1970s, what broad shape the final Convention would take. For example, it was plain that it would recognize coastal State rights over fish stocks in an Exclusive Economic Zone, within 200 miles of their coasts—a radical change to the '1958' law, which had limited exclusive fishery rights to twelve miles. States began to assert such rights unilaterally, establishing 200-mile fishing zones or claiming an exclusive economic zone with rights over all marine resources, as the negotiating texts envisaged. So many States adopted this course that there was a clear 'general practice accepted as law' supporting the 200-mile claims by the latter half of the 1970s, *before* the sequence of negotiating texts had generated the final Convention text in 1982. Nonetheless, the fact that the State practice accumulated around the UNCLOS III texts and was plainly intended to reflect them meant that the provisions of the 1982 United Nations Convention on the Law of the Sea crystallized that development in customary international law, and may be regarded as a clear articulation of the legal rules implicit in that body of State practice.

The third possible relationship between a treaty and customary international law contemplated in the *North Sea Continental Shelf* cases was that the treaty might pass into customary international law after its conclusion. In principle this is unremarkable. Customary international law results from the accumulation of State practice coupled with *opinio juris* focused upon an explicit or implicit norm. It does not matter where that norm is located. It might be articulated in something like the Truman Proclamation, or be implicit in parallel laws adopted by several States, for example. And there is no reason why that norm should not be set out in a treaty. If a treaty provision is taken up in State practice, with the necessary *opinio juris*, it may pass into customary international law.

The need for State practice is straightforward; but the need for *opinio juris* is more problematic. The question one asks in addressing the need for *opinio juris* is, does the State following this course of action consider that it is the expression of a rule of customary international law? For States Parties to the treaty, however, the obvious reason for a State to express a norm in its practice is that it is acting in conformity with the treaty, rather than in conformity with customary international law. As the Court noted in the *North Sea Continental Shelf* cases, it will therefore be difficult to prove the existence of the *opinio juris* necessary in order to translate the rule of treaty law into a rule of customary international law. It will not, however, be impossible to do so, as the *Nicaragua* case showed.

That case concerned Nicaragua's complaint that the United States was engaged in military and paramilitary activities against the Sandinista Government in Nicaragua. The United States said that it was acting in collective self-defence with El Salvador, which was itself the victim of armed intervention by Nicaragua. All three States were parties to the UN Charter (which is, of course, a treaty). But the United States' declaration accepting the jurisdiction of the International Court contained a reservation stipulating that disputes arising under a multilateral treaty are excluded from the Court's jurisdiction unless all treaty parties affected by the decision are parties to the case: and El Salvador was not a party to the case. The Court therefore could not rule on the United States' compliance with the UN Charter. If, however, the Charter rules in question—on non-intervention and the use of force—had passed into customary international law, the Court could apply the customary law rules. The Court set about the task of determining if this was indeed the case. It said in its *Nicaragua (Merits)* judgment that:

> The Court does not consider that, for a rule to be established as customary, the corresponding practice must be in absolutely rigorous conformity with the rule. In order to deduce the existence of customary rules, the Court deems it sufficient that the conduct of States should, in general, be consistent with such rules, and that instances of State conduct inconsistent with a given rule should generally have been treated as breaches of that rule, not as indications of the recognition of a new rule.

In the event, the Court was satisfied with rather little in the way of State practice (much of it in the form of declarations and General Assembly resolutions). It dealt swiftly, and somewhat obliquely, with the question analysed so thoroughly in the *North Sea Continental Shelf* cases, whether the conformity of States with the putative rules was the result of the fact that they were bound by the Charter to comply with them or the result of *opinio juris* concerning customary international law. The Court found that the adoption by States of various resolutions, and in particular the 1970 Declaration on Principles of International Law concerning Friendly Relations and Co-operation among States (UN General Assembly resolution 2625 (XXV)—the bracketed Roman numerals indicate the year in which the resolution was adopted, measured from the date of the foundation of the UN in 1945), evidenced the necessary *opinio juris*. Not surprisingly, it held that there were rules of customary international law corresponding to the Charter rules on the use of force and non-intervention.

The *Nicaragua* case shows that it is possible for treaty provisions to have a parallel existence as rules of customary international law; and the prohibition on the use of force in Article 2(4) of the Charter was a post-1945 development, so that the Charter cannot be regarded as having simply codified or crystallized a pre-existent rule of customary law. But there are not great numbers of treaties or treaty provisions that are likely to be so readily accepted as having a parallel existence in customary law. The Vienna Convention on the Law of Treaties is one example, most of whose provisions are regarded as reflecting customary international law. The 1982 Law of the Sea Convention (or at least Parts I–X of that Convention) is another. So, too, are a good number of the basic human rights provisions in treaties. Many of these instruments were regarded as actual or prospective codifications of whole areas of international law. But there is certainly no general presumption that even the most common provisions found in treaties, such as the provisions on investor protection contained in more than 2,000 treaties drafted in broadly similar terms, have passed into customary international law. Treaties and customary law have a close inter-relationship; but the fact remains that treaties, unless they are attempting to codify international law, are generally concluded because customary international law is regarded as insufficient for the needs of the parties. They are specific bargains, binding on the parties only.

2.2.8 TREATY COLLECTIONS

It is relatively easy to locate treaty texts. Article 102 of the UN Charter stipulates that no Member may rely on a treaty 'before any organ of the United Nations' unless the treaty has been registered with the UN. The vast majority are so registered and then published in the *United Nations Treaty Series*, in hard copy and on-line. The League of Nations performed a similar function with the *League of Nations Treaty Series*. Other international organizations publish treaties for which they are depositories. For example, the IMO is the depository for many multilateral treaties in the fields of shipping and marine pollution. In addition, many States publish the bilateral and multilateral treaties to which they are parties, in national series such as the *United Kingdom Treaty Series*.

Having considered customary international law and treaties, it remains to say something about the other sources of international law.

2.3 OTHER SOURCES OF LAW

2.3.1 GENERAL PRINCIPLES OF LAW

The third of the sources of international law listed in Article 38 of the ICJ Statute is 'the general principles of law recognized by civilized nations'. This source may appear to be inferior to treaties and customary international law: a stop-gap to which judges may revert if they fail to find a rule of treaty or custom that determines an issue before them. There is some truth in this view. It is easier, and more compelling, to determine cases by holding States to explicit rules to which they have signed up in a treaty and to rules of customary international law which bind all States. But general principles have an important place in international law and should not be underestimated.

In some respects they are uniquely useful. There are powerful legal principles, such as the rules of natural justice (the rules that each side in a dispute is entitled to be heard; that no-one may be a judge in his own cause; and so on), and doctrines such as estoppel and the 'clean hands' principle (that someone who has breached his obligations under an agreement may not ask a tribunal to enforce that agreement), which have not been codified in any international treaty. These principles are commonly used in national courts; but they rarely arise in State practice because diplomatic exchanges are not conducted like court pleadings. One State may point out that another has previously taken a different position on a certain matter, but it is unlikely that a diplomatic note would say explicitly that the other State is 'estopped' from changing its position. Estoppel is the language of the court-room lawyer, not of the diplomat. Accordingly, it is difficult to find sufficient State practice on the question of estoppel to form the basis of a rule of customary international law. Yet all lawyers know that estoppel is a basic tool of court-room law. Article 38(1)(c) lets such principles in to international law, as 'general principles of law recognized by civilised nations'. It enables international courts to employ such rules.

There is a related point, which concerns the connections between international and national courts and tribunals. The lawyers who practise in international tribunals almost invariably also practise in national tribunals. Many of the judges on international tribunals come from the ranks of those lawyers, and not infrequently from the ranks of national judges. Disputes before international tribunals have often been (or subsequently go) before national courts. National and international law are not separate systems, isolated one from the other. They are deeply interconnected, and the techniques and principles and practices of national laws permeate international law. The reference to 'general principles of law' in the ICJ Statute reflects the fact that although it routinely applies sources such as treaty and customary international law which arise relatively rarely in municipal courts, the International Court is still a member of the family of tribunals which together maintain the Rule of Law in the settlement of disputes. It may be International; but it is still a Court.

Not all municipal law principles and doctrines are suitable for translation onto the international plane. To take one obvious example, national legal systems commonly apply the rule that the validity of statutes may not be challenged by courts (except in circumstances where they can be challenged on grounds that may be set out in the constitution). If that rule were applied in international tribunals, it would in many cases be practically impossible for an international tribunal to find that a State had violated its international obligations. It is only those general principles that are apt for translation onto the international plane that may be so applied. It is, of course, a matter of appreciation whether any given principle is 'apt' for application in this way. What about the principles of legitimate expectation and of proportionality? What about pre-contractual representations, or the rules on self-defence? Arguments might be made either way. The right to have recourse to general principles of law gives international tribunals a powerful instrument for judicial creativity and innovation—though tribunals have, as yet, used it sparingly.

2.3.2 UNILATERAL ACTS OF STATES

Legal obligations can arise from simple utterances. When people, asked during a wedding ceremony if they take someone as their spouse, say 'I do' they do not simply make a statement of fact or intention. The utterance of those words has a specific effect, changing the legal relationship between the people concerned. By uttering those words they effect the act of marriage. Those words are an example of a particular category of speech acts, as they are known in linguistics. The speech acts in a marriage ceremony are a bilateral matter. The marriage is constituted by an exchange of vows, and the exchange is essential in order to make the marriage: if the groom says 'I do', but the bride says 'On reflection, I'd rather not', there is no marriage. There are, however, speech acts that are unilateral in character but which nonetheless achieve legal effects. The taking of an oath of allegiance, or an oath of office, or of the oath administered prior to the giving of evidence, are all instances of unilateral acts that have legal effects, changing the legal position of the person making the utterance.

International law has its own category of acts of this kind: unilateral acts that produce legal effects. The best known examples are the statements made by the President and the Foreign Minister of France in 1974, in which they stated that the atmospheric tests of nuclear weapons which France was then conducting in the Pacific were the last round of such tests and that future testing would be conducted underground (but still in the Pacific, rather than France). Australia and New Zealand had instituted proceedings against France in the International Court, seeking a declaration that the atmospheric tests were unlawful. France chose not to appear before the Court; and it was evident that France would not regard itself as compelled by any decision that the Court might take to abandon any tests that it considered essential to its security. The Court seized on the French statements, saying:

It is well recognised that declarations made by way of unilateral acts, concerning legal or factual situations, may have the effect of creating legal obligations. When it is the intention of the State making the declaration that it should become bound according to its terms, that intention confers on the declaration the character of a legal undertaking, the State being thenceforth legally required to follow a course of conduct consistent with the declaration.

The Court regarded the French statements as binding unilateral acts, with the result that France had bound itself as a matter of international law to cease atmospheric tests. The corollary of this conclusion was that France had voluntarily assumed the main legal obligation that Australia and New Zealand wished the Court to impose upon France, so the Court was able to dismiss the applications against France as moot.

Few readers have been convinced by this analysis. Some have argued that there was no established rule of international law that gave binding legal effect to public statements of this kind. There were, it is true, precedents that gave such effect to commitments made in the course of negotiations with another State which acted in reliance upon the statement; and it is a well-established legal principle that commitments made to a court during proceedings are legally binding. Estoppel and preclusion are also well-established legal doctrines. But none of these covered the case of the French declarations, and it is hard to find any basis in State practice or in the jurisprudence of international tribunals for the principle that the Court asserted in the *Nuclear Tests* cases. But the most potent objection is surely that there was no proof that France had intended the statements to be binding: they looked like simple statements of policy. It is hard to believe that France intended to bind itself legally by those statements, convenient as that assumption was as a way for the Court to avoid having to issue a judgment that would almost certainly have been ignored

by France. Indeed, a few years later in the *Frontier Dispute* case between
Burkina Faso and Mali the question of unilateral acts came before the
International Court once more, and the Court took the opportunity to
redefine the requirements for giving them binding legal force, doing so in
a manner that comes close to confining the *Nuclear Tests* principle to the
peculiar circumstances of that case.

Nevertheless, undoubtedly there are instances of binding unilateral acts.
Declarations of acceptance of the jurisdiction of the ICJ; the making of
reservations and interpretative declarations in respect of treaties; and the
declaration by coastal States of maritime zones, such as territorial seas
and customs zones, in the waters adjacent to their land territory, are all
examples. The International Law Commission undertook a study of
unilateral acts and in 2006 issued 'guidelines' relating to them, which reflect
the general approach of the International Court in the *Nuclear Tests* cases.
Yet there is a more general question which is being left largely unexplored:
whether it is enough to distinguish between 'binding' and 'non-binding'
unilateral acts. That distinction is stark. It is, presumably, a consequence
of the *Nuclear Tests* approach that France, being bound by its unilateral
declarations, had no legal right to depart from them. There is no indication
that France could *ever* have escaped the binding force of those declarations,
although common sense says that there must be circumstances in which it
could do so. But it might be better to regard all unilateral statements, including even 'non-binding' statements of policy as potentially having some legal
consequences, so that States would not in ordinary circumstances be
entirely free to reverse announced policies without notice. If a State did
make an unannounced reversal of policy, it might be liable to compensate
those who had reasonably acted in reliance upon the policies. This approach
would import into international law the doctrine of legitimate expectations,
which might be counted as a 'general principle of law recognized by civilized nations'. But this lies in the future. It is another possible growing
point; another possible way in which international law can continue to adapt
itself to changing circumstances and demands.

2.3.3 THE ROLE OF INTERNATIONAL ORGANIZATIONS IN LAW-MAKING

It is a trite proposition that the international legal system has no legisla-
ture; but there are many instruments adopted by international organiza-
tions that look suspiciously like legal texts. One, the Declaration on
Principles of International Law Concerning Friendly Relations and
Co-operation Among States in Accordance with the Charter of the United
Nations, looks almost like a statement of basic constitutional rules and

principles. Indeed, in the next chapter I will discuss its content in much those terms. But here I am referring to it not because of what it says but because of where it came from. It is a text adopted by the UN General Assembly as Resolution 2625 (XXV) in 1970. What legal force does that give it, and other resolutions adopted by the General Assembly?

Some resolutions of international organizations are binding. Resolutions on the admission of new Members, on the budget and other matters concerned with the internal economy of the organization are clear examples. But these are scarcely law-making resolutions. Some resolutions are, however, expressed in the language of legal pronouncements. To take two examples, General Assembly resolution 1514 (XV), the Declaration on the Granting of Independence to Colonial Territories and Peoples set out in some detail the right of self-determination of 'all peoples' and the consequences of that right for other States, and General Assembly resolution 2574 (XXIV) declared a moratorium on the exploitation of the resources of the deep sea bed beyond the limits of national jurisdiction (i.e., beyond the limits of national continental shelves). Are those resolutions legally binding?

It is tempting to say simply, no. Nothing in the UN Charter stipulates that such resolutions have the force of law, or even that they are binding upon the Members of the UN. Indeed, because the Charter does say (in Article 25) that Members 'agree to accept and carry out the decisions of the Security Council in accordance with the present Charter' one might infer from the absence of a similar provision concerning General Assembly resolutions that they were intended not to be binding. And, furthermore, an examination of the debates and drafts leading to the conclusion of the UN Charter would lead to much the same conclusion. But the matter is not quite so simple.

Resolution 1514 addresses the question of self-determination. Article 1(2) of the UN Charter stipulates that it is one of the Purposes of the United Nations to 'develop friendly relations among nations based on respect for the principles of equal rights and self-determination of peoples'. Article 1(2) binds UN Member States as a matter of treaty law. But what does Article 1(2) *mean*? What does respect for the principle of self-determination of peoples entail in practice? Resolution 1514 was adopted in 1960, when many present Members of the UN were still under colonial rule, by 89 votes to 0, with nine abstentions—Australia, Belgium, Dominican Republic, France, Portugal, South Africa, Spain, the UK, and the USA. True, the main (non-communist) colonial powers abstained: but no State actually voted against resolution 1514. We might therefore say that the resolution represents a consensus as to what the concept of self-determination means under the UN Charter.

To put it in treaty terms, we might regard the resolution as being similar to an agreement between the parties to a treaty regarding the interpretation of the treaty, which is one of the materials that must be taken into account in the interpretation of the treaty, according to Article 31(3) of the Vienna Convention on the Law of Treaties. The similarity is inexact, because we cannot tell from the face of the resolution that it was intended by those who voted for it to be an interpretation of the legal consequences of Article 1(2) of the Charter, even less that it was intended to be a binding interpretation. States may have voted for it for purely political reasons— as an expression of policy, not of law. The records of the General Assembly debate may give some insight into the motivation behind the resolution; but they will rarely be conclusive. Moreover, even if the resolution was intended as an authoritative interpretation of Article 1(2), only States that had voted for the resolution would clearly be bound by it. Nonetheless, unless States had plainly opposed the interpretation that it set out, it is likely that it would become an influential guide to the interpretation of the Charter provisions to which it relates.

There are other ways of looking at General Assembly resolutions. Recall the nature of customary international law. The traditional formulation says that customary international law consists of State practice coupled with *opinio juris*, and I referred earlier to the problem of prohibitive rules where the 'practice' element consists of *not* doing something. Take as an example the rule of customary international law that stipulates that no State may appropriate any area of the deep sea bed beyond the limits of national jurisdiction. That is the 'rule' that was articulated in General Assembly resolution 2574. No State has ever attempted to make such an appropriation: in other words, all States have always refrained from appropriating the deep sea bed. But that is not enough to make a rule of law. We plainly cannot assume that for every act that no State has (yet) undertaken there is a rule of customary international law forbidding such acts. It is the *opinio juris* that will make the position clear. States are not given to making abstract statements of law *à propos* of nothing. Declarations of *opinio juris* are responses to particular occasions; and one such occasion may be the adoption of a UN General Assembly resolution. Thus *opinio juris* may accumulate around UN General Assembly resolutions as it may gather around any other articulation of a putative rule of customary international law, and may transform rules set out in the resolution into rules of law. The *opinio juris* may be discerned from the debates in the General Assembly or from external sources, such as statements made outside the UN by governments in which they affirm that the resolution in question embodies a statement of the law. If the rule were 'generally' accepted, a rule of customary international law would emerge. I have given the example of a prohibitive rule of customary international law in order to make the point clearer. Resolutions of international organizations are one of the most obvious ways by which such rules may emerge. But there is no reason why the same analysis should not apply to any other kind of rule.

UN General Assembly resolutions may thus be the seeds of rules of customary international law, and acquire binding legal force. The normal rules applicable to customary international law would apply. For instance, States may persistently object to the emergent rule and therefore not be bound by it. Equally, in the early stages of the rule two or more States that have accepted it as law might be bound by it as between themselves. The fact that the text in question appears in a General Assembly resolution is, in truth, irrelevant. The text might as well have appeared in a unilateral declaration, such as the Truman Proclamation, or in a draft General Assembly resolution, or in some non-governmental statement, for example articles adopted by the International Law Commission (whose Articles on State Responsibility have been enormously influential and widely cited by tribunals) or by some other body such as the International Law Association (which adopted the influential Helsinki Rules on the Uses of the Waters of International Rivers in 1966).

Wherever the text is set out the legally significant factor is the assertion by a State that it regards the text as the statement of a binding rule of law. Assertions of that kind are more to be expected in some circumstances than in others. Circumstances in which the General Assembly has before it a resolution that 'declares' (or even better, 'solemnly declares') certain principles of an apparently legal nature are natural situations in which to look for, and often to find, evidence that the resolution was intended by some or all of the States to express rules of law. For instance, the International Court of Justice in the *Nicaragua* case was faced with the need to decide whether there was a rule of customary international law prohibiting the threat or use of force in international relations. It looked for *opinio juris* on the matter and held that:

This *opinio juris* may, though with all due caution, be deduced from, *inter alia* the attitude of the Parties and the attitude of States towards certain decided General Assembly resolutions, and particularly resolution 2625 (XXV) entitled 'Declaration on Principles of International Law concerning Friendly Relations and Co-operation among States in accordance with the Charter of the United Nations.' The effect of consent to the text of such resolutions cannot be understood as merely that of a 'reiteration or elucidation' of the treaty commitment undertaken in the Charter.

The Court did not explain why it thought that consent to (i.e., voting for) the text of the resolution should not be viewed as 'reiteration or elucidation' of the Charter obligation, but it probably understood this to flow from the unequivocal statement in the Declaration that 'The principles of the Charter which are embodied in this Declaration constitute basic principles of international law.'

There is another possibility. Votes for UN General Assembly resolutions might be regarded as instances of unilateral declarations. If a State votes for the resolution and the State's representative declares during the debate that he or she is voting for the resolution on behalf of the State because the resolution affirms a rule of customary international law, it is at least arguable that the vote might be regarded as a commitment by that State to that rule of law at least if it can be shown that the State making the declaration intends to become bound according to its terms. In this case, unlike the analysis that treats resolutions as the seeds of new rules of customary law, it is only those States that made the statement that would become bound by the terms of the resolution: no wider normative effect would flow from the 'unilateral declaration'.

The results of these analyses may be unexpected. When UN General Assembly resolution 2574 was adopted in 1969 the intention on the part of the States that promoted the resolution—mainly members of the 'Group of 77' developing States—was to create a prohibition that would prevent those few developed States which were then the only States technologically capable of exploiting the deep sea bed resources from engaging in such exploitation prior to the international regime which the Group of 77 was trying to negotiate (and which eventually was established in Part XI of the 1982 UN Convention on the Law of the Sea). But resolution 2574 was not inherently binding on all UN Member States under the Charter; it was not an authoritative exposition of any provision of the Charter; and on the 'customary international law' and 'unilateral declaration' analyses, the resolution could have had the effect of binding those States that voted for it (mainly Group of 77 States) but could not have bound those States that opposed it, as did practically all of the developed States at which the prohibition was aimed.

The explanations that I have given so far of the binding force of resolutions of the UN General Assembly all fit in to the classical framework of the sources of international law. The binding force is attached to analysis based on treaty law or customary international law and 'unilateral acts'. But there are other ways in which resolutions of international organizations can have normative force.

One such way is through the development of technical standards. Suppose that one State claims that another is interfering with the rights of passage of foreign ships by constructing port facilities protruding into the sea in a narrow international strait. The State constructing the works replies that it has left a fairway which is perfectly adequate to allow the passage of foreign ships. The first State responds that the fairway is too narrow. How is one to judge who is right? The International Court and other international tribunals before which the question may arise have very able lawyers sitting on them: but few, if any, of those judges could make an expert judgment on the minimum width of fairway necessary to accommodate the range of commercial and military vessels that may wish to exercise their right of passage. How, then, is the question to be settled? One approach is to refer to technical standards set by competent international organizations. For instance, the IMO adopts many standards relevant to shipping matters, at meetings composed of technically knowledgeable representatives from the governments of its Member States. It is natural for counsel before international tribunals to refer to such standards in support of their case, and equally natural for tribunals to refer to them in support of their judgments. This is indeed what happens. Standards set by bodies such as the IMO, the World Health Organization (WHO), the International Atomic Energy Agency (IAEA), the Food and Agriculture Organization (FAO), and the Codex Alimentarius are increasingly relied upon in order to give precise substance to international rules that are framed in general terms.

The discussion so far has pointed out various ways in which resolutions of international organizations can have a law-making effect. It is important to see this in perspective, however. Most resolutions do not have law-making effect. Most resolutions do not bind States or set out technical standards. Most resolutions are statements of policy or recommendations to governments and others. The UN routinely adopts resolutions promoting various interests—encouraging States to assist poorer States with technical and financial assistance, urging the advancement of colonial territories to self-determination, deploring discrimination, and so on. The majority of these are plain statements of policy; and while the resolutions of technical international organizations include a higher proportion of resolutions dealing with technical standards, most of them are also recommendatory or policy statements. But even these resolutions are not wholly without normative force.

Such resolutions are part of the body of 'soft law', that is, norms that are not themselves legally binding but form part of the broader normative context within which expectations of what is reasonable or proper State behaviour are formed. Some people also put into the category of soft law norms that are legally binding but which are expressed in vague terms, such as the duty not to 'hamper' the passage of ships through international straits, which stand in need of further particularization before they can be applied to decide concrete cases. I think it is unhelpful to regard such rules as 'soft law'. They are binding in their own terms; and even rules that appeared clear at the time that they were drafted may come over time to reveal a range of possible interpretations and become 'vague'. Better to confine the term 'soft law' to norms that are not binding but which colour the application of norms that are legally binding.

A good example is the 'precautionary principle'. Principle 15 of the 1992 Rio Declaration on Environment and Development stipulates that:

In order to protect the environment, the precautionary approach shall be widely applied by States according to their capabilities. Where there are threats of serious or irreversible damage, lack of full scientific certainty shall not be used as a reason for postponing cost-effective measures to prevent environmental degradation.

The Rio Declaration is not itself a legally-binding instrument. The terms in which Principle 15 is drafted are so vague as to make it difficult to regard it as a rule of any kind. How widely is 'widely applied'? What are the relevant capabilities of States, and how is the application of the precautionary principle to be calibrated in relation to them? In what contexts should the precautionary principle be applied? How can one know if a measure is 'cost-effective' if one lacks 'full scientific certainty' concerning the proposed measures, their effects, and the risks against which they are directed? But for all this uncertainty, the precautionary principle expresses a particular approach to questions clearly enough. And it is expressed in essentially normative terms: do not use scientific uncertainty as a reason for inaction, or something like that. So, while States and judges on international tribunals have not, as yet, appeared keen to treat it as a binding, legal obligation, they have referred to it as part of their reasoning in order to justify decisions that are aligned with the precautionary principle. (A good example can be found in the *Southern Bluefin Tuna* case in the ITLOS, in the Separate Opinion of Judge Laing.) The deployment of texts to bolster support for a conclusion that ultimately rests on other, binding rules is a classic use of 'soft law'.

There is a growing use of 'soft law' instruments: non-binding declarations, resolutions, recommendations, and the like. The reason is not hard to see. States are naturally reluctant to sign up to binding legal instruments, particularly in respect of such vaguely formulated provisions as Principle 15 of the Rio Declaration. But they may well see the desirability of a particular course of action and be willing to accept it formally, as a guideline or aim which they hope and intend to implement progressively as and when they are able to do so. A good example is the UN Food and Agriculture Organization's Code of Conduct on Responsible Fishing, which sets out a wide range of measures that States might adopt in order to reduce unlawful fishing and over-exploitation of fish stocks. Knowing that other States are working towards the imposition of similar measures on their own fisherfolk may be critical to the acceptability of the measures, and formal adoption of the soft law instrument may therefore be a very useful step. It is a mistake to think that simply because an instrument is not legally binding it has no value, and no effect upon State behaviour.

2.3.4 INTERNATIONAL LAW AND NON-LEGAL SOURCES OF NORMS

Law, as the Greeks and Romans knew well, is essentially a matter of rhetoric. It is a style of argument, where speech is deployed in order to persuade people to do or not to do something, in accordance with the speaker's wishes. No-one who has seen a very good (or a very bad) advocate in action could believe that courts simply have lines of legal authority drawn to their attention and then decide the case accordingly, or that a reference in a diplomatic note to some provision of a treaty or of customary international law will compel another State to concede that the law is against it. Disputes usually arise because there are at least two positions on the matter that can be argued rationally and reasonably. Almost invariably, cases are pursued in courts precisely because both sides think that they have enough chance of success to make litigation a rational option. Similarly, specifically legal argument in diplomatic exchanges generally reflects a belief that each side has an arguable legal case. In such situations, how is a tribunal to decide?

I hope that it comes as no surprise to learn that common sense, the intelligent analysis of the policy implications of the decision, and an elemental sense of justice are paramount considerations in choosing between the solutions that a tribunal might rationally adopt. These factors sit within a framework motivated by the fundamental desire for coherence— the desire to ensure that legal rules and decisions fit together, supporting and not conflicting with one another. That much may be obvious; but it may be less obvious that one consequence of this inevitable position is that extra-legal arguments and principles are inextricably intertwined with specifically legal norms in the application of the law.

These extra-legal or non-legal principles are often overlooked. Take, for example, the case of a claim by an investor that its investment has been treated in breach of a duty of 'fair and equitable treatment' set out in a bilateral investment treaty. The investor may complain that officials of the host State said that it could expect to be granted a licence to operate a waste plant in a particular location; or the investor might enter into a concession agreement with the host State on the assumption that the prevailing tax rules would continue to be applied. But what if local authorities in the region decide to refuse a licence to operate the waste plant, or the tax authorities adopt new tax laws which affect the profitability of the concession? Is that unfair or inequitable treatment? Clearly, that question cannot be answered by asking if the action of the State is *lawful*. One must ask if it is fair, and if it is equitable.

In asking those questions one is, in effect, referred to a system of normativity that lies outside the law. The answers will differ according to the conception of what is fair and equitable. If one measures the standard against the practice of a despotic State in which decisions announced by agents of the ruler will always be implemented, regardless of what the law may say, one may come to a result different from that which uses as its measure practice in a State where the Rule of Law is applied at all levels and a rule of law stipulates that public authorities can never be estopped in the context of decisions where they have a statutory discretion which they must exercise. Systems that have developed doctrines of legitimate expectations or of proportionality may suggest yet other results. In such cases there is a combination of elemental notions of fairness—'elemental' in the sense that the notion is not defined in terms of legal rules and doctrines, but rather in terms of the near-intuitive sense of fairness—with a broad framework of principles of fair behaviour that is posited, perhaps unconsciously, as the framework within which judgements on fairness are made.

This approach to fairness draws heavily upon ideas of fairness that are 'out there', circulating in those parts of international society that lawyers inhabit. And those ideas change over time. British lawyers no doubt took a slightly different view of fairness of the expropriation of private property after the British Government nationalized the coal industry and the health service. The fairness and reasonableness of a State refusing to prosecute, or even investigate, alleged corruption is (sadly) affected by the knowledge that influential States choose to abandon such investigations if they carry the risk of souring diplomatic relations with another State. The key point here is that these ideas of fairness and equity are not the product of law-creating processes. 'Fairness' and 'equity' are not concepts whose content is prescribed by law. They are extra-legal concepts to which the law refers at certain stages in legal reasoning. The corollary is that the content of 'fairness' and 'equity' is shaped by a much broader range of factors and processes than bear upon the creation of rules of law.

A good example is the concept of sustainable development. This is not a legal rule. It is a concept whose essence is the idea that it is good to exploit resources and carry on activities in such a manner that they could be carried on indefinitely. Fisheries should not be over-fished, but fished at sustainable catch levels; industries should not throw out pollution in unlimited quantities, but should discharge waste only on a scale and in a manner in which it can safely be absorbed. It is the idea that any given generation is in some sense (and not necessarily a very coherent sense) a trustee for future generations, obliged to hand on the world in as good a shape as it found it. This concept was first developed outside the legal context, as a political axiom in seminal documents such as the Brundtland Report.[8] The concept continues to be refined by political and moral philosophers, environmentalists, economists, and others. Lawyers continue to refer to it: prominent examples are Judge Weeramantry's Separate Opinion in the *Gabcikovo* case in the International Court, and the decision of the Supreme Court of the Philippines in the *Minors Oposa* case. But what they are referring to is not a legal norm but an interstitial norm—a non-legal norm, generated and developed by non-legal sources and processes, with a life of its own outside the law—which can nonetheless be used to assist legal argument. Thus, Judge Weeramantry used the (non-legal) concept of sustainable development to reconcile the legal norm that permits States to develop their economies and the potentially conflicting legal norm that forbids the causing of environmental harm. The legal norms coexist: and the manner of their co-existence is explained by reference to the non-legal concept of sustainable development, which reconciles the two legal norms.

Thus does the law sit within society. It has its own rules and procedures. But it can never be divorced from the general framework of normative argument in the society within which it operates. And this is as true of international law as it is of national law.

---

[8] World Commission on Environment and Development, *Our Common Future (The Brundtland Report)* (Oxford: Oxford University Press, 1987).

3

The Principles of the International Legal System

International law has something close to a constitutional document, or perhaps more exactly a manifesto: a statement of the fundamental principles upon which the international legal order is based. It is the Declaration on Principles of International Law Concerning Friendly Relations and Co-operation Among States in Accordance with the Charter of the United Nations, adopted by the UN General Assembly in 1970 as resolution 2625 (XXV). It was negotiated between 1962 and 1970, with all the attention to detail that would be expected in the negotiation of a major international convention. It was, moreover, adopted at the height of the Cold War, in the decade that saw the building of the Berlin Wall, the Cuban Missile crisis, the Vietnam War, and the break-up of the remains of the old colonial empires. And yet resolution 2625 was adopted without a vote, thus signalling that it represented a consensus. It therefore has a peculiar importance, as the irreducible core of principles upon which States that were diagonally opposed, and States that preserved their Non-Aligned status, could agree as the foundation of the international order.

The resolution sets out seven basic principles:

(a) The principle that States shall refrain in their international relations from the threat or use of force against the territorial integrity or political independence of any State, or in any other manner inconsistent with the purposes of the United Nations,

(b) The principle that States shall settle their international disputes by peaceful means in such a manner that international peace and security and justice are not endangered,

(c) The duty not to intervene in matters within the domestic jurisdiction of any State, in accordance with the Charter,

(d) The duty of States to co-operate with one another in accordance with the Charter,

(e) The principle of equal rights and self-determination of peoples,

(f)   The principle of sovereign equality of States,

(g)   The principle that States shall fulfil in good faith the obligations assumed by them in accordance with the Charter, so as to secure their more effective application within the international community.

These are principles and not rules. In the influential distinction drawn by Ronald Dworkin[1] rules have an all-or-nothing character but principles do not. Rules are applied by deciding if a case falls within the rule; and if it does, the rule stipulates what decision must be reached. For instance, if *x* is a member of the family of a diplomatic agent, *x* enjoys the privileges and immunities specified in Articles 29 to 36 of the 1961 Vienna Convention on Diplomatic Relations. There is no room for manoeuvre, no possibility of arguing that some of those privileges and immunities do not apply. Principles, on the other hand, are not all-or-nothing norms. They are rather reasons for reaching a conclusion, factors weighing in favour of a particular decision. A principle may, however, be displaced or superseded by another principle. For instance, while the principle that States should not use force against other States is firmly established in international law, that principle yields to the right of a State to use force to defend itself if it is attacked. The distinction between rules and principles, though controversial, is useful here because it indicates that the principles with which we are concerned may be invoked in any context as reasons for a particular decision. They have a pervasive importance that entitles them to be regarded as fundamental principles of the international legal system; and they underlie all of the other principles and rules discussed later in this book. Some of the principles in resolution 2625, such as the prohibition on the threat or use of force, have been developed in some detail and will be discussed in later chapters. But it is worthwhile examining the principles themselves, because of their fundamental significance.

3.1   THE PROHIBITION ON THE THREAT OR USE OF FORCE

First place is given in resolution 2625 to the principle that States shall refrain in their international relations from the threat or use of force. The scope of this principle is wider than may at first appear. As subsequent paragraphs of the resolution make clear, it prohibits, for example, not only

---

[1] Ronald Dworkin, *Taking Rights Seriously* (Cambridge, Mass: Harvard University Press, 1977).

armed aggression against other States, but also the use of force to violate
boundaries and armistice lines, the use of force in reprisals, and the organization or encouragement of irregular forces for incursion into another
State. The latter aspect is reinforced by the

duty to refrain from organizing, instigating, assisting or participating in acts of
civil strife or terrorist acts in another State or acquiescing in organized activities
within its territory directed towards the commission of such acts, when the acts
referred to . . . involve a threat or use of force.

The prohibition serves two functions. One is to establish the basic rule
that international disputes should not be settled by the use of armed force.
That principle is taken for granted now; but international society has been
organized on this basis for less than a century. The move towards this position began at the first Hague Peace Conference in 1899 when the major
powers agreed upon peaceful procedures for the settlement of international disputes 'with a view to obviating, as far as possible, recourse to
force in the relations between States' as it was put in the 1899 Convention
for the Pacific Settlement of International Disputes. While that
Convention did not forbid, or even limit, recourse to war it was intended
to promote peaceful settlement as the preferable alternative. Though
there were earlier agreements limiting the manner in which war might be
conducted, the first limitation upon the actual right to go to war did not
appear until the adoption of the Covenant of the League of Nations, the
predecessor of the United Nations, in 1919. As I explain further in
Chapter 8, the Covenant merely imposed a cooling-off period before
States could resort to force; but in 1928 the General Treaty for the
Renunciation of War (also known as the Briand-Kellogg Pact or the Pact
of Paris) went a stage further. Originating in a proposal by the French
Foreign Minister and Nobel Peace Prize Winner, Aristide Briand to the
United States' Secretary of State, Frank Kellogg, that the two States
should lead by example and make a formal renunciation of war, the Pact
was opened up for adherence by all States; and 65 of them did adhere. The
States Parties solemnly declared in the Pact:

in the names of their respective peoples that they condemn recourse to war for the
solution of international controversies, and renounce it as an instrument of
national policy in their relations with one another.

'War' turned out to be an elusive concept. There was some argument as
to whether the Pact prohibited uses of force falling short of war; and the
Pact was not a great success. It, and the League, appeared powerless in
the face of the international violence of the 1930s. It was this background

of limited and unsuccessful attempts to abandon and outlaw the use of force as an instrument of foreign policy that lay behind the absolute prohibition of the threat or use of force in international relations, expressed in the Article 2(4) of the UN Charter and elaborated at the beginning of resolution 2625.

That first function of the prohibition is addressed to the question, how should States go about the protection and advancement of their national interests? It is, one might say, the equivalent of the 'play nicely' edict issued to children in a playground.

The second function is much more specific, the equivalent of the firm word in the ear of the playground bully. It establishes a duty on each State not to threaten or use force against the territorial integrity or political independence of another State; and a correlative right for each State not to have force threatened or used against it. The second function is a matter of precise obligations owed by each individual State to each other individual State—one of the obligations that Iraq violated when it invaded Kuwait in 1990. Whereas the first function focuses upon the whole of international society and on the system of international law, the focus of concern here is on the violator and the victim. Moreover, the breadth of the duty and its extension to the prohibition of the fomenting of terrorist acts in other States is designed to underpin the integrity and inviolability of each State.

These two functions are not formally recognized as distinct aspects of the principle, which refers simply to the principle of the non-use of force in various contexts. But the conflation of the two functions can lead to confusion. It is sometimes said of particular uses of force that they are not aimed at 'the territorial integrity or political independence' of the State against which force is used, but are intended only to compel that State to comply with its international obligations. The Israeli raid on Entebbe airport in 1976, in which Israeli passengers were rescued from a hijacked jet, is one example. Such claims (whether or not they are legally valid) may address the rights and interests of the target State; but they do not address the broader community interest in the maintenance of the principle of the non-use of force in international relations. The central issue in practice is how and by whom a decision may be made that particular use of force is justified, given the individual rights, duties, and interests of the States using force and of the States against which force is used. How, in other words, can the international community release States from the obligation not to use force? There is a clear answer to this, which is that under the UN Charter force may be used only in self-defence or with the authorization of the Security Council. The issue, explored further in Chapter 8, is whether that clear answer is satisfactory.

3.2 THE DUTY TO SETTLE DISPUTES PEACEFULLY

The second of the principles set out in resolution 2625 is 'the principle that States shall settle their international disputes by peaceful means in such a manner that international peace and security and justice are not endangered'. At its heart this principle is essentially a corollary of the principle of the non-use of force; but it extends further. States are not obliged merely to refrain from using force to settle disputes: they are under a positive obligation to seek to settle disputes by peaceful means of their choice. This positive duty reflects the interest that all States have in the resolution of disputes that may run out of control and threaten international peace and security if they are not addressed and resolved timeously.

3.3 THE DUTY OF NON-INTERVENTION

The third principle is curiously entitled '[t]he principle concerning the duty not to intervene in matters within the domestic jurisdiction of any State, in accordance with the Charter'. This principle 'concerns' the duty, rather than simply stating what the duty is. It is one of the most potent and elusive of all international principles, whose importance warrants its quotation in full:

No State or group of States has the right to intervene, directly or indirectly, for any reason whatever, in the internal or external affairs of any other State. Consequently, armed intervention and all other forms of interference or attempted threats against the personality of the State or against its political, economic and cultural elements, are in violation of international law.

No State may use or encourage the use of economic, political or any other type of measures to coerce another State in order to obtain from it the subordination of the exercise of its sovereign rights and to secure from it advantages of any kind. Also, no State shall organize, assist, foment, finance, incite or tolerate subversive, terrorist or armed activities directed towards the violent overthrow of the regime of another State, or interfere in civil strife in another State.

The use of force to deprive peoples of their national identity constitutes a violation of their inalienable rights and of the principle of non-intervention.

Every State has an inalienable right to choose its political, economic, social and cultural systems, without interference in any form by another State.

Nothing in the foregoing paragraphs shall be construed as affecting the relevant provisions of the Charter relating to the maintenance of international peace and security.

This principle, which had been solemnly declared in UN General Assembly resolution 2131 (XX) (the Declaration on the Inadmissibility of

Intervention in the Domestic Affairs of States and the Protection of Their Independence and Sovereignty), again reinforces the principle of the non-use of force, in its second role as the guarantee of the integrity and inviolability of each State. It does so not by proscribing one particular form of pressure—the threat or use of force—but by forbidding *all* action that is intended 'to coerce another State in order to obtain from it the subordination of the exercise of its sovereign rights and to secure from it advantages of any kind'. Even the encouragement of such action is forbidden. In this way the principle affirms the central right of each State to independence and to self-determination: that is, the right freely to choose its political, economic, social, and cultural system.

To people accustomed to privacy and a right to individuality, the right to be secure against intervention may appear to be an obvious element of the international order. No matter what we may be thinking to ourselves, we do not go up to strangers and tell them that we think that the design of their coat is ugly and offensive; even less would we think of using force to make them change their attire. We would not ordinarily tell a stranger that we thought their choice of partner, or their way of bringing up their children, was dangerously misguided. Why should we feel any more entitled to intervene in the domestic affairs of foreign States?

This individualistic view carries over into the international field. The influential liberation theology of the 1980s[2] emphasized that while the problems of oppressed peoples around the world might be caused by a small number of States, industries, or other groups, liberation from oppression must be fought for and won by the oppressed themselves: liberation cannot be secured by foreign aid or foreign intervention. Something of this view survived in the reaction against the 2003 invasion of Iraq. Some accepted the argument that it was desirable that the Saddam régime be overthrown, but thought that this was a matter that should come from within Iraq, and neither imposed nor materially assisted by foreign States.

This individualistic view is, however, neither historically constant nor necessarily transposable into the normative structure of international relations. The focus on individual autonomy, rather than on a person's role and position in society, appears to be a characteristic that has grown within the past half-millennium. The priority given to the idea of individual

---

[2] See, e.g., Gustavo Gutiérrez, *We Drink From Our Own Wells* (Maryknoll, NY: Orbis Books, 1984). Gutiérrez wrote a study of Bartolomé de las Casas, the sixteenth century theologian whose writings touched on issues of international law and who engaged in the great Valladolid Debates of 1550–1551 with Juan Ginés de Sepúlveda, concerning the rights of the indigenous peoples of 'Latin' America: see *Las Casas: In Search of the Poor of Jesus Christ* (Maryknoll, NY: Orbis Books, 1993).

choice, and of the parallel right of each State to choose its own structure and destiny (which is often said to lie at the heart of the classical 'Westphalian' conception of Statehood) were corollaries of this movement. But while the idea of individual autonomy gained hold, the idea of *national* autonomy remained a relatively subtle and attenuated concept.

United States' doctrine illustrates this well. The Monroe Doctrine, enunciated by President James Monroe in his 1823 State of the Union Address, is often cited as an affirmation of the principle of non-intervention. In as much as it asserted that the European powers should not meddle in the affairs of American States—and notably the recently independent United States and the newly independent South American Republics— that is correct. But the Doctrine also asserted that any such meddling with States in the United States' 'hemisphere' (the Americas) might be regarded as a threat against the United States, against which the United States might react. This is evident in the text of the Doctrine:

In the wars of the European powers in matters relating to themselves we have never taken any part, nor does it comport with our policy so to do.

It is only when our rights are invaded or seriously menaced that we resent injuries or make preparation for our defense. With the movements in this hemisphere we are of necessity more immediately connected, and by causes which must be obvious to all enlightened and impartial observers.

The political system of the allied powers is essentially different in this respect from that of America. This difference proceeds from that which exists in their respective Governments . . .

We owe it, therefore, to candor and to the amicable relations existing between the United States and those powers to declare that we should consider any attempt on their part to extend their system to any portion of this hemisphere as dangerous to our peace and safety. With the existing colonies or dependencies of any European power we have not interfered and shall not interfere, but with the Governments who have declared their independence and maintained it, and whose independence we have, on great consideration and on just principles, acknowledged, we could not view any interposition for the purpose of oppressing them, or controlling in any other manner their destiny, by any European power in any other light than as the manifestation of an unfriendly disposition toward the United States.

The threat of a United States' reaction was spelled out in the 'Roosevelt Corollary', announced in President Theodore Roosevelt's remarkable 1904 Address to the Congress, which set out a vision of the role and responsibilities of the United States that anticipated attitudes which were asserted a century later. Roosevelt announced that the United States was ready 'to take action which in a more advanced stage of international relations would come under the head of the exercise of the international police', noting that 'a great free people owes it to itself and to all mankind not to sink into helplessness before the powers of evil'. He then continued to expound his reading and development of the Monroe Doctrine:

Our interests and those of our southern neighbors are in reality identical. They have great natural riches, and if within their borders the reign of law and justice obtains, prosperity is sure to come to them. While they thus obey the primary laws of civilized society they may rest assured that they will be treated by us in a spirit of cordial and helpful sympathy. We would interfere with them only in the last resort, and then only if it became evident that their inability or unwillingness to do justice at home and abroad had violated the rights of the United States or had invited foreign aggression to the detriment of the entire body of American nations. It is a mere truism to say that every nation, whether in America or anywhere else, which desires to maintain its freedom, its independence, must ultimately realize that the right of such independence can not be separated from the responsibility of making good use of it.

The United States' State Department has observed that the Roosevelt corollary 'inverted the original meaning of the [Monroe] doctrine and came to justify unilateral U.S. broadened in Latin America'.[3] But in truth Roosevelt simply spelled out what was truly a corollary of the original doctrine. All States are to be free from foreign intervention: the issue is, who will intervene to prevent such intervention. Talleyrand understood the point when he wrote of the concept of non-intervention, 'c'est un mot métaphysique, et politique, qui signifie à peu près le même chose qu'intervention'.

Non-intervention has thus long combined a basic principle that States should not meddle in one another's internal affairs with an ill-defined body of exceptions allowing intervention in circumstances where some essential interest of the intervening State is imperilled. The question is, what circumstances warrant intervention? There is a pragmatic answer, and a legal answer to that question. Some sense of the practical answer can be gained by considering the occasions on which intervention has taken place. Many instances from the years prior to the drafting of the Declaration of Principles spring to mind: among them are the United Kingdom–United States intervention in Iran in 1953 to assist in the overthrow of the Mussadeq regime; the Soviet interventions in Hungary in 1956 and Czechoslovakia in 1968; the intervention by United States and Belgian forces in Stanleyville in the Congo in 1964; the United States' interventions in Cuba in the Bay of Pigs 1961, and the Cuban Missile Crisis in 1962; India's intervention in the civil war in East Pakistan in

---

[3] <http://www.state.gov/r/pa/ho/time/jd/16321.htm>.

1971, from which Bangladesh emerged as an independent State; the United States' intervention in Chile to assist in the overthrow of President Allende's Government in 1973; Israel's intervention at Entebbe airport, Uganda in 1976; Tanzania's intervention in Uganda in 1979 to assist in the overthrow of Idi Admin; the United States' interventions in Grenada in 1979, and in Panama 1989; the NATO intervention in Kosovo in 1999; and the United States–United Kingdom intervention in Iraq in 2003. Readers with some sense of history will immediately appreciate that the list includes a range of episodes which differ widely in the context in which the intervention took place and the justifications that were offered for the intervention.

The interventions in Hungary and Czechoslovakia are generally regarded as attempts to prop up a particular brand of communism in Soviet satellite States. The interventions in the Congo in 1964 and in Uganda in 1976 were operations to rescue persons held hostage. The interventions in Bangladesh, Uganda, and Kosovo are often seen as instances of humanitarian intervention, where action was justified despite the non-intervention principle by the need to avert grave, large-scale suffering. The Iranian and Chilean interventions are often seen as naked attempts to preserve western economic interests. The Cuban interventions, and perhaps Chile and Panama also, appear to have been exercises in the maintenance of United States' hemispheric interests. And in the ghastly confusion of the 2003 invasion of Iraq, 'regime change' loomed large as a supposed justification—though that is less a justification than a description of the action taken.

Among those different circumstances some appear to have gained a measure of international acceptability. Intervention to rescue nationals, as in Entebbe, is one example; intervention to prevent a humanitarian catastrophe, as in Kosovo, is another. By no means all States have accepted the legality even of interventions in those narrow circumstances. Some States remain deeply concerned by any weakening of the non-intervention principle, fearing that it may lead to widespread interventions by powerful States for their own interests on one pretext or another. Even States such as the United States, which have a not inconsiderable record of intervention in third States, complain of interventions in the Middle East by States that are 'sponsors of terrorism'.

It is also sometimes said that there is a right to intervention in order to assist the process of self-determination (which is the subject of another of the principles in the 1970 Declaration), and in order to counteract intervention by another State—for example, in order to 'balance' support for one side in a civil war. These grounds are, however, much more controversial. Some such interventions might be justified as exercises of self-defence by the intervening State, and some on the basis that the intervention was requested by the government of the State in which the intervention takes place. In these two cases the intervention is characterized in such a manner as to fall within the scope of well-established rules of law.

Certain other kinds of intervention appear to be generally regarded as unlawful. Interventions to topple or install a particular regime, as in Hungary and Czechoslovakia and the Bay of Pigs fiasco, are prominent among them. But there is still much uncertainty in this area, partly because the lawfulness of an intervention turns upon the reasons for which it is undertaken and it is difficult to pinpoint the true reasons for State action. Furthermore, the reasons for State action are almost always manifold, with some possibly lawful reasons sitting alongside others that may be plainly inadequate as bases for the intervention; and the reasons given may themselves conceal very different motives for action.

In the light of this uncertainty within the concept, the broad principle of non-intervention is tolerable so long as States feel that the exceptions to it are broad enough, or narrow enough, to be reasonable. As Percy Winfield once wrote, 'the non-intervention rule appears to be a patent consequence of independence with a host of disorderly exceptions fastened on to it'.[4]

Thus far I have been concerned for the most part with armed intervention, of the kind that the International Court held in the *Nicaragua* case amounted to a violation of international law.[5] But, as I noted at the outset, the concept of non-intervention is much broader than this. The breadth of the principle was reflected in a further General Assembly resolution, 36/103; the Declaration on the Inadmissibility of Intervention and Interference in the Internal Affairs of States. That resolution sought to extend the scope of the principle, setting out a duty not to use economic aid as a tool of intervention, and obliging States to prevent the use of corporations under their jurisdiction and control as instruments of political pressure or coercion. The resolution, adopted by 120 votes to 22 with 6 abstentions, was opposed by many States, particularly the developed States against which such provisions were primarily directed, and cannot be regarded as stating or having passed in its entirety into customary international law. Nonetheless, though such 'interferences' may not amount to violations of the principle of non-intervention, they may be unlawful on some other ground.

[4] P.H. Winfield, 'The History of Intervention in International Law', 3 *BYIL* 130, at p. 137 (1922–1923).
[5] *ICJ Reports 1986*, p. 14 at paragraphs 202–209, 239–249.

Take, for example, the case of jurisdiction having extra-territorial effect, such as a law forbidding murder committed abroad by a national. That would be regarded as uncontroversial, even though it purports to criminalize activity within the jurisdiction of another State. But what of a law forbidding bigamy committed abroad by nationals, which might be thought necessary in order to prevent the avoidance of the bigamous liaisons inside the State that would arise as a result of marriages conducted outside the State? From the point of view of the legislating State this looks perfectly reasonable. But would it amount to intervention in the affairs of a State that permitted bigamous marriages? And what of a law that, say, criminalizes attacks on a religion. If such a law is applied extraterritorially, could the consequent limitation on freedom of speech in another State amount to intervention in that State? Or would a law criminalizing extraterritorial cartels amount to a denial of the right of the State where such a cartel is based and operates with the approval of that State, to choose its economic system? There is evidently a question in such cases of the propriety of the action taken; but the cases would not necessarily be regarded as instances of the violation of the principle of non-intervention. It is just as likely that they would be analysed in terms of the limits upon a State's jurisdiction, or of human rights.

That overlap is important, and I shall return to it later. For now, however, I shall let it rest, but underline the curious potency of this principle and its powerful internal contradictions.

3.4 THE DUTY TO CO-OPERATE

States have the duty to cooperate with one another, irrespective of the differences in their political, economic and social systems, in order to maintain international peace and security and to promote international economic stability and progress, the general welfare of nations and international cooperation free from differences based on such differences.

That formulation of the duty in resolution 2625 (XXV) may sound banal. Who would argue that States are entitled to pursue naked self-interest, regardless of the consequences for other States, or to obstruct action taken by other States? But the principle is more significant than it may initially appear.

First, the principle is notable for what it rejects, which is not simply the pursuit of national self-interest but the idea of a crusade. Some schools of thought within certain political ideologies, such as Communism, and within certain religions, such as Christianity and Islam, have a profound commitment to the conversion of the whole world. This is usually seen by the crusader as saving or liberating other people from sin or oppression or some other individual or social deformation. Some of those other people, blinded by the false consciousness of the proletariat (surely one of the most wonderful instruments of political analysis ever put at the disposal of governments and would-be governments) or its equivalent, may not wish to be saved or liberated; but that is no reason to call off the crusade. Such thinking is one of the core ideas against which the principle of non-intervention is directed; but it has an enduring currency and was the subject of an influential debate at the end of the twentieth century over the 'clash of civilizations'.[6] During the Cold War, in particular, it was widely believed that Communist States were constantly plotting to bring down the governments of Capitalist States and convert those States to communism, and *vice versa*. Indeed, the belief in China that the Soviet Union had gone soft in the global battle for communism was one of the main ideological reasons for the split between those countries in the 1960s. The Soviet attitude was pragmatic, and articulated in a legal context in the concept of 'peaceful co-existence',[7] i.e., the idea that rather than being locked in a permanent antagonistic struggle, the two great social orders could co-exist in a kind of sporting rivalry from which the superior philosophy (communism) would eventually and inevitably emerge triumphant. It is this idea that the principle of co-operation expresses. States may differ in their philosophies; but that is no reason why they should not work together for the good of all.

The duty to co-operate is so general that it is difficult to see how it can be enforced; but it can be instantiated. In other words, while it may be practically impossible to establish that a State is failing to co-operate in the broad aims of promoting international peace, security, economic stability and progress, and the general welfare of nations, it is certainly possible to establish a legal duty to co-operate in specific legal contexts and to measure a State's compliance with it. This is done, for example, in the United Nations Convention on the Law of the Sea, Article 123 of which stipulates that 'States bordering an enclosed or semi-enclosed sea should co-operate with each other in the exercise of their rights and in the performance of their duties under this Convention'. That obligation was the subject of litigation in the *MOX Plant* case, in which Ireland claimed that the United Kingdom was in breach of its Convention duties in being insufficiently co-operative in the framing and implementation of measures to defend against terrorist

---

[6] See Samuel P. Huntington, *The Clash of Civilizations and the Remaking of World Order* (London: Simon & Schuster, 1997).

[7] See, e.g., G. Tunkin (W.E. Butler, trans.), *The Theory of International Law* (London: George Allen & Unwin, 1974).

attacks on the United Kingdom's Sellafield nuclear plant on the shores of the Irish Sea and on ships carrying nuclear materials to and from that plant. Although that case was withdrawn from the UNCLOS tribunal in the wake of a ruling from the European Court of Justice that disputes over non-co-operation between EU States must go to the European Court, there can be no real doubt that tribunals can and will rule on compliance with such specific duties of co-operation.

The duties under the Law of the Sea Convention are paralleled in many other treaties, particularly treaties relating to environmental protection and shared resources. Among the most prominent instances are the 1990 International Convention on Oil Pollution Preparedness, Response and Co-operation, the 1989 Basel Convention on the Control of Transboundary Hazardous Wastes and their Disposal, the 1972 UNESCO Convention for the Protection of the World Cultural and Natural Heritage, the 1992 Helsinki Convention on the Protection and Use of Transboundary Watercourses and International Lakes, and the 1997 Convention on the Law of the Non-navigational Uses of International Watercourses.

In the field of shared resources there is at least a rudimentary rule of customary international law mandating co-operation between interested States. In the *Lac Lanoux* arbitration in 1957 the Tribunal, faced with a dispute over the proposed diversion of waters of the River Carol, which runs from Lake Lanoux through France and Spain, held that States are obliged to seek, by preliminary negotiations, terms for an agreement on the development of a shared resource which might affect other States sharing that same resource. It found no duty actually to reach agreement, much less a duty to refrain from the development unless the agreement of the other States is obtained beforehand. But there is here the reflection of a customary law duty of co-operation. It is well to think of it as a reflection, rather than a seed, of a customary law duty because in some contexts there is in State practice a more highly developed notion of co-operation. In civil law jurisdictions there is a well-established concept of *voisinage*, a legal regime that flows from the sociological phenomenon of the frontier—a concept distinct from that of the border. A frontier is an area around the border line between two States. As one text puts it:

frontiers are *outer-oriented*, with their attention directed to those areas of friendship and danger which lie beyond the state. Boundaries on the other hand are *inner-oriented*. They neither denote nor connote relationships. They are the physical manifestation of the sovereign limits of state territory and power.[8]

[8] Hastings Donnan and Thomas M. Wilson, *Borders. Frontiers of Identity, Nation and State* (Oxford; New York: Berg, 1999), p. 48.

In frontier zones there is a special need for co-operation, for example in the provision of public services such as roads, railways, electricity, water, and sewage disposal, in the pursuit of criminals, and in the use of shared resources—boundaries often follow the course of rivers. One area in which the principles of *voisinage* are particularly well developed in practice is the utilization of boundary waters. In Scandinavia, for instance, there is a long tradition of bilateral treaty-making on the subject, and of the institutionalization of co-operation by the establishment of binational mixed commissions with extensive executive and judicial powers.[9]

3.5 THE PRINCIPLE OF EQUAL RIGHTS AND SELF-DETERMINATION OF PEOPLES

The principle of equal rights and self-determination is stated in resolution 2625 to apply to 'all peoples'; it was addressed primarily to the situation of colonies and non-self-governing territories. The idea that colonies were entitled to independence had been widely accepted by the 1960s, particularly in the United Kingdom (the mood changed more slowly in the other colonial powers), even if it was driven more by a reappraisal of the economic costs and benefits of maintaining the colonial system than by a reappraisal of the moral and political arguments concerning colonialism.

In 1960 General Assembly resolution 1514 (XV) had declared the subjection of peoples to alien subjugation, domination, and exploitation a fundamental denial of human rights, and affirmed the right of all peoples to self-determination. Conscious of the potential of that principle for destabilizing international relations by encouraging distinct ethnic groups within States (such as the Basques in Spain and the Tamils in Sri Lanka) the General Assembly went on to declare in resolution 2625 that 'any attempt aimed at the total or partial disruption of the national unity and the territorial integrity of a country is incompatible with the Purposes and Principles of the United Nations'. That effectively limited resolution 1514 (XV) to the interpretation of self-determination which regarded the independence of former colonies within their existing borders as the natural expression of self-determination. The principle was affirmed in the 1966 International Covenant on Civil and Political Rights, and in the

---

[9] See Malgosia Fitzmaurice and Olufemi Elias, *Watercourse Co-operation in Northern Europe* (The Hague: Asser, 2004).

International Covenant on Economic, Social and Cultural Rights adopted in the same year, and is regarded as an essential condition for the effective guarantee and observance of individual human rights.[10]

How much further, beyond the colonial situation, does the principle of equal rights and self-determination reach? Certainly it reaches far enough to render unlawful the forcible occupation and annexation of inhabited territory, as the decision of the International Court made clear in the *East Timor* case. Beyond that, the position is unclear. The main problem lies in deciding what constitutes a 'people' entitled to the right. Before the people determine their future, someone must determine who are the people. Are the Palestinians entitled to self-determination? The Scots, the Welsh, the English, Texans, or Falkland Islanders? Attempts have been made to define the concept of a 'people'. A meeting of UNESCO experts in 1990 set out a working definition, referring to the common historical tradition, racial or ethnic identity, cultural homogeneity, linguistic unity, religious or ideological affinity. But the political implications of the principle are so great that all definitions are controversial. And once 'the people' is defined, who determines its future? If the Scots have a right to self-determination, do the inhabitants of England, Wales, and Northern Ireland also have a vote on the question? If the people of Northern Ireland are a 'people' for the purposes of self-determination, is the Catholic minority bound to accept the wishes of the Protestant majority? In 1967 Gibraltarians voted by 12,138 to 44 in favour of retaining the link with Britain, rather than passing under Spanish sovereignty. Does the principle of self-determination entitle the population of Gibraltar to change its mind? Is the United Kingdom obliged periodically to ask the Gibraltarians if they still wish to remain a British territory? There are no clear answers to these questions,[11] and the lack of certainty on such fundamental aspects of the principle underlines the fact that it was essentially a child of its time, rooted in the movement for decolonization and unsure of its role beyond that context.

3.6 THE PRINCIPLE OF SOVEREIGN EQUALITY OF STATES

The sovereign equality of States is a prominent element of the catechism of international lawyers, fundamental and unshakeable in theory but baseless and with few meaningful consequences in practice. Equality matters

---

[10] See General Comment 12 (1984) of the UN Human Rights Committee, <http://www1.umn.edu/humanrts/gencomm/hrcom12.htm>.

[11] See *Opinion No. 2* of the Arbitration Commission on the EC Conference on Yugoslavia, 92 *ILR* 167.

in a democracy, where everyone has one vote and the minority may be legally bound by the decisions of the majority. But there is no democratic structure on the international plane. True, the 'one State—one vote' principle prevails in most[12] international organizations; and in circumstances in which States decide to proceed by the 'consensus' procedure, any State, regardless of size or power, is able to block the adoption of a resolution. But as there is no international legislature through which the majority may impose its will on the minority, this point has rather less importance than it has in a municipal system.

What this principle does do is to articulate a principle that meshes with, and is arguably implicit in, the other principles set out in the resolution 2625 Declaration. If we ask which States are secure against threats or uses of force or benefit from the prohibition on non-intervention the answer is, each of them. No matter how great or small, each State is juridically equal. Nicaragua, with a population smaller than that of New York and a land area comfortably under 2% that of the United States, was able to bring the United States before the International Court of Justice to account for the alleged breaches by the United States of Nicaragua's rights under international law. True, the US decided to boycott the merits phase of that case (having lost its argument that the Court lacked jurisdiction): but that is a risk in any court. Powerful, slippery, or very popular defendants often succeed in escaping a summons to a court.

At one time the principle of sovereign equality was widely supported as the cure for the arrogance with which the Old Powers of Europe treated the newer, and less powerful States. Condescension and a certain *hauteur* may serve the grandees of government well in their dealings with their subjects at home, but they rarely work well when dealing with the brittle egos of the grandees of some other State. Diplomacy is easier and more effective if all are treated with equal courtesy. Of course, no-one believes that this reflects any real equality between States: neither the superpower nor the micro-State has any delusions about the distribution of power and influence on the international plane. There is an international pecking order as keenly appreciated as any feudal hierarchy: superpowers, regional powers, local powers, those surviving on alms, and the occasional eccentric who manages to operate at least temporarily outside the normal social rules. All have their international analogues.

---

[12] But not all. In several economic and financial institutions votes are allocated so as to reflect the differences in the wealth or financial commitment of the Member States. See Chapter 6 below.

The principle reflects a genuine belief that communities that have, through the accidents of history and diplomacy, acquired the status of Statehood have a right to be left alone to pursue their own economic, cultural, and political ambitions, at least as long as they do not upset their neighbours. It also embodies the presumption that in international organizations all States will have equal votes and equal access to the procedures and facilities of the organization, although that presumption may be rebutted and States may (and do) agree to establish organizations based on a different distribution of powers and rights. And it reflects the belief that as a matter of principle laws should apply to all States alike. The equal application of the law may seem to be an elementary proposition, an axiom of any legal system: but it is not. As I shall explain in the chapters dealing with the economic and environmental law, international law has developed a notion of what some scholars have called the 'duality of norms'— that is, the idea that in some fields it is unfair and unrealistic to impose the same legal obligations on every State. The burdens of improving and protecting the environment, or of moving further towards free trade, should be borne by those best able to carry them. One might say that in cases where differential obligations are imposed the law still applies equally, in as much as each State is equally bound by the rules that apply to it, and it is simply the range of applicable rules that varies from State to State. That is, of course, true; but only at a level of abstraction that conceals the practical reality, which is that in certain fields the principle of sovereign equality has been departed from because it has appeared to States to be in the interests of justice and the efficient promotion of global interests to do so.

3.7 THE PRINCIPLE OF GOOD FAITH

The final principle set out in the 1970 Declaration of Principles is that States shall fulfil in good faith the obligations assumed by them in accordance with the Charter. Not, you will notice, assumed *under* the Charter, but in accordance with the Charter. Obligations assumed under valid treaties and under customary international law are included.

This principle again may appear vacuous. Who would argue that a State is entitled to approach the fulfilment of its obligations in bad faith? But that view takes little account of cultural differences.

One of the free entertainments that London offers on a wet afternoon is the pleasure of going into a Knightsbridge store, taking an expensive jacket to the checkout desk, and starting to haggle with the sales assistant over the price. Behaviour that is perfectly normal and expected in the markets of Abijan or Jerusalem seems to rip a small hole in the social fabric of west London, producing a conversation that proceeds according to two quite different and irreconcilable sets of rules. The acceptance of laws is no less prone to the impact of cultural differences. Imagine how a foreign diplomat, whose education in English included the dissection of *The Merchant of Venice*, would see western conceptions of law. When Portia demands that Shylock take only his pound of flesh and not one drop of blood she is engaging in the kind of argument that gives lawyers the reputation of combining pedantry, slickness, and self-righteousness on a scale beyond the imagining of most mortals. Who would sign a treaty with Portia as the representative of the other party? Who would subscribe to a court where a lawyer could raise that sort of argument without fear of disciplinary action?

Conceptions of the nature and role of law vary significantly from culture to culture. In the west we are accustomed to the strict interpretation of laws, and the swift dismissal of cases in court. The idea that one party can be wholly responsible for a breakdown in contractual relations leading to a breach of contract is normal. In other cultures it may be different. Disputes are talked through; relationships survive breaches of particular obligations. The law is more flexible, more a guide towards a just solution than a procrustean bed within which social relations must be fitted.

The principle of good faith in resolution 2625 (XXV) has two aspects, and the first is to make plain that in international law literal interpretations and applications of legal instruments must not be allowed to defeat the evident intentions of those who made them. As I explained in the context of the law of treaties, the rule in international law is that texts are interpreted in accordance with their ordinary meaning in their context and in the light of their object and purpose. A good example of the application of the principle of good faith arose in the *Rainbow Warrior* arbitration between New Zealand and France. French agents had bombed the Greenpeace vessel, *Rainbow Warrior*, while it was in harbour in Auckland, New Zealand, in 1985 prior to a voyage on which it intended to protest against French nuclear tests in the Pacific. Fernando Pereira, a photographer on board the ship, died as a result of the attack. Two French government agents pleaded guilty to his manslaughter and to criminal damage, and were sentenced to three years in custody at a French military base on the Polynesian island of Hao, under an agreement between New Zealand and France which stipulated that they would be prohibited from leaving the island for any reason without with the mutual consent of both governments. Both agents were repatriated to France without New Zealand's consent, one (Alain Mafart) because of illness, the other (Dominique

Prieur) because she was pregnant and her father had a fatal illness. France said that the extreme urgency of the situation precluded attempts to obtain New Zealand's consent. The arbitral tribunal established to hear New Zealand's complaint that France had broken the agreement, found that France was under a duty to make a good faith effort to try to obtain the consent of New Zealand to the transfer of the prisoners, and that in the case of Captain Prieur France had failed in this obligation.[13]

The second purpose of the principle of good faith is simply to reinforce the point that States are bound by the law and by the treaty obligations that they assume. Simple as that point is, it encapsulates the essence of the Rule of Law in international society.

3.8 THE NATURE OF THE DECLARATION ON PRINCIPLES OF INTERNATIONAL LAW

The Declaration closes with a 'General Part', often overlooked, in which the General Assembly declared that:

In their interpretation and application the above principles are interrelated and each principle should be construed in the context of the other principles.

And it declared further that:

The principles of the Charter which are embodied in this Declaration constitute basic principles of international law, and consequently appeals to all States to be guided by these principles in their international conduct and to develop their mutual relations on the basis of the strict observance of these principles.

The interrelationship between the principles will be apparent from what I have said about them. The injunction to develop international relations on the basis of them requires a word of explanation. The declaration of the principles was, as the preamble to resolution 2625 (XXV) makes clear, an exercise in the 'progressive development and codification' of principles already implicit in the structure of the UN Charter, with the aim of promoting the realization of the purposes of the United Nations. The resolution was explicitly stated not to prejudice 'the provisions of the Charter or the rights and duties of Member States under the Charter or the rights of peoples under the Charter taking into account the elaboration of these rights in this Declaration'. In other words States may use

---

[13] See 82 *ILR* 499. In the case of Major Mafart the Tribunal decided by a 2–1 majority that France had not breached its obligation.

the principles progressively in order to advance, but not to impede, the purposes of the United Nations, which include the maintenance of international peace and security, the development of friendly relations among States based on respect for the principle of equal rights and self-determination of peoples, and the achievement of international co-operation on solving international problems of an economic, social, cultural, or humanitarian character.

In truth, the principles set out in the Declaration function more as policies than as normative principles. The principles of sovereign equality and good faith can barely be described as being norms in themselves, although they may be instantiated in, or in relation to, more specific norms that are derived from State practice or from treaties. That is not to say that none of the principles in resolution 2625 (XXV) could operate as substantive norms—there is clearly a substantive norm prohibiting the use of force, corresponding to the principle in the resolution, for instance. The point is rather that the principles operate *in the context of the resolution* not as rules but as policies. One might say that the 1970 Declaration of Principles defines the grain of international law, and instructs States to work with the grain rather than against it in developing international law. This is one of many examples of the need in legal analysis to be clear as to the kind of norm that one is dealing with, and its function in the particular context in which it arises.

3.9 STATE RESPONSIBILITY

The basic principles (or policies) of the international legal system determine the kind of system that international law is intended to sustain. But there is one crucial element missing. Resolution 2625 (XXV) says that States are bound to fulfil their obligations, and indicates what some of those obligations are; but it does not indicate what the consequences of a failure to fulfil those obligations might be. Consequences are important. I may decide that I should check my footnotes more carefully, or the principles of a religion may stipulate that I must act in a certain manner; but unless there are (or I believe that there are) some consequences of failing to do these things, they are merely aspirations or commitments rather than rules of conduct. If I fail to comply with them they are simply added to the lists of my failed resolutions. The same is true of the stipulations of international law. If no consequence attaches to their breach, we should question whether they are rules of law or statements of policy or aspiration. Examples abound. If one analyses the so called 'third generation' human rights,[14] such as the right to a clean environment, it is at the very least doubtful that they can properly be regarded as rights at all.

Those norms that are true rules of international law are secured by the principles of State responsibility. In the event that a State breaches the rule, it incurs responsibility to any State injured by that breach. That responsibility would typically be discharged by paying compensation for any injury suffered, or by apologizing for non-material injuries. When we talk of the State injured by the breach, it is often not literally the State. If a national—an individual or a corporation—of a State is injured by the act of another State in breach of international law, the national State of the injured person is, in effect, deemed to have suffered the wrong and may bring an international claim on behalf of the injured person (or, 'exercise diplomatic protection' in respect of the injured person, as it is often put— the phrases mean the same thing).

The Articles concerning State responsibility adopted by the UN International Law Commission in 2001, while not in themselves binding, closely mirror State practice and are mostly considered to represent customary international law. The Articles deal with a range of crucial issues. For instance, what counts as conduct of 'the State'? States are responsible for acts of their agents, such as the police, the military, and government officials, but not for the acts of private individuals (though States may be responsible for a failure to prevent acts of individuals). So, if I travel to another State and am assaulted by, say, a drunken football fan, the State is not responsible for that act. But if the State and its agents were aware that the assault was planned and made no effort to stop it, the State might be responsible—not for the assault, but for the failure to take reasonable steps to prevent it; and that failure would violate the duty of the State to take certain minimum steps to ensure the safety of those within its borders.

This much is plain. But as I mentioned in Chapter 2, there are difficult questions as to what counts as 'the State'. For example, if the religious hierarchy administers a system of courts and penal sanctions, is that an exercise of authority imputable to the State, for which the State bears responsibility, or is it the exercise of powers by a private voluntary association, for which the State is not directly responsible? Is a State responsible

---

[14] First generation rights are essentially civil liberties or 'negative rights', rules that tell States to refrain from certain conduct, such as denials of the right to life. Second generation rights are 'positive rights', such as rights to work or to form trades unions. Third generation rights are complex social rights which move beyond the first and second generation rights of individuals and which can only be realized through social institutions. Group rights and rights to a healthy environment or to peace, or to development are examples of third generation rights.

for the acts of a revolutionary movement trying to seize power? (The answer is, no—though here again the State may be liable for a failure to takes reasonable steps to protect foreigners against injury by revolutionary groups.) Does it make any difference if the revolutionaries succeed and become the government? (The answer is, yes: acts of insurrectional movements that become governments are considered to be acts of the State concerned.)

Another set of provisions in the Articles on State Responsibility addresses the question of the time at which a breach of international law occurs, drawing distinctions between completed breaches, such as uncompensated expropriations of foreign property, and continuing breaches, such as the continuing unlawful occupation of another State's territory. One reason that the distinction is important is that courts and tribunals may have jurisdiction only over disputes arising or subsisting after a certain date.

Two groups of the Articles are of particular importance for the development of international law. One concerns the responsibility of States for complicity in the wrongful acts of other States. Article 16 stipulates that a State which knowingly aids or assists another State in the commission of an internationally wrongful act is itself liable. A State which allows its territory to be used as a base for terrorist groups that attack third States, or allows its airfields to be used as a base for unlawful attacks on a third State, would fall within this provision. So, arguably, would States that provide foreign aid for projects such as the building of huge infrastructure projects such as dams, which are planned and executed in such a way as to violate rules of human rights law or environmental law. This development is particularly interesting, because it heralds the extension of legal responsibility into areas where States have previously carried moral responsibility but the law has not clearly rendered them responsible for the acts that they facilitate. Quite how much use will be made of this provision remains to be seen.

The second group of Articles that are of particular note is that containing the provisions on 'circumstances precluding wrongfulness'. These Articles provide that action taken, for example, in self defence, or in circumstances of *force majeure* or distress, are not merely excused (i.e., treated as unlawful but as excusable), but as not wrongful at all. Another example is necessity. The Articles provide that action taken by a State which is necessary to safeguard one of its essential interests, and which does not seriously impair an essential interest of another State, is not unlawful. As I mentioned in Chapter 2, international tribunals have yet to develop a settled view on what is necessary for the plea of necessity to succeed.

The remaining Articles on State responsibility deal with matters such as the problems of applying concepts of responsibility in circumstances where there are several claimants, or several respondents. These issues are particularly significant in the context of environmental and economic laws, where both the causes of injury and the effect of breaches may be widely spread. I shall say a little more about this in later chapters. The Articles also address in some detail the question of the precise meaning of the duty to make reparation, and the circumstances in which States are entitled to bring claims against one another—the question of standing to sue, as it would be described in domestic law.

It is through the concept of State responsibility that the international legal system acquires its basic coherence. We have primary, substantive, rules of international law; and we have in the rules on State responsibility rules that stipulate the legal consequences of violations of the primary rules. Both are necessary for a viable legal system to exist, as also are the rules governing the creation of legal obligations which I discussed in the previous chapter.

3.10 IMPLEMENTING STATE RESPONSIBILITY

It may be helpful at this stage to say something about the ways in which international responsibility is implemented—by whom, where, and how it is implemented. These topics are usually handled in textbooks under some such rubric as 'dispute settlement', and at the end of the account of the substantive rules of international law. Logically, there is a case for that; but it may tend to suggest that international law is a set of rules applied by tribunals to settle disputes, whereas I am trying to emphasize that international law is better regarded as an activity, a way of doing things, rather than as a set of norms.

3.11 PERSONALITY AND THE SCOPE OF APPLICATION OF INTERNATIONAL LAW

I need first to raise again the question, who does international law apply to? Who has rights and duties under international law? Textbooks usually answer that question by addressing the subject of international personality, and assert that international law was traditionally, up to around a century ago, regarded as inter-State law, so that the simple answer would have been that international law applied to States. I have already noted that even at that time that answer would have been inaccurate. States concluded agreements with principalities, cities, indigenous peoples, bodies such as the Order of St John, and others who would not have fitted squarely within the concept of a 'State'. And international law recognizes that international organizations can be legal persons within the international law legal system.

Broadly speaking, international organizations are comparable to corporations as persons in municipal law systems. In the *Reparations* case the International Court observed that '[t]he subjects of law in any legal system are not necessarily identical in their nature or in the extent of their rights, and their nature depends upon the needs of the community'. Thus, the Court considered that the United Nations must have the implied powers necessary for the performance of its duties, including the capacity to bring international claims on behalf of its agents injured during the course of their duties. This plainly gave the Organization some measure of international personality. This is not the same measure of personality that a State has: the United Nations cannot, for example, hold sovereignty over land, as a State could. (That is why disputed areas such as Jerusalem cannot be put under 'UN sovereignty', though they could be administered by the United Nations—as East Timor was administered by UNTAET, the United Nations Transitional Administration for East Timor—or on its behalf by a State—as Australia was the Trustee for the UN Trust Territory[15] of Papua New Guinea, prior to its independence.)

Similarly, international organizations have limited treaty-making power and other capacities. The International Court held in the *Nuclear Weapons* case that the World Health Organization (WHO) was not competent to request an Advisory Opinion on the question of the legality of the use of nuclear weapons by a State, because that question related not to the effects of the use of nuclear weapons on health, but to the legality of the use of such weapons in view of their health and environmental effects, and whatever those effects might be, the competence of the WHO to deal with them is not dependent on the legality of the acts that caused them. Accordingly, since international organizations do not have the general competence that States have, but only the limited powers implied by their specific functions (the 'principle of speciality'), the WHO was not competent to put the question before the Court. The UN General Assembly, on

---

[15] The Trusteeship system under Chapter XII of the UN Charter was the successor of the Mandate system under the League of Nations. Territories under trusteeship were to be nurtured to independence or to voluntary association with another State, as they might choose. The last UN Trust Territory was the Republic of Palau, which became independent in 1994, having been administered by the United States; but there is no reason why other territories should not be put under UN Trusteeship in the future.

the other hand, which had made a parallel request for an Advisory Opinion, was found competent to make the request; and the Court rendered an opinion as requested.

We might, therefore, say that international law applies to both States and to international organizations, albeit with some differences following from their different capacities. But even that would not accurately describe the scope of application of international law. I referred in Chapter 1 to the rights of individuals and corporations to make applications complaining that one of their rights under the European Convention on Human Rights has been violated, and to the hundreds of bilateral investment treaties that give a right to investors of one State to initiate arbitral proceedings against another State if they or their investment are mistreated. Does this mean that individuals and corporations also have 'personality' within the international legal system? Or should we treat them, as the older textbooks did, as 'objects' rather than as 'subjects' of international law? The question seems to me to be of little importance, and usually to be misconceived. The important question is always in some such form as, can X bring this particular claim against State Y in this particular forum? In these circumstances, whether or not we say that individuals are in some general sense 'persons' in the international legal system, or 'objects' or 'beneficiaries' of certain duties imposed on certain States, is really a matter of taste.

Personality is an inference from the legal rights, duties, and capacities that attach to an entity: the rights, duties, and capacities are not inferred from the personality. Whether or not an international organization that has a very narrow range of competences has sufficient capacity to count as an 'international legal person' is an arbitrary matter, depending entirely upon the stipulative criteria of personality that are chosen. But whatever the criteria, they have no practical value, because there are no consequences of meeting the criteria (other than featuring in the list of entities that do meet the criteria). The UN, for instance, is said by the ICJ to have international personality; but it cannot be a party to contentious cases in the Court because Article 34 of the Court's Statute limits its contentious jurisdiction to disputes between States. The answers to all important questions depend not upon knowing whether an entity is a person, but upon knowing whether or not it has the particular rights, duties, capacities, and so on that are in issue in the specific context in question.

There is a more fruitful approach to questions such as, who may implement international law and, who has rights and duties under international law? The plain fact is that on one level substantive international law consists of a bundle of rules and principles that are concerned with how people should behave; and those rules and principles can be *invoked* in argument by anyone—State, international organization, NGO, individual, corporation, parent, employee, or whomever. What *effect* that invocation has is a separate question, as is the question of access to the various forums in which the argument might be made. These points become clear when the position of international law in domestic legal systems and domestic affairs is considered.

3.12 INTERNATIONAL LAW IN DOMESTIC COURTS

In English law, customary international law is one of the sources of the common law.[16] Courts will draw on it to decide cases. So, for instance, the customary international law on State immunity was applied by the English courts prior to the enactment of the State Immunity Act 1978. (Not every rule of customary international law is apposite, and some will not be applied. For example, the House of Lords accepted that the waging of a war of aggression was a crime in international law, but declined to accept that a corresponding crime was thereby created in English law.)[17] Treaties, on the other hand, are not a source of English law. They must be transposed into English law by legislation if they are to be given effect as law in English courts. But these clear rules of English law did not prevent the frequent invocation of the European Convention on Human Rights in English courts at a time when the United Kingdom had ratified the Convention but not enacted it into domestic law. Nor was the invocation of the Convention without effect. As the House of Lords noted in *Ex parte Brind*,[18] there is a relevant canon of interpretation in English law, that 'the courts will presume that Parliament intended to legislate in conformity with the Convention, not in conflict with it'. The point applies more generally. Wherever possible, courts will interpret English law so as to conform with international law. That is fitting. If the courts were to decide cases in a manner that violated the United Kingdom's international obligations, the United Kingdom would incur international responsibility. In this way the courts play their part in discharging the State's legal obligations. Accordingly, even though the European Convention was not binding on the courts, its provisions influenced the way in which other rules of law were interpreted and applied. On the other hand, the constitutional position of the judges obliges them to uphold the laws of the land; and if Parliament clearly intends to legislate in a manner that is incompatible

---

[16] *Trendtex v Central Bank of Nigeria* [1977] 1 QB 529; *R v Jones (Margaret)* [2006] UKHL 16.
[17] *R v Jones (Margaret)* [2006] UKHL 16.   [18] [1991] 2 WLR 588.

with international law, it is right as a matter of general principle that the judges should uphold the will of Parliament.

In other countries the position is different. In the United States, for example, treaties have, under Article VI of the Constitution, a status equivalent to federal statutes; and 'self-executing' provisions (which are sufficiently clear and unequivocal, and intended to create rights and duties in individuals) will be enforced by the courts.[19] As in the United Kingdom, customary international law is a source of law in the United States. The classic statement of principle appears in the decision of the Supreme Court in *The Paquete Habana*, where it was said that:

[i]nternational law is part of our law, and must be ascertained and administered by the courts of justice of appropriate jurisdiction as often as questions of right depending on it are duly presented for their determination.

Each State (or more properly, each jurisdiction) has its own rules on the precise status to be given to customary international law and to treaties by its courts; but the general tendency is certainly to interpret and apply domestic law in conformity with international law wherever possible. As any 'person'—human or legal—in principle has access to national courts, it is not surprising that international law issues are frequently raised in national courts. A glance at the cases reported in *International Law Reports* or at the on-line *International Law in Domestic Courts* site,[20] many of which are concerned with the relationship between municipal law and international law, will give a good idea of the extent to which international law has permeated national legal systems.

Of course, not only courts are permeated by international law. One of the most startling aspects of the massive debate over the propriety of the invasion of Iraq by the United States and the United Kingdom in 2003 was the extent to which it was pinned to questions of the legality of the action under international law. In Parliament, in the press, and elsewhere illegality was generally seen as a serious argument against the propriety of the action, and (for those who took this view) legality as a serious argument in defence of the action. That is an instance of international law in action, of it being implemented by being used to frame debate. Indeed, the use of international law arguments *within* government, in the course of inter-departmental battles for the control of policy, is one of the most potent, if least visible, ways in which international law is implemented in practice.

---

[19] *Foster and Elam v Neilson*, 27 US 253 (1829); See *Fuji v California*, 217 F.2d 481 (1950), 242 F.2d 617 (1952), 19 *ILR* 312 (1952).
[20] <http://www.oup.com/online/ildc/>.

3.13 INTERNATIONAL LAW IN INTERNATIONAL TRIBUNALS

That is not to say that there are no important international tribunals applying international law. The largest number of pending claims before a single international tribunal is probably constituted by the backlog of applications to the European Court of Human Rights, which had around 90,000 cases pending at the end of 2006—a figure expected to rise to over 250,000 by 2010—although around 95% of the cases lodged with the Court are ultimately found to be inadmissible. Other human rights bodies, such as the Inter-American Commission and Court of Human Rights, have a very much smaller case-load, measured in dozens rather than in thousands. Outside the field of human rights (and aside from the special case of the European Court of Justice and the Court of First Instance, which are institutions of the European Communities—but like municipal courts still sometimes have to apply international law) the most active area at present, in terms of the number of tribunals and the number of cases outstanding before them, is probably investment arbitration. The international arbitral tribunals established to adjudicate upon alleged breaches of investors' rights secured by investment treaties.[21] decide the cases between the non-State applicants and the State respondents by applying international law, in much the way that the Iran–US Claims Tribunal, established after the 1979 crisis in American-Iranian relations precipitated by the unlawful detention of United States' staff in the embassy compound in Tehran, handled the 4,000 or so claims brought before it.

The United Nations Compensation Commission (UNCC), established by the UN Security Council in 1991 to determine claims against Iraq arising from the Iraqi invasion of Kuwait in 1990, is somewhat different. It is technically not a judicial, but an administrative, body. Security Council resolution 687 had determined in advance that Iraq was 'liable under international law for any direct loss, damage, including environmental damage and the depletion of natural resources, or injury to foreign Governments, nationals and corporations, as a result of Iraq's unlawful invasion and occupation of Kuwait', so that the UNCC is in principle only required to deal with questions of causation and quantum. In practice, however, it has been faced with some detailed argument on legal issues arising in some of the larger claims. By 2006 the UNCC had distributed over $20 billion, raised from a levy on Iraqi oil exports. The UNCC received more than 2.6 million claims, many

---

[21]   See the materials collected at <http://www.investmentclaims.com/>.

of them relatively small claims from expatriate Egyptian and Pakistani workers which it treated as a priority. The claims totalled $368 billion. The number of claims explains, even if it does not entirely justify, the procedures that the Commission was obliged to follow, which left Iraq with little opportunity to mount a proper defence.

The tribunals that I have just mentioned accept applications from individuals. There are others that do not. The most active of these are the International Court of Justice, to which I shall return shortly, and the World Trade Organization Dispute Settlement System, which saw about 350 cases brought before it in the decade after its establishment in 1995. Though the number of new cases each year is falling off a little, the WTO system is so busy that the adjudication of trade disputes can no longer be viewed as an abnormal or unusual occurrence. Other inter-State tribunals are less busy. The International Tribunal for the Law of the Sea (ITLOS) in Hamburg, established under the 1982 United Nations Convention on the Law of the Sea, has had only fifteen cases in its first eleven years. There is little sign of any increase in its workload, States appearing to prefer to resort to the ICJ or to *ad hoc* arbitral tribunals for the settlement of law of the sea disputes, although the possibility of litigants choosing their own five-person chambers of judges from the ITLOS might attract more cases to it. Even that tribunal looks busy compared to some: the European Nuclear Energy Tribunal has not had a single case in its fifty-year history.

Then there are the special cases of the international criminal tribunals: the International Criminal Tribunal for the Former Yugoslavia, the International Criminal Tribunal for Rwanda, both established by Security Council resolutions, and the International Criminal Court, established by the 1998 Rome Statute of the International Criminal Court as a standing international tribunal to complement the role of national courts in prosecuting genocide, crimes against humanity, and war crimes.

Apart from these standing tribunals, and others like them,[22] there are also *ad hoc* tribunals, constituted by States to resolve a specific dispute. Investment tribunals fall into this category, each tribunal being constituted for a particular case, there being no standing tribunal. Other prominent examples include the tribunals set up to determine the disputes over continental shelf delimitation between the United Kingdom and France,[23] to determine the dispute between France and the United States over air services,[24] and to determine the boundary and inter-State claims

---

[22] More tribunals are listed on the website of the *Project on International Courts and Tribunals*, <http://www.pict-pcti.org/>.

[23] 54 *ILR* 6, 139 (1977–1978).   [24] 18 *RIAA* 416 (1978).

between Eritrea and Ethiopia.[25] The last was organized by the Permanent Court of Arbitration—not really a court, but a permanent secretariat in The Hague that organizes arbitral proceedings.

One might ask why States sometimes prefer *ad hoc* tribunals to established bodies such as the International Court of Justice. The answers usually given are the ability to hand-pick the judges (each side picking an equal number, and the presiding arbitrator being chosen by agreement or appointed by a neutral appointing authority), the consequent possibility of a quicker decision (because the Parties can select arbitrators who do not have a great case-load through which they must work), and flexibility (because the two Parties can agree upon procedures with the tribunal, rather than being bound by the fixed rules of the court). There is something in these points; but it must be said that the ITLOS, for example, has an exemplary record for speedy decision, and that other standing tribunals can often act with expedition if the Parties so wish. Perhaps the ability to select a small tribunal is the key advantage, warranting the extra expense incurred in having to pay the arbitrators' fees instead of using the facilities of, say, the International Court (which is funded from the UN budget).

I turn now to the International Court. The Court has jurisdiction over two kinds of case. The first category is the Court's contentious jurisdiction. This is limited to inter-State cases: only States, and not other persons such as international organizations, may be Parties to contentious cases in the Court. The Court may hear:

any legal dispute concerning:

(a) the interpretation of a treaty;
(b) any question of international law;
(c) the existence of any fact which, if established, would constitute a breach of an international obligation.
(d) the nature or extent of the reparation to be made for the breach of an international obligation.[26]

All UN Member States are *ipso facto* Parties to the Court's Statute, and any of them is eligible to bring a case before the Court. If a State violates obligations under international law that it owes towards other States, any of those other States is entitled to complain and to obtain redress, usually in the form of a return to compliance by the State concerned and perhaps an apology and compensation for any injury caused.

---

[25] <http://www.pca-cpa.org>.
[26] ICJ Statute, Article 36(2).

The contentious jurisdiction of the International Court can only be invoked by and against States that have specifically agreed to submit to the jurisdiction of the Court: it is not enough that a State is a Party to the Court's Statute. There are several ways in which States may submit to the jurisdiction. They may accept the so-called 'compulsory jurisdiction' of the Court under Article 36(2) of its Statute—confusingly known as the 'Optional Clause'—by making a declaration that they accept the Court's jurisdiction without the need for any further agreement. That declaration may be made either unconditionally or subject to reservations, imposing time or subject-matter limits upon its application. The Court then has jurisdiction over a dispute identified in an application instituting proceedings if, but only if, the dispute falls within the scope of the acceptances of jurisdiction in the declarations of both Parties. Around 64 States have made such declarations, and the United Kingdom is the only one of the five permanent members of the UN Security Council to have a declaration in force, France having withdrawn its declaration after it was brought before the Court in the *Nuclear Tests* cases, and the United States withdrawing its declaration after the *Nicaragua* case. (Neither China nor Russia has ever accepted the jurisdiction of the Court under Article 36(2).) This is, of course, not really 'compulsory jurisdiction': it is a standing acceptance of the Court's jurisdiction in respect of all, or defined categories of, future disputes with other States.

The reservations to Optional Clause declarations can be extensive. The UK, for example, excludes from its acceptance of the Court's jurisdiction 'disputes with the government of any other country which is a Member of the Commonwealth with regard to situations or facts existing before 1 January 1969', thus excluding 'colonial' disputes. Potentially even wider are the reservations exemplified by the provision in Sudan's declaration, excluding from the Court's jurisdiction 'disputes in regard to matters which are essentially within the domestic jurisdiction of the Republic of Sudan as determined by the Government of the Republic of Sudan'. Such 'self-judging' or 'automatic' reservations are controversial. The best known was the United States' reservation, included as a result of the Connally Amendment during the passage of the declaration through the Senate. It purports to permit the State making the declaration to decide that any matter is within its domestic jurisdiction, but the Court has shown some reluctance to accept such reservations at face value.[27] It is a basic rule of international law that tribunals, once established, have the

---

[27] See the judgment and separate opinions in the *Norwegian Loans* case, *ICJ Reports 1957*, p. 9, and the *Interhandel* case, *ICJ Reports 1959*, p. 6.

power to interpret the texts that establish their jurisdiction; and there are surely some matters, such as boundary disputes, which the Court would be entitled to rule cannot, on any good-faith interpretation, fall within the domestic jurisdiction of a State.

Rather than make an Optional Clause declaration, many States prefer to decide on a case-by-case basis whether to go to the Court. Sometimes this is done literally, by concluding a special agreement or *compromis* with the other party to the dispute, providing for its submission to the Court. Hungary and Slovakia did this in the case concerning the *Gabčikovo-Nagymaros Project*, for example. Sometimes this is done by accepting ICJ jurisdiction in the dispute settlement clauses ('compromissory clauses') that are included in many treaties—and sometimes forgotten until another State invokes them. In this way jurisdiction is confined to questions concerning the interpretation or application of the treaty in which the clause is found. In the *Nicaragua* case the Court's jurisdiction was founded in part upon a 1956 Bilateral treaty between Nicaragua and the United States; the *Oil Platforms* case was brought by the United States against Iran on the basis of a compromissory clause in a 1955 Treaty of Amity between the two States; and the *Hostages* case was brought on the basis of compromissory clauses in the Vienna Convention on Diplomatic Relations, the Vienna Convention on Consular Relations, and other treaties.

It is also possible for a State to throw down the gauntlet, and institute proceedings in the Court in the hope that the other Party will accept the Court's jurisdiction even though it has not already submitted to it. This was done in the case concerning *Certain Criminal Proceedings in France* in 2002. Congo lodged an application with the Court seeking the annulment of French proceedings against the Congolese President and Minister of the Interior and others in respect of crimes against humanity and torture. To the surprise of those who thought that States avoid appearing in courts as respondents wherever possible, France decided to accept the ICJ's jurisdiction and defend the action.

The second basis of jurisdiction I have mentioned already. The ICJ may give Advisory Opinions where requested to do so by certain designated UN organs and specialized agencies, such as the General Assembly and Security Council. It did so, for example, in the *Reparations* case, the *Nuclear Weapons* cases, and the *Western Sahara* case, and also in the case concerning the *Wall in Occupied Palestinian Territory*. Advisory Opinions are authoritative statements of the law but do not technically bind any particular State because there is no State Party to the proceedings. It is quite wrong to regard them as mere recommendations having no legal weight. It is practically inconceivable that the Court would take a different view of the law in a contentious case from that which it had recently taken in an Advisory Opinion. Nonetheless, the theory is that the Advisory Opinion is given to assist the UN body in the discharge of its functions, with the International Court acting in its role as principal judicial organ of the United Nations and a member of the United Nations' family.

3.14 DIPLOMATIC PROTECTION OF NATIONALS

Many international obligations concern the way in which a State treats nationals of other States. There is in international law what is sometimes called an 'international minimum standard of treatment' for aliens, which obliges States not to treat them in a way that would:

> amount to an outrage, to bad faith, to wilful neglect of duty, or to an insufficiency of governmental action so far short of international standards that every reasonable and impartial man would recognize its insufficiency.[28]

A State may not arbitrarily imprison an alien, or confiscate property without compensation, or make no effort to protect aliens from foreseeable attacks by mobs, for example. But, while individuals are protected by these rules, they cannot be Parties to proceedings before the ICJ. When a person is injured in breach of such duties, it is the national State of the victim which may present an international claim against the wrongdoing State, on behalf of its injured national—which, in other words, may exercise diplomatic protection on behalf of the national. As it was put in one case:

> It is an elementary principle of international law that a State is entitled to protect its subjects, when injured by acts contrary to international law committed by another State, for whom they have been unable to obtain satisfaction through the ordinary channels. By taking up the case of one of its subjects and by resorting to diplomatic action or international judicial proceedings on his behalf, a State is in reality asserting its own rights—its right to ensure, in the person of its subjects, respect for the rules of international law.[29]

One consequence of this is that the individual has no right to diplomatic protection: it is for the State to decide in each case whether or not to pursue the claim. Another is that if the State does pursue the claim and recovers compensation, the individual has no absolute right to that compensation, which is the property of the State.

---

[28] The formula used in the much-quoted *Neer* case, *US v Mexico* (1926) 4 *RIAA* 60.
[29] *Mavrommatis Palestine Concessions* case, *Greece v UK* (1924) *PCIJ Reports*, Ser. A, No. 2, p. 12.

The nationality of individuals is determined by the law of the State that claims him as a national. In the *Nottebohm* case Liechtenstein sought to bring a claim before the International Court in respect of the mistreatment by Guatemala of Friedrich Nottebohm. He was a German national who— no doubt with an eye to the inconveniences which German nationality could entail during wartime—had become a Liechtenstein national (thereby losing his German nationality) during a very brief trip there in 1939, but had spent most of his adult life in Guatemala, where he maintained his business activities. While his Liechtenstein nationality would almost certainly have been treated as valid for the purposes of Liechtenstein's jurisdiction over him (he had, after all, freely chosen to take that nationality), the International Court held that Liechtenstein, given the absence of any real connection with Nottebohm, could not bring a claim in respect of his alleged mistreatment against Guatemala, with which he had very strong and long-lasting connections. The difference is that while jurisdiction was a matter between Nottebohm and Liechtenstein, the Court considered that a third State such as Guatemala could not be obliged to accept the consequences of such an artificial arrangement.

An individual may have two or more nationalities: for instance, the nationality of one or both parents, and in addition the nationality of the State where he was born. In these circumstances international law permits either or any of the national States to bring a claim against a third State, and permits the State with which he has the closest connection—the State of dominant nationality—to bring a claim against the other national State. If a person has no nationality (which might happen to children born to refugees temporarily within a State, for example), the International Law Commission has proposed that diplomatic protection should be exercisable by the State in which they are lawfully and habitually resident.[30]

The nationality of corporations is more problematic. Individuals may set up a corporation in a State whose nationality they do not have and with which they may have no real connection. It was established in the *Barcelona Traction* case, where Belgium tried to bring a claim in the ICJ against Spain on behalf of the 88% of shareholders in the Barcelona Traction Company who were Belgian, that where a wrong is done to a company it is the national State of the company, not that of the shareholders, which should bring the action, and that the nationality of a company is determined by its place of incorporation and/or the place where it has the seat of its management. In that case, the company was Canadian. This can be problematical where, as

---

[30] See Article 8 of the ILC Articles on Diplomatic Protection, 2006, <http://untreaty.un.org/ilc/texts/instruments/english/commentaries/9_8_2006.pdf>.

is often the case, foreign investors establish a subsidiary in the host State as a vehicle for the investment. If the host State mistreats the company, it will be mistreating one of its own nationals, and no other State will be able to complain. The Court in *Barcelona Traction* raised the possibility (without deciding the point) that in such circumstances the national State of the shareholders might be permitted to bring the action. Whether or not that is indeed the law, a similar result is achieved in many hundreds of bilateral investment treaties where foreign investors are permitted to initiate proceedings in respect of investments that they directly or indirectly own or control; and a similar possibility is admitted in Article 25 of the Convention establishing ICSID, which oversees many of the arbitrations arising from investment treaties.

Diplomatic protection is not confined to proceedings before a court or tribunal: it extends to all formal procedures by which one State seeks to implement the responsibility of another. And it may be exercised in respect of isolated wrongs to particular individuals or of much larger claims. Mass claims are often handled by special mechanisms established in the claimant State. Thus, when the United Kingdom pursued claims against China arising from damage to property and expropriations during the Communist revolution, the Foreign Compensation Commission, a body established under the Foreign Compensation Act 1950, first assembled details of all British claimants. The British Government then negotiated with China a settlement in respect of all those claims. The compensation paid (which was, as is practically always the case, significantly less than the total of the amounts claimed) was handed over to the United Kingdom; and the Foreign Compensation Commission then distributed the monies pro rata among claimants whom it determined to have provided sufficient proof of their losses.

3.15 INTERNATIONAL LAW OUTSIDE TRIBUNALS

I have described some of the main courts and tribunals in which international law is applied, but I emphasize that this is merely one way in which international law is applied. Consider a comparison with, say, company law. There are many thousands of companies, all organized on the basis of company law, mostly complying with the prescribed procedures for the appointment of directors, holding of meetings, making of contracts, filing of accounts, and so on. None of this requires any recourse to courts or tribunals: the law establishes the basic framework for corporate life, and it is largely observed. So, too, with international law. If a State fails at some point to observe its obligations, the usual response would be to put the matter right when the matter is drawn to its attention. If it does not do so immediately, the matter may be raised more formally, and negotiations may begin. There are few differences that are not resolved at this stage. If the Parties are unwilling to negotiate directly, sometimes a mediator or conciliator will be involved. The Secretary General of the United Nations, or officials in a regional organization, might offer to see if they can find an amicable way out of an impasse. A fact-finding commission may be established to clarify disputed facts. These are all ways of settling international disputes peacefully, as Article 33 of the UN Charter recognizes.

It may appear that the law is absent from these relatively informal procedures, and that the Parties are free to adopt solutions that ignore the law. That may be so in theory; but the reality is that the law, and perhaps the possibility of litigation, always sits in the background. The Parties will constantly be concerned to know what are the best and the worst alternatives to a negotiated agreement; and if there is a court or tribunal with jurisdiction over the dispute, the legal position will heavily influence the terms of the settlement. Even if there is no such tribunal, it is very likely that the argument that a State is in breach of its legal obligations will be prominent in exchanges between the Parties, and that any defences offered by the respondent State will likewise be couched in legal terms. Thus is international responsibility brought to bear. The most successful laws are those that do not require action before the courts to secure their observance.

4

States

4.1 INTRODUCTION: TERRITORIES, BORDERS, AND STATES

When we think of the world systematically we usually think of it as divided into States, like the differently coloured areas on an atlas; but the precise nature and the significance of that division are elusive, even in everyday experience. For many centuries prior to the modern period, people travelled across continents without encountering borders. There were in many places kingdoms or other polities: but they were defined, as it were, from the centre outwards. There would be one or more central cities, the seat of power; and the kingdom was an often ill-defined area beyond the city which was regarded as the territory of the king. For instance, a series of Hittite treaties concluded in the thirteenth century BCE define the lands and frontiers of kingdoms established by Hattusili III. They do so by referring not to lines, but to locations. It is said that Mount Hawa, and the city of Sanantarwa and the sinkhole of the city of Arimmata are the frontiers; but what is meant is that those locations are within the kingdom, and that the frontier in the sense of the boundary with neighbouring kingdoms lies somewhere in the areas connecting those locations. It is perhaps more accurate to say that these kingdoms had spheres of influence than that they had frontiers. Precise linear boundaries, such as those marked out by the shores of island kingdoms, or by man-made structures such as roads (Watling Street divided the England of Alfred the Great from the Danish territory in England) or structures such as the Great Wall of China and Hadrian's Wall, were the exceptions.

In the eighteenth century, in Europe at least, treaties were still being concluded that provided for the creation of buffer zones between two States, to be left as uninhabited wastelands with the consequence that there was no practical necessity to determine the precise line of the frontier. The Treaty of Constantinople between Russia and the Ottoman Empire in 1700, for instance, created a twelve-mile frontier zone between them in the Crimea. But as surveying and mapping techniques were refined later in the eighteenth century, the general trend in treaty practice shifted to the stipulation of much more precise boundaries, defined by physical markers. Some such markers were existing features such as rivers or roads, but others were specially installed by Commissions established to mark out the agreed boundary on the ground.

The drawing of lines was a shift in the perception of what it meant to be a State, which developed alongside the idea that the entry of foreigners and goods into the State should be systematically controlled. We tend to regard the twentieth century as the time in which the world shrank into a global village, as people, goods, and messages moved quickly and effortlessly across national boundaries. Paradoxically, it was the twentieth century that saw the major efforts to turn national boundaries that had been drawn on maps into physical obstacles to travel. Passports did not become universally common requirements to enter a State until the twentieth century. Prior to that time passports were usually not required to enter a State, but those who could afford it might carry passports in order to identify them as subjects of another sovereign or State, and perhaps secure them a degree of respect and safety that could not be taken for granted. Travellers in the eighteenth and nineteenth centuries roamed Europe, Asia, Africa and the Americas freely. As J.M. Keynes remarked, until 1914 a man

could secure forthwith, if he wished it, cheap and comfortable means of transit to any country or climate without passport or other formality, could despatch his servant to the neighbouring office of a bank for such supply of the precious metals as might seem convenient, and could then proceed abroad to foreign quarters, without knowledge of their religion, language, or customs, bearing coined wealth upon his person, and would consider himself greatly aggrieved and much surprised at the least interference.[1]

Security fears during World War One, underscored by the unprecedented movement made possible by the rapid development of rail travel, prompted the imposition of comprehensive mandatory requirements for passports and visas in order to cross frontiers. This was the decisive move that continues to mould our current perception of the division of the globe into pink, yellow, green, and blue areas between which we move passport in hand, although for many the effective 'border' of the State is no longer at its periphery but at its heart, in the bowels of one of the State's international airports.

There are three concepts at work in what I have said so far: first, that of the territory of the State, which is an area; second, that of the border of the

---

[1] John Maynard Keynes, *The Economic Consequences of the Peace* (London: Macmillan, 1919), Chapter 2.

State, which is a line having adjacent to it a vaguer 'frontier' zone; and third, that of the State itself, which is a legal concept that denotes the political society that is based in the territory. Each is a legal concept, though not only a legal concept. Geographers and political scientists, for example, also use these concepts, although not always in the same way that international lawyers use them. Each of the concepts has a different role; and I shall say a little about each in turn.

4.2   STATE TERRITORY

First, the concept of State territory. The underlying question addressed here is, how do we know that this piece of territory belongs to this State rather than to another?

The concept of the State is rooted in the concept of control of territory. The purpose and role of every State is to control activities within its borders so far as possible, or more accurately to ensure that activities within its borders are not regulated by any other State. That idea is expressed in international law through the concept of sovereignty. International law speaks of a State 'having sovereignty' over its territory, rather than 'owning' that territory. As it was put by the Swiss Professor Max Huber, the arbitrator in the *Island of Palmas* case, which concerned the conflicting claims of the USA and the Netherlands to a Pacific island,

Sovereignty in the relations between States signifies independence. Independence in regard to a portion of the globe is the right to exercise therein, to the exclusion of any other State, the functions of a State.

Huber referred not to what independence *is* but to what sovereignty *signifies*; and the contrast is interesting. In international law, discussions of sovereignty commonly focus on the principles of non-intervention in the affairs of other States, prohibitions on the use of force and coercion, the principles of sovereign equality and sovereign immunity, and the like, all of which are said to be in some sense dependent upon or derived from the concept of sovereignty (though I suspect that the relationship is precisely the opposite, and that sovereignty is a concept extrapolated from these components).

Sovereignty is an elusive concept—in philosophical terms, an essentially contested concept—with a complex genealogy as a topic of debate in political theory. It makes sense to discuss the likely effect of a particular policy or action on the 'sovereignty' of a State; and that normally entails references to a knot of concepts centring on two inter-related ideas—the formal independence of decision-making of the State, and its freedom to exercise that independence in practice. It is less clear that the concept of sovereignty has much use in international legal reasoning. It appears to add little, if anything, to the legal consequences that flow from its component principles, such as non-intervention. But the practice is to express the relationship between a State and its 'own' territory in terms of the State's sovereignty over its territory, with the consequence that one State may be sovereign and another may actually occupy the territory, as China was sovereign over the territories that Britain leased from it in Hong Kong, and Cuba is sovereign over the US base at Guantanamo, for example.

It is tempting to begin discussions of State territory by explaining how it is that States first came to have the legal right to possess their territory. Such a perspective is nonsensical. The world did not begin as a *tabula rasa*, gradually portioned out as States were established. Every person, every nuclear and extended family, every tribe, needs its private space. Family lands, kingdoms, and States emerged as groups, first establishing their control over central areas and then reaching out towards other centres of control. Borders emerged where the powers of neighbouring States, attenuated by distance from the centres of power, contested with each other and reached a kind of low-level equilibrium, rather as drying mud cracks into distinct tiles. The border was like a political isobar, the line along which the desire and capacity of each of the adjacent rulers to expand his territory more or less balanced the determination of his neighbour to hold on to his own lands.

International law is not concerned with the mythical histories by which States first gained their territory; but it does speak of the processes by which sovereignty over territory changes hands, and it operates a presumption against disturbing states of affairs that have long existed peacefully—of letting sleeping dogs lie. If we ask what right a State—say, the United Kingdom or India—has to its territory, the answer given by international law is pragmatic. It has its territory (or, more accurately, the State is recognized as having sovereignty over its territory) because so far as we can tell it has acquired that territory by processes that are recognized as lawful.

There is nothing peculiar in this. In domestic law our right to land depends in most cases upon the fact that we paid for it, or inherited it, or acquired an interest in it by marriage. The same will be true of the person from whom we acquired it, and of the person from whom they acquired it, and so on. The fact that we may not be able to explain how the land came to be owned by someone, say, more than three hundred years ago does not matter. The critical point is that the land is now regarded by the community at large as the property of the people who have acquired it.

There may, in fact, have been defects in title at some point. But international law has a robust approach to this possibility. International law must work with the world as it is, and make the best of what the position is now. It is not the role of international law to give redress to centuries-old grievances. This pragmatic approach is implemented through two powerful concepts: intertemporal law and prescription.

4.3 INTERTEMPORAL LAW AND THE MODES OF ACQUIRING TERRITORY

The doctrine of intertemporal law says that the legal effect of conduct is to be determined in accordance with the law as it was at the time of the conduct. For example, since the outlawing in the mid twentieth century of the use of force in international relations it has been unlawful to gain territory by the use of force (even force used in self-defence).[2] But large areas of the globe were incorporated into the States of which they are now part as a result of uses of force. According to the doctrine, however, if territory could lawfully be gained by force at the time that those areas were acquired by force, the State had and still has good title to them.

There is another side to the doctrine. It requires that States keep up with the changing demands of the law. It is sometimes said (probably wrongly) that during the fifteenth century territory could be acquired by discovery or by papal grant. If an expedition sent out by a State 'discovered' an island and claimed it, the island would belong to the State. It is also said that land could be acquired by papal grant. In 1493 the (Spanish) Pope Alexander VI, exercising the exclusive power of the papacy to authorize 'missions to the heathen', issued papal bulls, including the famous bull *inter caetera*, which granted to Spain:

all islands and mainlands found and to be found, discovered and to be discovered towards the west and south, by drawing and establishing a line from the Arctic pole, namely the north, to the Antarctic pole, namely the south, no matter whether the said mainlands and islands are found and to be found in the direction of India or towards any other quarter, the said line to be distant one hundred leagues towards the west and south from any of the islands commonly known as the Azores and Cape Verde.

Lands already in the possession of a Christian king were excluded from the grant. Portugal, then competing with Spain in its colonial expansion,

---

[2] Because the right of self-defence extends only as far as the removal of the threat. Hence, for instance, claims that Israel is entitled to retain lands seized during wars in which it acted in self-defence are misconceived.

was dissatisfied with the grant and in a diplomatic coup succeeded in renegotiating its terms in the 1497 Treaty of Tordesillas, fixing the boundary 'at a distance of three hundred and seventy leagues west of the Cape Verde Islands'. Spain took the lands to the west, and Portugal those to the east of the line. (So it is that Portuguese is spoken in Brazil and Spanish elsewhere in Latin America.) In fact, the dominant view came to be that neither discovery nor papal grant was truly a source of legal title. As international law developed it became accepted that in order to acquire title to territory it was necessary actually to occupy it. Simple discovery or papal grant was not sufficient, if it ever had been, to confer title; and States would have had to maintain their title in accordance with the developing law. Discovery, for instance, would have had to be followed up by occupation.

There are other antique 'modes of acquisition' as they are known of territory in international law. Much territory has over the centuries been ceded by one ruler to another, often in the context of a marriage. Bombay and Tangier, for example, were part of the dowry of Catherine of Portugal when she married Charles II of England in 1662. The Habsburgs were particularly good at acquiring territories in this way, giving rise to the dictum '*Bella gerant alii; tu felix Austria nube*'—'Let others wage war; but you, happy Austria, marry'. The phrase is sometimes attributed to Matthias I Corvinus, the fifteenth-century king of Hungary and Bohemia who spent much of his reign gaining territory the hard way, using armed force, which was for many centuries the main process by which rulers expanded their lands.

Some territories were 'sold', in the sense that they were ceded by one State to another for monetary compensation. The United States acquired Louisiana from France for 60m francs, Florida from Spain for $5m, and in what were even better bargains Alaska from Russia for $7.2m and Texas, New Mexico, and Northern California from Mexico for $15m. It is sometimes said that the biggest real estate deal in history was the Louisiana Purchase of 30 April 1803 (or the tenth day of Floréal in the eleventh year of the French Republic: revolutionaries tend to believe that when their own lives are transformed by the acquisition of power, everyone else's life should also be given a new beginning). It was not: it was a cession of territory, together with its citizens and with rights of political control and governance, in exchange for monetary compensation. These were not 'sales' of land in the domestic sense. Private purchasers can only ever buy a legal interest in land: a freehold or leasehold. The ultimate property rights always vest in the State as sovereign. Indeed, it is the law of the State that creates and secures the legal interests of private landowners. Thus, no State can ever be bought up by private buyers. If all the land in the United Kingdom were purchased by a foreign State, the United Kingdom would still remain under British sovereignty. The critical question is not who owns the real estate in the territory, but who governs, who is sovereign over it.

Yet other territories have been exchanged. Sardinia was exchanged for Sicily, between the Duke of Savoy and the Habsburg Emperor Charles VI. More recently, Belgium and Germany transferred parcels of frontier land in the 1950s in order to create a more practical border.

In all these cases, however, the mere abstract transfer of land would be insufficient to transfer title if the former sovereign continued to treat the territory as its own and the new sovereign did nothing to assert its own sovereignty over the territory. One might almost say that cessions and sales of territory were merely the factual background which in practice ensured that the occupation by the new sovereign—the transferee—was not challenged by the former sovereign, and that it was the assertion of its rights by the new sovereign that was the effective cause of the change of sovereignty.

Title to territory not already under the sovereignty of some other recognized State[3]—*terra nullius*, as it is known—could be acquired simply by occupying it. States adopted the position that the first State to 'take' the land should have title to it, and applied this approach with some enthusiasm during the era of European 'discoveries' of foreign lands in the sixteenth and seventeenth centuries. This pragmatic solution was given a degree of dignity by resting it on an analogy with the Roman law right to acquire *res nullius*—a thing belonging to no-one—by *occupatio*, that is, the taking of possession of a *res nullius* with the intention of becoming its owner. Classical Roman law appears not to have applied the concept of *res nullius* to land, except in the case of islands emerging from the sea: but no matter. International law has always owed more to *bricolage* and pragmatism than to the cold logic of bloodless scholarship. As long as effective control was established over the territory in question in the name of an existing State (or occupation *à titre de souverain*, as it is known), that was sufficient to confer sovereignty.

'Effective control' meant simply the area that could in practice be controlled from the occupied area. Typically, occupation of a coastal strip would give effective control over the hinterland, unless that control was contested by an indigenous power or a rival State. The degree of activity needed to establish effective control over uninhabited or sparsely inhabited territory was much less than that needed in inhabited territory.

---

[3] I deal with the question of recognition below.

It is sometimes supposed that the European States marched into Africa, Asia, and the Americas and announced that they were acquiring uninhabited lands to be brought under their sovereignty by occupation. That is not so. Lands occupied by communities which stood their ground and dealt with the colonizers, were generally not regarded as unoccupied. Much of the process of colonization was conducted through agreements with the indigenous populations of the colonized territories;[4] and elaborate legal and theological arguments were developed in an attempt to legitimize the colonial endeavour. While there was no doubt a good deal of chicanery and threats or uses of force, the appearance of consent was regularly sought. Many of the agreements were trade agreements, often concluded with local political leaders by the Chartered Companies instructed by European governments in the seventeenth and eighteenth centuries to occupy foreign lands in the name of the Crown. Over the years the network of such treaties and contractual agreements became overlain with layers of governmental activity: legislation and taxation, for instance, applied to the colonial territory, so that title to the territory became consolidated through the display of effective and unchallenged control— the display, in short, of sovereignty.

These distinctions between modes of acquiring territory are a modern superimposition upon the historical record. The distinction between acquisition of territory by occupation and acquisition by agreement, for instance, was often blurred. Each European power had its characteristic ceremony of possession to signify the commencement of the assertion of effective control. In South America Christopher Columbus, following instructions from the Spanish King and Queen, planted their standards in the ground and solemnly declared the land under Spanish authority. Elsewhere in South America the French organized elaborate processions, at the climax of which the Tupi Indians themselves placed the French flag in the land. In North America, the Dutch (like the Portuguese) made meticulous maps; while Sir Humphrey Gilbert summoned 'both English and strangers' to witness his taking possession of the harbour of St John in Newfoundland 'and 200 leagues every way', by a ceremony in which his commission from Queen Elizabeth was read and he 'had delivered to him (after the custome of England) a rod and a turf[5] of the same soile', whereby the land became:

a territorie appertaining to the Queene of England, and himself authorised under her Majestie to posesse and enjoy it. And to ordaine laws for the government

---

[4] See *Mabo v Queensland* (1988) 83 *ALR* 14, (1992) 107 *ALR* 1; 112 *ILR* 412, 457.
[5] i.e., a twig and a lump of soil.

thereof, agreeable (so neere as conveniently might be) unto the laws of England: under which all people coming thither hereafter, either to inhabite, or by way of traffique, should be subjected and governed.[6]

Such ceremonies persist today. Rockall, a rock approximately the size of a tennis court lying about 250 miles west of the Outer Hebrides, was annexed by the United Kingdom in 1955 by a boarding party from HMS *Vidal*, who cemented a small plaque onto the rock to record the event.[7] Occasional visits since then have sufficed to maintain British sovereignty over the rock.

The need to occupy territory as sovereign meant that in the eyes of international law private individuals could not establish their own States. The Chartered companies that occupied foreign lands were acting in the name, or at least under the authority, of whichever State had granted the charter. More unusually, a private person, James Brooke, was given a kingdom in Sarawak by the Sultan of Brunei, where he was installed as the White Rajah in 1842. (The Law Officers in the United Kingdom subsequently advised that as a matter of British constitutional law the Queen was legally competent to permit one of her subjects to assume the sovereignty of a foreign State, and to recognize him as such.) Sarawak was eventually relinquished to the United Kingdom as a Crown colony in 1946 by Brooke's great-nephew.

4.4 PRESCRIPTION

Whatever defects there may have been in the original title of a State to a particular parcel of territory, they can be cured by time and acquiescence, thereby building up a title based on prescription. Gibraltar offers a good example. Title to 'the town and castle of Gibraltar, together with the port, fortifications, and forts thereunto belonging' was ceded by Spain to Great Britain by Article X of the Treaty of Utrecht, 1714. There is, however, a spit of land, where Gibraltar's airstrip lies, between the foot of the rock of Gibraltar and the present frontier fence with Spain. In the 1960s Spain claimed that this land was not part of the territory ceded in 1714. The United Kingdom considered that it was ceded in 1714 but also asserted an

---

[6] Richard Hakluyt, ed. by Janet Hampden, *Voyages and Documents* (London: Oxford University Press, 1958), p. 257. These ceremonies are analysed in the fascinating study by Patricia Seed, *Ceremonies of Possession in Europe's Conquest of the New World 1492–1640* (Cambridge: Cambridge University Press, 1995).

[7] See James Fisher, *Rockall* (London: Geoffrey Bles, 1956). States tend to want sovereignty over such tiny, god-forsaken rocks and islets (i) to stop any other State getting them, and (ii) because they may claim maritime zones around them.

alternative title, based on the fact that the strip has been under exclusive British jurisdiction since at least 1838 and that successive Spanish Governments acquiesced in the situation and forfeited any title to the area concerned which they may at one time have possessed.[8]

Britain also claims that the cession of 1714 included the territorial sea around Gibraltar, a claim which Spain, Portia-like, disputes on the ground that no mention of the surrounding sea appears in the Treaty of Utrecht. In order to prevent this claim from dying through acquiescence, Spain has protested against the British claim and engaged in other actions such as sending a Spanish warship into the territorial sea and launching a helicopter from it—something that foreign ships in the territorial sea cannot lawfully do without the consent of the coastal State, and thus an implicit assertion that the waters are Spanish. It is an elegant example of the use of symbolic acts to delimit sovereignty—a kind of twentieth-century ceremony of possession.

Prescription is international law's way of deciding when it is appropriate to draw a line under the untidiness of history. If a State has been in peaceful possession of a parcel of territory for some time, it will be regarded as having acquired good title to that parcel unless its right to possession is challenged. Challenges may take many forms—diplomatic notes, symbolic acts such as the Spanish helicopter flight, attempts to refer the dispute to an international tribunal, and so on. Some claims are kept alive for a long time by such moves, and the acquisition of title by acquiescence is blocked. For example, Guatemala claims half of the territory of Belize; Portugal apparently still claims that the village of Olivenza is owing to it under an 1815 agreement concluded at the Congress of Vienna; and for many years Cambodia maintained a claim to Khmer Krom, an area in the south of Vietnam. But now that a State may programme a computer to fax a note of protest every year, there must surely come a time when mere verbal protests are not enough and some more decisive action, such as an invitation to refer the dispute to the International Court, must be taken if a claim by a State not in possession of the territory is to be kept alive. One cannot say how long that time might be, whether decades or centuries, though the period is likely to be shorter in the case of near and inhabited areas than of distant or uninhabited ones simply because one would expect a swift protest in respect of the occupation of areas where the challenge to the claimant State's effective control is most direct.

---

[8] *Gibraltar: Talks with Spain, May–October 1966*, Cmnd 3131, p. 62. For a Spanish view see the decision in *Exequatur Procedure Goran U*, No 1768/1998; Aranzadi RJ [*Referencia de Jurisprudencia*] 2001/3968; ILDC 130 (ES 2001).

Moreover, if third States, acting unilaterally or perhaps through a body such as the United Nations, recognize the title of the State in possession, that will count towards the building of its title. What is at work here is a process of 'historical consolidation', the term used by the International Court of Justice in the *Anglo-Norwegian Fisheries* case to describe the process by which nineteenth-century Norwegian decrees were effective to give Norway title to certain coastal areas when its title to those areas was challenged by the United Kingdom. The Court held that the decrees had not given rise to any opposition on the part of foreign States and should therefore 'reap the benefit of general toleration, the basis of an historical consolidation which would make it enforceable against all States'. Here again one sees the underlying concern of international law not to disturb a peaceful state of affairs. If the international community recognizes a claim as valid, that will be a powerful argument in favour of its objective validity. This follows from the realities of the position. If all other States recognize that the parcel of territory belongs to State A and not to State B and act on that basis, the abstract question of title is of relatively little importance. And if the dispute does go for adjudication it is likely that the tribunal will make a decision that accords with the position that all or most third States regard as correct.

That last point raises another issue. Questions of territorial title are decided on balance. International tribunals are concerned with what is known as 'relative title'—which of the competing claims is stronger—rather than some absolute standard of title. This must be so. If two States litigate over a particular parcel of territory and a third State which has a claim remains silent, its claim would be extinguished by its acquiescence. The position is more complex and uncertain if the third State raises its claim but does not wish, or is not allowed, to join the litigation. International tribunals have a doctrine of 'indispensable parties' and might refuse to adjudicate in such circumstances, as the International Court of Justice refused in the *East Timor* case to rule upon the validity of a treaty between Australia and Indonesia in the absence of Indonesia, which had not accepted the ICJ's jurisdiction.

4.5 OCCUPIED TERRITORIES, DECOLONIZATION, AND *UTI POSSIDETIS*

The account so far may all sound rather medieval, as though parcels of land could be traded, ceded, and conquered, with inhabitants going to bed in Germany and waking up to find themselves in Poland. There has, indeed, been a good deal of such activity over the centuries. But it does not sit well with the principle of self-determination, enshrined in the UN Charter and the 1970 Declaration of Principles of International Law. As Judge Dillard put it in his Separate Opinion in the *Western Sahara* case, according to 'the cardinal restraint which the legal right of self-determination imposes . . . [i]t is for the people to determine the destiny of the territory and not the territory the destiny of the people'. Self-determination now operates as a significant restraint on the right of States to transfer territory.

It has come to be accepted that parcels of territory should not be transferred contrary to the wishes of the inhabitants, expressed in exercise of their right of self-determination. Accordingly, dispositions of territory are now generally preceded by a plebiscite. Thus, in the case of the Western Sahara, which had been claimed both by Morocco and by Mauritania (though Mauritania withdrew its claim in 1979), the United Nations has for more than twenty years been trying to organize a referendum on the fate of the territory. It has been unsuccessful so far because of the refusal of Morocco, which has virtually annexed the territory, to accept the possibility of an independent Western Sahara, which is the solution advocated by the Frente Polisario, the Sahrawi independence movement and Government-in-exile of the Sahrawi Arab Democratic Republic (SADR). Referenda have been held more successfully in other places, such as Timor and Gibraltar; and the principle of self-determination remains very much alive. It is frequently invoked by independence movements, and lies behind the United Kingdom's political commitments not to transfer the Falklands/Malvinas to Argentina against the wishes of the inhabitants. Plebiscites, particularly popular in the 1920s, have also been held in circumstances in which the question of the unification of smaller areas with neighbouring States has arisen, for example in the Saarland (reunited with Germany in 1955), and in Northern Ireland (which voted in 1973 to remain part of the United Kingdom).

The principle of self-determination has usually been applied in situations where the transfer of discrete bundles of territory, such as former provinces, is in issue. The break-up of the Former Yugoslavia and the separation of Eritrea from Ethiopia are two examples from the 1990s, both involving the holding of plebiscites. International law is, however, keen to preserve international stability. Practice on the question of secession is not consistent, but broadly speaking while the right of former colonies to secede from the colonial power is clearly established, there is no clear right under international law for parts of an independent State to secede. The one exception lies in the context of the dissolution of former federal

States, such as the USSR and Yugoslavia; but in the former case the secession of the various republics occurred by agreement and through constitutional processes within the USSR, and in the latter case the handling by the international community of the secession of the various republics appears to have been largely determined by the need to contain the escalating violence in the Former Yugoslavia.[9]

It is clear that wherever there is a decolonization or secession or other separation of parts of a State, the separation takes place within the pre-existing boundaries. This is known as the principle of *uti possidetis*, originally deployed when the Latin American colonies achieved their independence. By becoming independent republics within the former colonial boundaries they ensured that no pockets of abandoned territory were left which the European States could colonize anew. There is another aspect to the doctrine. Respect for these administrative boundaries means that it is highly unlikely that, for as long as the current legal principles apply, any new State can be founded except by means of the achievement of independence of a 'people' within the boundaries of an existing administrative unit or units.[10]

4.6 GOVERNING WITHOUT SOVEREIGNTY

Thus far I have focused upon the territory of States, which is subject to their sovereignty. (I have treated the matter as if territory is always under the sovereignty of a single State, but it is possible for sovereignty to be shared—as, for example, in the Anglo-Egyptian condominium in the Sudan from 1899 to 1955, and the Anglo-French condominium in the New Hebrides (now Vanuatu) from 1914 to 1980.) There are, however,

---

[9] See James Crawford, *The Creation of States in International Law* (2nd edn., Oxford: Oxford University Press, 2006), Chapter 9.

[10] As I write, the memory of Thomas Baty bears down. Baty was an English international lawyer who emigrated to Japan and became a legal adviser to the Japanese Ministry of Foreign Affairs, and published several texts on international law. Baty, a transvestite, also wrote novels under the name of Irene Clyde and gave a good deal of his money for the promotion of radical feminist publishing. Narrowly escaping a charge of treason after he remained in Japan during World War Two, he died in Japan, and is buried in Tokyo. His book *International Law in Twilight* (Tokyo: Maruzen Co., 1954) is one of the most remarkable international law texts ever published. It calls for 'the dethronement of the masculine', the quelling of arrogance by 'the according of world-wide acclaim to the Feminine as supereminent', and ends with the haunting words, 'behind the Freedom and behind the Dictators flows serenely the eternal tide of loveliness'. Baty had an exceptional ability to identify correctly the critical questions of international law, and to propose answers to them that were completely the opposite of the way in which international law in fact developed. The sentence to which this note is appended may suffer the same fate.

other rights over territory, not amounting to full sovereignty. These are rights of government and control possessed by one State over territory that remains technically subject to the sovereignty of another.

International leases are one example. For many years the United Kingdom exercised effective control over Hong Kong, but not entirely in the United Kingdom's capacity as a sovereign State. The island of Hong Kong was a Crown Colony, ceded to Great Britain by China in the 1842 Treaty of Nanking, and British Kowloon and Stonecutters Island were ceded in the 1860 Treaty of Peking. They were occupied and controlled by the United Kingdom *à titre de souverain* and were territory under British sovereignty. But the New Territories on the Chinese mainland adjacent to Hong Kong island were only leased by the United Kingdom from China, for a period of ninety-nine years under the 1898 Treaty of Peking. They were occupied and controlled by the United Kingdom in its capacity as an international lessee, not as sovereign. The site of the United States' naval base at Guantanamo Bay is another example, leased from Cuba under treaties of 1903 and 1934. It appears to have been precisely the fact that the base was not under US sovereignty, and therefore thought by the US Government not to be within the geographical scope of the legal protections afforded by the US Constitution, which made Guantanamo attractive as a place in which to detain without trial people alleged to be suspected terrorists. As is often the case, invocation of the letter of the Law and indifference to the practical implication of its principles marched hand in hand.

Another exceptional case of occupation and control of territory not being exercised *à titre de souverain* arises in the context of belligerent occupation; that is, the occupation of enemy territory that occurs during and after armed conflicts. Thus, while West Germany (as the Federal Republic of Germany—FRG) and East Germany (as the German Democratic Republic—GDR) became separate States, Berlin was occupied and controlled for decades after the end of the Second World War by the military authorities of the victorious Allied States. Technically, Berlin remained under the sovereignty of the 'old' pre-war Germany but under Allied military occupation, and was governed by the Allied Kommandatura who had the right to adopt laws and maintain courts in the City. In 1978, two GDR citizens, Hans Tiede and Ingrid Ruske, hijacked an aircraft flying from Gdansk to East Berlin and forced it to land at Tempelhof Airport in West Berlin, which was under the control of the United States' Air Force. Western States had recently ratified several treaties concerning hijacking—the 1963 Tokyo Convention on Offences and Certain Other Acts Committed on Board Aircraft, the 1970 Hague Convention for the

Suppression of Unlawful Seizure of Aircraft, and the 1971 Montreal Convention for the Suppression of Unlawful Acts Against the Safety of Civil Aviation. The two latter Conventions obliged their States Parties either to extradite alleged hijackers or to submit the cases to their own prosecuting authorities—the so-called *aut dedere, aut judicare* obligation. The German policy at the time, however, was to support those fleeing oppression in the GDR, and neither option fitted comfortably with that policy. The case was therefore handed over to the Allied Kommandatura for trial in the US Military Court for Berlin, under Judge Herbert Stern.[11] The judge, in a remarkable display of judicial independence and integrity, ruled that the accused were entitled to a jury trial and to procedural safeguards under United States' law, despite vigorous arguments to the contrary by counsel for the United States.

The main rules of belligerent occupation were codified in the Regulations attached to the 1907 Hague Convention Respecting the Laws and Customs of War on Land. Those rules were designed for situations in which the belligerents would withdraw to their own territory shortly after the hostilities ended, so that territory came once more under the control of the relevant sovereign State. They were not designed for long-term occupations of the kind that have existed in the Palestinian Territory (by Israel) and Iraq (by the United States, the United Kingdom, and a handful of others), where the occupying army functions as a long-term (albeit temporary) peacetime government. States need to consider the revision of this area of the law.

4.7 BORDERS AND FRONTIERS

The development of faster transport and communications, and of vast State apparatuses employing a significant proportion of the population, has made it possible to create State borders on land (and to some extent at sea) which are reasonably secure. The unusual phenomenon of (usually communist) States wishing to fence their own citizens in, rather than merely to keep undesirable aliens out, coupled with an obsession with national security that has grown steadily in the wake of two world wars and the attacks of 11 September 2001, have combined to produce a system of borders that in some parts of the world take the forms of practically impenetrable barriers, although in other parts of the world the frontier is

---

[11] Stern published an account of the trial in his book *Judgment in Berlin* (New York: Universe Books, 1984), subsequently made into a film. The judgment in the case is reported at 86 FRD 227.

marked by no more than an increased risk of treading on a land mine or
of arrest or shooting by any military patrol that might happen to be in
the area.

The borders of a State extend around its land, sea, and air territory. The
legal principles governing the determination of borders are, of course,
those same principles that govern title to territory. The border is where the
limit of one State's territory meets the territory of another State. As I
mentioned in the previous chapter, in some legal systems a distinct regime
for border areas (i.e., frontiers) is recognized, notably the regime of *voisinage*. This regime has few hard rules, beyond obligations of co-operation
and consultation between the neighbouring States and communities in
relation to projects that may affect those on the other side of the border.
There may be jointly administered infrastructure facilities, such as water
and power distribution systems, and co-operation between neighbouring
police forces; and there are often many small courtesies and concessions
such as bilingual road signs and expedited passage rights for frontier
workers, shared access to common resources, and the like, sometimes
formalized in treaties and sometimes organized informally. The 1990
International Convention on the Protection of the Rights of All Migrant
Workers and Members of Their Families, is one example of a multilateral
attempt to improve the position of this subset of commuters, though a
great deal more has been done within regional economic integration
organizations such as the European Community. The most help has come
from the 1985 Schengen Agreement, which abolished systematic border
controls between the (currently fifteen) participating States, permitting
practically free movement between their respective territories.[12]

The question of rights over airspace under international law first
became an issue with the use of aircraft for military purposes. Balloons
had been used by Austria in an attempt to bomb the defenders of Venice in
1849, but it was only at the end of the nineteenth century that reliable
technology was developed. By the time of World War One the legal issue
could no longer be ignored. The French fighter ace, Georges Madon,[13]
was interned in Switzerland in April 1915 having flown into Swiss airspace in fog. This amounted to an assertion of sovereignty by (neutral)
Switzerland over its airspace; and that position was generally accepted
and embodied in the 1919 Paris Convention on Aerial Navigation. The

---

[12] Austria, Belgium, Denmark, Finland, France, Germany, Iceland, Italy, Greece,
Luxembourg, Netherlands, Norway, Portugal, Spain, and Sweden.
[13] Madon shot down 41 aircraft during the war. He was killed in 1924, aged 32, when he deliberately crashed his malfunctioning plane in order to avoid injury to spectators at an air show.

sovereignty of States over the airspace lying vertically above their land and sea territory is confirmed by the Chicago Convention on International Civil Aviation 1944. There is no international agreement on the point where national airspace ends and outer space begins, although a commonly used criterion is the lowest point of a satellite orbit, around 50 to 60 miles from the earth. Outer space may not be appropriated by any State; but there is a growing need for some rules to maintain order there. Quite apart from the threat of the use of outer space for military purposes (although the stationing of weapons of mass destruction in outer space or on the moon or other celestial bodies is forbidden by the 1967 Treaty on the Principles Governing the Activities of States in the Exploration and Use of Outer Space, which is regarded as reflecting customary international law), there are estimated to be around 5,000 satellites currently in orbit, not to mention other bits and pieces that have fallen off rockets; and that number will doubtless increase as businesses work to bring the blessings of 900-channel television to the whole globe and governments struggle to ensure that our every move can be tracked. Even though outer space is an awfully big place, earth orbits are starting to become a little crowded.

States—coastal States—also have sovereignty over an area of sea as an automatic adjunct of their sovereignty over their land territory. The twelve-mile territorial sea extends from the coastal State's baselines (normally the low-water mark, but straight baselines are notionally drawn across bays, river-mouths, and some other features), and is under the sovereignty of the coastal State. Boundaries with the territorial seas of neighbouring States are fixed by agreement, failing which a boundary line equidistant from the nearest points on the baselines of the respective States is used. The State's sovereignty over its territorial sea is, however, subject to a right of innocent passage for ships of all States. That is to say, they may sail through the territorial sea as long as they do not threaten the peace, good order, or security of the coastal State. There is no such right of passage through a State's land territory or airspace. Landlocked States must negotiate rights of passage through neighbouring States if they wish to have access by air or land—by road, rail, river, or canal—to the sea, and there are many agreements concluded for this purpose. Particularly notable are the treaties governing navigation on international rivers, such as the Danube and the Rhine, and more general instruments such as the 1921 Barcelona Convention and Statute on the Regime of Navigable Waterways of International Concern. There are many international agreements concerning road, rail, canal, and multimodal transport; and surprisingly little written (at least by public international lawyers) on this aspect of international law. Air transport, by contrast, has a very highly developed system of international agreements that has been extensively analysed. The framework for these agreements is provided by the 1944 Chicago Convention on International Civil Aviation, and rights for commercial airlines to overfly and land in other States are regulated by a network of bilateral 'Bermuda agreements', as they are known.

Coastal States also have more limited rights over other maritime zones, notably the continental shelf and the 200-mile exclusive economic zone (EEZ), in which the coastal State has exclusive rights over marine resources (such as fish, oil, gas, and gravel) and their exploration and exploitation, and jurisdiction in respect of marine pollution and marine scientific research. These rights do not, however, amount to sovereignty, and the zones in question are not part of the territory of the State. Beyond the 200-mile EEZs of States lie the high seas, which are broadly speaking free for use by all States in the same way that outer space is free for use by all.

4.8 THE STATE

I have been talking about the territory of the State. But power is not geographically limited; and there is more to a State than its territory. It is not, however, easy to say exactly what more there is to a State than its territory.

One of the most frequently quoted definitions of a State is that found in the 1933 Montevideo Convention on Rights and Duties of States, one of a remarkable series of texts emanating from the Pan American Union, predecessor of the Organization of American States. Article 1 of that Convention stipulates that:

The state as a person of international law should possess the following qualifications: (a) a permanent population; (b) a defined territory; (c) government; and (d) capacity to enter into relations with the other states.

That definition was a child of its time, and reflects none of the preoccupation with self-determination, democracy, and legitimacy which characterized discussions of Statehood later in the twentieth century. But it is a good place to start because while its four criteria have been added to, no-one has suggested that any of them is dispensable.

4.9 THE POPULATION

The first requirement refers to the population of a State. Unless there is someone to be governed, there is no State. It does not matter much how many people there are. The populations of current Member States of the

United Nations range from around 1.3 billion (China) to less than 12,000 (Tuvalu)—the Holy See/Vatican City (population 932) is a 'Non-member State maintaining a Permanent observer mission at UN Headquarters'. There are more people reported missing each week in the United States than the entire population of Tuvalu; but both are sovereign States, with the same number of votes in the United Nations. There may be some point at which the international community would draw the line. For example, if the Pitcairn Islands (population, 45) were to become independent and seek admission to the United Nations, States might re-examine the relationship between the principle of sovereign equality and common sense. The population must be reasonably stable. They may wander around within the country, like the nomadic people of the Western Sahara, but they must have some degree of social cohesion; a transient, dissociated population (such as the groups of fisherfolk who reside on certain otherwise unoccupied islands on a seasonal basis) is not enough.

Most of those who live in a State will be its citizens, its nationals, though there will almost certainly also be nationals of other States, and perhaps also people who have no nationality. The relationship of nationality is important in international law, particularly (as was seen in Chapter 3) in the context of diplomatic protection and, as I shall explain, of jurisdiction. It is therefore worth exploring the concept in a little more detail.

4.10 NATIONALITY

The nationality of persons, ships and aircraft is determined not by international law but by national law. As the International Court observed in the *Nottebohm* case, where the validity of an unusually swift acquisition of Liechtenstein nationality was in question, it is in principle for each State to decide who are its own nationals. In the case of individuals, most States ascribe nationality to those who are born within their territory (the *jus soli*), or who have one or both parents with the nationality of the State (the *jus sanguinis*). Furthermore, it is generally possible to acquire nationality by naturalization. For jurisdictional purposes this ascription of nationality to individuals is likely to be determinative, unless perhaps a State attempts to impose its nationality upon individuals who do not want it and have no real connection with the State. The nationality of corporations is usually determined, as I noted in Chapter 3, by the place of incorporation or of the seat of the management, or some combination of the two.

In the context of the nationality of ships, Article 91 of the 1982 United Nations Convention on the Law of the Sea requires that there be a 'genuine link' between the ship and its flag State. In practice, despite an unsuccessful attempt in the 1980s to secure international agreement on the implementation of this principle,[14] many 'flag of convenience' ships sail (often for tax reasons) under the flags of States with which they have no real connection. This practice reinforces the view that each State is free to determine the conditions for the grant of its nationality. Nevertheless, in circumstances where access to resources (such as quotas of fish catches) or other privileges are granted on the basis of the nationality of ships tribunals may in future revisit this question and, as the International Court did in the *Nottebohm* case, say that the grant of nationality by a State is not necessarily determinative in every context. It would strain the concept of nationality if a shipowner, denied benefits such as access to fish stocks under one flag, could circumvent the restrictions simply by re-flagging his vessel in another State.

4.11 STATELESSNESS

Although Article 24 of the International Covenant on Civil and Political Rights declares that 'every child has the right to acquire a nationality', some unfortunate people have no nationality. They may have been born in a State that refuses to give its nationality to some people born within its territory—for example, the children of refugees[15]— or a woman may have lost her nationality on marrying a foreigner, and then lost his nationality upon divorce. Such Stateless people are at a grave disadvantage. They have no national State which they are entitled to enter and reside in if no other State will accept them, and they may be denied many of the rights of citizens, such as the right to work or own land or receive welfare benefits. Two Conventions have sought to ameliorate their position. One seeks to reduce the incidence of Statelessness by guaranteeing everyone born in a territory the right to the nationality of that State if they would otherwise be Stateless, and by prohibiting the withdrawal of nationality on a change of status, such as divorce, if that would leave the person Stateless.[16] States Parties to the other Convention guarantee certain rights, such as the right to some basic welfare provision, and the same right to work as is 'accorded to aliens generally in the same circumstances' to Stateless persons.[17]

---

[14] See the 1986 UN Convention on Conditions for Registration of Ships, 7 *Law of the Sea Bulletin* 87 (1986). The Convention is not in force.

[15] But note that the categories of Stateless persons and of refugees are not co-extensive.

[16] Convention on the Reduction of Statelessness, 1961, 989 UNTS 175.

[17] Convention Relating to the Status of Stateless Persons, 1960.

4.12 THE TERRITORY

I have already discussed the territory of a State, and there is little more
to be said. As in the case of populations, there are wide differences of
scale between States. Russia has around 17 million square kilometres of
territory, Monaco about two square kilometres—much less than the area
lost annually to coastal erosion in Louisiana. And, as David Harris
remarked, the Holy See 'whatever domain it may have elsewhere, has less
than 100 acres on earth'.[18] But, as they say, size does not matter: all count
as sovereign States.

The reference to 'defined territory' signals a requirement that the
State should have reasonably determinate borders. During a civil war, for
example, a rebel government may manage to establish effective control
over part of the State and to command the obedience of a part of the
population; but if the conflict continues and the borders of the area under
rebel control ebb and flow, there will not be a sufficiently defined territory
to support a claim to Statehood. It is not necessary that the borders be
wholly determined: India and Israel are two of several States that achieved
Statehood when their precise boundaries remained in dispute.

4.13 THE GOVERNMENT

The third *Montevideo Convention* criterion of Statehood is the existence
of a government. This means an effective government in control of
the territory and population that form the basis of the State. In order to
be a government some degree of constitutional order is necessary. In 1933,
Justice Pound asked 'As a juristic conception what is Soviet Russia? A band
of robbers or a government?'[19] Given those alternatives, it would be
relatively easy to place putative governments on one or other side of
the line. The surprising thing is that this Montevideo criterion is not
more discriminating and demanding. Why not require that the government be representative or democratic, for example? While the natural
reluctance of government representatives at international conferences to
spell out the criteria for their own legitimacy has delayed the articulation
of a clear and generally accepted statement along these lines, the fact is

---

[18] David Harris, *Cases and Materials on International Law* (6th edn., London: Sweet &
Maxwell, 2004), p. 100.

[19] *Salimoff & Co. v Standard Oil Co. of New York*, 262 NY 220 (1933). He answered, 'We all
know that it is a government. The State Department knows it, the courts, the nations and the
man on the street.'

that there is a trend towards requiring a minimum standard of legitimacy and constitutionality from a government if the entity that it governs is to be accepted as a State. There is more to be said about this, but it is an aspect of a broader question, not confined to the nature of the government; and so I shall postpone discussion of it until I have dealt with the fourth and last of the 'Montevideo' criteria.

4.14 INDEPENDENCE: THE CAPACITY TO ENTER INTO RELATIONS WITH THE OTHER STATES[20]

The fourth criterion, 'the capacity to enter into relations with the other states', is paradoxical. It is set out as a condition of Statehood, but it might more properly be regarded as a consequence of Statehood. Clearly, an entity will not be able to enter into State-to-State relations unless it is a State. The paradox may seem to be resolved on one level by referring to the notion of recognition. An entity may have all of the attributes of Statehood, but if other States refuse to recognize it as a State and to deal with it as such, it will in practice not be possible for it to enter into relations with other States. But that throws us into a circular argument: how does one State know if another entity is a State and to be dealt with as such?

The position makes more sense when one views this criterion as emphasizing the question of *capacity*. The very next Article in the Convention stipulates that 'the federal state shall constitute a sole person in the eyes of international law'. That gives a clue to its meaning. Component units of federal States, such as Texas, Ontario, and New South Wales, have permanent populations, defined territory, and effective governments, but they are not sovereign States in international law because they lack the capacity to act on the international plane. The conduct of foreign relations is a function of the federal government, not of provincial or state governments. If the Government of Scotland or of Texas were to violate some rule of international law, for example by imposing laws requiring unlawful discrimination, it would be the United Kingdom or the United States that would be responsible, and the matter would be handled through the British Government in Westminster or the federal Government in Washington DC. Accordingly, under the Montevideo Convention, although a political subdivision of a State may meet the first three criteria, it will not meet the fourth. If a subdivision were entitled to conduct

---

[20] Often misquoted as 'the capacity to enter into relations with other states', omitting the definite article, which appears in the definitive version of the text. See 165 *LNTS* 19.

foreign relations, it would be eligible to be a distinct State as a matter of international law, even if as a matter of constitutional law it was linked to, and in some respects subordinate to, another government or governments. Thus, Texas is not a sovereign State[21] as a matter of international law, but the constituent States of the European Union and of the Commonwealth of Independent States are. The fact that some provincial and other non-State units do in fact maintain international dealings does not invalidate this point. The Government of Quebec,[22] for example, maintains overseas delegations and has extensive dealings with foreign governments; but it is not treated by them as a sovereign State.

Occasionally this question of independence arises in respect of entities that do not purport to be parts of other States. The classic example is that of the *Bantustans* that formerly existed in South Africa, such as Transkei and Ciskei. The *apartheid* regime in South Africa declared these enclaves within South African territory to be 'independent' States, so as to push a large part of its black population beyond its legal borders. No other State in the world recognized them as States, because they were patently not independent. They were puppets of the South African Government.

In the case of the South African *Bantustans* that was not a difficult conclusion to reach. But how far does it go? What, for instance, of the provisions in the Compact of Free Agreement between the Marshall Islands and Micronesia and the United States which give the Government of the United States 'full authority and responsibility for security and defense matters in or relating to the Marshall Islands and the Federated States of Micronesia' and stipulate that in recognition of that authority and responsibility 'the Governments of the Marshall Islands and the Federated States of Micronesia shall consult, in the conduct of their foreign affairs, with the Government of the United States'? Can these States, which are Member States of the United Nations, properly be regarded as independent of the United States? Can the Marshall Islands, with its population of about 60,000 souls—under half the size of Oxford—maintain an effective independent foreign policy, operating in the United Nations and its agencies in New York, Geneva, and elsewhere? If so (and some awkward questions would arise in the General Assembly if the answer were, no), what does that say about the requirement of independence? It seems that the notion of independence is a highly legalistic

---

[21] Although it was from 1836 to 1845, prior to joining the United States of America. The Legation of the Republic of Texas was in St James's Street, and is now occupied by the wine merchants, Berry Brothers and Rudd.

[22] See the *Reference Re Secession of Quebec* (1998) 161 *DLR* (4th) 385; 115 *ILR* 536.

one, in contrast to the bold approach of the majority judgment (adopted by eight votes to seven) rendered by in the Permanent Court of International Justice when it was called upon to decide whether the 1931 Protocol providing for an Austro-German customs union violated the stipulation in the 1919 Treaty of Saint-Germain that 'the independence of Austria is inalienable'. The Court distinguished between the formal preservation of Austrian independence and the 'reality' of the position, and held that the customs union was calculated to threaten Austria's economic independence. The minority, in contrast, considered that the Protocol merely called for an assimilation of the tariff and economic policies of the two States, and for each State to see that the interests of the other were not violated by the conclusion of any treaty with a third State. The contrast between the two approaches is striking.[23]

Why has the international community apparently preferred the formal to the 'realist' approach to the question of independence? The main reason is historical. The modern law on Statehood was forged in the context of two great political shifts: the decolonization movement, and the break up of the Soviet empire, when more importance was attached to the right to independence than to the demand for internationally effective governments. These developments have modified the traditional criteria of Statehood.

4.15 LEGITIMACY

State practice has also developed so as to indicate that in addition to having a stable population, defined territory, effective government, and the capacity to engage independently in international relations, a candidate for Statehood is expected to satisfy an additional requirement of 'legitimacy'.

The main implication of the requirement of legitimacy is that the entity must have emerged towards Statehood in a manner that is consistent with the principle of self-determination. That explains why the Unilateral Declaration of Independence by the all-white minority Smith regime in the British colony of Southern Rhodesia in 1965 was not regarded as leading to the creation of a new State, even though it fulfilled all of the Montevideo criteria.[24] Only when adequate representation of the black majority population was secured did the country move to independent Statehood, as Zimbabwe, in 1970. Conversely, it is the inability of

---

[23] PCIJ, Ser. A/B, No. 41, at pp. 52–53, 83, 85.
[24] It might be said that it lacked independence, because as a matter of United Kingdom law it remained a (rebellious) colony. But the declaration of independence would have cured that, because there is no requirement that a new State should have come into existence in

international law to deny the right of self-determination to even the smallest colonies that seek it which explains the number of micro-States in the United Nations. While self-determination is an admirable principle on which to base the government of a territory, it is less clear that it is a good basis on which to structure international political and economic relations. The steady growth of regional political and economic groupings and organizations reflects the pull of reality: many micro-States lack the resources necessary to function both independently and effectively on the international stage.

It is sometimes suggested that there is a second aspect of legitimacy, a 'right to democracy'[25] and that an aspirant to Statehood will not be regarded as such if its government, no matter how 'effective' in its control of territory, is hopelessly undemocratic. Many jurists are not convinced that there is, or perhaps even that there should be, any such right; and rather more take the view that even if there were, it should not operate as a condition of Statehood. That is not to say that the appraisal of the nature of the government is of no significance. It will certainly affect the attitude of other States towards it, and significantly affect its chances of survival. This brings me to the question of recognition.

4.16 RECOGNITION: WHERE PRINCIPLE AND EXPEDIENCY MEET

There used to be a great doctrinal debate over the effect of recognition. If an entity fulfilled all of the criteria of Statehood but no-one recognized it as a State, would it be a State? The Montevideo Convention itself answered the question clearly:

Article 3

The political existence of the state is independent of recognition by the other states. Even before recognition the state has the right to defend its integrity and independence, to provide for its conservation and prosperity, and consequently to organize itself as it sees fit, to legislate upon its interests, administer its services, and to define the jurisdiction and competence of its courts.

The exercise of these rights has no other limitation than the exercise of the rights of other states according to international law.

    . . .

accordance with constitutional procedures which formerly applied to the territory. If there were, international law would be in a state of permanent denial regarding revolutionary change.

[25] See, e.g., 'Promotion of the right to democracy', Commission on Human Rights Resolution 1999/57.

Article 6

The recognition of a state merely signifies that the state which recognizes it accepts the personality of the other with all the rights and duties determined by international law. Recognition is unconditional and irrevocable.

In other words, Statehood was a 'fact'; and the act of recognition simply recognized the fact of the existence of a State.

But others took a different view. Some argued that recognition was a further criterion of Statehood, or implicit in the requirement of the capacity to enter into relations with other States. Others argued that the existence of the fact of Statehood had to be determined by someone, and that only States could make that determination, so that the 'fact' of a State's existence was established only when it was recognized. However it was explained, the point was that recognition was constitutive of Statehood, not merely declaratory of it.

It is now generally accepted that the declaratory theory is correct—that is, that it is the most accurate description of what goes on in State practice in relation to the recognition of States. The question was faced directly by the Arbitration Commission established in 1991 under the chairmanship of Robert Badinter, a distinguished lawyer and former French Justice Minister, to advise the European Communities on the grant of recognition to the constituent republics of the former Yugoslavia as that federation broke up. In a faintly medieval process, questions were posed to the Badinter Commission by Lord Carrington, chairman of the European conference on Yugoslavia. In the course of its response to one question the Commission stated unequivocally that 'the existence or disappearance of the State is a question of fact; . . . the effects of recognition by other States are purely declaratory'.[26] It went on to describe the conditions of Statehood and the relevance of the internal governmental structure. It said that it considered:

(b) that the State is commonly defined as a community which consists of a territory and a population subject to an organized political authority; that such a State is characterized by sovereignty;

(c) that, for the purpose of applying these criteria, the form of internal political organization and the constitutional provisions are mere facts, although it is necessary to take them into consideration in order to determine the Government's sway over the population and the territory.[27]

On this view the crucial question is the four traditional criteria (territory, population, government, sovereignty) are fulfilled. The question of the

[26] Opinion No. 1, 92 *ILR* 162.   [27] Opinion No. 1, 92 *ILR* 162.

internal structure and legitimacy of the government is relevant only to the question whether the nascent State is likely to last. But this injects one crucial element into the calculation. It is not enough for an entity to display the criteria of Statehood at the instant of its birth: it must be likely to survive.

A second element was reflected in the European Communities' 1991 Declaration on the Guidelines for the Recognition of New States in Eastern Europe and the Soviet Union. The operative part of the Declaration merits quotation in full:

The Community and its Member States confirm their attachment to the principles of the Helsinki Final Act[28] and the Charter of Paris,[29] in particular the principle of self-determination. They affirm their readiness to recognize, subject to the normal standards of international practice and the political realities in each case, those new States which, following the historic changes in the region, have constituted themselves on a democratic basis, have accepted the appropriate international obligations and have committed themselves in good faith to a peaceful process and to negotiations.

Therefore, they adopt a common position on the process of recognition of these new States, which requires:

— respect for the provisions of the Charter of the United Nations and the commitments subscribed to in the Final Act of Helsinki and in the Charter of Paris, especially with regard to the rule of law, democracy and human rights

— guarantees for the rights of ethnic and national groups and minorities in accordance with the commitments subscribed to in the framework of the CSCE[30]

— respect for the inviolability of all frontiers which can only be changed by peaceful means and by common agreement

— acceptance of all relevant commitments with regard to disarmament and nuclear non-proliferation as well as to security and regional stability

— commitment to settle by agreement, including where appropriate by recourse to arbitration, all questions concerning State succession and regional disputes.

---

[28] The 1975 Helsinki Final Act of the Conference on Co-operation and Security in Europe set out the basic principles for inter-State relations in Europe, then still locked in the Cold War. See 14 *ILM* 1292 (1975), and < http://www.osce.org/item/15661.html >.

[29] The Charter of Paris for a New Europe, 1990. See < http://www.osce.org/documents/mcs/1990/11/4045_en.pdf >. This great clarion call declares that the signatory States 'undertake to build, consolidate and strengthen democracy as the only system of government of our nations' and affirms the central importance of human rights and economic liberty. Largely ignored at the time of its adoption, future generations may see in it the clearest affirmation of the values of the North American-European community ('from Vancouver to Vladivostok') in the late twentieth century.

[30] The Conference on Co-operation and Security in Europe, now the Organization for Co-operation and Security in Europe. < http://www.osce.org/ >.

The Community and its Member States will not recognize entities which are the result of aggression. They would take account of the effects of recognition on neighbouring States.

The commitment to these principles opens the way to recognition by the Community and its Member States and to the establishment of diplomatic relations. It could be laid down in agreements.[31]

The Declaration is an interesting phenomenon. Recognition, the Badinter Commission had asserted, is declaratory; but still, someone must do the recognizing. The law lays down the criteria, but in this Declaration the States assert that their common position on recognition 'requires' indications concerning the good behaviour of aspirant States; and in doing so they impliedly affirm that recognition is a matter of discretion, something that they are entitled to withhold. Then the third step: they identify the factors relevant to the exercise of that discretion— though not committing themselves to anything other than the 'opening of the way' to recognition if the conditions are satisfied.

What is one to make of all this? Legally, the position may appear to be confused and unclear. The reality is more straightforward.

Recognition is undoubtedly a political instrument. When would-be States emerge in a non-consensual way from the territory of existing States, whether it be by attempted secession or by the break up of the former State, there is always a time during which it is unclear whether the attempt to establish the new State will succeed. The existing State will be resisting the attempted breakaway, often by the use of armed force or attempts to isolate the new entity politically and economically. During this period the attitude of third States is enormously important. If, say, the EU or the USA or Russia announces that it recognizes the new entity as a State and will give it economic or other assistance, it is much more likely to survive than if they all say that they will have nothing to do with it. That is one practical effect of recognition. A second practical effect is that recognition creates the possibility of formal diplomatic relations. It announces that the recognizing States are ready to deal on a State-to-State basis with the entity, exchanging diplomatic representatives, accepting it as a party to multilateral treaties, and so on. When the new State is widely recognized, it will no doubt apply for membership of the United Nations. The decision of the General Assembly, acting on the recommendation of the Security Council, on the admission of the entity as a Member State of the United Nations is in practice the definitive seal on the Statehood of the new State.

[31] 4 *EJIL* 72 (1993).

Recognition is, therefore, an important step. But timing is everything. Premature recognition, before the entity truly fulfils the criteria of Statehood, is not only legally incorrect, it amounts to intervention in the internal affairs of the State from which the new entity is attempting to break away. Among other legal effects, recognition of a seceding entity would convert a rebellion or civil war, which the former sovereign has every right to attempt to suppress, into an international conflict, in which third States should not intervene and in which the former sovereign would be bound by the UN Charter prohibitions on the threat or use of force. This was the difficulty that faced the European States as they watched the break up of the Former Yugoslavia. Some thought the recognition of Croatia and Slovenia premature, although most thought that the European States were simply recognizing the reality of the situation.

Recognition may, on the other hand, be unduly delayed even where the entity plainly meets the factual criteria for Statehood. Israel was not universally recognized as a State even after its admission to the United Nations in 1949. Denial of recognition might amount to the impeding of the right of a people to self-determination. There can be no real doubt, however, that an entity which meets the factual criteria of Statehood—population, territory, government, and independence—is entitled to the basic rights of a State, such as the right not to be attacked, and to be free from foreign intervention. Other rights that flow from participation in treaty regimes will, of course, be denied to it until such time as it is permitted to become a party to the relevant treaties. It will, therefore, have a diminished and lonely life: but not one entirely without legal rights. In short, one might say that recognition is declaratory of Statehood but constitutive of the possibility of participating fully in the international community.

Entities that meet the factual criteria of Statehood may endure for years without recognition. It seems, for example, that Somaliland is in this position; so, too, is Palestine. The reason is often that it is thought that recognition of the entity would not assist a durable solution to the problems of the area.

There have been many self-proclaimed States that have failed to meet even the basic criteria for Statehood. The names, mostly forgotten, given to these fantasies range from Abaco, an island in the eastern Bahamas where one Michael Oliver attempted to establish a libertarian State in 1973, to Zoutpansberg in what is now Mozambique, where João Albasini tried to establish a nation in the 1850s. If suitable land could not be found, the more determined nation-founders have sometimes built their own. Michael Oliver (the same) tried to establish the State of Minerva as a tax haven on a platform built on a submerged coral reef in the South Pacific in 1971; but he suffered a crushing defeat, reportedly at the hands of a Tongan prison work detail that had been sent out to pull down the Minervan flag.

There are also converse cases: entities that objectively appear to meet all the criteria of Statehood, but which seem not to wish to be a State. Taiwan is the classic example. Taiwan is the last stronghold of the nationalist Government of the Republic of China, pushed back during the Communist revolution. But the Taiwan Government regarded itself as the legitimate government of the whole of China and, indeed, occupied China's seat at the United Nations until 1971, when it was expelled and replaced by the Government of the People's Republic of China. Since then the question of independence or reunification with China has been controversial in Taiwan, which has not unequivocally asserted its separation from China. The People's Republic of China strongly opposes independence for what it regards as Taiwan Province, and third States have sought to avoid aggravating the dispute. Nonetheless, Taiwan has dealings with foreign States and international organizations very much like those of an independent State, and is represented abroad by (non-diplomatic missions). For instance, in the United States the CIA website—which places Taiwan out of order in its otherwise-alphabetical list of States, between Zimbabwe and the European Union—records that 'unofficial commercial and cultural relations with the people on Taiwan are maintained through an unofficial instrumentality—the American Institute in Taiwan (AIT)—which has offices in the US and Taiwan'.

The road to Statehood is a one-way street. Once an entity has become a State it will remain one, no matter how useless and ineffectual its government might become. In an article in 1934 Thomas Baty asked, 'Can an anarchy be a State?', and the answer under current doctrine is, yes.[32] Somalia, despite the anarchic conditions that obtain there and the lack of any real government, remains a State. While this position is doctrinally clear, it has been increasingly questioned in recent years. The idea of the 'failed State' has emerged, with the suggestion that if a State does collapse someone might have to step in to reconstitute it. Not surprisingly, there is concern that the label (which begs a great many questions as to what should count as a definitively 'failed State', as opposed to a State in difficulties) might easily become an excuse for foreign intervention and neocolonialism. It is difficult to see that the notion of a failed State does not imply the permissibility of some sort of intervention, of a kind that would

---

[32] Thomas Baty (see fn 10), 'Can an Anarchy be a State?', 28 *AJIL* 444 (1934). True to form, Baty thought that the answer should be, no.

be unlawful under the established principles of international law. On the other hand, the absence of any such right may cause serious difficulties. For example, the prohibition on the pursuit of pirates from the high seas into a State's territorial sea, or of criminals across a land frontier, derives from the duty not to infringe the sovereignty of the State into which they flee. The proper course is to allow that State to arrest them, or to seek its consent to pursuit. But if there is no functioning government in the State, neither possibility is available. Should the principles of State sovereignty and non-intervention stand, or should they be put aside to allow effective law enforcement? It is a difficult and troubling question; but one which has to be faced.

Any 'failure' in such cases would in any event almost certainly be the failure of the government rather than of the State. Governments come and go; but even if they come to power by unconstitutional means, such as a *coup*, the personality of the State is wholly unaffected. Other States have to decide whether they will have normal government-to-government dealings with the new regime; and this gives rise to questions of recognition similar to those concerning the recognition of States. Here, the element of political discretion is particularly pronounced, but the underlying approach in most cases is based on the principle of effectiveness. If the government is in effective control of the territory and of the machinery of the State, and is governing with the consent of (most of) the people, and appears willing to comply with its international obligations, it will generally be recognized—although many, perhaps most, States do not now make formal declarations of recognition of a foreign regime but simply decide on the nature of dealings that they are prepared to have with it. There may be a wide range of unofficial dealings, outside the normal channels of formal international diplomacy, even with an 'unrecognized' regime.

4.17 RECOGNITION AND STATEHOOD IN DOMESTIC LAW

I should say a little about the handling of questions of Statehood and recognition in domestic legal systems, because it is different from the approach adopted in international law and the differences cast an interesting light on the role of the courts in the conduct of foreign affairs. Each State will regulate these questions under its own national law, but the position in English law is broadly typical of that adopted in many States.

Recognition of a State is an act of great political significance. Municipal courts tend to avoid taking a position on the question, preferring to follow the Executive. If the Executive recognizes it, it is a State: if the Executive does not recognize it, it does not exist. Thus, the English courts refused to accept that the German Democratic Republic (GDR) was a State in 1967,[33] or that the South African *Bantustan* of Ciskei was a State in 1986,[34] because the Government provided Executive Certificates to the courts indicating that it had not recognized the entities. The so-called State could therefore not be a plaintiff, defendant, or otherwise a party to proceedings in English courts. Furthermore, the acts of the government of the purported State were in principle regarded as a nullity, because there was no State of which it could be the government. But the courts in those cases avoided the creating of legal blank spaces on the world map by treating the acts of the governments concerned as acts of the Soviet Union and of South Africa respectively. The *Carl Zeiss* decision on the GDR has been criticized as an artificial device to avoid the undesirable consequences of non-recognition; but that is not a fair criticism. Rightly or wrongly, it was generally perceived in the United Kingdom that the Government of the GDR was in fact directed by the authorities in Moscow, and that the authorities in Ciskei were in fact the puppets of Pretoria. The courts simply applied what appeared to many people at the time to be a common-sense solution, disturbing as that might appear to legal formalists.

Pragmatism has gone further in some circumstances. The one substantive section of the Foreign Corporations Act 1991 stipulates that a corporation having corporate status under the laws of a territory that is not a recognized State is nonetheless to be treated as a legal person if those laws are 'applied by a settled court system in that territory'. Had the Act been in force, corporations established under the laws of the GDR in the 1960s, or of Ciskei in the 1980s, would have been recognized as corporations with personality, capable of suing and being sued in English courts. The Act follows the approach of a dictum of Lord Denning in *Hesperides Hotels v Aegean Holidays Ltd*,[35] itself reflecting a much older line of authority in United States' courts suggesting that routine administrative acts of unrecognized entities should be given legal effect. That policy springs from the laudable belief that individuals should not suffer unnecessarily as a result of political upheavals. If effect is denied to, say, a divorce granted under laws enacted by an unrecognized government, people who thought themselves legally divorced under the laws of the country where they may have spent their whole lives could find themselves not divorced; and if

---

[33] *Carl-Zeiss-Stiftung v Rayner & Keeler Ltd* [1967] AC 853.
[34] *Gur Corp v Trust Bank of Africa (Government of the Republic of Ciskei, third party)* [1986] 3 All ER 449.
[35] [1978] QB 205.

they remarry, they might commit bigamy.[36] Better to allow such routine laws to be given effect, even if more 'political' laws, such as expropriatory decrees, are regarded as nullities.

The problems that arise from denying effect to the laws of an unrecognized State can arise also if laws are enacted or some other action is taken by an unrecognized government within a recognized State. This was the problem in the *Republic of Somalia* case.[37] The plaintiffs claimed to be the Government of Somalia and entitled to dispose of funds in England belonging to the Republic of Somalia. Prior to 1980 this question would have been answered in English Law by asking whether the regime had been recognized by the British Government as the government of Somalia. But in 1980 the United Kingdom announced[38] that it would no longer formally recognize governments, largely because formal recognition of regimes that had come to power unconstitutionally had sometimes been misinterpreted as a sign of approval by the United Kingdom, even though British doctrine regarded recognition as a matter of facing facts—if someone could give a convincing answer to the question, 'who's in charge here?' the United Kingdom would recognize them as the government, at least if they seemed likely to remain in charge for a while, whether or not it approved of them.[39] Under the new policy, which conforms with that adopted by most other States, the United Kingdom no longer formally recognizes the regime but simply decides what dealings, if any, it will have with the regime. The United Kingdom might, for example, refuse to have diplomatic relations with the regime, and oppose its participation in international conferences, but ask it for information or assurances concerning the safety of British citizens in the country. If a question arose as to whether the regime was in law the government of the State, it would be left to the courts to decide. The *Republic of Somalia* case sets out the approach that a court will follow in taking that decision. If the putative government is constitutionally appointed, there is no problem. If it is not, the court will look to 'the degree, nature and stability of administrative control' that the government exercises over the territory, the nature of any dealings that

---

[36] See *Adams v Adams* [1971] p. 188.

[37] *Republic of Somalia v Woodhouse Drake & Carey Suisse SA* [1993] QB 54, 94 *ILR* 608.

[38] Hansard, H L Debates, vol. 48, cols, 1121–22, 28 April 1980; 51 *BYIL* 367 (1980).

[39] There was a difference between *de facto* and *de jure* recognition of States and governments. As Brierly put it, 'Recognition *de facto* is provisional; it means that the recognizing government offers for the time being to enter into relations, yet ordinarily without cordiality, and without the usual courtesies of diplomacy.' : *The Law of Nations* (6th edn., Oxford: Oxford University Press, 1963), p. 147. *De jure* recognition signalled a belief that the State or government was 'lawfully established', and a proper member of international society, with whom cordial relations would not be inappropriate.

the British Government has with it, and in marginal cases the extent of international recognition that the government has been given. The views of the Executive are no longer determinative on these questions, although they will naturally be given considerable weight.

4.18 STATE SUCCESSION

When new States emerge (whether following decolonization or the break up of another State or in some other way, such as by the fusion of two States, or the transfer of part of one State into another) they come with a history: and there is an important question as to how much of that history binds them. Are they bound by treaties entered into in respect of their territory by the former sovereign? Do they have rights under such treaties? Are they entitled to a share of the wealth (and the debts) and the archives, of the former sovereign? These are the questions of State succession. They have acquired great importance in the context of the break-up of the former Soviet Union, Yugoslavia, and Czechoslovakia. The disposition of the Soviet warships and missiles, for instance, is one of the practical questions that has had to be addressed.

The law in this area is complex, and the rules vary according to the manner in which the new State emerges: States formed by absorption or merger of two previous States are not in the same position as States formed by the dismemberment of one predecessor State. There is a multilateral treaty dealing with some aspects of the question,[40] but much of the law remains unclear and controversial. Speaking broadly, it can be said that there is wide (but by no means unanimous) approval for the principle that successor States are not automatically bound by the treaties of their predecessors, except in the case of provisions defining borders, and perhaps other provisions that apply to specific locations so as to create, as it were, rights and duties *in rem*. The broad principle of succession to public property and debts is generally admitted, but questions of the extent to which that principle applies, the way that shares of debts and property should be calculated, and other such crucial matters, remain controversial.

This, then, is the State: a synthesis of people, territory, and government, which establishes a distinct public order in the exercise of its sovereign right to self-determination. In the next chapter I shall explain how that public order is put in place.

---

[40] The Vienna Convention on Succession of States in Respect of Treaties, 1978.

5

Inside the State

5.1 STATE JURISDICTION

The essence of a State lies in the entitlement of the handful of people who constitute the government, and the legislature (if that is not controlled by the government), of the State to force everyone within the State to do what the government want them to do. All sorts of groups and entities can tell us what to do in particular contexts. I could be excommunicated, dismissed by my employer, or refused treatment by my dentist. But only 'the State' can do all of this and in addition do anything else that it wishes, backing up its desires in relation to my behaviour by the threat that if I do not comply the police, court bailiffs, and if I am exceptionally resistant the armed forces, will coerce me into compliance—and, moreover, be regarded as acting *legitimately* when doing so. 'The State' shapes all aspects of our lives by what it compels us to do and what it leaves us free to choose. It may decide whether to adopt one State religion or to allow many or none; whether to allow private ownership and private enterprise or to place all economic activity directly in the hands of the State. It may mandate equality of treatment for the sexes or forbid it by imposing discriminatory laws. The choices are infinite, and the societies that governments construct differ subtly but importantly.

In a libertarian State the government can enforce its chosen constraints on the lives of individuals largely by action within its own borders; but only largely. If the State wishes to maintain active competition within the economy it may wish to ban cartel agreements which fix prices or divide up markets. But if the officers of companies based in the State can travel to a neighbouring State and incorporate a business and make such an agreement, a strictly territorial approach to regulation of the economy will not be effective. The government will need to regulate extra-territorial activity. But whose extra-territorial activity? If I am a citizen of the State, the government may decide that it is appropriate that I should obey the State's laws wherever I might be. But is that appropriate? There are good reasons why I should not participate in an extra-territorial cartel that aims to carve up the national market, and why I should not commit murder or marry bigamously abroad, but is there any reason why I should not buy cannabis, or guns, or disrespectful cartoons of the Prime Minister or the Prophet, if it is legal to do those things in the State where I happen to be? This is the question of the proper reach of a State's jurisdiction.

Jurisdiction is the right to prescribe and enforce rules against others. A State has 'prescriptive' or 'legislative' jurisdiction, which it exercises by enacting laws. Some laws establish rights (such as the right to welfare support) or duties (such as the duties to pay taxes, and not to steal, and not to operate cartels); others, such as the law of contract or family law, establish the conditions upon which individuals may themselves create certain rights and duties; yet other laws determine the status of persons or things (such as minors, 'goodwill', and intellectual property). Together the laws define, and in large measure constitute, the nature of a particular society. States also have 'enforcement jurisdiction', that is, the right to enforce their laws by deploying the police, courts, bailiffs, and other agencies in order to compel compliance with the law and punish non-compliance. The question for international law is how far the State's jurisdiction reaches.

Parents tend to have an instinctive sense of jurisdictional limits. If children misbehave in our houses, we feel entitled to tell them off. We feel entitled to reprimand children who stand outside our house throwing stones into it, and children inside throwing stones at people in the street outside, and to tell off our own children wherever they may be. And there are some activities of children so gross and unacceptable that we feel entitled to intervene, whoever and wherever the perpetrator might be. We do not, on the other hand, generally reprimand querulous and noisy children in supermarkets, no matter how great a contribution to the public good that would be; nor do we relieve them of lollipops and crisp packets, no matter how important that might appear to be in their fight against obesity. The police, however, may reprimand anyone, anywhere. Why should there be these differences?

There is plainly some concept of *interest*, of *locus standi*, at work here: a concept wrapped up in the idea of there being circumstances in which one may properly act and circumstances in which one should mind one's own business. The international law concept of jurisdiction maps on to my domestic analogy with remarkable accuracy.[1]

Let me begin by considering the limits of a State's legislative jurisdiction, its jurisdiction to prescribe laws. I shall use the language of the criminal

---

[1] This may reflect a deep structural characteristic of human social interaction; or it may be no more than a coincidence.

law to illustrate the points for the most part, although the principles apply to all 'public' laws that make up the public order of the State including, for example, tax and competition laws.

5.2 JURISDICTION OVER TERRITORY

The most obvious basis upon which a State exercises its jurisdiction is the territorial principle, that is, the principle that by virtue of its sovereignty over its territory the State has the right to legislate for all persons within its territory. And, as in the case of the stone-throwers, that jurisdiction extends to people (regardless of their nationality) inside the territory who engage in conduct that is consummated and has its main effects outside the territory. The bomb on Pan Am Flight 103 is said to have been loaded at the airport in Malta, and therefore within Malta's jurisdiction, even though the aircraft was American and the bomb exploded over Lockerbie in the United Kingdom. Conversely, acts initiated abroad that have effects within the territory—the stones thrown in from outside the garden—are within the jurisdiction of the territorial State. The United Kingdom had jurisdiction over the Lockerbie bombers, even though the bomb was put on board in Malta.[2]

Jurisdiction based upon the occurrence within the territory of one of the elements of which the crime (or other conduct) is made up is well established, but how far can this approach go? Customs laws have made it an offence for ships to enter the territorial sea having broken a bulk cargo into smaller packages (action which is usually the prelude to smuggling); and laws on lorry-drivers' maximum hours will take into account hours worked outside the territory. But what if it were made an offence for anyone 'to enter the country having consorted with terrorists'? That would amount to an assertion of jurisdiction over the worldwide acts of everyone who happened to set foot in the country. Such an approach could destroy the fundamental conception of municipal law as a territorial phenomenon, linked to the public order of a particular State.

Further problems arise where the link between the extra-territorial and intra-territorial conduct is more tenuous. Suppose that a number of corporations in Europe and Japan agree to fix the prices at which trucks are sold to buyers in Zimbabwe, but that they have no agents or active sales campaigns in that country, merely responding passively to orders that come from there. Could Zimbabwe properly assert jurisdiction over them,

---

[2] These two variants of territorial jurisdiction are known as 'subjective' and 'objective' territorial jurisdiction, respectively.

and criminalize the cartel? What if they agree not to supply customers in Zimbabwe at all, so that there is no activity within the State at all? And what if the cartel members were encouraged, but not obliged, by their national governments not to trade with Zimbabwe at the time? Or if their national governments had imposed mandatory sanctions against Zimbabwe?

Two issues are entwined in those questions. One is the proper reach of a State's laws; and the other is the question of how we should deal with cases where a State clearly has jurisdiction, but its exercise would conflict with freedoms, policies, or laws of other States. Let me start with the question, are such activities within the reach of a State's jurisdiction?

In the absence of any element of intra-territorial conduct, some States have asserted jurisdiction over conduct that 'has an effect' within the territory of the State. This 'effects doctrine' has been controversial, for instance when used by US authorities to break up cartels formed lawfully by non-US companies outside the United States. Some such cartels have been organized with the explicit approval and encouragement of the national States of the companies concerned, and the companies have engaged in no actual activity whatever within the United States; but because they affected world prices (which US consumers might have to pay) the cartels have been held to have an impact on the United States and so to fall within its jurisdiction.[3] While many States have protested against some uses of the effects doctrine, there is a growing acceptance of the need for some such extension of jurisdiction in order to regulate effectively the activities of transnational businesses. The emphasis has shifted from objections to unilateral exercises of jurisdiction and towards attempts to find a framework for international jurisdictional co-operation in the fields most affected.

5.3 MARITIME JURISDICTION

Territorial jurisdiction ordinarily applies within a State's land, sea, or air territory; but other areas are also subject to a State's jurisdiction. Seaward of its twelve-mile territorial sea, a State is entitled to exercise jurisdiction in three other zones. States may assert jurisdiction for customs, fiscal, sanitary, and immigration purposes in a contiguous zone that extends a further twelve miles seaward beyond the territorial sea. This is not part of the territory of the State: it is simply under its jurisdiction, and then only for the limited purposes stated. Though some States have claimed jurisdiction

---

[3] See A. V. Lowe, 'Blocking Extraterritorial Jurisdiction', 75 *American Journal of International Law* (1981), pp. 257–282.

for other purposes, such as security, in the contiguous zone those claims are widely regarded as unwarranted by international law and accordingly ineffective to impose obligations on foreign ships in the area.

Contiguous zones have to be claimed but the second major maritime zone, the continental shelf, exists automatically by operation of law. It gives coastal States exclusive rights over the exploration and exploitation of the natural resources of the seabed seaward of the territorial sea out to the limit of the geomorphological continental margin. The continental shelf, as a legal institution, was created by the development in customary international law that began with the 1945 Truman Proclamation; but it is now largely subsumed within the third major maritime zone, the exclusive economic zone (EEZ), which extends 200 miles from the coast and is the centrepiece of the 1982 UN Convention on the Law of the Sea. In the EEZ the coastal State is entitled to claim exclusive jurisdiction to regulate the exploration and exploitation of all resources, including fish, oil, gas, and gravel. Coastal States may also assert jurisdiction over marine pollution and scientific research in the EEZ.

5.4 JURISDICTION OVER NATIONALS

Jurisdiction almost certainly began as a personal, rather than a territorial, link. Individuals would owe allegiance to a king or other leader and he in turn would owe them a duty of protection. As his subjects they would be subject to his jurisdiction, bound to abide by the commands that he issued. In very early English law, for example, the King's Peace appears to have been a local phenomenon, attaching originally to certain places such as the King's court and the great highways.[4] Anyone breaking the peace could be brought before the King's justices and punished. Only later did royal control become so extensive and pervasive that the entire realm was regarded as being within the King's Peace. In international law terms we would say that jurisdiction based on nationality preceded jurisdiction based on territoriality.

The jurisdiction of a State over its own nationals is well established in international law but rarely used, because States generally have little interest in what their nationals do outside the State. In English law, bigamy, murder, and a handful of other offences may be committed by nationals

---

[4] The extent was defined by some curious formulae. 'The king's peace shall extend thus far from his gate, where he is in residence, in all four directions from that place, that is to say, three miles, three furlongs, the breadth of three acres, nine feet, the breadth of nine hands and nine grains of barley': L.J. Downer (ed. and trans.), *Leges Henrici Primi* (Oxford: Oxford University Press, 1972), p. 121.

extra-territorially. One important variety of nationality jurisdiction gives States jurisdiction over all ships and aircraft that sail or fly under the State's flag. This is sometimes treated as a kind of quasi-territorial jurisdiction; but it is better to regard it as a quasi-national jurisdiction in order to resist the temptation to regard ships and aircraft as pieces of floating or flying territory of the State, which they are not. Not all laws that apply within a State's territory will necessarily apply to its ships and aircraft. There is a presumption in English and American law, for example, that statutes apply only within territorial limits. If statutes are to apply beyond those limits, for example to aircraft in flight, this must be stipulated.

National jurisdiction is particularly important in places beyond the territorial jurisdiction of any State. The three main examples are the high seas beyond the limits of maritime zones claimed by States, Antarctica (which, under the 1959 Antarctic Treaty, may not be appropriated by any State),[5] and outer space. If jurisdiction is to be exercised in these places it must be on some basis other than territoriality. The practice is to subject ships and aircraft on the high seas, and spacecraft in outer space, to the exclusive jurisdiction of the State of registry, and to attach a nationality to camps and expeditions in Antarctica so as to reinforce the possibility of the exercise of national jurisdiction.

One recurrent problem arises from attempts to assert jurisdiction over foreign branches and corporate affiliates of domestic corporations. For example, the US sanctions imposed upon Libya in 1986 included a freeze on Libyan assets in 'the possession or control of US persons including overseas branches of US persons'.[6] The freeze applied to Libyan funds held in a London branch of a US bank, Bankers Trust, which was bound under English law to pay monies out of the account on Libya's instructions and bound under US law not to pay out those monies. The English court affirmed the bank's duty to pay, and a potentially embarrassing conflict between the British and American authorities was averted by a US Treasury decision to license Bankers Trust to make the payment. The episode illustrates both the potential reach of the nationality principle and the problems that arise where the rules applicable to nationals conflict with those applicable under the territorial principle.

Some States apply a variant of national jurisdiction known as 'passive personality' jurisdiction, under which the State may apply its laws to persons who injure its nationals. For instance, a US citizen who injures a Greek

---

[5] National claims to segments of Antarctica that predated the 1959 Antarctic Treaty were suspended by the Treaty.

[6] *Libyan Arab Foreign Bank v Bankers Trust Co.* [1989] QB 728.

citizen in a road traffic accident in New York might be made subject to Greek law, and summoned to defend his action before Greek courts.[7] The convenience of this for tourists and others injured abroad is evident; but it must be startling to receive a summons from a State in which one may never have set foot to answer a charge of injuring one of its nationals. It is a form of legal imperialism; and the validity of this basis of jurisdiction is controversial, and it is rarely relied upon in practice. To the extent that safeguarding the interests of nationals travelling abroad is an important social goal, one wonders whether it is not better met by travel insurance.

5.5 PROTECTIVE JURISDICTION

Territoriality and nationality are not the only bases of jurisdiction. Every State has jurisdiction over conduct, wherever and by whomever it is carried out, that threatens its essential security interests. For long this basis was narrowly construed, covering offences such as the counterfeiting of the State's currency and other serious threats to the State's existence. But in the 1980s States began to use it as a basis for the assertion of extra-territorial jurisdiction over drug-traffickers and other attempts to subvert customs and immigration laws.[8] In the present climate this convenient facility for extending the jurisdiction of the State is likely to prove increasingly attractive to governments.

Treaties addressing various aspects of terrorism have already moved in this direction.[9] For example, Article 9(2) of the 2005 Convention on Nuclear Terrorism, having affirmed States' jurisdiction over offences in their territory or on their ships and aircraft, provides that:

A State Party may . . . establish its jurisdiction over any such offence when:
- (*a*) The offence is committed against a national of that State; or
- (*b*) The offence is committed against a State or government facility of that State abroad, including an embassy or other diplomatic or consular premises of that State; or
- (*c*) The offence is committed by a stateless person who has his or her habitual residence in the territory of that State; or
- (*d*) The offence is committed in an attempt to compel that State to do or abstain from doing any act; or
- (*e*) The offence is committed on board an aircraft which is operated by the Government of that State.

---

[7] See, e.g., the *Digest of United States Practice in International Law 1975*, p. 339.

[8] See, e.g., *US v Gonzalez*, 776 F. 2d 931 (1985).

[9] See <http://www.un.org/terrorism/instruments.html>.

Paragraph (a) is an application of the passive personality principle, uncontroversial here because it is established by agreement. Paragraph (c) is an extension of nationality jurisdiction, albeit arguably unnecessary: if a State were to assert jurisdiction over a stateless person, there would by definition be no State that could object that its rights had been violated. But paragraphs (b), (d), and (e) are more noteworthy here. They address what might be called the *Achille Lauro* problem. In 1985 an Italian cruise ship in Egyptian waters was hijacked by terrorists supporting the Palestinian cause. They killed one of the passengers, Leon Klinghoffer, who was a United States citizen and Jewish. The hijackers were trying to bring pressure upon Israel to release Palestinian prisoners. Whereas Egypt (as the territorial State) and Italy (as the State of registry of the ship) had jurisdiction over the hijacking, the State against whom the attack was primarily directed—Israel—had no jurisdiction over the hijacking under the established bases of jurisdiction in international law. Paragraphs (b), (d), and (e) above provide, as between the States Parties, a basis upon which targeted States that cannot assert jurisdiction based on territoriality or nationality may rely. Such developments in treaty law may foster a parallel development in customary international law, perhaps as an extension of the protective principle.

5.6 UNIVERSAL JURISDICTION

Some crimes are regarded as so serious that all mankind has a legitimate interest in repressing them, and all States have the right under international law to criminalize them and to put alleged offenders on trial. That, in essence, is what universal jurisdiction is. Piracy is the archetypal example and it illustrates another part of the rationale for universal jurisdiction, which is the difficulty faced by any one State in apprehending suspected offenders. On the high seas, where ships are in principle subject to the jurisdiction only of their flag State (so that, for example, Spain could not arrest a pirate ship flying the Dutch flag if it was outside Spanish waters), the problems were clear. Crimes against humanity, serious war crimes, and genocide are also generally regarded as falling within the principle, and possibly torture and slavery, too.[10] The United Kingdom asserts universal jurisdiction over the offence of knowingly causing a nuclear explosion without authorization.[11]

---

[10] See the Princeton Principles on Universal Jurisdiction, 2001, <http://www1.umn.edu/humanrts/instree/princeton.html>.

[11] See the Anti-terrorism, Crime and Security Act 2001, ss. 47, 51.

While the existence of a category of offences subject to universal jurisdiction is firmly established, its scope, and the persons to whom it applies, is controversial. Courts in a number of European States have asserted jurisdiction on this basis over foreign government officials accused of torture and crimes against humanity, and have named other officials as witnesses in the proceedings. The result, as General Pinochet found, is that foreign travel may end in arrest on very serious criminal charges relating to acts committed in their home State. Some States whose officials face these charges have protested. (If their home government positively wished to prosecute its officials for their misdeeds, it is likely to have taken action itself.) They object that exposure to arrest impedes the movement of officials, and that charges against government ministers or Heads of State violate their immunity. Several cases objecting to the exercise of jurisdiction by European courts in these circumstances have come before the International Court.[12] In the *Arrest Warrant of 11 April 2000 (Democratic Republic of the Congo v Belgium)* case, the Court held that the arrest warrant issued against the incumbent Minister for Foreign Affairs of the Congo did not respect his immunity from criminal jurisdiction under international law, and Belgium was ordered to cancel the warrant.

Those cases in the International Court illustrate the political friction that can be generated by exercises of universal jurisdiction; but another, more fundamental, issue must also be considered. Criminal law serves the interests of a community. Not all laws are enforced with equal vigour all of the time. Sometimes the police may direct particular effort into action against drugs or knife crime, or into completing their paperwork, and turn a blind eye to other crimes, such as prostitution or traffic offences. They will usually be guided by the wishes of the community that they serve, expressed through a Police Committee or some similar system for political control and accountability. The exercise of universal jurisdiction may detach the decision concerning the desirability of prosecuting a particular offence from the community most affected by it, and transfer the discretion to prosecute to a foreign authority which may know little of circumstances in the State directly affected and understand even less. This is also an objection against the establishment of international criminal courts with prosecutorial discretion. Some issues need to be addressed internationally,

---

[12] In 2000, the Congo filed a claim against Belgium in the case of *Arrest Warrant of 11 April 2000 (Democratic Republic of the Congo v Belgium)*, *ICJ Reports 2002*, p. 3. The case of *Certain Criminal Proceedings in France (Republic of the Congo v France)*, was filed in 2002, and in 2007 Rwanda filed a claim against France relating to warrants issued by French courts in connection with the shooting down in 1994 of an aircraft carrying the Heads of State of Rwanda and Burundi.

rather than by each State, because it is the essence of universal jurisdiction that it should serve an agreed community interest and not simply the particular interests of any individual State: but who determines the community interest?

5.7 OTHER EXTRA-TERRITORIAL EXTENSIONS OF JURISDICTION

Legislators try to draft laws that are not easily circumvented, and sometimes frame laws in ways that do not fit within any of the established bases of jurisdiction. There was for many years a tiresome, and in my view fatuous, debate over the question whether a State claiming jurisdiction on some novel basis is obliged to justify its claim, or whether those opposing it are obliged to prove that international law specifically prohibits the claim in question. But there is no recorded instance of a State attempting to prove the existence of such a prohibitive rule, and it would be astonishing if there were. If a State seeks to apply its law to persons or conduct which appear to have no real connection with the State, other States are entitled to ask what right it has to do so. Thus, in 1982, when the US tried to prevent the acquisition of militarily valuable US technology by the Soviet Union, making it a criminal offence for anyone, anywhere, to export to the Soviet Union goods containing more than a certain proportion of components or technology of US origin, European States objected. The main European Community protest—the 'Comments' of 12 August 1982[13]—are a classic statement of opposition to excessive jurisdictional claims.

One of the most extraordinary jurisdictional claims ever made is that contained in the US Military Order of 13 November 2001, which sought to prohibit the making of *habeas corpus* and similar applications to foreign or international courts on behalf of the individuals incarcerated in the United States' base at Guantanamo Bay, Cuba. The Order stipulated that:

the individual shall not be privileged to seek any remedy or maintain any proceeding directly or indirectly, or to have any such remedy or proceeding sought on the individual's behalf, in (i) any court of the United States, or any State thereof, (ii) any court of any foreign nation, or (iii) any international tribunal.[14]

Peace groups in, say, the remotest villages of West Wales could violate that Order merely by asking the Inter-American Court of Human Rights,[15] or

---

[13] 21 *ILM* 891 (1982).

[14] <http://www.whitehouse.gov/news/releases/2001/11/print/20011113-27.html>.

[15] Which, to its credit, acted anyway: see 41 *ILM* 532 (2002). And see the decision of the US Supreme Court in *Rasul v Bush* 542 US 466 (2004).

the UN Human Rights Committee to take up the question of the legality of the detention of the Guantanamo prisoners.

5.8 TREATY-BASED JURISDICTION

Despite the resistance to excessive jurisdictional claims, there is a general recognition that territorial jurisdiction is an inadequate basis for regulating problems of the modern world such as international crime, terrorism, cartelization, and pollution. But it is also appreciated that no matter how wide it casts its jurisdictional net no single State or small group of States can effectively regulate matters without the co-operation of other States. The emphasis is firmly upon international co-operation, secured by treaty agreements which allocate jurisdiction and responsibility among States Parties.

Co-operation of this kind exists in many fields. The fight against terrorism is one prominent example. A set of treaties[16] deals with various aspects and manifestations of terrorist activity, ranging from aerial hijacking to hostage-taking, nuclear terrorism, and terrorist financing. The general pattern is that each State Party agrees to criminalize conduct specified in the Convention and to assert jurisdiction over such crimes as are committed in its territory or on one of its ships or aircraft or by one of its nationals. States Parties also assert jurisdiction over those crimes if they are committed by a person found within its territory whom the State does not extradite to another State Party having jurisdiction over the crime. In this way a kind of treaty-based universal jurisdiction is established between the Parties.

Under such treaties States are obliged either to extradite persons within their territory accused of the crime, or to submit the case to their own authorities for the purposes of prosecution: this is the '*aut dedere, aut judicare*' obligation. The Conventions thus address a number of different aspects of the problem: they stipulate which bases of jurisdiction must be applied by States Parties to the Convention crimes, (and may also list further, optional bases of jurisdiction), and so ensure that there is no jurisdictional gap which might prevent the prosecution of an alleged offender; they oblige States to act in respect of suspects found within their territory; and they establish a basis for the international transfer of accused persons through the mechanisms of extradition.

---

[16] See <http://www.un.org/terrorism/instruments.html>.

5.9 COMPETING AND CONFLICTING JURISDICTION

The co-existence of various bases upon which legislative jurisdiction might be exercised creates the possibility of competing and conflicting claims to jurisdiction. In the *Achille Lauro* hijacking both Egypt and Italy had jurisdiction, and jurisdiction might have been claimed by other States, such as the national State(s) of the hijackers and—in the view of some States—the national States of the victims. Any of these States could try the accused, if it managed to apprehend them.

5.10 EXTRADITION AND LEGAL CO-OPERATION

If an accused person is detained by one State, another State having jurisdiction over the alleged offence may seek his extradition. Though they are entitled to do so, most States will not extradite suspects unless they have an extradition treaty with the requesting State. The need for a treaty, as a matter of the law or policy of the requested State, usually flows from a desire to ensure that no-one is sent to face imprisonment and trial in another State without a showing of some cause (normally a *prima facie* case against the accused) and without giving the person concerned an opportunity to apply to a court to oppose the extradition. This process has been subverted by the 'irregular rendition' of persons by covert flights, apparently organized by the United States with the complicity of other States in Europe and elsewhere, between secret detention facilities. The numbers and identities of the persons, and the evidence and charges (if any) against them, were not publicly known, and they were effectively beyond the protection of the law.

Extradition law varies from State to State but some common principles appear in most extradition treaties.[17] Extradition is available only for serious offences, as defined in the treaty. Under the 'double criminality' principle, extradition is granted only if the conduct with which the accused is charged would amount to an offence under the laws of both the requesting and the requested State. If extradition is granted, the 'speciality' principle stipulates that the person may be tried only for offences listed in the extradition warrant unless the requested States consents to other charges, and the person must have the opportunity to leave the State after trial and sentence before any further charges are brought. The laws of some States, such as Russia, forbid the extradition of their nationals.

---

[17] In the European Union a European Arrest Warrant has replaced extradition procedures.

In the nineteenth century international support for revolutionary freedom-fighters in various States led to the development of the 'political offence' exception, according to which extradition would be refused if it was sought for political reasons such as the punishment of opposition politicians, or in respect of a political offence, such as criticizing the government. This creates difficulties in handling extradition requests in respect of alleged terrorists. Their offences are archetypically 'political', but some of their methods lie far beyond the limits of tolerable conduct. The solution is international (but not universal) agreement that certain crimes, such as indiscriminate bombings, will not be treated as political crimes for extradition purposes. The 1977 European Convention on the Suppression of Terrorism, adopted during the days of ETA, the IRA, and the Baader-Meinhof Group and Brigate Rosse, is a prominent early example.

In addition to the network of bilateral and regional extradition agreements, there are also networks of treaties on judicial co-operation, and on co-operation between law enforcement agencies. These are generally designed to facilitate the obtaining and exchange of information and evidence. On the global plane, for example, the United Nations Crime and Justice Information Network and the United Nations Office on Drugs and Crime provide the focus for a good deal of international co-operation, as does the better-known Interpol. There is also an extensive and well-used network for international assistance in judicial co-operation in non-criminal matters.

This is an appropriate point at which to mention the growth of international criminal law. States do not always wish to try or to punish suspected criminals, no matter how serious their offences. They may wish to draw a line under the past; they may sympathize with the criminal; they may fear that a trial would generate serious domestic unrest. But it may be thought by some, within the State or elsewhere, that the perpetrators of the offences should not escape trial. There is a deep social need, epitomized by the work of the Nuremburg Tribunal, to prove, document, and record heinous wrongdoing, so that the victims can tell their story and the facts cannot later be denied, and so that those found guilty should not escape condemnation and punishment. This is the thinking behind the establishment of the international criminal courts.

Two *ad hoc* international courts were established by the Security Council to try those accused of serious crimes in the Former Yugoslavia and in Rwanda. Elsewhere, courts have been established on a different model—the tribunals in Cambodia and Sierra Leone, for example, are hybrid national/international tribunals, with a combination of national and international judges but integrated into the national legal system. The International Criminal Court (ICC) itself, established under the 1998 Rome Statute, is the first standing international criminal tribunal. Its role is complementary to that of national criminal courts: it will be the forum for prosecutions only in instances where national courts are not themselves handling the case, and in this way any State can keep cases out of the ICC by prosecuting them itself. Nevertheless, the ICC has been strongly opposed by the United States because US personnel are particularly exposed to the Court, given the extent of US military operations and participation in international peacekeeping around the world. The US has, moreover, insisted that many States sign agreements not to hand over United States personnel to the ICC. The ICC is now beginning its work, but it is unlikely ever to wrest large numbers of cases from national courts.

5.11 RESOLVING JURISDICTIONAL CONFLICTS

Where competing jurisdictions collide it has been necessary to devise some way of resolving the conflict. There is some support for the view that as a general rule the State asserting jurisdiction on the basis of territoriality should have preference over those relying on, say, nationality; but that is of little assistance in circumstances where a number of States appear to have an important and equal interest in asserting jurisdiction. Three broad approaches have been adopted to these more difficult jurisdictional conflicts.

First, courts have sought to exercise principled self-restraint in asserting jurisdiction. The United States' courts, in cases such as *Hartford Fire Insurance Co. v California*, have laid down principles that indicate the circumstances in which they should refrain from exercising jurisdiction and should leave a matter to be regulated by the authorities in another State. Not surprisingly, given the oath that judges take to uphold their national law, this approach has not led to any significant retrenchment of jurisdictional claims—although sensitivity on the part of courts to the rights and interests of other States is welcome. A second approach has been to try to harmonize national laws so as to eliminate the substantive policy conflicts that make the abstract phenomenon of overlapping jurisdiction problematic. In the area of competition law, where divergences in national policies have in the past been particularly troublesome, there has been a clear convergence of policies in recent years, assisted by progress in securing international agreement over trade matters generally. And third, there are international agreements which address jurisdictional conflict

directly, providing procedures for the negotiated settlement of cases
where there is a clash of regulatory requirements. The 1991 EC/US
Competition Co-operation Agreement and 1998 EC/US Positive Comity
Agreement are examples.[18]

5.12 ENFORCING JURISDICTION

In addition to a State's legislative jurisdiction, its right to prescribe laws,
there is the question of the right to enforce laws by arresting, trying, and
punishing people. The exercise of enforcement jurisdiction is an exercise
of State sovereignty, and the rule that governs it is simple. No State may
exercise its enforcement jurisdiction in the territory of another State
without that State's permission. So, if a suspect escapes over the border
into a neighbouring State, high-speed chases by police cars must stop; and
if the police wish to get the suspect back they must fill in the forms necessary for an extradition application. So clear and fundamental is this
principle that courts of one State will not even enforce the penal laws
of another State, because to do so would be to promote an exercise of sovereignty by another State in the territory of the forum.[19]

There are agreements which permit the authorities of one State to pursue and arrest suspects in places within the jurisdiction of another State.
In the Caribbean, for example, there are 'shiprider' agreements, under
which US law-enforcement officers may be stationed on the police or
naval vessels of another Caribbean State, or may pursue suspects into the
territory and territorial sea of the other State.[20] There is a similar regional
agreement, the 2003 Agreement concerning Co-operation in Suppressing
Illicit Maritime and Air Trafficking in Narcotic Drugs and Psychotropic
Substances in the Caribbean Area (the Aruba Convention).

5.13 IMMUNITIES

There are limitations upon the exercise of a State's jurisdiction over
certain persons. Diplomats, though obliged to obey the laws of the States
to which they are accredited, may not be arrested. Their immunity is one
of the oldest of rules of international law, now enshrined in the 1961

---

[18] See <http://ec.europa.eu/comm/competition/international/bilateral/background/
us1_en.html>.

[19] See *Huntington v Attrill* [1893] AC 150; *Rio Tinto Zinc Corporation v Westinghouse Electric
Corporation* [1978] AC 547.

[20] See the 2007 International Narcotics Control Strategy Report, <http://www.state.gov/
documents/organization/80968.pdf>.

Vienna Convention on Diplomatic Relations and the 1963 Vienna Convention on Consular Relations. Heads of State and of government, and some others such as foreign ministers, enjoy a similar immunity. The rationale is that immunity from a State's enforcement jurisdiction is necessary in order to prevent the harassment of diplomats and ministers, impeding the discharge of their official duties and the conduct of international relations. More limited immunity is enjoyed by minor officials and employees and family members.

If a diplomat is suspected of having committed an offence or of engaging in activities incompatible with their status, he may be declared *persona non grata* and be expelled from the receiving State. Many suspected spies have been expelled in this way over the years. Once a person ceases to be a diplomat he loses his entitlement to immunity, except in respect of his official acts, for which the immunity persists.

States also enjoy immunity from enforcement jurisdiction, in this case based on the rationale that because States are equal sovereigns no State can be obliged to submit to the jurisdiction of another's courts, although States are free to submit if they choose. Whereas diplomatic immunity is tied to the discharge of the diplomat's functions, the different rationale of State (or sovereign) immunity led naturally to the conclusion that the immunity was absolute. As States engaged increasingly in commerce, however, it was thought that they should be subject to the same rules as other traders. Accordingly, a doctrine of restricted immunity arose, limited to the non-commercial acts of governments. It was given effect in English law by the rightly celebrated judgment of the Court of Appeal in the *Trendtex* case, and codified and consolidated in the State Immunity Act 1978. Under the Act it is presumed that foreign States are immune from the jurisdiction of English courts, but that immunity is withdrawn in specified circumstances, including non-commercial transactions and the causing of death or personal injury or damage to property by acts or omissions in the United Kingdom. Even if the State can, under one of the statutory exceptions, be brought before the court (or chooses to submit to the jurisdiction of the court), it remains immune from the exercise of enforcement powers. It cannot be fined or have its representatives imprisoned, and execution may not be levied against its property except in respect of property that is used for 'commercial purposes'.

The State Immunity Act does not apply to criminal law, and there is much discussion as to the extent to which States are immune from actions in respect of serious breaches of international criminal law, such as the crimes of genocide and torture. The *Pinochet* litigation established that immunity has its limits, and that the immunity of former Heads of State does not extend to acts of official torture. The rationale of the House of Lords' decision in that case[21] is not wholly clear, with their Lordships producing a range of different explanations for their decision. Subsequently, in the case of *Jones v Saudi Arabia* the House of Lords made it plain that the *Pinochet* decision should be understood in the context of the specific provisions of the 1984 Torture Convention, and not as an instance of a general principle that immunity does not subsist in respect of grave crimes and breaches of fundamental human rights.

5.14 OTHER LIMITATIONS ON THE EXERCISE OF A STATE'S JURISDICTION

Immunities under international law are the clearest limitation upon the exercise by a State of its jurisdiction, but they are not the only limitation. There are other things that a State is forbidden by international law to do, which go to the question of legislative as well as enforcement jurisdiction.

The most obvious example is the international law of human rights. There are rights that are regarded as being so fundamental, so much a necessary part of what it is to be a human being, that they can never be denied or withdrawn. Indeed, one might regard them as being not merely rights of individuals but as limitations upon the legal power of governments.

The substantive provisions of international human rights law are mostly set out in treaties. The centrepiece is the so-called International Bill of Human Rights, which consists of the 1948 Universal Declaration of Human Rights, the 1966 International Covenant on Economic, Social and Cultural Rights, and the 1966 International Covenant on Civil and Political Rights and its two Optional Protocols. Many other treaties also set international standards: for example, the Conventions on Genocide, on Refugees, on the Elimination of Discrimination against Women, and on the Rights of the Child. Regional agreements, such as those in Europe, the Americas, and Africa, overlay the global texts, as do sectoral agreements such as those adopted by the International Labour Organization to protect people in the context of employment. In addition, there are agreements that stipulate rights not for individuals but for groups of people, such as the 1992 European Charter for Regional or Minority Languages, and the 1995 European Convention for the Protection of National Minorities. Not all of the provisions of these treaties have passed into customary international law; many bind only the States Parties, but

---

[21] *R v Bow Street Metropolitan Stipendiary Magistrate, ex parte Pinochet Ugarte (No. 3)* [2000] 1 AC 147.

nevertheless impose a significant limitation upon what a State may do in exercising its jurisdiction.

Supervisory mechanisms exist under a number of the Conventions, which establish bodies to which reports must be made and which monitor the implementation of the Convention and compliance with its provisions. Their reports have a powerful political impact, but the committees are not courts and they do not have enforcement powers. The European Convention on Human Rights, and its Inter-American and African equivalents function in a more traditionally judicial fashion, hearing particular complaints. It is also possible under the domestic laws of some States to sue for breaches of international human rights obligations. The most famous example is the Alien Tort statute in the United States, under which those injured by violations of the Law of Nations may initiate claims. That statute is, however, something of an historical anomaly (it was enacted in 1789), and it is interpreted narrowly, so as to apply to a very limited range of customary international law rights.[22]

Finally I should mention the international minimum standard of treatment for aliens. Every State is obliged to accord a basic minimum level of protection to aliens and their property within its territory. States must take reasonable steps to preserve the safety of aliens, so that measures that exposed them to particular risks, for example, by inflaming racial hatred, would violate international law. States may not expropriate alien property except on a non-discriminatory basis, for a public purpose, and against proper compensation, for another example. The notion of what 'proper' compensation is has been controversial, but it is now generally accepted that it must reflect the market value of the property taken and be paid at the time of the taking or shortly afterwards and in a convertible currency. Laws that do not fulfil these criteria will violate international law. These substantive limitations upon States' powers are being supplemented by international standards set out in multilateral treaties on a wide range of subjects—the control of trade in narcotics is one instance—so as to create what is in effect an agreed, 'contractual' supplement to the standards of public order, by which States Parties are bound. Such agreements are an increasingly important component of the public orders of the States in which we live and travel. Together with the limitations on States' jurisdiction they set the constraints within which governments may impose their rules upon the world.

---

[22] *Sosa v Alvarez-Machain*, 159 L. ED. 2d 718 (2004).

6

The Global Economy

6.1 INTRODUCTION

Around the turn of the millennium the British Government published two reports: *Eliminating World Poverty: A Challenge for the 21st Century* (1997), and *Eliminating World Poverty. Making Globalization Work for the Poor* (2000).[1] They noted that around 1,300,000,000 people, almost one in four of the world's population, live in abject poverty, on less than $1 a day. Britain's goal was to halve that proportion by 2015. The 1997 report identified two necessary elements for the achievement of that goal: an agreed set of international policies and principles which promote sustainable development and environmental conservation, and the political will to deal with global poverty. The 2000 report identified further elements, including improved health and education, technical assistance, flows of private investment, more open trade, sustainable development, and effective action against corruption.

The idea that international law has a significant role in the redistribution of wealth on an international scale dates back no more than a few decades. There have been grandiose attempts to reform the global economic order. The Charter of Economic Rights and Duties of States is the outstanding example. Adopted by the UN General Assembly in 1974 as resolution 3281 (XXIX),[2] the Charter sought to 'promote the establishment of the new international economic order, based on equality, sovereign equality, interdependence, common interest and co-operation among all States, irrespective of their economic and social systems', in order to create the conditions for 'the attainment of wider prosperity among all countries and of higher standards of living for all peoples'. The provisions of the Charter had little effect, but attention was increasingly focused on the role of international law in international economic relations.

[1] Cm 3789 (1997) and Cm 5006 (2000).
[2] By a majority of 120 votes to 6 with 10 abstentions (the opponents and abstainers including the leading economies in Europe, Canada, Japan, and the USA).

That role is facilitative: there is no sense in which international law requires States to redistribute wealth or establish fairer terms of international trade. International law is simply the means by which States resolved to do those things can establish a robust framework of commitments to do so. When they create such a framework, they transform the stage. It ceases to be an area in which action is dictated by the free play of foreign policies and the laws of the market and becomes an area governed by rules and procedures. As the 2000 report put it, 'where there are no rules, the rich and powerful bully the poor and the powerless. In a globalising world, poor countries need effective, open and accountable global institutions where they can pursue their interests on more equal terms'.

Until the middle of the twentieth century, the involvement of international law in trade matters was essentially confined to the tasks of ensuring access for the major industrial States to foreign markets, and to protecting the investments made in foreign States by investors from industrialized States. The shameful episode of the Opium Wars of 1839 to 1842 and 1856 to 1860 epitomizes this insalubrious phase of legal history. British armed forces forced the opening up of China to British trade, with the particular aim of exporting opium to China.[3] The opium trade was an essential element in Britain's colonial enterprise, paying for British imports of tea and silk. Britain was said to be shipping one ton of opium each day from India to Chinese ports prior to the Chinese ban on opium imports in 1839. In the treaties of Nanjing (1842), Tianjin (1858), and Beijing (1860) China was forced to open up certain named 'treaty ports' to foreign traders and to accept imports of opium once more, in what was widely trumpeted as a victory for free trade.

In the Chinese Wars we see international law used to draw a cloak of legitimacy over policies imposed by force: the overseas trading interests of major powers were secured in treaties that had the appearance of freely negotiated contracts. Not all trading arrangements of this period were so startlingly hypocritical. The nineteenth century saw the conclusion of many bilateral treaties of Friendship, Commerce and Navigation (FCN treaties)—in which the States Parties opened up their territories for trade with one another, and commonly guaranteed Most Favoured Nation treatment to one another (that is, guaranteed that nationals of the other State would receive in respect of rights of establishment, liability to customs duties, and other matters covered by the treaty, treatment no less favourable than that given to nationals of the most favoured third State).

---

[3] The irony of giving Britain the responsibility for leading the counter-narcotics campaign to eradicate the Afghan opium trade in 2002 passed largely unnoticed.

The 1853 Argentina–United States FCN Treaty[4] is a typical example, signed for the United States by Robert C. Schenck, who later became a General in the United States Civil War, a member of the Alabama Claims Commission, and the Ambassador to Great Britain, where he introduced the game of draw poker to England before being summoned back to America because of his involvement in an alleged share fraud.

Bilateral treaties were the most numerous of international trade agreements in the nineteenth century and the first half of the twentieth; but there were multilateral agreements which sought to establish global rules in certain areas. The need to agree upon common standards for telegraphic equipment, for instance, led to the conclusion of a number of regional agreements and, in 1865, to the creation of the International Telegraph Union (ITU). That body later took on responsibilities under the 1906 International Radiotelegraph Convention, and became the International Telecommunication Union, which survives as a Specialized Agency of the United Nations. Similarly, the Universal Postal Union (UPU) was formed in 1874 in order to bring some order to international mail services.

While the creation of the ITU and UPU might be regarded as predictable responses to the imperatives of international commerce, the establishment of the International Labour Organization (ILO) at the Paris Peace Conference in 1919 was more unusual. As Article 23 of the Treaty of Versailles records, the States Parties agreed to 'endeavour to secure and maintain fair and humane conditions of labour for men, women, and children, both in their own countries and in all countries to which their commercial and industrial relations extend'; and the ILO was set up for that purpose. The pressures for its creation were a mixture of humanitarian concerns for the welfare of working people, a desire to ensure that disillusioned workers did not follow the example of their Soviet brothers and sisters and produce, in the words of the ILO Preamble, 'unrest so great that the peace and harmony of the world are imperilled', and a concern that States that did implement social reforms would not find their competitive position undercut by States that permitted more primitive labour practices and standards. This combination of motives is reflected in the structure of the ILO, which is unusual in not consisting entirely of representatives of governments. Its governing body consists of 28 representatives of governments, 14 representatives of employers and 14 representatives of workers. The representatives of the different interests frequently speak and even vote against one another,

---

[4] <http://www.yale.edu/lawweb/avalon/diplomacy/argentina/argen02.htm>.

although unanimous votes from individual States are more common than might be supposed. The ILO monitors the performance of Member States in labour matters, and has complaints procedures which, like the ILO itself, include representatives of government, workers, and employers. The procedures have been invoked, for example, in relation to the prohibition which used to exist upon trade union membership by employees of the UK Government Communication Headquarters (GCHQ), an intelligence-gathering facility.

The organizations discussed so far were all established by inter-State agreement; but many international arrangements were established by private enterprises. The chartered companies, such as the East India Company, the Hudson's Bay Company, and the Dutch East India Company, all established in the seventeenth century, had exercised quasi-governmental powers in the territories that were effectively controlled by them. Elsewhere, cartels were formed to align production and demand in some industries, particularly those concerned with the production of primary commodities, usually at a level that optimized the profits of the participants. Some were very efficient. It is said, for example, that the inter-company agreements limiting whale catches were more effectively imple-mented than the conservation measures adopted by the International Whaling Commission (IWC), because whaling companies knew that their profits depended directly upon the application of reasonable quotas whereas those negotiating inter-State agreements tend to accept unreason-ably high quotas in order to placate their domestic industries. Enterprises also made arrangements less directly serving the profit motive. They set technical standards, to ensure the compatibility of goods: the International Electrotechnical Commission (IEC) was established for this purpose in 1906, for example. They adopted common forms and procedures in order to streamline commercial and banking operations; and they worked for the harmonization of national laws.

All of these functions are now reflected in international arrangements adopted by States. There are commodity agreements that aim to stabilize prices by matching production and demand; conservation regimes that aim to ensure that over-exploitation of commodities does not jeopardize sustainable development; agreements to reduce technical barriers to trade; and organizations charged with pressing forward the agenda of har-monization of laws and procedures. Even matters that had traditionally been the preserve of national governments, such as the imposition of taxes and customs duties, the grant of monopolies and State subsidies for industry, and the control of money supply and convertibility, were the subject of increasing international co-operation in the period before 1945.

The legal landscape changed after World War Two. The creation of the United Nations Organization might be regarded as a second attempt at the achievement of the political goals of the League of Nations: but the economic institutions that were designed as part of the post-war international structure carried formal inter-State co-operation into a new phase. One may speculate on the reasons. Perhaps it was the widespread view that World War Two was a result of economic pressures created by the Versailles settlement after World War One, the hyperinflation of the 1920s, and the great economic depression that began in 1929. Perhaps it was the simple fact that rebuilding the many States whose economies had been severely damaged by World War Two demanded a wide-ranging economic programme. Or perhaps the moves simply made sense, as a way of improving the functioning of the world economy. But for whatever reason, the attempts to rebuild the international (or at least, the European–North American) order after World War Two were as much economic as political. The European Community sprang from the idea that binding France and Germany, and in particular their coal and steel industries, to one another was the best way of avoiding another European war; and the creation of what was planned as the triumvirate of the World Bank, the International Monetary Fund, and the International Trade Organization was intended to induce prosperity and peace on a global scale.

6.2 THE CREATION OF THE BRETTON WOODS SYSTEM, THE GATT, AND THE HAVANA CONFERENCE

In August 1941, in the depths of World War Two, President Roosevelt of the United States and Winston Churchill, Prime Minister of Great Britain, met on the USS *Augusta*, anchored off Argentia, Newfoundland. Their purpose was to agree upon the manner in which the United States, still formally neutral in the War, would assist the Allies. The terms that they agreed were not published; but they did make a press release. It set out the basic principles of international relations to which the two countries were committed, including the principle of self-determination and self-government (which the United Kingdom did not consider to apply to British colonies)[5] and two provisions directed at economic reform. They committed their respective countries 'to further the enjoyment by all States, great or small, victor or vanquished, of access, on equal terms, to

---

[5] Leo Amery, Secretary of State for India, declared later in 1941 that calls to apply the Atlantic Charter provisions of self-government to India were 'a typical example of loose thinking'.

the trade and to the raw materials of the world which are needed for their economic prosperity' and announced their 'desire to bring about the fullest collaboration between all nations in the economic field with the object of securing, for all, improved labor standards, economic advancement and social security'.

Those provisions were vague but this did not matter, because the purpose of the Atlantic Charter, as the press release was grandly named, was to signal to the Axis powers the solidarity of the signatories, Britain and the United States. But the Atlantic Charter did reflect the view that the regulation of the international economy was essential for a stable peace. In July 1944 representatives of forty-four governments, including the United States, (Communist) Russia, (non-Communist) China, the United Kingdom and countries in the British Commonwealth, and France, met in the New Hampshire resort of Bretton Woods to discuss ways of promoting international economic stability.

The Bretton Woods conference established three commissions, one to draft the Articles of Agreement of the International Monetary Fund (IMF), a second to draft the Articles of the International Bank for Reconstruction and Development (IBRD, better known as the World Bank), and a third to consider other means of international financial co-operation. The drafts were adopted in the astonishingly short time of three weeks; and the IMF and IBRD Articles of Agreement entered into force on 27 December 1945.

The 'trade' element of the system was negotiated separately. Negotiations between the United States and the United Kingdom from 1943 onwards led to a proposal in a 1945 US paper on 'Proposals for Expansion of World Trade and Employment' for the establishment of an International Trade Organization and an agreed set of principles on a wide range of matters related to international trade, such as tariffs and non-tariff barriers, trade quotas, subsidies, most-favoured-nation treatment, and cartels. A conference was convened in 1946 under the auspices of the recently-established United Nations Economic Council to draft a text which was submitted to the UN Conference on Trade and Development held in Havana in November 1947 and became the Havana Charter.[6] At the same time tariff-cutting negotiations were held in the 'Geneva Round' negotiations of 1947, which produced the General Agreement on Tariffs

---

[6] One of the great mysteries of international law is how an original copy of the Havana Charter, bearing the signatures of the plenipotentiaries (and with the Polish representative's signature apparently crossed out) came to rest in a food cupboard in a house in Liverpool. It is now in the Bodleian Library, Oxford, with a note by Sir Adam Roberts describing the circumstances of its discovery.

and Trade (GATT). The GATT recorded both the agreed tariff concessions and other agreed principles for the conduct of international trade, and was opened for signature in October 1947.

The proper focus of the 1947 Havana Conference[7] was controversial. Questions such as the permissibility of discriminatory trade preferences (for example, the 'Imperial Preference' applicable to trade within the British Empire) were fiercely debated. The original free-trade model was subjected to more and more qualifications, and the idea of creating another international organization, of questionable value to US trade interests, faced increasing opposition in the US Congress. The Truman Administration decided in 1950 that it would not put the Havana Charter to Congress for adoption, and the project collapsed as other States took the lead from the United States. The GATT did, however, survive. It had been applied since 1948 on a provisional basis, pending the anticipated entry into force of the Havana Charter and establishment of the ITO; and it continued to be applied 'provisionally' for the best part of half a century, until it was superseded by the World Trade Organization.

The establishment of the IBRD, the IMF, and the GATT marked the beginnings of a serious attempt to make the international economy a rule-based system, rather than a power-based system in which the most powerful players in the international markets prospered at the expense of the weak. To see how these rules operate (or at least were intended to operate) it is necessary to look in a little more detail at this trio of institutions.

6.3 THE WORLD BANK

The roles of the World Bank and the IMF are sometimes confused, no doubt because both of them appear to some to epitomize the reactionary forces of international capital. The distinction is simple: as Keynes is reputed to have said, the Bank is a fund, and the Fund is a bank. In crude terms, the World Bank is a source of funding for States, while the IMF acts to preserve the stability of the international monetary system by overseeing exchange rates and the convertibility of currencies.

The aim of the international community in establishing the World Bank was to make long-term financial aid available at reasonable rates to restore war-damaged economies and to promote sound industry and increase industrial and agricultural production in developing countries. The World Bank's primary function, set out in Article 1 of its Articles of

---

[7] To be carefully distinguished from the 1946 Havana Conference, at which Lucky Luciano presided over a meeting of American gangland bosses.

Agreement, is 'to assist in the reconstruction and development of territories of members by facilitating the investment of capital for productive purposes'. It does so by arranging or guaranteeing loans made to States by private sector banks, and where private capital is not available on reasonable terms by making relatively long-term (typically 5 to 10 year) investment loans to States to finance economic and social development projects from its own resources. Those resources come in small part from subscriptions of Member States, but largely from the sale of the Bank's own bonds in international capital markets. Those bonds, backed by the contributions that the Bank is entitled to call upon from Member States, are regarded as secure investments; so the Bank is using its reputation and economic strength to obtain money at low rates from the market which it can then lend on to States which could borrow from the market only on much less advantageous terms. The Bank also provides shorter-term (1 to 3 year) development loans to support policy and institutional reforms in States; and it operates a number of funds from which grants can be made.

The scale of Bank operations is large. Each year it makes loans, (or grants, in the case of the very poorest countries), totalling around $20 billion. Lending policies were influenced by political factors during the Cold War, but the Bank now tries to take decisions based upon the viability of the project and its value to the State in question. Discipline is tight. If a State fails to make repayments, after one month the Bank puts a bar on any further loans, and after two months it stops further payments on existing loans.

All banks, if they lend money on a project, will try to ensure that the project is viable and that the sums lent can be recovered, or at least that the borrower can meet the interest payments. That is what happens when one obtains a mortgage from a bank and one's earnings and savings are measured by the bank and a surveyor is sent round to value the property. Similarly, the World Bank will try to ensure that the project is properly planned and properly authorized under the law of the State concerned. But it goes further. Its own internal operational policies and procedures, which are published, require that it check that the project conforms to a range of social, economic, and environmental guidelines, such as the minimization of environmental harm and the avoidance of forced relocations of indigenous populations that might arise in the context of a large dam project, for example. There is a considerable correspondence between these guidelines and basic principles of human rights and environmental law.

Adherence to the Bank's guidelines is monitored by the Independent Evaluation Group, which also has oversight of operations in other international financial organizations. There is an important and imaginative procedure for dealing with complaints, established in 1993. Any two or more people in the country where the Bank-financed project is located may complain that the Bank has violated its own policies and procedures and thereby caused harm to their material interests. If the local people cannot complain, bodies such as NGOs may complain on their behalf. Complaints are investigated by the three-person World Bank Inspection Panel, which reports on the Bank's adherence to its policies and proced-ures, in accordance with guidelines contained in the 1999 'Clarification' of the role and functions of Panels. Though the Panels, which had handled about forty cases by 2006, are non-judicial and some cases turn on factors such as the scientific adequacy of environmental assessments, it is evident from the published reports that legal argument has an important role. In the 2005 report on the *Colombia: Cartagena Water Supply* project, for example, there is detailed discussion of the conformity of the project with instruments such as the 1983 Cartagena Convention for the Protection and Development of the Marine Environment of the Wider Caribbean Region, compliance with which was one of the conditions of the Colombian licence to proceed with the project. If the Panel finds that a project is incompatible with the Bank's policies and procedures, the man-agement and the Board of Executive Directors of the Bank decide what remedial action will be taken. It may include withdrawal from the project, as was the case in respect of the *China Western Poverty Reduction Project*, where a 2000 Panel report found non-compliance with environmental and human rights norms. In this way, even though Panel reports are not bind-ing, Bank monitoring procedures have become an important instrument for securing compliance with international law.

6.4 THE IDA AND THE IFC

The IBRD is one of the World Bank Group of international organizations, whose other members complement the activities of the Bank. The International Development Association (IDA) provides long-term inter-est-free or concessional loans and grants to the poorest countries (defined in 2006 as those with a per capita GNP of under $1,025) and is the largest source of international donor funds for basic social services. It also pro-vides assistance to countries in danger of 'debt distress'—that is, an inability to service loans from richer States, banks and international organizations. The International Finance Corporation (IFC) is the 'pri-vate sector arm' of the World Bank, promoting sustainable private sector development in developing countries by providing loans or equity invest-ments, typically in the $1m to $100m range, and technical advice and assistance. It invests in circumstances where private institutions will not invest alone, and creates financial products designed to meet the needs of the developing world. While it charges market rates, it can structure loans so as to make repayments easier to bear.

The two remaining members of the World Bank Group are rather different. The International Centre for the Settlement of Investment Disputes (ICSID) and the Multilateral Investment Guarantee Agency (MIGA) are both closely linked with the protection of private investment in foreign States. This may appear to mark a departure from the main focus of the Bank's activities; but that is not really so.

6.5 FOREIGN INVESTMENTS, THE ICSID, AND MIGA

ICSID was established by the World Bank in 1966, with the aim of promoting flows of private investment—foreign direct investment or FDI, as it is known—in order to stimulate international development. It was widely thought that investors were deterred from making investments in many States by fear of non-commercial risks such as expropriation and regulatory interference with the investment. Why make an investment of many millions of dollars if the host State could simply announce that it was being expropriated (or 'nationalized' or subjected to a programme of 'indigenization', to use some of the more genteel synonyms)?

If such action were taken against an investment, investors would have little chance of any effective remedy. Even setting aside the concern that national courts would tend to side with the government against the foreign investor, expropriations and other legislative interferences could not be overturned unless they violated some constitutional law in the host State, and this is unlikely to be the case. Against the background of the mass expropriations by the Communist regimes in China and eastern Europe, and of the anti-colonial currents of the 1960s, it is not surprising that corporate executives, who saw their responsibilities as making profits from secure investments and not as the development of new economies by speculative ventures, took a cautious view of investment in the developing States. And, as the World Bank Executive Directors put it, '[t]he creation of an institution designed to facilitate the settlement of disputes between States and foreign investors can be a major step toward promoting an atmosphere of mutual confidence and thus stimulating a larger flow of private international capital into those countries which wish to attract it'.

Disputes of that kind were, up to that time, handled in a cumbersome way. Investors who failed to find a remedy in the host State's national courts could turn to their own national governments and ask them to take up the case on their behalf on the plane of international law—to exercise the right of diplomatic protection. As a matter of international law it would be no defence for the host State to say that it had acted throughout in accordance with its own laws and decrees (which, of course, the host State government could make as it chose), and in principle international law requires that full reparation be made for losses caused by its breach.

There were, however, two major problems with this approach. First, it was difficult to persuade governments to take up the claim. Most cases are complex, and to persuade a government official to assimilate volumes of detailed evidence on the making, taking, and valuation of a foreign invest-ment, and then to draw up a claim against a foreign State, is hard. To persuade the corresponding official in the accused State to receive the claim and reciprocate with a detailed response is doubly difficult. And the moment has to be right. If relations between the two States are good, the claimant State may be reluctant to spoil them by raising the claim. If relations are bad, the respondent State is unlikely to be co-operative. The investor may have an enviably simple view of matters, wanting only its money: but States have more complex inter-relationships, spanning a wide range of economic, political, and social and other matters. If one claim is pursued, or paid, who else will expect the same treatment? If a particular State measure is attacked as unlawful, what will that imply if the State wishes to take a similar action itself in future? Did the investor not know the risks? Were they not built into its calculations of costs and profits? Has it not made enough in the past, and is it not making enough elsewhere, to cover these losses?

The second major difficulty lay in pinning down precisely what host States could and could not lawfully do to investments. It was clear that international law forbade expropriation of foreign investments unless the expropriation was for a public purpose, was non-discriminatory, and adequate compensation was provided. That was a view reflected in the 1962 Resolution on Permanent Sovereignty over Natural Resources, UN Assembly resolution 1803 (XVII). But what did those terms mean? Is the expropriation of, say, British companies as a protest against some aspect of British foreign policy an expropriation for a 'public purpose'? Is a policy of confiscating foreign-owned farms, but not farms owned by citizens of the State, discriminatory, if it is part of a process of indigenization? Is compensation from which the host State deducts a sum in respect of what it says are excessive profits earned in the past by the investor nonetheless 'adequate'? Are environmental laws that make it almost impossible for a factory to operate at a reasonable profit tantamount to expropriation?

Governments are less keen to take up claims that are legally doubtful, particularly where large sums of money are claimed, than they are to pursue clear violations of international law.

Given such difficulties it is not surprising that, compared with the scale of expropriations in Russia, China, and States in eastern Europe and elsewhere, relatively few cases of unlawful interference were pursued on the plane of international law. Some were. In the mid nineteenth century Britain successfully claimed against Greece for the taking of land belonging to the historian George Finlay, which had been enclosed in King Otho's garden. At about the same time, and, with the added urgency that the arrival of British warships to blockade Greek ports brought to the affair, Greece paid over £5,000 in compensation for damage caused by a mob to the property of Don Pacifico, the Portuguese consul in Athens who had, by the happy accident of his birth in Gibraltar, acquired British citizenship and the protective interest of one of the most aggressive foreign ministers of the time, Lord Palmerston. Palmerston declared, during the Parliamentary debate on the Don Pacifico affair, 'As the Roman, in days of old, held himself free from indignity, when he could say, *Civis Romanus sum*, so also a British subject, in whatever land he may be, shall feel confident that the watchful eye and the strong arm of England will protect him from injustice and wrong.' One could barely wish for a better, or more florid, expression of the principle of diplomatic protection.

Pace Palmerston, the truth is that governments have never relished the systematic protection of the property of their nationals abroad. Instances of governments taking up single claims are rare. Among the best known are the *Chorzów Factory* case, in which the Permanent Court of International Justice ruled on the expropriation of property of German companies by Poland, and the *Anglo-Iranian Oil Company* case, which the United Kingdom tried unsuccessfully to bring before the ICJ (which found that it lacked jurisdiction over the dispute) following the nationalization of the oil industry in Iran by Prime Minister Mossadegh in 1951.

It has been more common for governments to deal with claims *en masse*. For example, American claims arising from revolutionary action in Mexico between 1910 and 1920 were dealt with in a bilateral treaty concluded by the two States in 1923.[8] The claims were submitted to a three-person Commission, which foreshadowed the Iran-US Claims Tribunal established to determine claims arising from the Islamic Revolution in Iran in 1979. Other claims have been handled by agreements in which the claimant government negotiates a lump-sum settlement of all outstanding claims

---

[8] 18 *AJIL* (Supp.) 143–146 (1924).

with the respondent government. The sum is paid over and distributed *pro rata* among claimants. In the United Kingdom the Foreign Compensation Commission, mentioned in Chapter 3, has carried out this role, and it has analogues in other States.

In all these cases the national government of the claimant has been involved either in directly pursuing the claim or in the establishment of a commission in which the claimant can pursue it. But large-scale investors sought a more expeditious approach to dispute settlement, removing the need to persuade their governments to espouse their claims. This was done by including in agreements between the investor and the host State a provision requiring the submission of disputes arising out of the investment to arbitration. Each party had the right to refer a dispute to arbitration, and each had an equal right to participate in the appointment of the tribunal, usually by appointing one of three arbitrators (the third, non-party arbitrator being appointed by agreement or by a neutral third party designated in advance). This was the pattern followed in cases such as the *Lena Goldfields* arbitration, brought by an English company against the Soviet Union in 1930,[9] and the cases brought against Libya by the western oil companies BP, Texaco, Calasiatic, and Liamco, whose property had been nationalized by Colonel Qaddafi in the 1970s.

The great advantage of these 'mixed' (State/non-State Parties) arbitrations is that they leave control of the litigation in the hands of the actual claimant. There is no need to involve the claimant's national government at any stage. The arbitration may, moreover, be conducted in private, and its outcome and even its existence kept confidential. This reduces concerns that other governments or investors may invoke the claim and its settlement as a precedent in future negotiations. Risks of delay and bias in the host State's national courts are avoided. The availability of arbitration of this kind increases the confidence of investors in the security of their investments, and thus facilitates the making of foreign investments.

It was these advantages that the World Bank sought to harness in the ICSID Convention, in order to encourage foreign direct investment. While ICSID itself does not conduct any arbitrations—the ICSID Convention functions as a framework within which individual arbitrations are organized as the need arises—the involvement of ICSID is a matter of great importance.

---

[9] See V.V. Veeder, 'The *Lena Goldfields* Arbitration: The Historical Roots of Three Ideas', 47 *ICLQ* 747–792 (1998).

Arbitral tribunals, composed of arbitrators appointed by the parties to the dispute, have the power to settle the dispute definitively, but they do not have the coercive powers of courts to compel the production of evidence, make orders for the protection of assets, and so on. Nor, unlike courts, can they issue orders for the enforcement of arbitral awards by the attachment of property. Arbitral tribunals may need the assistance of courts in order to perform their duties effectively. Courts also assert a supervisory jurisdiction over arbitral tribunals. They may remove arbitrators for misconduct, and quash arbitral awards that are seriously flawed, for example because the arbitral proceedings did not meet the standards of natural justice. The 1985 UNCITRAL Model Law on Arbitration and the UK Arbitration Act 1996 illustrate the relationship between courts and arbitral tribunals. But the corollary of this helpful relationship of support and supervision is that disgruntled parties may use applications to courts as a means of delaying the arbitral process and the finality of arbitral awards. In the ICSID Convention, the States Parties agreed to a different, self-contained system which allows no resort to any other remedy, and no exercise of diplomatic protection by the investor's host State. 'Interference', as it may be seen, by national courts is averted. ICSID awards may not be challenged in national courts, and national courts are obliged to recognize and enforce those awards. No record is kept of compliance with ICSID awards, but the prominence of the process (secured by ICSID's practice of publishing the fact that a dispute has been referred to arbitration, even though the actual proceedings themselves may be kept private) and the fact that the system operates under the auspices of the World Bank, appears to result in a very high degree of voluntary compliance with awards by losing States.

The ICSID Convention leaves two crucial gaps to be filled by other instruments. One is the consent of the Parties—the investor and the host State—to go to arbitration, which is essential in every case. Consent may be given in various ways. It may be contained in a dispute settlement clause in an investment contract, or the State may make an open offer to investors to take disputes to ICSID arbitration by a provision in its national investment law or in a bilateral investment protection treaty (or BIT), though the treaty provisions only apply to nationals of the States Parties.

The second gap in the ICSID Convention is that it says nothing about the substantive rights and duties of investors and host States. Customary international law protects the property of aliens against uncompensated and arbitrary expropriations and against damage resulting from a failure of the State to provide the minimum protection of alien property from malicious damage. BITs secure those protections and go further. Their precise provisions vary, but most of the 2,000 or so BITs now in existence protect investments against treatment by the host State which is not 'fair and equitable'. That is a striking extension of protection, because it provides a guarantee against unfair and inequitable treatment even if that treatment is in accordance with the host State's law. Tribunals are developing a concept of fair and equitable treatment that includes, for instance, a requirement that host State authorities behave transparently towards investors, giving adequate publicity to laws and administrative procedures and practices. While BITs protect only foreign investors, and not the host State's own citizens, the requirements of transparency are concerned with the ways in which governments are structured and operate, and so have a significant influence on the whole system of governance within the State.

One crucial question is, how does one distinguish between legitimate regulation on the one hand and unfair and inequitable treatment on the other? May a host State impose price controls, or additional taxes, on a foreign investor if that significantly reduces its profitability? Or would that violate the BIT? There is, as yet, no comprehensive and coherent doctrine that establishes the boundaries of permissible regulation. The scores of investment tribunals now hearing cases are taking decisions that will define the nature of the responsibilities of States towards foreign investment and have a substantial influence upon the nature of international economic relations.

BITS set out the rights of investors. They do not set out the rights of the host State, and some have thought that this evidences an unacceptable bias in the system. There have been attempts to set out the duties of investors. In 1974, at the same time that the Charter on Economic Rights and Duties of States was being drafted, the UN Centre on Transnational Corporations (UNCTC) was established, following a report on *Multinational Corporations in World Development* commissioned by the UN's Economic and Social Committee (ECOSOC). The UNCTC worked for many years on the preparation of a UN Code of Conduct for Transnational Corporations, which would have set out the responsibilities of foreign investors towards host States and their people and economies; but enthusiasm for the rhetoric of the new international economic order waned as States studied the fine print of drafts of the Code and the economic realities bore in upon them. The effort was abandoned in 1992, when the work of the UNCTC was transferred to UNCTAD—the UN Conference on Trade and Development—which continues to produce expert reports on the subject.

Other bodies have had more success in adopting codes of conduct with a narrower focus. For example, in 1976 the Organization for Economic

Co-operation and Development (OECD), a group of market-economy countries including Australia, Canada, Japan, Korea, Mexico, the European States, and the USA, produced the *Declaration and Decisions on International Investment and Multinational Enterprises*, since revised, which has proved an influential statement of investors' responsibilities. In 1977 the ILO produced the *Tripartite Declaration of Principles Concerning Multinational Enterprises and Social Policy* (the 'MNE Declaration'), a voluntary code agreed by representatives of employees, employers, and governments. And in 2003, the UN ECOSOC adopted a statement of *Norms on the Responsibilities of Transnational Corporations and Other Business Enterprises with Regard to Human Rights*. The most ambitious is the UN's *Global Compact*, launched in 1999, which sets out ten 'universal principles' in the areas of human rights, labour, the environment, and anti-corruption. The Compact sets an agenda and basic standards of behaviour towards which companies, NGOs, and governments will work. By 2006 around 2,500 businesses in 90 countries had adhered to the Compact; and perhaps more significantly, in an attempt to maintain the integrity of the Compact the UN had removed 335 companies from the list of participants because they had failed to submit the required annual Communications on Progress on Implementation of the Principles. There are also many voluntary sectoral codes, which may have only limited success in bringing about an age of corporate moral purity but do at least signal an awareness that companies have social responsibilities.

The real point concerning the balance between the rights of investors and the rights of host States, however, is that the balance of individual legal documents—or even of the whole collection of legal instruments—has little relevance to the issue. There is no more point in seeking a balanced BIT setting out investors' duties than there is in amending the Universal Declaration on Human Rights to include provisions on the duty to pay taxes and obey the law. Corporations may be powerful; some have wealth far exceeding that of many States: but most do not. All governments have the power to make laws and demand obedience to them, and that is how the rights and legitimate interests of States are most effectively protected—not by making general proclamations that companies ought to behave as good citizens, true as that may be.

Foreign investors are not merely tolerated: they are actively encouraged. Governments advertise the advantages of locating facilities in their countries: cheap labour, low taxes, generous development grants, low tariffs, and so on. Governments also seek to assist outward investment. Many States have bodies such as the United Kingdom's Export Credit Guarantee Department (ECGD) which provide investment insurance and co-ordinate policies through the Berne Union. Exporters pay a premium to insure themselves against non-payment of their bills, expropriation by foreign governments, and other non-commercial risks. The one member of the World Bank Group not yet discussed does the same on the international plane. The Multilateral Investment Guarantee Agency (MIGA) was established in 1988 in order to promote foreign investment and international development. It provides technical assistance on investment issues to developing States, and is available to mediate in investment disputes. It is perhaps best known as a provider of insurance against political risks, including losses resulting from war risks, expropriation, the imposition of currency transfer restrictions, and non-payment of judgments or awards against a host State arising from the breach or repudiation of a contract. Cover is available for investors from the 167 States Parties to MIGA who wish to invest in developing countries that are themselves members of MIGA. MIGA offers insurance cover of up to 90% of the value of the investment, up to $200m, often acting in partnership with public bodies, such as the ECGD, and with private insurers.

There were plans, pursued within the OECD from 1995 to 1998, for another international organization, the Multilateral Agreement on Investment (MAI). It was intended that the MAI would be open to all States and would 'provide a broad multilateral framework for international investment with high standards for the liberalisation of investment regimes and investment protection and with effective dispute settlement procedures'. Following widespread criticism of the draft text for the MAI, which was thought excessively favourable to investors and burdensome for governments, the attempt to establish the MAI was abandoned at the end of 1998, shortly after the new French Government withdrew from the negotiations.

The development of BITs is proceeding in a different direction. Rather than strengthening international protections of investments, governments are becoming more sensitive to the constraints that BITs impose upon their regulatory powers and their ability to steer the development of their economies. Investment protection is increasingly seen not as an aspect of the duties of a State towards citizens of another State, but as an aspect of the network of economic relations that each State has with others. High levels of protection are seen as benefits rather than rights, to be negotiated and traded against concessions in other areas, such as market access; and some sectors of the economy may be excluded altogether from the protections of the BIT, at least in respect of the national treatment provisions. The investment protection provisions are integrated with provisions based upon the General Agreement on Trade in Services (GATS), to which I will refer shortly. While these trends can be seen even in early BITs, they are more clearly evident in the generation of BITs exemplified by the 2004 United States Model BIT.[10]

6.6 THE IMF AND THE INTERNATIONAL MONETARY SYSTEM

In 1986 *The Economist* magazine devised a scheme for measuring Purchasing Power Parity, i.e., the price in different currencies of a stipulated basket of goods that constitutes the 'standard'. Economic theory has it that in the long run the price of such a standard basket should equalize around the world. If the price in the USA, converted into pounds, is lower than the price in the United Kingdom, enterprising traders will export the goods from the United States, thus increasing demand and raising prices there, and import them into the United Kingdom, thus increasing supply and lowering prices here. In theory, therefore, the prices of a standard commodity in different currencies should give some indication of the relative values of those currencies—of their exchange rates.

The Economist used a Big Mac as a standard, because of its ubiquity (it is available in well over 100 countries) and its uniformity (hold the relish and it is more or less the same everywhere). Today, a Big Mac costs $3.10 in the United States, 10.5 yuan in China, and £1.94 in the United Kingdom, for example. Measured against the Big Mac standard, therefore, 1 yuan is worth $0.29, and £1 is worth $1.60. In fact, hamburgernomics provide an inaccurate guide to exchange rates because the simple conversion does not take account of a range of factors that affect price. Different labour costs, transportation and storage costs, rents and business overheads, and taxes, all affect the picture. But the idea is plain enough.

Problems with storage and perishability make the hamburger unattractive as an international monetary standard; but gold has been used to serve the same role. The value of many currencies has in the past been pegged to the value of gold or silver. In the early eighteenth century Sir Isaac Newton, then Master of the Royal Mint, defined the weight of gold and silver that was to be included in English coins; and in 1844 the Bank Charter Act defined the value of England's paper currency in terms of its convertibility into gold. As Sir Robert Peel said during the Parliamentary debate on the Bill, 'according to practice, according to law, according to the ancient monetary policy of this country, that which is implied by the word "Pound"

---

[10] < http://www.state.gov/e/eb/rls/othr/38602.htm >.

is a certain definite quantity of gold with a mark upon it to determine its weight and fineness, and . . . the engagement to pay a Pound means nothing, and can mean nothing else, than the promise to pay to the holder, when he demands it, that definite quantity of gold'. The relative values of the pound and other currencies similarly linked to the value of gold could thus be easily calculated.

From about 1880 to 1913 there was widespread adherence to the gold standard among major economies. The economic model in its simplest form predicted that if a State spent more on imports than it had earned in exports, gold would flow out of the country, interest rates would rise, spending would decrease, and equilibrium would be restored. Conversely, a State into which gold flowed could increase the money supply because it held more gold to back its paper currency, and would see falling interest rates, increasing spending, and an economic boom. In this way any dis-equilibrium in the balance of payments between a State and its inter-national customers and suppliers would, in theory, correct itself. Of course, the system never worked like this. Not all States were on the gold standard (or the gold-exchange standard, in which a currency was pegged not to gold but to another currency which was itself pegged to gold). In those that were, the economic contraction and fall in wages that would, under this theory, follow an outflow of gold were slow to occur: workers do not willingly accept pay cuts, and governments tend to intervene in the economy to soften the impact of economic downturns. The 'Invergordon Mutiny' of 1931, in which British Navy personnel refused to perform their duties in protest at a cut of around 10% in the pay of naval ratings, which had been imposed as part of an emergency budget measures intended to stop the outflow of gold from the United Kingdom, was a good example of the social realities that could interfere with the theory of the gold standard.

The system could not cope with the strains that arose from World War One. States spent more on armaments than they had in the bank, and printed more and more paper money to cover the costs. Germany had to borrow from the United States to pay the swingeing reparations that it owed to France and the United Kingdom, which in turn owed the United States debts arising from the war. Money circulated in what one historian called 'a ridiculous cycle of indebtedness which, by its very nature, tended towards a crash'.[11] The crash came in 1929 and precipitated the Great

---

[11] David Thomson, *Europe Since Napoleon* (London: Penguin, 1966), p. 682. After the 1932 Lausanne conference had reduced German reparations payments to about one-eighth of the former level, the British Government stopped repayments of Britain's debt to the United

Depression—an episode whose effects were on a scale comparable to that of the Great War itself. Millions, particularly in the United States, lost their jobs and their homes and possessions in the ensuing economic chaos. States were forced off the gold standard, which was completely abandoned by 1937. Currencies were allowed to float against one another with exchange rates determined by the market, over which governments struggled, largely ineffectually, to exercise some influence. Unlike the position when exchange rates were fixed to gold and economic imbalances saw massive outflows of gold from States, with direct effects upon internal economic activity in States, changes in floating rates affected the external value of the currency but allowed governments greater scope to regulate their domestic economies, at least in the short term. Yet the system was clearly in crisis; and the inability of the governments to cope with the economic upheaval that followed World War One was a major cause of the Second.

A key aim in the plans for post-war economic reconstruction was the creation of a stable international monetary system in which States were once more obliged to maintain more or less fixed exchange rates and to take corrective measures to deal with economic imbalances. The discipline would be imposed by a legal framework, binding States to conform to the mechanism, which would operate through a permanent international institution. This in itself was a significant change: in the days of the gold standard there had been no such binding international obligations underpinning the international monetary system. The policy was explained at Bretton Woods by United States Treasury Secretary Henry Morgenthau:

Today the only enlightened form of national self-interest lies in international accord. At Bretton Woods we have taken practical steps toward putting this lesson into practice in monetary and economic fields.

. . .

What are the fundamental conditions under which the commerce among nations can once more flourish?

First, there must be a reasonable stable standard of international exchange to which all countries can adhere without sacrificing the freedom of action necessary to meet their internal economic problems.

States. It believed that the Roosevelt administration had agreed to this, but Congress refused to accept any such agreement so that Britain's original repayment obligation stood. One historian noted that 'the British had practised the unilateral repudiation of an international agreement which they were to condemn so sternly when practised against them by de Valera or Hitler': A.J.P. Taylor, *English History 1914–1945* (Oxford: Oxford University Press, 1965), pp. 335–336.

This is the alternative to the desperate tactics of the past—competitive currency depreciation, excessive tariff barriers, uneconomic barter deals, multiple currency practices, and unnecessary exchange restrictions—by which governments vainly sought to maintain employment and uphold living standards. In the final analysis, these tactics only succeeded in contributing to world-wide depression and even war. The International Monetary Fund agreed upon at Bretton Woods will help remedy this situation.

The monetary mechanism was established by the Articles of Agreement of the International Monetary Fund drafted at Bretton Woods. The system was based upon adjustable pegged rates or 'par values'. Each Member was obliged to declare a par value for its currency, expressed in terms of gold or of the US dollar (which was itself defined in terms of gold, initially at $35 per ounce), and was then obliged to intervene in the markets, for example by buying or selling gold or other currencies, in order to maintain the exchange rate within a narrow (1%) margin in either side of the par value. If that value became unsustainable, and a devaluation or revaluation of the currency was necessary in order to correct a fundamental disequilibrium in the balance of payments, a State could change the par value of its currency, but only after following the prescribed procedure for consultation within the IMF.

This system operated until the late 1960s, when economic pressures forced the devaluation of several currencies and it became plain that the rigidity of the existing IMF provisions on exchange rates was unsustainable. In 1976 the Fund adopted the Second Amendment to its Articles of Agreement; and when that amendment entered into force in 1978 the legal rules within the IMF came into line with what was already the situation in reality and exchange rates floated freely, determined by the market. That is not to say that government intervention in the market has ceased. Many governments attempt to control exchange rates in order to iron out fluctuations in the value of their currency or to maintain its relationship to some other currency: but this is a matter of choice, and not of obligation as it was under the original IMF scheme. The IMF maintains a system of surveillance—monitoring and consultation—in respect of exchange rates. The principles that it expects Members to observe were set out in a 1977 *Decision on Surveillance over Exchange Rate Policies*:

A. A member shall avoid manipulating exchange rates or the international monetary system in order to prevent effective balance of payments adjustment or to gain an unfair competitive advantage over other members.

B. A member should intervene in the exchange market if necessary to counter disorderly conditions, which may be characterized inter alia by disruptive short-term movements in the exchange value of its currency.

C. Members should take into account in their intervention policies the interests of other members, including those of the countries in whose currencies they intervene.

The 1977 Decision set out the surveillance procedures, which culminate in miscreant States being invited to have 'discussions' with the Fund's Managing Director.

The IMF Articles of Agreement also address the question of exchange control restrictions. Under Article VIII of the Fund's Articles of Agreement, Members are bound, subject to certain exceptions, not to impose restrictions on the making and payment of current international transactions (as distinct from capital transactions) without the approval of the Fund.

States might run short of foreign currencies needed to buy imports. In those circumstances the IMF can act as a source of international liquidity by lending the foreign currency to the State in difficulties. At Bretton Woods there had been a split between the scheme proposed by the British economist John Maynard Keynes[12] and that proposed by the United States Treasury economist Harry Dexter White.[13] Keynes sought a Fund which would have the power to create liquidity by issuing a new world currency, which Keynes would have named the Bancor, in much the way that central banks created liquidity by issuing paper currency. Keynes proposed that the responsibility for resolving problems of international indebtedness should lie with both debtor and creditor nations: trade surpluses would be taxed in order to encourage States in surplus to buy from States in deficit. Keynes' plan envisaged a Fund—he would have called it the International Clearing Union—with around $30 billion in assets at its disposal. White, who thought that the prime responsibility for restoring equilibrium should lie on debtor countries rather than on those in surplus, proposed a more modest scheme, based on funding of around $5 billion and not reliant on the creation of a new international currency. The IMF Articles as adopted were close to White's conception, and the liquidity that the IMF makes available comes from within the system rather than by the creation and issue of a new currency.

On joining the IMF each State was assigned a quota or subscription, of which in most cases one-quarter was to be paid in gold and three-quarters

---

[12] Celebrated associate of the Bloomsbury group and author of the observation, of cardinal importance to all theoreticians of macro-economics, that 'in the long run, we are all dead'.

[13] Later accused of passing secrets to the Soviet Union in a hollowed-out pumpkin, White died of a heart attack in 1948 shortly after testifying before the House Committee on Un-American Activities of the US Congress.

in its own currency. If a State needed foreign currency it could borrow from the Fund using its drawing rights, which were calculated on the basis of its quota. Borrowing was effected by the State 'buying' the foreign currency from the Fund using its own currency. States could in practice freely borrow within the amount of the 'gold tranche' of their quota; but beyond that, and within the 'credit tranches' as they were known, limits were placed on borrowing by Article V of the IMF Articles. For example, a Member could generally borrow only up to 25% of its quota in any twelve-month period, and only up to 200% of its quota in total, unless the Fund waived the limitations. Members were also obliged to 'repay' an IMF loan within a certain time by repurchasing their currency using gold or other Members' currencies.

Gold is a finite resource, and could not long meet the demands of a growing international economy for liquidity.[14] Nor could the United States dollar, which was the major international trading currency and which in the 1960s was still convertible into gold. If more dollars were printed, confidence that they were adequately backed by gold would inevitably fall. On the other hand if more dollars were not added to the monetary supply the world economy would move into a state of deflation and instability. This dilemma had been identified by the economist Robert Triffin in his testimony to the US Congress in 1960, and he proposed to address the problem by creating additional liquidity in the form of a new monetary reserve unit. That course was followed in 1968 when the IMF Articles of Agreement were amended and Special Drawing Rights (SDRs) were created. The SDR is a purely abstract conception, a unit of account, originally defined as being equivalent to 0.888671 grams of fine gold, which was then the value of one US dollar. With the collapse of the system of fixed exchange rates, however, the method of calculating the value of an SDR was changed. It is now calculated by adding together the values (expressed in US dollars at prevailing exchange rates) of defined amounts of a defined 'basket' of currencies, which has the effect of smoothing out fluctuations that might occur if only one currency were used as the basis. The basket consisted in October 2006 of €0.41, plus 18.4 Japanese yen, plus £0.09, plus US$ 0.63; and one SDR was worth about £0.79, US $1.46, or €1.71.

The shift from gold, which has intrinsic value, to the SDR may be seen as a shift to what is a fundamentally legal basis for the international monetary system. The system is held together by the legal definitions, obligations, and procedures that make up the IMF system.

---

[14] Revaluing gold was not a practical option. It would have benefited only those States that held gold, such as the Soviet Union and South Africa, and was opposed by the United States.

SDRs were distributed among IMF Member States in proportion to their quotas. The liquidity of the Fund also benefited from the General Arrangements to Borrow (GAB) set up by the Group of Ten (G-10) industrialized countries in 1962 and regularly renewed, in order to permit the IMF to borrow their currencies, and the New Arrangements to Borrow adopted after the Mexican debt crisis of 1994 by the IMF and twenty-six Member States and institutions to make supplementary funds available to prevent or cope with exceptional threats to the stability of the international monetary system.

The needs of States vary and the IMF has been active in developing loan arrangements, known as 'facilities', to address specific issues. For example, there is a Compensatory Financing Facility (CFF), created in 1963 to help States cope with falls in export earnings or increases in the price of imported cereals, and emergency assistance for coping with natural disasters, a Poverty Reduction and Growth Facility (PRGF) available to low-income countries, and an Enhanced Structural Adjustment Facility (ESAF) to assist States in making structural reforms to revitalize their economies.

Borrowing is a good means of overcoming cash-flow problems, but it is of little long-term benefit to poor and chronically weak economies. The Fund has, since 1996, joined the World Bank in the Heavily Indebted Poor Countries (HIPC) initiative, which aims to ensure that no State has an unmanageable burden of debt to governmental or private creditors, and the Multilateral Debt Relief Initiative (MDRI), which provides for debt relief of up to 100% on certain debts owed to the IMF, the IDA, the World Bank's African Development Fund (AfDF), and the Inter-American Development Bank (IDB).

Borrowing from the IMF is subject to Fund approval, and this has been the occasion for one of the more controversial aspects of the Fund's operation: conditionality. There was no mention of conditionality in the original IMF Articles, but as Keynes had noted, there was enthusiasm in the United States for the view that the Fund 'should exercise something of the same grandmotherly influence and control over the central banks of member countries, that these central banks in turn are accustomed to exercise over the other banks within their own countries'. As I have mentioned, Fund approval was necessary for the imposition of currency controls and borrowing by Member States. This approval was far from automatic. In 1952 the Executive Directors of the Fund decided that Fund approval should be conditional upon the request being consistent with Fund policies. That involved an assessment by the Fund of the underlying economic problems and of whether the policies the Member would pursue would be adequate to overcome them. The practice of making 'stand-by arrangements' developed, under which the IMF gave an assurance that the Member would be permitted to draw funds within a set period, originally six months. These stand-by arrangements are subject to conditions for access to IMF resources, set out in Letters of Intent drawn up by the borrowing State; and this conditionality became a primary instrument by which the IMF influenced economic policies in Member States.

Many delegations at Bretton Woods, including the British, had strongly resisted giving the IMF this influence, and this opposition explained the absence of the idea of conditionality from the original IMF Articles. But the IMF is a pragmatic organization. It is not organized according to the myth of sovereign equality, with each Member having an equal vote. Votes are proportionate to quotas. At present, the United States has 371,743 votes (the EU countries together have even more), and Bhutan has 313. While most States are tolerant of rhetorical gestures in the General Assembly and other political bodies, because words are cheap, they have a more guarded approach when it comes to money. States that want help from the IMF are expected to adopt sound policies; and what is 'sound' is determined by the economic theories that are in fashion from time to time in the most powerful States. Conditionality accordingly came to be seen as an instrument for the manipulation by western capitalist States of the economies of others. A report to the US Congress in 2000 (the 'Meltzer Report') wrote that:

Transformation of the IMF into a source of long-term conditional loans has made poorer nations increasingly dependent on the IMF and has given the IMF a degree of influence over member countries' policymaking that is unprecedented for a multilateral institution. Some agreements between the IMF and its members specify scores of required policies as conditions for continued funding. These programs have not ensured economic progress. They have undermined national sovereignty and often hindered the development of responsible, democratic institutions that correct their own mistakes and respond to changes in external conditions.

The conditionality system was put on to a formal basis in the First and Second Amendments to the Fund's Articles, and is the focus of much attention. The Fund itself reviewed the operation of its conditionality policies and issued a revised set of *Guidelines on Conditionality* in 2002. The broad policies are that Fund loans should contribute to solving the Member's balance of payments problem without recourse to measures destructive of national or international prosperity, and to achieving medium-term external viability while fostering sustainable economic growth. It is hard to disagree with those aims; but the more detailed policies pursued by the IMF can be more controversial. The Fund applies a principle of 'parsimony', according to which 'program-related conditions should be limited to the minimum necessary to achieve the goals of the Fund-supported program, to monitor its implementation, and to implement specific provisions of the Articles of Agreement or policies adopted under them'. Nonetheless, the Fund's concerns can be far-reaching. It lists a range of matters on which codes and standards have been laid down, which it regards as material to its surveillance responsibilities and other operations: accounting; auditing; anti-money laundering and countering the financing of terrorism (AML/CFT); banking supervision; corporate governance; data dissemination; fiscal transparency; insolvency and creditor rights; insurance supervision; monetary and financial policy transparency; payments systems; and securities regulation. The Fund also seeks to ensure that its operations are consistent with international environmental and human rights law. Serious failures to meet standards can result in a withdrawal of Fund support. For example, the Fund suspended a $216 million loan to Kenya in 1997 because Kenya had failed to take adequate steps to combat corruption. This approach is a notable example of the indirect enforcement of international rules. The 'corporate governance' standards, for instance, are the OECD's *Principles of Corporate Governance*, and the AML/CFT standards are the Financial Action Task Force's (FATF's) *Forty Recommendations*. Their adoption by the IMF is a powerful mechanism for securing their application in States that would probably not otherwise choose to implement them.

While much good comes from the encouragement of sensible disciplines and practices in States with financial difficulties, there is still strong criticism of the IMF's policies. In a memorable intervention in the debate, Joseph Stiglitz wrote in 2000, 'I was chief economist at the World Bank from 1996 until last November, during the gravest global economic crisis in a half-century. I saw how the IMF, in tandem with the U.S. Treasury Department, responded. And I was appalled.' His essential complaint was that the Fund failed in its diagnoses to distinguish between different kinds of economic problem, and persisted in administering inappropriate remedies. That takes the subject into realms of economic policy in which I have no expertise; but it is difficult not to think in such circumstances of the questions of international responsibility that might arise.

Lenders and borrowers run the risk that the borrower may be unable to repay the loan. There is, of course, always the possibility of rescheduling loans by revising the timetable for repayments and sometimes by reducing them. On the international plane this is a matter often handled by the Paris Club, an informal group of nineteen governments, including the

United States, Japan, Russia, Canada, Australia, and several European States, that are large lenders to other States. It considers the rescheduling of debts on a case-by-case basis, though within the framework of agreed principles, operating by consensus, and applying conditionality in much the same manner as the IMF. Paris Club negotiations rescheduled more than $500 billion in international debt between 1983 and 2006. There is an equivalent body, the London Club, which provides a framework for the renegotiation of debt owed to commercial lenders.

In extreme cases rescheduling cannot accommodate the economic difficulties facing a State, and it may default on financial obligations and fall into a situation that would be called insolvency were it to befall a corporation. Municipal law carefully regulates insolvency so as to give priority to certain creditors, such as employees, in access to whatever funds the insolvent corporation may have. The corporation moves into a form of administration which ensures that large and powerful creditors do not seize assets or force repayment of their loans at the expense of the weak (or those who allow the debtor more time before insisting on repayment). There is no comparable system for States. Moreover, the problems for States are much greater. States increasingly raise loans by issuing government bonds rather than by entering into loan agreements with banks or foreign States. But bonds are tradable securities, and bondholders may be both very numerous and very difficult to identify. A negotiated variation of the loan contract, of the kind that the London and Paris Clubs effect, may be wholly impractical, especially in the context of a full-blown economic crisis. There is a clear need for some agreed international mechanism to deal with these situations, and it has been the subject of proposals within the IMF for a Sovereign Debt Rescheduling Mechanism (SDRM). Despite the attention that is being given to this matter, however, it is likely to be some years before any such mechanism is agreed.

I have concentrated so far on the agreements that establish the architecture of the international monetary system. There are many other agreements of cardinal importance.[15] There are monetary unions, such as the European Union with its Euro, the Eastern Caribbean Currency Union with the Eastern Caribbean dollar, and the CFA Franc of the Communauté financière d'Afrique—the eight countries of the Union Économique et Monétaire Ouest Africaine (UEMOA). These have complex rules for the co-ordination of the economic policies and the banking

---

[15] See Rosa M. Lastra, *Legal Foundations of International Monetary Stability* (Oxford: Oxford University Press, 2006).

regulation and supervision systems of the participating States. There are regional development banks, such as the European Bank for Reconstruction and Development, the African Development Bank, the Asian Development Bank, and the Inter-American Development Bank. All of them invest in projects and ventures, often within the private sector, in their respective regions. Together with the World Bank group, they are often referred to as the Multilateral Development Banks (MDBs).

There are other institutions concerned less with lending than with the supervision and smooth operation of the international monetary system. The Bank for International Settlements (BIS), which is the oldest of the international financial institutions, established in 1930 to assist with reparations payments following World War One, is a focus for international banking co-ordination and the development of financial standards. The Financial Action Task Force (FATF), established by the G-7[16] in 1989, has produced some very important guidelines and principles on money laundering and terrorist financing which have led to significant changes in the financial regulations of many States. A similar organization, the Caribbean Financial Action Task Force (CFATF), has been set up to focus on money laundering in that part of the world and its links with the illegal narcotics trade.

There is much else that could be written about the intricate web of international, regional, and national financial institutions which constitutes the international monetary system; but now it is necessary to turn attention to the other major component of international economic law—the international trade system and the WTO.

6.7 THE INTERNATIONAL TRADING SYSTEM

The adoption of the General Agreement on Tariffs and Trade (GATT), on a provisional basis in 1947, pending the entry into force of the proposed International Trade Organization, has already been noted. Now it is time to say a little more about what the GATT was and what it did.

Throughout the nineteenth and twentieth centuries, debate over international economic problems focused on trade barriers. In England the Corn Laws were introduced by the Importation Act 1815 in order to protect English farmers from being undermined by cheap foreign imports. The Corn Laws in turn were opposed by the free trade movement as a

---

[16] Strictly, the G-7 is the meeting of the Finance Ministers and Governors of the Central Banks of Canada, France, Germany, Italy, Japan, the United Kingdom, and the United States.

protectionist measure which served only to maintain the profits of landowners, and were eventually abolished in the face of the Irish potato famine. Much the same debate over the desirability of protectionist laws has been rehearsed time and time again in different States and in the context of different industries.

There had been a network of bilateral trade treaties before the First World War, and its effect was magnified by the widespread use of MFN clauses which obliged each State Party to give the other treatment that was at least as good as the treatment given to the 'most favoured' third State. This relatively liberal period of international trade was brought to an end by the Great War and the tariffs, export prohibitions, exchange controls, and other trade restrictions that came in its wake. It is understandable that those who in the 1940s began the planning of a new international order, having come through the Great Depression but still embroiled in World War Two, should look back to the halcyon days of free trade, peace, and prosperity.

The theory of comparative advantage asserts that overall welfare and economic efficiency—though not necessarily economic justice—is maximized if everyone, and every State, does what they are very best at doing, even if some States are better at everything than other States. It had become a matter of economic orthodoxy in the non-communist world, appearing to be a self-evident truth. Textbooks gave persuasive examples. A man may be the only lawyer, and also the most efficient gardener, in town; but rather than divide his time between practising law and digging his garden it makes sense for him to practise law full-time and to pay some-one else to dig his garden, even though the gardener he employs is less efficient than the lawyer would have been. On the international scale, it may be that both wheat and coffee could be grown in Canada and in Uganda; but it is still more efficient, and more will be produced in total, if Uganda concentrates upon growing coffee, and Canada upon growing wheat, and they trade products.

If reality were so simple, all States would cheerfully accept free trade and the maximized welfare that it promises. The fact that States do not do this indicates that there is something missing from the theory.

There are a number of deficiencies in that simple theory of comparative advantage. Protectionist measures may permit domestic industries to thrive, which under free trade would wither in the face of cheap imports. Imports may be opposed by the government in the public interest—for example because it thinks it imprudent to rely upon foreign suppliers of certain strategic goods such as staple foods, energy, or military equip-ment, or because it wishes to nurture an infant industry as yet too weak to compete internationally, or because it wishes to preserve traditional industries such as fishing in order to preserve employment and local communities. There are also theoretical objections to the theory of comparative advantage. In the mid nineteenth century the economist Robert Torrens pointed out that a State could impose an 'optimal tariff' and maximize its own welfare, even though there would be an adverse effect upon global efficiency and welfare. It is this belief that intervention in international trade may secure real advantages for large States that provides an economic justification for their governments to move away from the pure free trade model. In the 1930s, for instance, tariffs were raised by many States: the Smoot-Hawley Act raised US tariffs to their highest ever levels in order to protect farmers. Thus, while it was always clear that the new order for the post-war world would be based upon the principle of free trade, there remained the critical question of the precise scope of that principle and the manner in which it would be applied. The answers were given in the General Agreement on Tariffs and Trade, drafted as an off-shoot of the Bretton Woods exercise, and the initial embodiment of the modified free trade principle.

6.8 THE GATT AND THE WTO

The GATT rests on a handful of clear and simple principles. The first is that restrictions on international trade should be minimized (but not eliminated) and should be transparent. Trade restraints must be imposed in the form of tariffs, which must be published. Non-tariff barriers to international trade, such as quotas and import or export licences, are in principle not permitted to GATT Contracting States (GATT Article XI). (The GATT was technically an agreement and not an international organization: had it been an organization, Congressional approval would have been needed for its adoption by the United States. Accordingly, it did not have 'Members' but only Contracting Parties, who are referred to as CONTRACTING PARTIES in uppercase font when they are acting collectively.)

The second principle is that trade concessions are multilateralized. That is to say, each GATT Contracting Party must apply its tariffs to all other Contracting Parties on a Most Favoured Nation ('MFN') basis (GATT Article I). This is not simply a matter of principle; it is an essential element of the structure and development of the GATT system. It is too difficult to negotiate tariffs bilaterally in the modern world. This is partly a question of numbers: even in 1945 the number of bilateral negotiations that would have been necessary would have rendered the task practically unmanageable. It is also a matter of the dynamics of negotiations. If a State looks for an equivalent concession to balance each tariff reduction that it makes in relation to imports from another State, further reductions will soon become impossible because the other State has run out of meaningful reductions to offer: bilateral tariff reductions can only be balanced on the basis of whatever the actual trade between the two States is, and that trade itself may be very limited and unbalanced. But by conducting negotiations collectively, among all Contracting Parties, this limitation is avoided. States do not seek to ensure that they balance the tariff reductions with each and every other State: they offer tariff reductions as contributions to an overall package in which State A's concessions may be met by little or nothing in return from State B, but any such detriment or imbalance is corrected by the aggregate of benefits that State A receives from States C, D, and so on. This makes it much easier to negotiate substantial tariff reductions.

Negotiations proceed between the main producing and consuming nations, and concessions are then extended to all by the operation of the MFN clause. This is a good example of the role of international law in the international trading system. It is the legal articulation, definition, and application of the MFN principle that underpins and gives precision to what might otherwise be a rather vague international understanding. The GATT CONTRACTING PARTIES have met in a series of negotiating 'rounds', in which tariff concessions and other trade restraints were agreed. The tariff concessions are incorporated in Schedules which are annexed to the GATT and which are binding on the State making them. Tariff 'bindings', as they are known, were the heart of the original GATT negotiations. At the end of the Uruguay Round, which lasted from 1986 to 1993, developed countries had bound 99% (measured in terms of the number of different kinds of goods, as fixed by internationally agreed customs classifications) of the goods in which they trade, developing countries had bound 73%, and 'transition economies' (that is, countries in the process of transformation from centrally-planned into market economies) had bound 98%. Those figures should be compared with the situation prior to the opening of the Uruguay Round, when the respective percentages were 78%, 21%, and 73%.

The third principle underlying the GATT is that once goods are admitted to a State they must be treated in the same way as 'like domestic products' (GATT Article III). Internal taxes and regulations within a State may not discriminate between imports and like domestic products. Much energy is devoted to determining whether products are alike. Are strong beer and weak wine 'like products'? Are cheap brandy and expensive luxury brandy 'like products'? Are cars with a high petrol consumption and cars with low petrol consumption 'like products', and does it matter if the former are largely imported and the latter are largely domestically produced, so that any differential taxation would favour domestic producers? These are not purely technical questions of classification. They implicate the basic rights of a State to use tax and trade measures as ways of achieving social object-ives. States are not entitled to maintain discriminatory taxes in breach of GATT Article III; and as I shall explain, the WTO operates an effective dis-pute settlement system to address allegations of breach.

This picture of a non-discriminatory free trade system may sound too good to be true; and it is. The commitments were not total. According to the Protocol of Provisional Application, by virtue of which the GATT was applied 'provisionally' (pending the entry into force of the Havana Charter), Contracting Parties were obliged to apply GATT Part II, which dealt with matters such as internal taxation, dumping, and quantitative restrictions on trade, only 'to the fullest extent not inconsistent with exist-ing legislation'. Existing discriminatory laws were thus 'grandfathered' in the original GATT.

There were also very extensive exceptions to those obligations that were established in the GATT. The exceptions were of various kinds. As might be expected, GATT CONTRACTING PARTIES were entitled to impose import and export controls for reasons of public welfare (Article XX). These provisions have featured prominently in disputes over import restrictions that States have taken ostensibly for environmental reasons (such as the *Tuna* and *Shrimp* cases against the United States); but the exceptions have been interpreted carefully, so as to ensure that environ-mental measures do not become disguised restrictions on trade. GATT also permits trade controls for security reasons (Article XXI), so that export bans on computers and armaments, for example, may be permissi-ble. GATT Article XXIV accommodated political realities by permitting the establishment and operation of customs unions and free trade areas, such as Benelux, within which free trade would operate between the Members, which would maintain a common trade frontier towards third States. Article XXXV permitted States to oppose the entry into force of the GATT *vis-à-vis* any other State. That provision has been used by more than sixty States for various reasons, including the opposition of India and Pakistan to trade relations with apartheid-era South Africa, and the use of Article XXXV by many States for commercial reasons against Japan on its accession to the GATT in 1955.

Three major exceptions were contained in GATT Articles XII, XIX, and XXV. Article XII permitted the imposition of import quotas in order to safeguard the State's balance of payments—a necessary concession when the GATT was drafted, because fixed exchange rates still prevailed under the IMF scheme. Article XIX, sometimes called the 'safeguards clause' or 'escape clause', permitted controls to choke off unforeseen import surges that threatened serious injury to domestic industries producing like products. In practice, Article XIX measures were rarely taken, States preferring to resort to what were known as 'grey area' measures, notably Voluntary Export Restraints (VERs—also known as Voluntary Restraint Agreements or VRAs) which were estimated to be around ten times as numerous as Article XIX measures. Under VERs, the exporting State would voluntarily restrict its exports of certain products at the request of an importing State troubled by the effect of the imports upon its economy. The best known were the VERs on Japanese steel and automobile exports to the United States, which endured for many years, and the Multifibre Agreement (MFA), which applied to about 80% of world textile exports and provided for quotas on textile imports into developed States from developing States (though not from other developed States). More generally, GATT Article XXV.5 permitted a two-thirds (now three-fourths) majority of the CONTRACTING PARTIES to waive any GATT obligation, and this provision was used on many occasions in order to permit preferential treatment for trade with certain States, and particularly developing countries (although the United States benefited from a very wide waiver in 1995 regarding agricultural products).

Other exceptions were narrower. Article I of the GATT permitted, as an exception to the MFN principle, the maintenance of existing preferences, such as the 'Imperial Preferences' under which imports from the British Dominions and colonies were admitted to the United Kingdom on special terms—a concession for which the United Kingdom had fought hard. Article XI.2 permitted the maintenance of quantitative restrictions on trade in agricultural products, and Article XVI permitted subsidies for exported primary products, including agricultural goods. These provisions, which gave a measure of protection to strong agricultural interests in developed States, set the stage for much criticism of the GATT and the international trade order. While there is widespread agreement that agricultural protectionism is expensive and inefficient and seriously distorts trade patterns, it must not be thought that abolishing the GATT exceptions that permit this protectionism would be an unequivocal benefit to developing States. If protectionist measures were abolished, for example, prices would rise. One might think that this would enable developing States to increase their exports: but Africa has become a net importer of food, and if the liberalization of trade in agriculture is considered in isolation, Africa might come out worse than it is under the existing rules.[17]

While these exceptions may appear as no more than concessions to vested interests of developed States, they established the principle of differential treatment within the structure of the GATT and thus facilitated the amendment of the GATT to accommodate the particular needs of developing States. This move was heavily influenced by the proponents of the 'New International Economic Order',[18] who argued that the fact that all States were treated equally did not mean that they were being treated fairly. The need for some modification to the terms of the GATT had been recognized in 1958, in the Haberler Report. The decisive movement occurred 1964 to 1965, when the UN Conference on Trade and Development (UNCTAD) drafted a new Part IV (Trade and Development) of the GATT, providing for non-reciprocal 'special and differential treatment' for developing States. (Such States are actually called 'less-developed States' in GATT Part IV, in accordance with the then-prevailing orthodoxy. There is no WTO definition of a 'developing State'. Each Member decides for itself whether it is 'developing' or 'developed').[19] Part IV acknowledged the need for 'positive efforts designed to ensure that less-developed Contracting Parties secure a share in the growth in international trade[20] commensurate with the needs of their economic development'; and developed Contracting Parties undertook 'to accord high priority to the reduction and elimination of barriers' to trade in products of particular interest to developing States. Part IV accepted that there was a problem, even if it did little to address it. More concrete steps were taken in the form of Article XXV.5 waivers, and in particular in the two waivers given in 1971 which permitted the creation of the generalized system of preferences for developing States (GSP) and tariff preferences on trade between developing countries, as exceptions to the general MFN obligation. The two 1971 waivers were put on a permanent

---

[17] See the African Union's 2003 Declaration on Agriculture and Food Security in Africa, <http://www.africa-union.org/root/au/Documents/Decisions/hog/12HoGAssembly2003.pdf>.

[18] See M. Bedjaoui, *Towards a New International Economic Order* (New York: Holmes & Meier, 1979), and M. Benchikh, *Droit international du sous-développement* (Paris: Berger-Levrault, 1983) for trenchant analyses of the position of developing States in international law.

[19] The World Bank does have such a definition. Countries with a gross national income (GNI) of $825 or less in 2004 were classified as low-income economies, those with a GNI per capita of $825–$3,255 as lower-middle-income economies, those with a GNI of $3,255–$10,066 as upper-middle-income economies, and those with a GNI of over $10,066 as high-income economies. See <http://devdata.worldbank.org/wdi2006/contents/Usersguide.htm>.

[20] Article XXXVI.3. Not, it will be noted, a 'share in international trade commensurate with the needs of their economic development'.

basis in 1979 in a Decision of the CONTRACTING PARTIES known as the 'Enabling Clause'.

The GATT system as described above functioned for around a quarter of a century, but the system needed to be developed to meet the demands of the major trading nations. As tariffs were progressively reduced, the relative importance of non-tariff barriers to trade (NTBs) increased, and became a focus of concern. NTBs included matters such as technical standards (the need for different plugs and voltages on electrical equipment in different countries is an example), and government subsidies, against which imports might be unable to compete. During the Tokyo Round negotiations (1973 to 1979) 13 supplementary agreements were concluded, dealing with non-tariff barriers such as technical barriers to trade, dumping, subsidies and government procurement, and with other matters such as safeguard measures, dispute settlement, and Differential and More Favourable Treatment for developing countries. These were known as the plurilateral agreements or codes, because there was no obligation for all GATT CONTRACTING PARTIES to accept them: participation varied from agreement to agreement—GATT à la carte.

The Tokyo Round Codes paved the way for the ambitious negotiations in the Uruguay Round (1986 to 1994). Those negotiations made a fundamental shift in the focus of the GATT Contracting Parties, moving beyond concern with trade in goods to bring in the 'new areas' such as intellectual property rights, investment, trade in services, and the linkages between trade and environmental concerns. The discussions were difficult and protracted but—somewhat surprisingly—they succeeded. Indeed, they not only added very significantly to the basic GATT framework, they produced a complete overhaul of the system; for it was from the Uruguay Round that the World Trade Organization (WTO) sprang into existence in 1994 and rapidly achieved near-global acceptance. In 2006 it had about 150 members, including almost all the major trading States. China acceded in 2001; and negotiations on the terms of Russia's accession began in 1995, the lengthy discussions consisting of detailed examination of the compatibility of Russia's laws and practices with the whole range of WTO rules to which it would accede.

The WTO is a real international organization: no longer is international trade organized under the aegis of the provisional and incorporeal GATT. The continuity between the WTO and the GATT, however, is very plain. Indeed, the 1994 Marrakesh Agreement establishing the WTO is remarkably short: under a dozen pages. The last page, however, is a list of annexes, and it is here that the real work is done. Thus, the first annex is the General Agreement on Tariffs and Trade, 1994. That consists of the

1947 GATT 'as rectified, amended or modified by the terms of legal instruments which have entered into force before the date of entry into force of the WTO Agreement'—what European Community lawyers would call the GATT plus the *acquis*. Then there is a list of Agreements. Those relating to trade in goods include the agreements on sanitary and phytosanitary measures (the SPS Agreement), on textiles (superseding the MFA), technical barriers to trade (the TBT Agreement), trade-related investment measures (the TRIMS Agreement, which addresses matters such as requirements that goods produced in a State must have a certain proportion of local components), subsidies and countervailing measures (the SCM Agreement), and on safeguards. In addition, there is the General Agreement on Trade in Services (GATS), and the Agreement on Trade-Related Aspects of Intellectual Property Rights (TRIPS). There is also the Understanding on Rules and Procedures Governing the Settlement of Disputes (the Dispute Settlement Understanding or DSU) and the Trade Policy Review Mechanism (TPRM). All WTO Parties are obliged to accept the foregoing agreements. The list of annexes closes with four plurilateral trade agreements, whose acceptance is not mandatory, on trade in civil aircraft, government procurement, dairy products, and bovine meat.

These agreements revise and consolidate the work of the Tokyo Round, and provide a much broader legal framework for trade regulation than has previously existed on a global scale. The GATS, for instance, regulates the very important services sector and, like the GATT before it, regulates both access to markets and the treatment of service providers once they have been admitted to foreign markets. It covers four 'modes of supply' of services: cross-border supply, such as international telephone services; consumption abroad, as when tourists travel to foreign destinations; commercial presence, for example when a law firm establishes a foreign office; and movement of natural persons, where an individual travels to work abroad. In principle (derogations are permitted for what should ordinarily be a maximum of ten years), services are subject to the MFN obligation; but beyond this governments have an almost unlimited right to choose what commitments they assume under the GATS. They may, for example, make commitments only in respect of certain sectors and certain modes of supply; and within those areas they may stipulate what degree of market access and national treatment they undertake to provide. Like the GATT, the intention is that trade should become progressively liberalized as States negotiate more and more commitments—or, to put it another way, as they progressively remove barriers to the international trade in services. The GATS does permit the withdrawal of commitments after three years, but the expectation is that the overall trend will be towards greater liberalization. The GATS itself has a series of annexes dealing with particular sectors, including financial services and telecommunications; and work is proceeding on detailed regulation in other sectors such as maritime transportation.

Much of the regulation under the WTO is highly technical in nature, but there are nonetheless great issues of principle being worked out, particularly through the work of the WTO panels and the WTO Appellate Body, which decide disputes concerning the interpretation of application of the 'covered agreements'—that is, WTO Agreement and its associated Agreements—which cannot be settled by the consultation procedure provided for in the DSU. Two controversial areas stand out. One is the question of the standards of review of governmental action. If the government of a Contracting Party decides that a particular measure, such as a ban on the sale or importation of a product, is necessary on health grounds, how should a WTO panel approach the task of reviewing the decision? This is a task comparable to the review of governmental action under human rights instruments, and is generating a rich jurisprudence on concepts such as proportionality and legitimate expectations. The second is the range of 'trade and . . .' topics, such as trade and human rights, and in particular the question of trade and the environment. The striking of a balance between trade restraints legitimately imposed for environmental reasons and restraints ostensibly adopted for environmental reasons but causing an unnecessary or unacceptable restriction on the basic trade rights under the WTO is a matter of great delicacy and importance. Of course, even these issues involve much technical WTO law; but here one finds much good lawyer's law. For example, there are very close parallels between the notion of 'like products', which underpins all of the WTO prohibitions on discrimination, and the notion of substitutable products in competition law; and as this youthful body of international law develops one sees it being knitted into the broader fabric of longer-established areas of the law—although some fear that the special characteristics of areas such as international trade law are leading to a degree of fragmentation in international law.[21]

Trade law is a fast-moving area, in part because of the WTO provisions on dispute settlement. These represent a major improvement on procedures under the 1947 GATT, which required a consensus (including the Respondent) in favour of action. The WTO Dispute Settlement Understanding provides that if the obligatory consultations between

---

[21] The ILC is studying the question of fragmentation in international law.

disputing parties fail to resolve a dispute, a complaining party has a right to require the establishment of a dispute settlement panel composed of three or five independent experts chosen in consultation with the parties to the dispute. The panel's report is adopted unless there is either a consensus of WTO Contracting Parties against adoption, or the report is successfully appealed to the WTO's Appellate Body. If an adopted report finds a violation of WTO obligations, the offending State is obliged to bring the measures in question into line with those obligations and to implement whatever remedial measures the panel (or Appellate Body) proposes. If it fails to do so within a reasonable time, the complaining party may seek the authorization of the Dispute Settlement Body to take countermeasures by suspending concessions equivalent in amount to the level of the violation. The presumption in favour of the establishment of dispute panels and the adoption of their reports has made the WTO DSU an effective and popular mechanism. By 2006, 350 disputes had been referred to the mechanism.

In fact, the dispute settlement procedure does not depend upon the concept of a violation of WTO rules. As GATT Article XXIII makes plain, a complaint may, indeed, be made that another Party has violated a WTO agreement; but a Party may also make a 'non-violation complaint', that is, a complaint that a benefit that it expected to receive under a WTO agreement is being nullified or impaired by a measure taken by another Party, whether or not that measure violates a WTO rule. For example, in the *EC–Oilseeds* case the United States complained that the benefit of EC tariff concessions on oilseed imports had been nullified and impaired by EC subsidies payable to processors in respect of purchases of EC-produced oilseeds but not payable with respect to purchases of the imported like product. The panel found that the subsidy was both a violation of GATT Article III.4 and an impairment of the benefit expected under the tariff concessions. There is a third category of action, similar to the non-violation complaint: the 'situation complaint'. This was intended to cover circumstances where expected benefits were nullified or impaired by a macroeconomic emergency, such as a general economic depression or a collapse in the price of a commodity; but the provision has not been used in practice. The distinction between violation complaints and non-violation complaints is one of the characteristics of the WTO dispute settlement procedures, and is a subtle mechanism for aligning those procedures with the economic realities of concern to WTO Contracting Parties.

The WTO continues to act as a key forum for international economic debate and negotiation. In 1999 a WTO Ministerial Conference in Seattle was intended to have launched a new round of negotiations, but the conference was disrupted by thousands of protesters. The protests were directed at a number of targets: globalization; capitalism; the democratic deficit in the WTO; and more generally, the perception that the WTO and the government representatives attending the meeting were not doing enough to address issues of global poverty and deprivation. The Battle of Seattle captured the spirit of the times, and was followed by many similar protests and movements aiming at the End of Poverty.[22] The protests reinforced the position of those who saw global poverty as the most pressing international problem. The resumed session convened in 2001 in Doha, and the Doha Round came to be perceived as the Development Round.

The Doha Declaration of 2001 identified a range of topics for negotiation, many of them clustering around the issues of implementation of WTO rules by developing States and the role of international trade in 'the promotion of economic development and the alleviation of poverty'. While ending global poverty might have been a latent goal, attention was focused on more proximate targets. The phasing out of developed States' agricultural subsidies is the key issue. Developing countries were also greatly concerned by issues such as the effect of the protections afforded to intellectual property rights of pharmaceuticals under the TRIPS Agreement upon their ability to procure medicines to combat AIDS and other diseases. The Doha 'Declaration on the TRIPS agreement and public health' addresses that question. In it the WTO Ministers affirmed the right of States to grant compulsory patent licences and asserted that:

We agree that the TRIPS Agreement does not and should not prevent members from taking measures to protect public health. Accordingly, while reiterating our commitment to the TRIPS Agreement, we affirm that the Agreement can and should be interpreted and implemented in a manner supportive of WTO members' right to protect public health and, in particular, to promote access to medicines for all.

International economic law has entered a new phase. Governments have an increasingly clear and sophisticated view of the social and political implications of even the most abstruse technical rules. Much of the credit for that development rests with the remarkable generation of lawyers who, during the past twenty or thirty years, have developed real expertise in difficult areas of the law that were practically unknown to their predecessors; and it is one aim of this short book to encourage others to follow them.

---

[22] The title of a widely read book by Jeffrey Sachs (*The End of Poverty, How we can make it happen in our lifetime* (London: Penguin, 2005)).

6.9 COMMODITY AND ENERGY AGREEMENTS

Artificial barriers to international trade can be removed: basic laws of economic behaviour cannot. Prices for primary products can fluctuate widely. Demand for tin may fall as aluminium cans supplant cans made from tin-plated steel; supplies of wheat may fall because of poor weather: and prices may fall or rise accordingly. Such fluctuations may of course harm individual producers and consumers, by leaving them with less money. But the fluctuations also have a seriously disruptive macroeconomic effect. They impede long-term planning and investment by States and by corporations engaged in the associated trades, which cannot predict their income in future years. Mechanisms that can reduce price fluctuations materially help planning and economic development.

The best-known such mechanism is the Organization of the Petroleum Exporting Countries (OPEC). Established in 1960, OPEC was originally designed by its Member States to counteract the economic power of the 'seven sisters', the oligopoly of international oil companies that dominated the international oil market. Recognition of the interdependence of international economies, and of the seriousness of the crises that interruptions of energy supplies might trigger, led OPEC to assume a crucial role in stabilizing the oil market, so helping oil producing States to maintain a reasonable rate of return on their investments and ensuring that the supply of oil to consumers is reasonably predictable. Whether it can maintain that stabilizing role, now that production from non-OPEC countries such as Russia have expanded, is open to considerable doubt.

OPEC is a producer cartel; but broader-based mechanisms have been devised for other commodities. The International Tin Council (ITC) is the most notorious. It was established in the 1950s and operated under a series of International Tin Agreements, which sought to stabilize prices within agreed limits through the maintenance of a buffer stock. Tin was sold from the stock when prices rose above a certain level, and bought into the stock when prices fell below a lower intervention level. The ITC was permitted to borrow money for the purposes of buffer stock operations, and to settle export quotas for producer States. Clearly, the system is sustainable over the long term only if the upper and lower intervention prices are fixed so as to be in line with long-term supply and demand. The constitution of the ITC facilitated this strategy: it was composed of producer and consumer States. The votes within the group of producer States were allocated on the basis of each State's share of world tin production, and the group of consumer countries had an equal number of votes, apportioned on the basis of their share of consumption. Decisions required a majority within each of the two groups. Thus, neither producers nor consumers alone could control the organization, but the largest producers and consumers together could do so. Unfortunately, the ITC tried to maintain prices at a level that was unsustainable in the face of falling demand for tin and it became insolvent in 1985, sparking off a round of litigation over the responsibilities of ITC Member States for the many millions of pounds that the Council owed.[23]

Other commodity agreements have survived, if only by adopting a less ambitious strategy. The International Coffee Organization (ICO), which is also organized on the basis of parity between the group of producers and the group of consumers, has since 1963 promoted the development of a stable market for coffee, and is increasingly active in the promotion of sustainable development and of diversification on the part of producers. Over the years it has introduced and abandoned quota mechanisms to influence prices, in the light of the prevailing market conditions. The International Cocoa Organization (ICCO) performs a similar function, but has not operated a pricing mechanism for many years. There are other, similar, organizations operating, in relation to sugar and tropical timber for instance.[24] But the days of market regulation and buffer stocks appear to have passed. The International Natural Rubber Organization (INRO) was probably the last international commodity organization to operate a buffer stock, and it was agreed in 1999 to wind up that stock. The difficulties in maintaining economic mechanisms flowed from several factors, including market instability, limited support for the organization from States, and disagreements over pricing policies and the division of the benefits that higher prices might bring. While there had been willingness to assist in the operation of market mechanisms—the IMF, for example, created a Buffer Stocks Financing Facility in 1969, and a Common Fund for Commodities was established in 1980 for various purposes including the financing of buffer stocks—the emphasis now is firmly on working within market disciplines to promote sustainable development and stability in relation to commodity markets.

---

[23] Among the related cases see *J H Rayner (Mincing Lane) Ltd v Department of Trade and Industry* [1990] 2 AC 418.

[24] See the list of organizations at <http://ro.unctad.org/commodities/partners.htm>.

The International Grains Council (IGC) exemplifies this approach. After the Great Depression of the 1930s there were several attempts to conclude an international wheat agreement which would secure supplies and support prices. Like other commodity agreements, the mechanisms for intervening in the wheat market were not wholly successful. The emphasis was shifted to transparency, market information, and technical assistance as means of adjusting to changing market conditions. More significantly the IGC, which again is composed of both producer and consumer States, administers two conventions: the 1995 Grains Trade Convention (GTC) and the 1999 Food Aid Convention (FAC). The former is concerned with the monitoring and development of markets in grains, and the latter with securing a predictable system of international food aid. Between the two conventions, the IGC is concerned both with grain as a tradable commodity and resource, and as a social necessity for feeding the world's population. One hesitates to refer to a holistic approach to commodities; but the IGC is moving in that direction.

One final group of agreements that falls under this broad heading is that concerned with energy supplies. Though OPEC continues its work in the oil sector, there is no comparable organization regulating the market in coal, gas, or nuclear power. There are, however, organizations concerned with ancillary aspects of energy supply. The International Energy Agency (IEA) was established during the 1973 to 1974 oil crisis, initially to co-ordinate emergency responses between the member States to energy shortages. It now has a broader responsibility for the formulation of energy policy and the development of sustainable energy strategies, and it is playing a significant role in the response to the problems of climate change. The Energy Charter Treaty and its secretariat were established in the 1990s to promote energy co-operation among the Eurasian States—essentially, to find ways of obtaining secure supplies of energy for western Europe from the east (though the members now include Australia and Japan). The Energy Charter Treaty has a particular importance in underpinning and providing legal protection for the extensive investments that have been made in the energy sector since the 1990s. Finally, and of particular importance for those who doubt the ability of the wind turbine to power the world economy, the International Atomic Energy Agency (IAEA) provides the one global mechanism for the monitoring and verification of uses of nuclear power. More familiar during the crises over real or imagined nuclear weapons programmes in Iraq, Pakistan, and North Korea as a pawn in Great Power politics, the IAEA has a crucial role in ensuring that the energy needs of the future can be met safely.

6.10 REGIONAL ECONOMIC ARRANGEMENTS

I have concentrated up to this point upon global regimes; but there is much, and often more visible, activity on a regional level. Regional economic integration agreements, in particular, are often expressions of a regional solidarity that extends well beyond the purely economic sphere.

The European Union is the obvious and most highly developed instance. There are three elements or 'pillars' in the Union. The first is the European Community, which secures economic integration and also addresses social and environmental issues. This aspect has been the keystone of European integration since the European Economic Community (EEC) was established in 1957, to sit alongside the European Coal and Steel Community (ECSC) and the European Atomic Energy Community (EAEC). (The institutions of those three bodies were merged in 1967.) The other two pillars of the Union are the Common Foreign and Security Policy, which seeks to foster common positions among the Member States on foreign relations and military matters, and the Police and Judicial Co-operation in Criminal Matters pillar. In addition to the Council, which consists of representatives of the Member States, the Union has a Parliament, with more extensive powers of irritation than of legislation, and a Court of Auditors which, by 2006, had refused for eleven consecutive years to sign off the Community's accounts. Above all, the Community has an unelected Commission which plays the central role in the formulation and implementation of Community policy and exercises enormous power. The European Community is a party to many international agreements and often attends conferences alongside Member States, causing some concern that the European States are over-represented—a view based largely upon the misconception that the interests of the Commission, which represents the Community, and the Member States are necessarily the same.

The European Community is unusual in combining the elements of a customs union, within which goods and services may in principle move freely, with more far-reaching provisions guaranteeing freedom of movement for workers and capital, and a single currency, the Euro, which has been adopted by about half of the Member States. There is a remarkable degree of harmonization of laws and supranational legislation, which aim to create a single market within the Union, producing something close to a federation of Member States. Other regional organizations have, as yet, more confined functions; but several of them have ambitious programmes of regional integration.

In West Africa the fifteen Member States of the Economic Community of West African States (ECOWAS), founded in 1975, revised the ECOWAS Treaty in 1993 so as to introduce significant supranational elements. It is complemented by the Union économique et monétaire ouest-africaine (UEMOA), and by the Banque Centrale des Etats de l'Afrique de l'Ouest (BCEAO). While the primary purpose of ECOWAS is to 'promote co-operation and integration, leading to the establishment of an economic union in West Africa', it also makes a very significant contribution to regional peacekeeping and security. For instance, it established an armed observer group, the Economic Community Cease-Fire Monitoring Group (ECOMOG), in 1990 to monitor and stabilize the situation in the midst of the civil war in Liberia. The Common Market for Eastern and Southern Africa (COMESA), which replaced the preferential trade area that had been established in 1981, also has supranational elements modelled on those in the European Community treaty. It has a supranational Court, based in Khartoum, now delivering judgments. The Southern African Development Community (SADC) is pressing ahead with a programme of integration, but the East African Community (EAC) and Union du Maghreb Arabe (UMA) have moved less far along the road of economic integration.

In the Americas there are some highly developed organizations. The North American Free Trade Agreement, (NAFTA), made by Canada, Mexico, and the United States in 1992 and in force since 1994, is a complex and detailed legal framework for trade and investment between the three States. In the south, the Mercado Común del Sur (MERCO-SUR—Southern Common Market), established in 1991 by Argentina, Brazil, Paraguay, and Uruguay and joined in 2006 by Venezuela, is similarly a highly developed organization. It has adopted a series of codes and protocols on various aspects of business regulation, investment protection, and dispute settlement. There are several other international economic organizations in Latin America. The Caribbean Community (CARICOM) and the Andean Community (CAN) are the most prominent; but others such as the Sistema de la Integración Centroamericana (SICA) and the Sistema Económico Latinoamericano y del Caribe (SELA) are active in promoting regional and subregional integration. An ambitious plan to create a Free Trade Area of the Americas (FTAA), which would embrace thirty-four American States from Canada and the United States, through the Caribbean and central America, down to Chile and Argentina, encountered opposition from trade unions, NGOs and other groups, and failed to achieve the 2005 target date for adoption. The plan appears to have been effectively abandoned in 2006.

Economic integration is also proceeding in other regions. There is a Gulf Co-operation Council (GCC) in the Middle East, which promotes regional co-ordination and integration across a wide range of economic and cultural fields. The Association of Southeast Asian Nations (ASEAN), has a similarly broad remit, as does the Pacific Islands Forum; while the South Asian Association for Regional Cooperation (SAARC) co-ordinates economic and developmental policies among its Member States. The Asia-Pacific Economic Cooperation (APEC) is working to achieve free and open trade and investment in the Asia-Pacific region by 2010 for developed economies and 2020 for developing economies; and the Asian Development Bank (ADB) plays an active role in promoting economic co-operation in the region.

6.11 FINAL OBSERVATIONS

Short as this survey of international economic law has been it has, I hope, given a sense not only of the considerable international activity in this field but also of the extent to which international economic relations are becoming rule-based rather than power-based. The world is closer than is widely recognized to a situation in which States can sue each other for economic injuries inflicted upon them. Among Nicaragua's complaints in its International Court case against the United States in 1984 was the interruption of its trade. Nauru, in 1989, complained to the Court about the mismanagement of its economy while it was under Australian administration. Cases were launched under Bilateral Investment Treaties against Russia and Argentina for losses suffered by foreign investors during the financial crises in those two States. And there are scores of cases being pursued through the WTO dispute settlement mechanism. There are many opportunities for claims to be based on the ways in which States manage economic crises; and there are many cases exploiting those opportunities.

While there is no doubt a significant degree of overlap and consequent inefficiency among international organizations, as there is in every sphere of human activity, this development is, by and large, a good thing. As I noted at the beginning of this chapter, quoting one of the more lucid analyses in recent British foreign policy, 'where there are no rules, the rich and powerful bully the poor and the powerless'. But it is not only a matter of economic justice—indeed, it is in large part not a matter of economic justice at all. The international rules are best seen not as largely ineffectual attempts to produce a fairer world, but rather as reasonably successful attempts to lubricate the wheels of international trade and the international economy. Their success is not that they make things fairer, but that they make things easier. It remains a matter for the governments of the world, and their citizens, to use the available mechanisms to make the world a fairer place.

7

The Global Environment

7.1 THE ENVIRONMENT AND THE LIMITATIONS OF LAW

There are two main models of legal relationship. In the first, someone injured by the wrongdoing of another sues the other. In the second, action is taken by a representative of the society against the wrongdoer in the public interest. These are the paradigms of private and public law, exemplified by civil and criminal law respectively, within national legal systems. They depend upon the ability to identify a wrongdoer and a victim or a representative of the public interest. But the paradigms cannot always easily be sustained within the international legal system; and there is no better example of this than the difficulties that arise in environmental law.

Take, for instance, the case of global warming. Greenhouse gases include carbon dioxide, methane, and nitrous oxide, and also some of the gases that have been used in refrigerators and aerosols as substitutes for the chlorofluorocarbons (CFCs) that are an acknowledged cause of harm to the ozone layer. Greenhouse gases are a cause of global warming. But *whose* emissions of greenhouse gases cause global warming? If a complaint is made that the United States or the United Kingdom is failing to prevent emissions from its territory, the allegedly wrongdoing State may respond that it is not the emissions from its own territory but those from other States that cause global pollution, or that the State's own emissions are no more than a tiny fraction of greenhouse gases released around the world. So who should be sued? May the action be brought against any polluting State, and if so is each polluter liable for all damage caused by global warming or only for its proportionate share of pollution? And how would such a proportionate share be calculated if, for example, some States that are now relatively light polluters have a long history of heavy pollution, while some of today's heavy polluters have no such history? And what of States that may emit pollutants but which have natural or man-made carbon sinks, such as extensive forests, which absorb more carbon dioxide than the State emits?

Similar problems arise when the position of possible claimants is considered. Must a claimant prove that it has actually been injured by global warming caused directly by a particular named respondent, or is it enough that the harm is caused by global warming in general? Indeed, is it really necessary that an actual injury be shown, or may a claimant such as the Maldives (average height above sea level, approximately one metre; highest point, Wilingili island, 2.4 metres above sea level) say that if it is to survive the impact of melting polar ice and rising sea levels it cannot afford to wait for actual injury to be sustained? And what if no injured or potentially injured State chooses to pursue an international claim concerning massive environmental pollution; must the pollution go unchecked, or may some other State, itself unaffected by the pollution, pursue the matter?

Both sets of problems arise from the same basic cause: the diffusion of injury and of responsibility among large numbers of potential claimants and respondents. In domestic contexts such situations are typically addressed through taxation. Communications, defence, education, and health care and similar public goods, which many people need occasionally or in small measure but which are too expensive for individuals to buy, are centrally procured and the cost spread widely among potential beneficiaries. On the international plane, however, there is no body with the authority to impose global taxes—or, indeed, to represent the global public interest in litigation over environmental pollution.

Environmental regulation frequently involves difficult, and sometimes very controversial, questions of science; and those usually concern the predicted, rather than the past, consequences of State action. This, too, causes problems. Whose opinion on the science is to be accepted? Is each State entitled to take its own view? Is it, like a criminal trial, not a matter of finding authoritative results but of devising satisfactory processes, so that a State that has put in place a formal procedure for considering scientific questions such as the environmental impact of a proposed industrial development would be said to have satisfied its international obligations even if its advisers reached a view on scientific questions that subsequently proves to be wrong?

Given these complications it is not surprising that international environmental law was slow to develop. Environmental lawyers sometimes claim early cases, such as the *Behring Sea Fur Seal* arbitration in 1893, as early stirrings of the subject. The *Fur Seal* case arose when the United States, having purchased Alaska from Russia in 1867, granted to the Alaska Commercial Company monopoly rights to take the fur seals. The value of the monopoly was greatly reduced by Canadian fishermen taking the seals on the high seas outside United States waters, with the result that the herds that congregated annually on land in Alaska became severely depleted. The United States and Great Britain (as the State responsible for Canada's actions at that time) agreed to take the matter to arbitration. The United States claimed to be acting not merely in order to protect the United States fisherfolk, but as trustees 'for the benefit of mankind' in managing the seal stock. Although the United States claim was rejected by the Tribunal, which upheld the right of all States to take fish on the high seas, the pleadings in the case do foreshadow some of the bold arguments that were being deployed by environmentalists for a full century.

The finding of the *Behring Sea Fur Seal* tribunal that the United States had no right to regulate high seas fisheries unilaterally had been anticipated by the United States and Great Britain in the treaty by which they established the tribunal. That treaty stipulated that if the arbitrators found that 'the concurrence of Great Britain is necessary to the establishment of Regulations for the proper protection and preservation of the fur-seal in, or habitually resorting to, the Behring Sea', the arbitrators should themselves draft the necessary regulations; and this they did. These regulations also anticipated some of the devices used in later environmental instruments. They created a sixty-mile zone around the Pribilov Islands in which sealing was banned, and a larger zone in which the ban applied only at certain times of the year. Sealing vessels were required to be licensed, but none of the constraints applied to fishing from canoes by the indigenous peoples. Britain and the United States enacted the regulations in their laws, but the defects of the scheme quickly became apparent. The seals migrated beyond the zones created in the regulations and were followed by sealers. Moreover, the measures applied only to British and American sealing vessels, and nothing prevented sealing by other States or, indeed, the reflagging of British and American ships under foreign flags in attempts to evade the ban. Japan, in particular, availed itself of the opportunity offered by the statutory limitations on British and American sealing in the Behring Sea to catch the seals.

The episode illustrated two basic constraints that still limit the effectiveness of environmental regulations. First, regulations could not be imposed by some supranational authority upon all participants in the exploitation of the resource, because there was no such authority. The measures had to be adopted by agreement between the national States of the persons concerned. Secondly, even when the agreement was made, it was impossible to prevent the problem of the 'free rider' who is not bound by the restraints imposed by the agreement and is free to reap the benefits produced by the restraints on parties to the agreement.

An obvious solution was to have an agreement between all the States whose nationals were engaged in the exploitation of the fishery. The United States proposed this, and Japan and Russia agreed to begin negotiations. Britain, however, feared the impact of extended restrictions on sealing upon Canadian fishing interests, and refused to join in the negotiations, prompting the US Ambassador in London, John Hay, to observe that 'I had always thought of English diplomacy as overbearing and pigheaded, but I never imagined it was tricky and tortuous.' Intensified Japanese sealing and a severe decline in the seal stock crippled the Canadian sealing industry and forced Britain to the negotiating table. James Bryce, the British Ambassador to the United States, proposed a bilateral agreement between the two States under which Canada would suspend sealing in return for a share of the US catch. The agreement was to enter into force only when all four sealing States had agreed upon a ban on catching seals at sea. In 1911 the four States agreed on a multilateral treaty that proved very effective: the Pribilov seal stock tripled in size in the first six years, and by 1940 it had grown from the 1911 figure of approximately 125,000 to 2,185,136 animals. The treaty continued in force, despite World War One and the Bolshevik Revolution, until 1940, when Japan's withdrawal brought it to an end. A revised treaty was adopted in 1957 and it remained in force until 1984, when opposition in the United States to sealing prevented US ratification of a protocol which would have renewed the treaty.

One commentator has written of the 1911 Treaty that:

the treaty succeeded by changing the rules of the game, by restructuring the relationships among the countries. In particular, five tasks needed to be achieved, each necessary for success, but each also almost useless should any of the others fail. The treaty needed to: (1) create an aggregate gain, a reason for all countries to come to the bargaining table; (2) distribute this gain such that all countries would prefer that the agreement succeed; (3) ensure that each country would lose by not participating, given that all the others agreed to participate; (4) provide incentives for all the parties to comply with the treaty; and (5) deter entry by third parties.[1]

The gains to the parties from participating in the 1911 Treaty were clear enough. The seal stock would survive and recover, whereas extinction of the stock through overfishing was the likely result of international inaction. The difficult part was providing the incentive to comply with the treaty restrictions on catches, and deterring catches by non-party States. The peculiar nature of the trade in seal skins made a solution possible. Practically all commercial processing of the skins was undertaken in

---

[1] Scott Barrett, 'The North Pacific Fur Seal Treaty and the Theory of International Cooperation', Chapter 2 of *Environment and Statecraft—The Strategy of Environmental Treaty-Making* (Oxford: Oxford University Press, 2005), p. 33. The foregoing account owes much to this paper.

London,[2] and if traders were denied access to the London market there was little point in catching and skinning the seals. The treaty therefore stipulated that only skins certified as having been taken in accordance with the treaty could be imported into any of the Member States. Here, too, the 1911 treaty foreshadowed later developments, creating a device that has been used in other environmental treaties in order to overcome the 'free rider' problem.

The Behring State Fur Seal episode epitomizes the limitations under which international law continues to labour in efforts to establish effective environmental regulations. But it could have been very different.

The tribunal approached the matter as one essentially concerned with the scope of coastal States' rights over areas of the high seas adjacent to their territorial waters. From that perspective the legal position was clear. For more than two centuries the dominant view had been that the high seas were free for use by ships of any State, and not subject to regulation by coastal States. There was debate over the exact distance to which coastal jurisdiction over adjacent waters extended; but the basic principle of the freedom of all States to use the high seas was firmly established. This principle was of considerable importance to European powers, whose freedom to trade with overseas colonies was dependent upon the freedom to navigate around the oceans without interference from coastal States, and who had built up considerable naval, merchant, and fishing fleets.

The *Behring Sea* Tribunal could, however, have taken a different view. It could, for example, have decided that the United States had some kind of property right in the seals when they were in herds on its land territory, and that taking seals on the high seas was a violation from outside United States territory of those rights.

Alternatively, it could have taken up the United States' idea of a kind of 'trusteeship', and said that precisely because the seals were a common resource, available to be caught by all States on the high seas, the United States (as the State on whose territory they bred) had a particular obligation to take measures to protect and manage that common resource. Or it

---

[2] It was a colourful trade. 'In the London fur trade grown men were employed in the 1890s to bring seal skins to plasticity by jumping on them. "It is a curious sight, on entering a room, to see a row of . . . tubs each with its Jack-in-the-box bobbing up and down", wrote one of Booth's investigators. "Every man is naked except for a vest, and a rough cloth which is tied round his waist and attached to the rim of his barrel. With hands resting on either ledge up and down he treads, and earns 20s to 25s piece-work. Skins cured by this process are said to be softer and silkier".' Samuel Raphael, 'Workshop of the World: Steam Power and Hand Technology in mid-Victorian Britain', *History Workshop Journal* 1977, No.3, pp. 6–72, at p. 46.

could have inverted that approach and held that although all States had a right to catch seals on the high seas, that right had to be exercised with due regard for the rights of others who have an interest in the seals and was subject to obligations not to take so many seals as to extinguish the resource. That obligation, it might have said, could be secured by agreement between all interested States; but in the absence of such agreement it could be secured by measures adopted unilaterally by the 'breeding' State. Or it could have taken an altogether more imaginative approach, distinguishing between the incidents that attach to private property on the one hand and to common property and to collective (State-owned) property on the other hand. It might, for example, have said that whereas private property entails rights to use and dispose of the goods as the owner might choose, collective property cannot be used in such a way but must be managed with a view to its sustainable development, for the benefit of all present and future users.

The fact that the *Behring Sea* Tribunal did not take any of these approaches might be the result of a tribunal fearful of innovation and opting for the safe ground of a conservative analysis, or serving the broader interests of powerful States in maintaining the freedom of the seas, or heavily influenced by the analogy of the treatment of animals under the game laws in municipal legal systems. Explanations can be given at different levels of analysis of the motivation and reasoning of the tribunal, and none is likely to capture all of the truth. What is plain is that it is unrealistic to suppose that decisions of this kind are motivated by the cynical self-interest of States and the lawyers upon whom they bestow their favours and patronage. It is a question of world-view, of *weltanschauung*. This is not simply a matter of belief about the exhaustibility of resources. It is a question of who carries the responsibility for the management of resources, what those responsibilities are, and to whom they are owed.

7.2 ALTERNATIVE APPROACHES

The alternative approaches that I have outlined, and which the *Behring Sea* Tribunal might have taken, mark out some of the main avenues along which international environmental law subsequently developed. The two main lines are what might be called the 'transboundary harm' approach, and the 'trusteeship' approach, and these were pursued alongside the classical route of environmental management by international agreement, exemplified by the handling of the fur seal dispute.

7.3 TRANSBOUNDARY HARM

The transboundary harm approach was followed in one of the best-known of international environmental cases, again involving Canada and the United States, the *Trail Smelter* arbitration. More of a saga than a case, the dispute arose from the operation of a lead and zinc smelting plant established by United States investors in Trail, British Columbia, in 1896, and later sold to Canadian investors. Emissions of sulphur from the smelter, which had risen by 1927 to around 9,000 tons per month, fell as acid rain and were causing significant damage to the Columbia River valley in the State of Washington in United States. The United States complained, and in 1928 the matter was referred to the International Joint Commission (IJC) established under the 1909 Canada–US Boundary Waters Treaty. The IJC appointed two scientists to investigate, and heard testimony from interested parties and from counsel. It recommended that Canada pay the United States $350,000 for damage caused up to 1931, and also recommended other ameliorative measures. The United States remained dissatisfied by continuing pollution from the smelter, as were the residents of the affected areas of Washington. No remedy was available in the Canadian courts because under Canadian law the courts would not take jurisdiction in cases of damage to foreign land. Accordingly, in 1933 the two States agreed in a Convention signed in April 1935 to submit to an arbitral tribunal the question whether the smelter had caused damage in the State of Washington after 1931, and if so whether and how the smelter should refrain from causing damage, and what compensation should be paid. Article IV of the 1935 Convention stipulated that:

The Tribunal shall apply the law and practice followed in dealing with cognate questions in the United States of America as well as international law and practice, and shall give consideration to the desire of the high contracting parties to reach a solution just to all parties concerned.

The Tribunal was, in other words, directed to apply United States domestic tort law, 'as well as international law and practice'. The inevitable result of this choice of law clause, in the wake of the prior IJC recommendation that Canada compensate the United States for pre-1932 pollution (confirmed as an obligation of the United States in Article 1 of the 1935 Convention), was that the case would be characterized as one of nuisance, with liability attaching to those who caused damage.

   The Tribunal said that 'the law followed in the United States in dealing with the quasi-sovereign rights of States of the Union, in the matter of air pollution, whilst more definite, is in conformity with the general rules of international law'. That was true; but the basis in international law which the Tribunal compared with United States law was remarkably slender. It was essentially confined to the elementary proposition that a State owes a duty to protect other States against injurious acts by individuals from within its jurisdiction. As the Tribunal noted, the real difficulty is in knowing what is deemed to constitute an injurious act. It observed, in an unusually frank explanation by a tribunal of its reasoning process, that:

No case of air pollution dealt with by an international tribunal has been brought to the attention of the Tribunal nor does the Tribunal know of any such case. The nearest analogy is that of water pollution. But here, also, no decision of an international tribunal has been cited or found.

There are, however, as regards both air pollution and water pollution, certain decisions of the Supreme Court of the United States which may legitimately be taken as a guide in this field in international law, for it is reasonable to follow by analogy, in international cases, precedents established by that court in dealing with controversies between States of the Union or other controversies concerning the quasi-sovereign rights of such States, where no contrary rule prevails in international law and no reason for rejecting such precedents can be adduced from the limitations of sovereignty inherent in the Constitution of the United States.

That reasoning is notable for the willingness of the Tribunal to treat two independent sovereign States on a par with constituent components of federal States. Theorists might say that the Tribunal was in effect positing the existence of a public order in which the two States were to be treated as having common interests, and to which a unified public interest applied, as it does within a federal State. That would be in contrast to the crude atomism of the 'States as co-existing independent communities' view of international law exemplified by the notorious dictum of the PCIJ in the *Lotus* case, that 'rules of law binding upon States emanate from their own free will. . . . Restrictions upon the independence of States cannot therefore be presumed.'

Whatever the validity of the claim of a constitutional shift in the *Trail Smelter* award, it certainly adopted an approach more focused upon the notion of shared resources, and more concerned with the custodianship of those resources, than the *Behring Sea* award had been. That development is reflected in the fact that the Tribunal also referred to two other, extra-legal, factors: the 'desire of the high contracting parties to reach a solution just to all parties concerned', and the fact that 'great progress in the control of fumes has been made by science in the last few years'. The reference to progress in science, which the Tribunal said 'should be taken into account', is particularly striking. It is hard to read it as saying anything other than 'we can protect the environment, therefore we should'.

The Tribunal held that:

under the principles of international law, as well as the law of the United States, no state has the right to use or permit the use of its territory in such a manner as to cause injury by fumes in or to the territory of another or the properties or persons therein, when the case is of serious consequence and the injury is established by clear and convincing evidence

The Tribunal also held Canada liable to pay compensation, in modest amount, to the United States, and it set out a detailed operating regime for the smelter based upon experiments and trials conducted during the three years between its first, 'temporary' decision in 1938 and its final, definitive award in 1941. The particularity of the regime is remarkable: it specified, for instance, that:

If the Columbia Gardens recorder indicates 0.5 part per million or more of sulphur dioxide for three consecutive twenty minute periods during the non-growing season and the wind direction is not favorable, emission shall be reduced by four tons of sulphur per hour or shut down completely when the turbulence is bad, until the recorder shows 0.2 part per million or less of sulphur dioxide for three consecutive twenty minute periods.

The award provided for the establishment of a tribunal made up of three scientists, which would have the power to make final decisions if the parties could not agree upon any amendments or suspensions of the regime that either of them might request. It is rare to find tribunals entering so fully into the detailed examination and prescription of technical standards, even if (like the *Trail Smelter* Tribunal), they are assisted by scientists; but the Tribunal's approach is one that has been emulated in later agreements.

Given the terms of the agreement between the two States to refer the matter to arbitration, and the context of the dispute, which was not so different from inter-State disputes within one of the two federal States parties to the litigation, this approach by the Tribunal to the characterization of the dispute, and its result, are not surprising. Why should it have mattered whether the pollution in Washington State emanated from British Columbia or Montana? Why should there be liability and compensation in one case but not the other? But the conclusion was, if not startling, at least significant.

Compare the *Trail Smelter* award with the *Behring Sea* award. In both, the 'injurious acts' complained of were not inherently unlawful: in the one case, the operation of an industrial plant in Canada, and in the other sealing on the high seas—both perfectly lawful activities. In both cases there was a claim for injury made by a State, effectively acting as custodian or representative or trustee of the national interests damaged by the pollution rather than as the representative of individual claimants. In both cases the pollution was a transboundary phenomenon. In the *Trail Smelter* case activity in one State caused injury in another. In *Behring Sea*, activity on the high seas caused injury in a(nother) State. But it is hard to see why harm emanating from the high seas should be any more acceptable than harm emanating from the territory of another State.

The two cases can, of course, be reconciled; but that is not the point. The point is that the *Trail Smelter* decision opened up a line of reasoning that imposed international liability for transboundary pollution, and admitted environmental arguments onto the stage of international law in their own terms, without attempting to force them into the straightjacket of traditional legal conceptions of right, duty, and property.

7.4 TRUSTEESHIP AND THE COMMUNITY RESOURCES APPROACH

The other approach that the *Behring Sea* Tribunal might have taken, based upon the United States 'trusteeship' argument, is an altogether more radical development. It represents a fundamental shift in the perception of the relationship of States towards shared resources and their responsibilities towards them. By 'shared resources' I mean not only what are sometimes called, with the faintly depressing woolliness that characterizes some of the writing on international environmental law, 'global commons', such as the high seas and outer space, but also resources that may at any given moment be within the jurisdiction of one State (within its territory or territorial sea), but which are liable to move so as to come within the jurisdiction of another State—fur seals, fish, and air are examples.

The clearest example of this development in legal thinking is found in the provisions of the 1982 UN Convention on the Law of the Sea that regulate fishing. Throughout the eighteenth and nineteenth centuries the rule generally applied in the European States and their colonies was that the coastal State had an exclusive right to fish in its territorial waters and that all States had the right to fish on the high seas beyond territorial waters. There were, it is true, variations. Some States claimed wider territorial seas than others, or a wider territorial sea for the purposes of fishery regulation than for other purposes. But these variations were minor, and it was generally accepted that however the zones were structured, coastal States had no jurisdiction over foreign vessels fishing more than twelve miles from the coasts. This created a dichotomy: exclusive fishing rights, and the possibility of full coastal State control, within the territorial sea or exclusive fishery zone, but a free-for-all on the high seas. True, each State could regulate fishing vessels sailing under its flag on the high seas; but why would it wish to do so? Limiting the catch taken by its own vessels would simply leave more fish for others to catch; and it would probably lead at least some fishermen to move their vessels to a different, less restrictive, flag.

The first attempts to codify the Law of the Sea addressed this problem. At the League of Nations Codification Conference in 1930, it had been impossible to secure international agreement on an extension of the right of the coastal State to regulate fisheries beyond its territorial sea. Opposition from States with distant-water fishing fleets, and with other strategic interests in keeping their ships on the high seas free from coastal State interference, precluded it. In 1958, at the first United Nations Conference on the Law of the Sea, a Convention on Fishing and the Conservation of Living Resources of the High Seas was prepared. It was based upon the principle that all States had the right to fish on the high seas, although it recognized that a coastal State had 'a special interest in the maintenance of the productivity of the living resources in any area of the high seas adjacent to its territorial sea', and it obliged States to co-operate in regulating high seas living resources so as to make it possible to achieve:

the optimum sustainable yield from those resources so as to secure a maximum supply of food and other marine products. Conservation programmes should be formulated with a view to securing in the first place a supply of food for human consumption.

If nationals of two or more States were engaged in exploiting a fishery, conservation measures were to be adopted by agreement among the States. If agreement proved impossible, an adjacent coastal State could impose non-discriminatory conservation measures. Disputes were to be settled by *ad hoc* Commissions, which would review the scientific evidence and determine if non-discriminatory measures should be upheld.

That Convention was not a great success. It failed to meet the demands of coastal States for extended jurisdiction over adjacent waters, and the practical need to reach agreements in order to safeguard particular stocks was being addressed with some success by local and regional agreements on fisheries. The Convention attracted only thirty-seven ratifications (including Switzerland), and was soon overtaken by events.

Pressure from coastal States to permit them to regulate fishing in high seas areas adjacent to their coasts was one of the factors that led to the massive revision of the law undertaken by the Third UN Conference on the Law of the Sea between 1973 and 1982. The resulting 1982 United

Nations Convention on the Law of the Sea adopted a novel approach to conservation of fish stocks. It allowed States to extend their jurisdiction over fisheries out to 200 miles from the shore. In practical terms, that no doubt appeared to be its major innovation in this field. But the real innovations appeared in the details of the regime that applied within the 200-mile zone. Instead of ascribing exclusive jurisdiction to the coastal State, with the implication that it could do as it pleased with the fish stocks under its jurisdiction, the Convention created a more balanced regime in which rights and duties go hand in hand. It is a regime that is in many ways closer to the idea of 'trusteeship', with which the United States had tried unsuccessfully to lure the *Behring Sea* tribunal, than to municipal law concepts of property ownership.

The coastal State has the sovereign right to manage living resources within its 200-mile exclusive economic zone (EEZ), but is obliged 'to promote the objective of optimum utilization' of those resources. The State must determine, 'taking into account the best scientific evidence available to it', what the total allowable catch of living resources in its EEZ is, and then determine how much of that catch it can itself take. Any surplus of the allowable catch which it cannot itself take must be made available to other States, with a certain priority for developing, land-locked and geographically disadvantaged States,[3] on terms to be agreed with the coastal State. Thus, the coastal State has in effect only a 'first priority', a right to take as much of the total allowable catch as it wishes, before allowing in others. The intention is that in this way the full potential of the living resources will be utilized without the danger of over-exploitation, against which the coastal State is specifically required to guard. In the case of anadromous species (such as salmon), which ascend rivers in order to spawn, and catadromous species (such as eels), which leave freshwater to spawn in saltwater areas such as the wide Sargasso Sea, the 'freshwater' State has 'the primary interest in and responsibility for' the stock, which may only be caught within its EEZ.

The coastal State can charge other States for access to the surplus. In 2004, the EU paid €86 million to Mauritania for access to its EEZ, for example. There is much debate as to the fairness of the terms on which these agreements are made and on the efficacy of the measures taken to prevent overfishing. It is said by some that fishing licences that authorize a certain number or tonnage of foreign fishing vessels to have access to an

---

[3] i.e., States with short coastlines (e.g., the Democratic Republic of the Congo: land area, 2,267,600 sq km; coastline, 37 km), or whose maritime zones are blocked in by the zones of neighbouring States (e.g., Jordan, Singapore, and Slovenia).

EEZ are much less effective conservation measures than licences that directly limit the size of catch that can be taken; and that licensing often leads to foreign vessels taking fish out of the region for processing, so that the coastal State loses out on the development of the parts of the fishing industry that add most value to the catch; and it is said that the buying of licences by the flag State may amount to a subsidy (possibly unlawful under the WTO rules) to its fishing industry, which may harm the development of fish catching, processing and marketing industries in the coastal State.

There is also much debate over the efficacy of conservation measures. The problems begin with uncertainty over the data on the size of fish stocks. Estimates of stock size are derived by extrapolation from data taken at particular places at particular times; but there is frequently controversy as to how representative the data is of the situation elsewhere in the seas. As far as conservation techniques are concerned, there may be debates as to whether the best approach is to set minimum mesh sizes for nets (which are designed to allow small young fish to swim through, and stay in the fishery to breed and grow), or to specify closed areas or closed seasons in which fishing is banned, or to allow in a certain number or tonnage of fishing boats for a certain number of fishing days, or to permit the catching of a certain tonnage of fish. Each approach may have a crucially different impact. Moreover, States tend to be reluctant to accept *any* measures which impose heavy burdens upon their own fisherfolk, particularly if they see or suspect that fisherfolk from other States are receiving what might be considered to be more favourable treatment—and, of course, the fishing lobby in each State tends to suppose that fisherfolk from other States will cheat and disobey any measures that are imposed. All fishing lobbies tend to press for quotas that scientists regard as too high to be sustainable; but gaining agreement on conservation measures is no easy matter, even if the scientific basis for them is clear and accepted by those involved in the industry.

Then there is the problem of by-catches. A quota may be set for one species, but the nets may drag out many other species, too; and fish that are too small for commercial sale or are of the wrong species may be thrown back, usually dead, into the water. Estimates are hard to make, but by-catches are thought to amount to something between 18 million and 40 million tonnes of fish each year—perhaps one quarter of the total fish catch. Perhaps the greatest problem, however, is that of Illegal, Unregulated and Unreported fishing (IUU fishing). Monitoring fish catches is not as easy as monitoring, say, opium crops or poaching on a wildlife reserve; and the rewards for ignoring fishery laws can be high—luxury fish such as the

Patagonian Toothfish can be worth well over $1,000 each. The sheer size of the oceans makes effective policing at sea an extremely difficult task, and attention is focused on monitoring the land-based trade in valuable fish. Programmes such as the Catch Documentation Scheme introduced under the 1980 Convention for the Conservation of Antarctic Marine Living Resources (CCAMLR) in Antarctic waters appear to be having some success; but criticisms of the efficacy of conservation measures remain valid.

There is much in these, and other, criticisms that casts doubt on how far the regime under the 1982 Convention is achieving its objectives. But the central point is clear: under the Convention rights of ownership are firmly welded to responsibilities for securing the optimum and sustainable development of living resources within the State's maritime zones. This principle is being supported by initiatives taken in international organizations. For example, the Food and Agriculture Organization (FAO), the UN body with primary responsibility for fisheries, adopted a Code of Conduct for Responsible Fisheries in 1995, and prepared an International Plan of Action to Prevent, Deter and Eliminate Illegal, Unreported and Unregulated Fishing in 2001. Both are statements of general principles and best practice; but they signal a serious attempt to bring proper resource management to the world's main commercial fisheries, and also a sensitivity to the special positions of developing countries and of artisanal fisherfolk.

This, then, is the second approach that is emerging: a redrawing of the fundamental nature of the rights and duties of States in respect of marine living[4] resources which, in broad terms, they 'own'. It sits alongside the concept of transboundary environmental harm as one of the two main developments in international environmental law. Much of the work in this field is, however, still done by the conclusion of agreements between interested States. Treaties regulating fishing were being concluded in the nineteenth century. The fisheries around the Channel Islands were regulated in a treaty between Great Britain and France in 1839, and the States Parties to a multilateral treaty made in 1882 sought to improve the policing of fisheries in the North Sea by giving reciprocal rights to board and search fishing vessels, for instance. States have much experience of co-operative resource management in this area.

Fisheries treaties are concerned with the rational use of shared goods; but much the same legal problems arise in the fight against shared evils, such as disease and pollution. International co-operation in the fight

---

[4] There is no duty of optimum or sustainable development of non-living resources, such as oil.

against disease has a long history. From the fourteenth century onwards there were established practices in Europe for dealing with plagues by means of quarantines, imposed by a *cordon sanitaire*.[5] The cholera and influenza epidemics of the 1830s prompted attempts to convene an international conference to focus on co-operation in the field of healthcare and disease control. This was the period in which the pioneering work in the field of public health, sanitation and epidemiology was undertaken by Edwin Chadwick, John Snow, and others whose contribution to the welfare of mankind is as monumental as it is now neglected. Their work represented an alternative approach, opposed to the quarantines which were regarded in Britain as inconvenient interferences with trade and movement and ineffective against the spread of disease. There was a tendency to see diseases as pestilential visitations from 'abroad'—one of the early (1851) conventions referred to measures against 'a disease reputed to be importable'. That view fitted the idea of the quarantine as a defensive measure. But as the precise patterns of epidemics were studied more closely it became clear that some diseases, at least, were home-grown, and that quarantines offered no defence against them.

The first International Sanitary Conference was convened in Paris in 1851 (by which time there had been further epidemics of influenza, typhus, typhoid, and cholera). The success of that conference was limited. The resulting Convention was ratified only by France, Portugal, and Sardinia; and Portugal and Sardinia subsequently withdrew. The threats, however, remained, as repeated outbreaks of cholera showed. Indeed, they increased as steam-powered ships made communication faster and easier, particularly after the opening of the Suez Canal in 1869. Scientific knowledge also increased rapidly, and by the 1880s the 'germ theory' of disease had displaced the view that diseases sprang from bad air or 'miasmas'. The coincidence of need and understanding facilitated progress; and after a number of international conferences, States began to agree upon ways of combating the spread of these deadly human diseases, little more than a decade after they had taken swifter action to protect European vines from *phylloxera*.[6] In 1892 an International Sanitary Convention concerning cholera was adopted at a conference in Venice; and in 1897 a Convention

---

[5] It is an interesting question whether these practices were so uniform, and whether the expectation of their implementation was of such a nature as to generate a rule of customary international law. If so, this would be a relatively rare early example, in the field of what we would now call the Law of Peace, of a customary international law rule that is not a claim to a right or to immunity.

[6] The first treaties to address diseases of plants appear to have been the Convention Respecting Measures to be Taken Against *Phylloxera Vastatrix* of 1878 and its 1881 revision.

concerning the plague was adopted. 1902 saw the establishment by American States of the International Sanitary Bureau (ISB), succeeded by the Pan American Sanitary Bureau in 1923 and subsequently restructured as a regional office of the World Health Organization (WHO), itself established as a UN specialized agency in 1948.

International health conventions focused on the early notification of outbreaks of diseases. For many years only cholera, plague, and yellow fever were notifiable, but a revision of the International Health Regulations by the WHO in 2005 in the light of the fears of worldwide epidemics of Severe Acute Respiratory Syndrome (SARS) and of avian influenza A (H5N1) obliged WHO States to report all events that may constitute a 'public health emergency of international concern' (PHEIC) and public health risks outside their territory that may cause international disease to spread, so that co-ordinated international responses may be organized. Human diseases have been the primary, but not the only, focus of attention. For example, the International Convention for the Campaign against Contagious Diseases of Animals was concluded in 1935, and the International Convention on the Protection of Plants, in 1929, and, spanning the animal and plant kingdoms, the Convention Regarding the Organisation of the Campaign against Locusts, in 1920—this last Convention, anticipating the trans-boundary *Trail Smelter* approach, obliging States Parties to 'take the necessary measures against locusts liable to damage the crops of neighbouring States'.

Generations to come, looking at the record of treaty-making in the century and a half that followed the devastating epidemics of the mid nineteenth century, may wonder why it was that States put such energy into the international regulation of shipping, telecommunications, trade, taxation, and warfare, and relatively little into international co-operation to contain and eradicate diseases that killed many millions of people each year—and even that limited effort focused upon protecting the peoples of Europe and North America. Some explanations may be offered for the lack of treaties on co-operation over human diseases. Perhaps the most important is that the shift from the focus upon quarantine to a focus on public health left most of the responsibility for the taking of concrete steps in the hands of individual States, responsible for their own territories. There is less need for international co-operation than there would be if the necessary preventive measures straddled international boundaries. Another reason is that the international community of physicians and healthcare workers is quick to transmit news of new techniques and products, and to adopt them (although the access of poor States to expensive pharmaceuticals protected by intellectual property rights remains an acute problem, addressed but only partly resolved in the WTO Doha Declaration on the TRIPS Agreement and Public Health). Put another way, the non-State channels are very effective in public health, as they tend to be in other technical fields, so that the need to secure international co-operation by making treaties is reduced. A third factor is the existence of regional and international organizations, such as the Pan American Health Organization (PAHO) and the WHO, which continuously inform and consult with relevant individuals and organizations in their Member States.

7.5 CHANGING ATTITUDES TO THE ENVIRONMENT

So far I have concentrated upon developments in the pre-1945, pre-UN era; and for a reason. The picture after 1945 is very different, so much so that it is tempting to think that the Depression, the troubles of the 1930s, and World War Two in some way wrought a profound change in the attitude of governments towards 'the environment' in its broadest sense— that is, to the natural world upon which their philosophies and fantasies are played out. Whether or not that is so, there are identifiable causes of a shift in views of the environment. Two stand out. First, the massively increased ability of mankind to exploit natural resources, and the parallel appreciation that all of these resources—including those that repro- duce—are exhaustible. And second, the realization that large parts of the land, sea, and air were becoming seriously degraded by pollution, erosion and other processes, in a manner that not only threatened human health and the very survival of the ecosystem but, as the escalating costs of pollu- tion could not be contained by governments, also threatened serious disruption to commercial and industrial activity on the way.

The initial steps in the post-war world were tentative. Attention was initially focused on the reconstruction of States battered by the War and on getting the United Nations and the international trade and financial institutions operating satisfactorily; and the Cold War impeded global co-operation in many fields. That is not to say that no treaties were being made at this time. There were many, some of substantial and enduring importance, on a wide range of broadly environmental topics: plant protection, the protection of wild birds, the regulation of fishing, the regulation of nuclear energy, and international watercourses. But the great leap forward in environmental law came rather later, in 1968 when, on the initiative of the Swedish Government, the UN General Assembly adopted resolution 2398 (XXIII).

Resolution 2398 (XXIII) began by noting 'that the relationship between man and his environment is undergoing profound changes in the wake of modern scientific and technological developments'. It listed the main international organizations involved with environmental matters, and spoke of the need for intensified action to address this important and urgent question, and for the creation of a framework within which it could be addressed within the UN system. The resolution then announced the convening of the United Nations Conference on the Human Environment, to be held in 1972 in Stockholm. Environmental issues are now so much a part of everyday debate that it is difficult to imagine a world that appeared oblivious to those concerns. But for those of us brought up in the 1950s, when schoolchildren were sent off to clinics for sun ray treatment as a substitute for the real sun that struggled patiently against the smogs of the industrial cities (which could be so dense that visibility could sometimes be nil),[7] environmental concerns first intruded upon our consciousness with an awkward, and not entirely convincing, novelty. It was not until 1956 that the first Clean Air Acts were introduced in the United Kingdom, in response to the Great Smog of 1952; and it was 1970 before the Environmental Protection Agency (EPA) was established in the United States. The Stockholm Conference brought these issues to the fore.

7.6 THE STOCKHOLM DECLARATION 1972

The immediate fruits of the 1972 Conference were, as might have been predicted, the adoption of a sonorous Declaration and the establishment of a new international organization. The Stockholm Declaration sets out 26 'Principles', more reminiscent of a creed than of a legal instrument. At first sight they appear to sit firmly in the genre of sanctimonious platitudes which seems to be the natural dialect of international organizations. 'Man has the fundamental right to freedom, equality and adequate conditions of life in an environment of a quality that permits a life of dignity and well-being, and he bears a solemn responsibility to protect and improve the environment for present and future generations' (Principle 1); 'The non-renewable resources of the earth must be employed in such a way as to guard against the danger of their future exhaustion and to ensure that

---

[7] The UK Meteorological Office records that during the great smog of December 1952 the visibility in the Isle of Dogs in London was at times nil. The fog was so thick that people could not see their own feet.

benefits from such employment are shared by all mankind' (Principle 5); 'Rational planning constitutes an essential tool for reconciling any conflict between the needs of development and the need to protect and improve the environment' (Principle 14); 'International matters concerning the protection and improvement of the environment should be handled in a cooperative spirit by all countries, big or small, on an equal footing . . .' (Principle 24): that sort of thing. But in the midst of this orgy of sententious vacuity, some important markers were laid down.

One is the frequently quoted Principle 21:

States have, in accordance with the Charter of the United Nations and the principles of international law, the sovereign right to exploit their own resources pursuant to their own environmental policies, and the responsibility to ensure that activities within their jurisdiction or control do not cause damage to the environment of other States or of areas beyond the limits of national jurisdiction.

That is a concise restatement of the *Trail Smelter* principle coupled with an affirmation of the principle of permanent sovereignty over natural resources—an assertion of the link between rights and duties. Other principles found in the Stockholm Declaration were more novel and more pointed. Three stand out. First, the assertion in Principle 9 that:

Environmental deficiencies generated by the conditions of under-development and natural disasters pose grave problems and can best be remedied by accelerated development through the transfer of substantial quantities of financial and technological assistance as a supplement to the domestic effort of the developing countries and such timely assistance as may be required.

Second, the assertion in Principle 10 that:

For the developing countries, stability of prices and adequate earnings for primary commodities and raw materials are essential to environmental management, since economic factors as well as ecological processes must be taken into account.

And third, a principle which builds upon those two affirmations of the links between aid, trade and the environment, and which specifically acknowledges the particular problems of developing States. Principle 23 stated that:

Without prejudice to such criteria as may be agreed upon by the international community, or to standards which will have to be determined nationally, it will be essential in all cases to consider the systems of values prevailing in each country, and the extent of the applicability of standards which are valid for the most advanced countries but which may be inappropriate and of unwarranted social cost for the developing countries.

Principles 9 and 10 locate the debate on the environment clearly in the context of the international economy. They recognize that the safeguarding of the environment needs money and technology and that these will have, broadly speaking, to flow from the North to the South, and that the long-term preservation of the environment depends upon States developing secure and sustainable economic bases. This may appear trite; but it was not a self-evident proposition. It would have been possible to say that each State must ensure that activities in its own territory do not harm others—the *Trail Smelter* principle—and leave it at that. Environmental concerns could have been left on an essentially bilateral basis, with the polluted looking to the polluter for remedial action. But the Stockholm Declaration treats the matter as one of global concern and recognizes that effective solutions to environmental degradation require a great deal of international co-operation. The belching factories and waste tips of the European industrial revolution arose because that was the cheapest way to industrialize; and there is no obvious reason why a developing State should not now choose to follow a similar route. In short, safeguarding the environment was recognized as a global problem which had to be addressed by every State; and those States lacking the money or technology to move away from activities that degraded the environment had to be given economic and technical assistance to help them to do so.

Principle 23 is immensely significant in a different way. It asserts that the law should not necessarily be applied in the same way to every State, rejecting the principle of formal equality according to which like cases should be treated alike.[8] Indeed, it is close to the dictum of Karl Marx in his *Critique of the Gotha Programme*: 'From each according to his abilities, to each according to his needs.' The responsibilities of rich States may be different from those of poor States. For political scientists, this is a recognition of an obvious and inescapable fact of life, which must be faced if there is to be progress in global co-operation over the environment. For lawyers, this is a fundamental shift in the formal structure of the legal system, coinciding with efforts to force a similar shift in the area of international economic law by creating a New International Economic Order based in part upon the idea of the 'duality of norms'.[9]

Both the shift from the bilateral to the multilateral approach and the idea of common but differentiated responsibilities are aspects of what

---

[8] Often attributed to Aristotle, in his *Nichomachean Ethics*, although this precise thought does not appear to be there. The earliest formulation of the aphorism appears to be Cicero, *Topica*, 23: '*Valeat aequitas quae paribus in causis paria iura desiderat*'—'Let equity prevail which requires equal rights for equal cases'.

[9] See Chapter 6, above.

might be seen as a movement away from the private and towards the public law paradigm upon which I remarked at the opening of this chapter. But while the significance of the identification of environmental degradation as a 'public' issue cannot be denied, it was not treated as a matter to be handled on the level of *global* public order, in the way that structure of international trade was globalized in the WTO. This is evident when the institutional structure established as a result of the Stockholm conference is considered.

December 15, 1972, marked a landmark in the development of international environmental law. It saw the adoption by the UN General Assembly of nine resolutions bearing on the subject, including resolution 2997 (XXVII) under which the United Nations Environment Programme (UNEP) was established. UNEP has a Governing Council and a small Environment Secretariat: but UNEP is what it says it is, a programme, like the UN Development Programme (UNDP) or the World Food Programme (WFP), rather than an organization such as the World Meteorological Organization (WMO). This reflects the nature of its work. resolution 2997 itself noted that:

responsibility for action to protect and enhance the environment rests primarily with Governments and, in the first instance, can be exercised more effectively at the national and regional levels.

Simple practicality dictates this approach. Pollution problems vary widely, and so will the actions needed to remedy them. The main problems facing the enclosed waters of the Baltic are not those facing States on West Africa's Atlantic coast; the nature of land-based pollution in Europe, both on land and in its great rivers, is different from that in the Caribbean. And in any event, the difficulties of reaching agreement between States on co-ordinated action are obviously reduced if the number of States involved is kept small.

These points are reflected in the pattern of treaty-making in the years following the 1972 Stockholm Conference. The major treaties are regional and the list is long. Among the examples are the 1972 Oslo Convention on Dumping at Sea and the 1974 Paris Convention on the Prevention of Marine Pollution from Land-Based Sources, combined in the 1992 Convention for the Protection of the Marine Environment of the North-East Atlantic (OSPAR); the 1978 Kuwait Regional Convention for Cooperation on the Protection of the Marine Environment from Pollution; the 1983 Cartagena Convention for the Protection and Development of the Marine Environment of the Wider Caribbean Region; the 1981 Abidjan Convention for Co-operation in the Protection and Development of the Marine and Coastal Environment of the West and Central African Region; the 1985 ASEAN (Kuala Lumpur) Agreement on the Conservation of Nature and Natural Resources; and the 1986 Noumea Convention for the Protection of the Natural Resources and Environment of the South Pacific Region.

This catalogue of regional initiatives gives some sense of the focuses of international action on the environment; but it does not give the whole picture. During the two decades following Stockholm some major international instruments of (at least potentially) global scope were adopted. In the field of marine pollution, I have mentioned the 1982 UN Convention on the Law of the Sea, which functions as a framework within which sit more specialized and detailed agreements, such as the 1973 Convention on Marine Pollution from Ships (MARPOL), adopted under the auspices of the International Maritime Organization (IMO), a UN specialized agency. This strategy of adopting a broad agreement defining basic aims and procedures and then setting out detailed standards and commitments in further agreements and protocols has been used successfully in several environmental contexts. It enables States to make progress on broad issues without being delayed by disagreement on fine details, and permits the revision from time to time of detailed regulations without the need to renegotiate an entire treaty. Thus, the Vienna Convention for the Protection of the Ozone Layer was adopted in 1985, and detailed provisions on the emission of CFCs were introduced in the Montreal Protocol in 1987, which has itself been amended and adjusted several times.

Other notable multilateral conventions of this period addressing problems of environmental degradation include the 1979 Convention on Long-range Transboundary Air Pollution (LTRAP), the 1989 Basel Convention on the Transboundary Movement of Hazardous Wastes (which regulates the trade in toxic waste, much of which was being sent to Eastern Europe and to developing countries for disposal in order to avoid the strict environmental regulations of Western Europe and North America), and the 1992 UN Framework Convention on Climate Change, under which the Kyoto Protocol was adopted in 1997.

There were also agreements that focused upon other aspects of the environment. In 1972 UNESCO sponsored the Convention for the Protection of the World Cultural and Natural Heritage, in order to identify, conserve, and present to the public both man-made and natural sites of outstanding importance. The listed sites (which in 2007 included 644 cultural, 162 natural, and 24 mixed sites in 138 States Parties) include well-known sites such as the Great Wall of China, the Pyramids, and the Great Barrier Reef, less-known sites such as the Hypogeum in Malta, sites virtually untouched by man, such as Henderson Island in the Pitcairn group, and some sites for which protection came too late or ineffectually, such as the Old Bridge in Mostar (destroyed in the 1990 Balkan wars; now reconstructed), the Old City in Warsaw (flattened by the Nazis after the 1944 Warsaw Uprising; now reconstructed), and the Buddhas of Bamiyan (destroyed by the Taliban in 2001; still rubble). Wildlife gained protection under instruments such as the 1973 Convention on International Trade in Endangered Species of Wild Fauna and Flora (CITES), which protects around 5,000 species of animal and 28,000 species of plant by requiring and controlling the supply of licences for trade in the protected species or products made from them. Migratory species are given special protection under a 1979 Convention; and wetlands (broadly defined to include estuaries, swamps, fens, lakes, rivers, and paddy fields) are given some protection under the 1971 Ramsar Convention. States Parties are pledged to promote the conservation of listed wetlands of international importance, and to promote 'as far as possible the wise use of wetlands in their territory'. The United Kingdom listed the island of Diego Garcia as such a wetland. It gave the island over to the United States in the 1970s for use as a military base.

7.7 UNCED, THE RIO DECLARATION, AND AGENDA 21, 1992

By the 1990s governments were better informed on environmental issues and more concerned to grapple seriously with them. They recognized that while agreements on specific topics and regions were important ways of pinning States down to precise and measurable obligations, environmental issues tend to form part of a complex inter-connected web. The need for a more integrated approach was reflected in the declarations produced by the 1992 UN Conference on Environment and Development (UNCED), also known as the Rio Conference or the 'Earth Summit'. One clear sign of it is the Convention on Biodiversity, adopted at the Conference. That Convention aims to conserve biological diversity, and to encourage the sustainable development of biological resources and the fair and equitable sharing of the benefits arising from them. It is the biodiversity itself—'the variability among living organisms from all sources including, *inter alia*, terrestrial, marine, and other aquatic ecosystems and the ecological complexes of which they are part', as Article 2 of the Convention puts it—that is the focus, rather than any particular species. Put another way, by obliging States to co-operate in and plan for 'the conservation and sustainable use of biological diversity', the Convention obliges them not only to conserve all species but also to safeguard the ecological balance between them. At the same time it is recognized that States have the right to exploit their natural resources: the Convention does not seek to put an end to development. One controversial aspect of this right concerns control over the exploitation of the biological resources, such as rare plants in rain forests, whose medicinal and other properties are known only to indigenous peoples.[10] It is feared that western companies will appropriate that traditional knowledge and tie it up in intellectual property rights. Western companies, on the other hand, are fearful of the Convention provisions which require the transfer to developing countries on fair and most favourable terms of technology relevant to the conservation and sustainable use of biodiversity. The latter concern is a major reason for the non-ratification of the Convention by the United States. Despite these reservations, progress continues to be made. The Biodiversity Convention was supplemented in 2000 by the Cartagena Protocol on Biosafety, which seeks to protect biodiversity from threats posed by Living Modified Organisms (which are practically the same as Genetically Modified Organisms or GMOs) by requiring the 'Advanced Informed Agreement' of States before they import such organisms.

This integrated approach, protecting habitats rather than species, is increasingly widely adopted. In 1991 a Convention on the Protection of the Alps and in 2003 another on the Protection of the Carpathians were concluded. They aim to conserve the ecosystems and cultural traditions of those areas, and to manage the threats resulting from development and tourism. In 1992 the European Community adopted the Habitats Directive, which has been a powerful and influential tool of environmental conservation.

The broad and integrated is evident also in two other key documents emanating from the Rio Conference. The first is the Rio Declaration on Environment and Development, which sets out principles designed to reconcile environmental and developmental needs. The Declaration is notable for its insistence on sustainable development, a concept which unites the ideas of custodianship of the earth's natural resources and of the duty of each generation to leave the earth in a reasonable state for future generations, and which is a pivotal concept in contemporary environmental law.[11] A UN Commission on Sustainable Development was established in 1992. The Declaration also sets out, as Principle 15, another central concept: the precautionary approach (or precautionary principle):

In order to protect the environment, the precautionary approach shall be widely applied by States according to their capabilities. Where there are threats of serious or irreversible damage, lack of full scientific certainty shall not be used as a reason for postponing cost-effective measures to prevent environmental degradation.

[10] Also the subject of another convention, the 2001 Treaty on Plant Genetic Resources.
[11] Its coherence is another matter. See my contribution, 'Sustainable Development and Unsustainable Arguments' in Alan Boyle and David Freestone, *International Law and Sustainable Development* (Oxford: Oxford University Press, 1999), pp. 19–37.

The principle should not need to be declared; but States have a sorry history of refusing to take action to protect health and the environment for as long as there is the slightest uncertainty about the need for urgent action.

The second key UNCED document is *Agenda 21*, a somewhat overblown text that opens with the words 'Humanity stands at a defining moment in history.' The document contains much conference verbiage, but also contains many carefully considered proposals on ways to tackle 'the delicate balance between environmental and developmental concerns' in the twenty-first century. It places much emphasis on mechanisms to monitor the actual implementation of agreed principles; and the UN Commission on Sustainable Development itself reviews progress on the implementation of Agenda 21 and the Rio Declaration.

In 2002, 12,625 accredited governmental and non-governmental representatives[12] met in Johannesburg at the World Summit on Sustainable Development, organized by the Commission on Sustainable Development, in order to review progress on the Rio agenda. Despite general acknowledgement that the situation on both the environmental and developmental fronts was deteriorating alarmingly, there were few concrete results. The delegates produced a political Declaration, in which one of the final paragraphs reassuringly declared, 'We commit ourselves to act together, united by a common determination to save our planet, promote human development and achieve universal prosperity and peace' and set out a detailed Plan of Implementation. It is difficult to avoid cynicism; but progress is being made. The need for action to make development sustainable is widely accepted by governments, businesses, and individuals, and is becoming a normal part of their decision-making. Increased data collection and reporting is clarifying areas where urgent action is most needed. Above all, the subject is at the top of the international agenda and, in many developed countries, also towards the top of the domestic agenda. These are all essential preconditions for further progress, and are all radical improvements on the position forty years earlier.

7.8 TECHNIQUES

Let me turn to the question of the implementation of the legal agreements that have been concluded. I have indicated some of the topics with which they deal: marine and atmospheric pollution; dumping of wastes;

---

[12] According to some estimates 45,000 people participated in the Conference and parallel events. More than twenty States or territories have populations under 45,000.

preservation of species and habitats. Here I will focus on the techniques that they employ to achieve their aims.

7.8.1 PROHIBITIONS

The instinctive reaction to undesirable behaviour is to ban it; and some environmental treaties do this. The Montreal Protocol ban on the use of chlorofluorocarbons (CFCs) is an example, effective partly because of the strength of the evidence of the harm caused by CFCs to the ozone layer, but more particularly because alternative, and profitable, technology was already available. That is not always the case, and total bans are not always feasible. Successful environmental regulation must not only be principled but also practical: States will not ratify international agreements that impose unrealistic obligations upon them. Furthermore, the world can absorb a certain amount of pollution. Thus, the 1973 MARPOL Convention does not prohibit the discharge of all oil by ships at sea: it limits the discharge of oily waste to 30 litres per nautical mile while the ship is travelling, subject to overall limits on the total discharge; and it prohibits discharges entirely in certain vulnerable areas. The sea is reckoned to be able to cope with these levels of discharge. The limitations were, moreover, phased in over a period of years to enable shipowners to fit equipment to their vessels that would enable them to operate within the limits. Law and technology reinforce each other in this area. As new technology enables the reduction of harmful emissions, into the sea or soil or atmosphere, it becomes practicable to forbid or limit the discharges and require use of the technology. And the more the law regulates pollution, the more profitable investment in the development of new, efficient, cost-saving technology becomes.

7.8.2 SETTING TARGETS

A second strategy is the setting of targets. Rather than impose bans on pollution, States commit themselves to achieve a certain reduction in emissions. The 1985 Sulphur Protocol to the 1979 LRTAP set a target of a 30% reduction on 1980 levels in sulphur emissions, which cause great damage in the form of acid rain. The Parties met their targets, reducing omissions by over 50%. A second Sulphur Protocol was adopted in 1994, adopting a more flexible approach, setting long-term goals for the achievement of critical loads—i.e., 'the concentration of pollutants in the atmosphere above which direct adverse effects on receptors, such as human beings, plants, ecosystems or materials, may occur, according to present knowledge'—and tailoring the targets to the particular circumstances of each State Party. The Protocol has an Implementation Committee to monitor compliance.

The LRTAP experience shows realism rearing its head. It is, within limits, better to accommodate the particular needs of certain States and have them inside the regime than to adopt a stricter approach which will result in them not joining the regime. This is the difficulty facing the 1997 Kyoto Protocol, adopted under the Framework Convention on Climate Change. It, too, sets targets for emissions of greenhouse gases from developed States, and has innovative mechanisms to help achieve them. Each State Party has an emission standard expressed in tonnes of carbon, but States may buy and sell units (so-called 'emissions trading'), or engage in joint implementation projects for reducing emissions or increasing carbon sinks (e.g., by planting suitable trees) or gain credits by participating in the Clean Development Mechanism and engaging in emission-reducing projects in developing countries. These quasi-market mechanisms have introduced flexibility into the implementation of the carbon targets, and spawned an entire secondary industry dedicated to the promotion of carbon trading in its various forms, which will contribute to the pressure for compliance. Even so, the United States, currently the largest emitter of greenhouse gases, decided not to ratify the Kyoto Protocol despite great pressure from other States concerned at the impact of global warming. Its main concerns were that developing countries (including large emitters such as Brazil, China, and India) were not subject to binding targets, and that the target set for the United States would harm its industry. Opponents of ratification have questioned the validity of the scientific data and analyses that support the view that emissions cause global warming, and have also questioned whether the modest reductions required under the Kyoto Protocol can have any significant impact upon global warming.

7.8.3 INFORMATION AND INFORMED CONSENT

Prohibitions and targets are constraints upon State behaviour. A third approach is more subtle. It leaves governments and others to decide what action they will take but insists that the decision be taken with knowledge of the environmental consequences. This is the international equivalent of labelling food with lists of ingredients and leaving shoppers free to choose whether to buy. The 1989 Basel Convention on the Control of Transboundary Movements of Hazardous Wastes is one example. It requires exporters of specified waste products to give written notification of an intended international movement of waste to the designated authority of the intended importing State, which may then permit (conditionally or unconditionally) or prohibit the movement. The 1998 Rotterdam Convention on the Prior Informed Consent Procedure for Certain

Hazardous Chemicals and Pesticides in International Trade has a similar mechanism. It aims to promote shared responsibility and co-operative efforts among Parties by facilitating information exchange. Parties are required to adopt a policy of prohibiting, permitting, or permitting subject to conditions imports of hazardous chemicals listed in an Annex to the Convention; and exporting Parties must notify other Parties of intended exports of chemicals that are banned or severely restricted. States enforce import and export bans within their own territories.

This information-based approach is becoming more generalized. The 1998 Århus Convention on Access to Information, Public Participation in Decision-Making and Access to Justice in Environmental Matters sets minimum standards for Parties regarding the disclosure of information and participation in environmental decision-making, and on the availability of judicial remedies for review of environmental decisions and challenges to breaches of environmental laws. The rights extend to all members of the public, without the need to show some special interest, and to NGOs.

7.8.4 ENVIRONMENTAL IMPACT ASSESSMENT

Closely related to the information-sharing approach is the strategy promoted by the 1991 Espoo Convention on Environmental Impact Assessment in a Transboundary Context. It requires States Parties to conduct environmental impact assessments of certain kinds of development, such as the construction of large dams or of paper pulp plants exceeding a specified capacity, while they are at the planning stage, and to notify other States that may sustain environmental effects from the development. The public in its own territory and in territories likely to be affected by the development must be given the opportunity to participate in the decision-making process. A Protocol adopted in 2003 extends these provisions and requires assessments at a much earlier stage in a State's development planning process.

7.8.5 LICENSING

A feature of many treaties is that regulated activities must be licensed by the State Party in whose territory they take place. Exports of wastes for transmission to other States, or for dumping at sea, are required to be licensed, for instance. This mechanism is designed to ensure that governments establish a national bureaucracy that can routinely monitor compliance with the treaty obligations. For the most part, this works well, with businesses accepting the national regulations as one more set of rules within which they must operate. But like all schemes that require government approvals, it is open to evasion and the pernicious effects of corruption.

That is one reason why the international efforts to combat corruption, such as the 2003 UN Convention Against Corruption and the various OECD initiatives, including the 1997 Convention on Combating Bribery of Foreign Public Officials in International Business Transactions, are so vitally important in this, as in all other, fields.

7.8.6 MONITORING AND REPORTING

Many treaties require States Parties to collect and publish data and information on their implementation of their treaty obligations. This keeps the attention of governments on the need to fulfil the obligations and may shame them into doing so, and also makes available to interested parties a clear and updated account of progress, so that the need for further or different action can be considered. Monitoring is the dominant mechanism for international supervision of environmental obligations.

7.8.7 SAFE PROCEDURES AND CLEANING UP

Unlike pollution known to result from routine industrial processes, some pollution is accidental. Treaties address this aspect of the problem in two ways. First, many treaties and other (non-binding) instruments require or advise the adoption of safe procedures and technology to minimize the risk of accidental pollution. I have mentioned MARPOL and its requirements for the fitting to ships of technology (such as crude oil washing, double-bottom hulls, load-on-top systems, and other exotica) that should obviate most accidental pollution. Similarly, the International Atomic Energy Agency lays down extensive standards on nuclear safety. Secondly, where there is serious pollution someone must try to clear it up. Several international treaties address this issue. The 1990 International Convention on Oil Pollution Preparedness, Response and Co-operation, and the IAEA Conventions on Assistance in Case of a Nuclear Accident or Radiological Emergency, and on Early Notification of a Nuclear Accident, adopted in 1986 after the explosion at the Chernobyl power plant, are instances.

7.8.8 LIABILITY

Finally, there is the question of implementation of environmental obligations by the imposition of liability. This brings me full circle to the question with which this chapter opened: who can sue whom for breaches of environmental obligations? There is no satisfactory answer to this question in relation to widely distributed causes of environmental damage; but in cases where damage is caused by identifiable persons liability can be imposed.

Since the 1970s the basic principle has been that the polluter pays. There is no great reliance on that principle as an enforcement mechanism: the emphasis is, rightly, on prevention and cure. Nonetheless, several treaties address liability because it is likely to be a practical issue in the case of very serious incidents, where claims against those responsible are likely to be large and complex. In relation to oil pollution, for example, the response has been to couple strict liability with a limitation of liability, and with provision for the establishment of a compensation fund in the courts of a single State before which all claims arising from a single incident must be brought. The 1992 International Convention on Civil Liability for Oil Pollution Damage follows the pattern set by its 1969 predecessor in adopting this procedure. The 1963 Convention on Civil Liability for Nuclear Damage also provides for strict (in fact, absolute) liability coupled with limited liability. The reason for limiting liability is that it makes it possible to insist upon, and to obtain, insurance cover for the activities in question. By spreading the risk in the insurance market it is possible to obtain greater cover than is likely to be available to any single operator. Furthermore, because insurance is expensive operators will seek to keep its cost down as much as possible. Specialist insurers are well aware of international standards on safe equipment and operating procedures and will commonly insist on compliance with these as conditions of the insurance. In this way the insurance system reinforces the basic standard-setting approach in international instruments.

7.9 THE BROADER VIEW

As a postscript I should re-emphasize the point that although this chapter has looked at specific legal instruments and initiatives, the current trend in international law is to see environmental issues as inextricably bound up with questions of trade and development. Action in those other fields is of immense importance in the pursuit of environmental goals. For example, World Bank lending policies require assessment of the environmental impacts of projects for which Bank support is sought. An understanding of international environmental law requires close attention to these other fields, too.

8

The Use of Force

8.1 INTRODUCTION

Some regard it as a curious, if not paradoxical, idea that international law should seek to regulate war and the use of force. It appears almost perverse to use the instrumentality of the law in an attempt to regulate the precise manner of violent killing and destruction of property. The idea might be criticized from two angles. Some may say that killing and the destruction of property are wrong, and that they should not be lent the colour of legitimacy by accommodating them within the law, and particularly not by establishing rules that make it permissible to use force in this way. What is the point of the 1868 St Petersburg Declaration Renouncing the Use, in Time of War, of Explosive Projectiles Under 400 Grammes Weight?[1] Does someone killed or maimed by a projectile care how heavy it was? Is it all right to kill someone with an explosive projectile over 400 grammes in weight? Should there be battlefield wardens checking the weights of projectiles, like weights and measures inspectors in municipal market halls?

Others may say that when the very existence of institutions and moral principles of fundamental importance is under grave threat they must be defended, and whatever is necessary for their defence must be done. This is the view reflected in the 'War is hell' view, associated with General Sherman's justification for the swathe of destruction that he cut through Georgia during the American Civil War, and more recently with US Defense Secretary Rumsfeld's observation that 'stuff happens', in response to complaints of looting during the 2003 invasion of Iraq. From this perspective, all fault lies with those who committed the original wrongs against which force is used (always defensively: no modern State has a Ministry of Offence). If shocking violence occurs during a conflict, blame those who caused the conflict, whether they caused it by attacking another State or by conducting themselves in such a manner that the

---

[1] Reproduced in Adam Roberts and Richard Guelff, *Documents on the Laws of War* (3rd edn., Oxford: Oxford University Press, 2000), p. 53.

'international community' was obliged to intervene militarily to safeguard international security, life, freedom, or other basic values.

Both criticisms have some force; but both are fundamentally flawed as criticisms of the role that has been given to international law in the context of the use of force. That role is based on the premise that there will be occasions on which governments will consider the threat to fundamental values, principles, and interests so great that lethal force must indeed be used to protect and preserve them. But that is a very different matter from saying that situations arise in which moral rules are suspended or inapplicable. Whatever one might think about the Vietnam war in the 1960s and 1970s, or the intervention in Kosovo in 1999, or the invasion of Iraq in 2003, it cannot be said that they were, taken as a whole, wanton acts of violence, even if there were individual acts of wanton violence during the course of each of those episodes. Those uses of force were all launched to safeguard some value that was thought sufficiently important to warrant asking or ordering people to die and to kill for. One might think those values wrong, or the means chosen to advance them profoundly misconceived. The conflicts might be regarded as fundamentally immoral and illegal, or as having involved disproportionate force, or in some other way defective. But they were not unprincipled. And if force is used to secure or advance values and principles, that force must itself be consistent with those principles. It makes no sense to fight to preserve freedom by imposing slavery on others; and it makes no sense to seek to preserve the 'civilized' values of human dignity and human rights by the use of torture and gratuitous and indiscriminate suffering. Whatever the moral justification for the use of force might be, that moral justification will—if it is to be coherent—entail limitations upon the circumstances in which force may be used and the manner in which it is used. As it was put in the 1863 *Instructions for the Government of Armies of the United States in the Field*, applied during the American Civil War, 'Men who take up arms against one another in public war do not cease on this account to be moral beings, responsible to one another and to God.'[2]

This view of the role of law in war has a long history, and is profoundly rooted in moral argument, as Michael Walzer demonstrated in his brilliant study *Just and Unjust Wars*.[3] Until the twentieth century, the regulation of war was one of the main concerns of international law, and

---

[2] Article 15, <http://www.yale.edu/lawweb/avalon/lieber.htm#art1>.
[3] Michael Walzer, *Just and Unjust Wars. A Moral Argument with Historical Illustrations* (3rd edn., London: Allen Lane, 1977).

one of the most ancient. In Chapter 20 of the book of Deuteronomy, some of the Mosaic rules for the conduct of war are set out. One says:

> When in the course of war you lay siege to a town for a long time in order to take it, do not destroy its trees by taking an axe to them, for they provide you with food; you must not cut them down.

Essentially the same rule appeared many centuries later in the Hague Regulations on the Laws and Customs of War on Land, annexed to 1907 Hague Convention No. IV,[4] where Article 55 provides that:

> The occupying State shall be regarded only as administrator and usufructory of public buildings, real estate, forests and agricultural estates belonging to a hostile State and situated in the occupied country. It must safeguard the capital of these properties, and administer them in accordance with the rules of usufruct.

The 1907 Hague Regulations remain in force, under the umbrella of one of the 1949 Geneva Conventions on the Laws of War, and the principles that they set out have applied to regulate the rights and duties of occupying forces such as the Israeli army in the Occupied Territories of Palestine and the American and British forces in occupied Iraq. This rule of the Law of Belligerent Occupation has applied in that part of the Middle East for the best part of three millennia.

Other rules have a comparable antiquity. Rules against the killing of prisoners appear as a settled part of the law of war, whose disregard at Agincourt was censured.[5] Heralds and envoys were regarded as inviolable, and entitled to be treated well: 'Don't shoot the messenger' has long been as much a principle of the laws of war[6] as it is of moral responsibility.

Underlying such rules are the twin principles of military efficiency and economy of means. Those principles relate to the manner in which force—war—is to be used. They are principles of the *jus in bello*, the law that applies *in* a war, and regulates the conduct of the war. This body of law is also known as the Law of Armed Conflict, or International Humanitarian Law. The terms are synonymous; but with the decline of classical learning '*jus in bello*' may seem obscure, and 'International Humanitarian Law' has a slightly Orwellian ring, to my ear—although the latter term does emphasize one very important aspect of this body of law, of rapidly growing importance, which is that in

---

[4] Reproduced in Adam Roberts and Richard Guelff, *Documents on the Laws of War* (3rd edn., Oxford: Oxford University Press, 2000), p. 73.

[5] See Shakespeare's *Henry V*, Act 4, scene 7, lines 1-11.

[6] See Articles 32 to 34 of the 1907 Hague Regulations on the Laws and Customs of War on Land.

modern conflicts the role and responsibilities of the armed forces are likely to extend well beyond the cessation of fighting and into the period of reconstruction and re-establishment of the social structure in areas blighted by the fighting. I shall use the term 'the Law of Armed Conflict' (which is the title given to the current British manual of military law).[7]

The rules of the Law of Armed Conflict do not address the question of the circumstances in which it is permissible to go to war and to use force. That question is addressed by the *jus ad bellum*, the law that regulates the right to resort to war. The *jus in bello* and the *jus ad bellum* developed separately from one another as legal concepts, although the two bodies of rules are closely related and there is a very long history of moral analysis of the rightness of resort to war, epitomized by the 'just war' tradition. It was only in the twentieth century that there arose specifically and distinctly legal constraints upon the right of States to have resort to war, although there had for many centuries been recognition of the need for a moral justification for the waging of war. For this reason, it is convenient to consider the two sets of rules in turn, dealing first with the law on the use of force—the *jus ad bellum*—and then with the Law of Armed Conflict.

8.2 THE USE OF FORCE IN INTERNATIONAL LAW

Until the beginning of the twentieth century, the dictum of Clausewitz, that war is the continuation of politics by other means, was an observation as accurate as it was elegant. States had armies; and the armies were instruments to be used. Not that the troops were unwilling. In a world still without the excitement of radio or television, and with practically no cinema, the army retained a certain glamour. British troops still wore scarlet uniforms in battle in Africa in the 1880s; and a cavalry charge promised the incarnation of masculine virtue and the thrill of existential risk combined with the prestige of self-sacrifice in the service of truth and justice. The path of duty was the way to glory. People volunteered to fight in their thousands. But human kind cannot bear too much reality. In the annals of human tragedy and catastrophic misjudgement there are few images as poignant as those of the crowds of young volunteers waving from the troop trains as they set off for Flanders in 1914, and the photographs of those same men as they faced the stupefying, incomprehensible, carnage of battles such as the Somme, where a million casualties were

---

[7] Ministry of Defence, *The Manual of the Law of Armed Conflict* (Oxford: Oxford University Press, 2004).

sustained—20,000 British dead on the first day—in a horrific struggle in which the front between the opposing armies was pushed across less than eight miles of pulped earth in five months.

The decimation of an entire generation—and even in the 1950s, there were few in Europe who did not hear first-hand accounts of the horrors of the Great War or of the losses of friends and family—galvanized governments. There was a realization that the War represented a monumental failure of policy, diplomacy, and military strategy. Even before the end of the War, United States' President Woodrow Wilson declared in his famous 'Fourteen Points' speech that the United States' goal in the War was that:

the world be made fit and safe to live in; and particularly that it be made safe for every peace-loving nation which, like our own, wishes to live its own life, determine its own institutions, be assured of justice and fair dealing by the other peoples of the world as against force and selfish aggression. All the peoples of the world are in effect partners in this interest, and for our own part we see very clearly that unless justice be done to others it will not be done to us.[8]

In that context he called for the establishment of 'a general association of nations . . . under specific covenants for the purpose of affording mutual guarantees of political independence and territorial integrity to great and small states alike'. The product of that call was the League of Nations, predecessor of the United Nations, whose Covenant was adopted in 1920. Ironically, the United States' Senate refused to accept the Covenant, and the United States never became a member of the League.

The Covenant was the first serious attempt to place general legal constraints upon resort to war. In the nineteenth century there had been bilateral treaties in which the States Parties declared their eternal friendship and renounced war with each other;[9] but these had little practical impact upon the development of international law.[10] In 1899, the Powers of the day had concluded a Convention on the Pacific Settlement of International Disputes (revised in 1907 at The Hague Peace Conference), which provided for various peaceful means of adjusting international disputes. But war remained an option. For example, there were provisions

---

[8] <http://usinfo.state.gov/usa/infousa/facts/democrac/51.htm>; and in Franz Knipping, Hans von Mangoldt, and Volker Rittberger, *The United Nations System and its Predecessors* (Oxford: Oxford University Press, 1997), vol. II, p. 181.

[9] e.g., Article I of the 1868 Costa Rica–Nicaragua Treaty of Peace and Friendship, reproduced with other examples in William R. Manning, *Arbitration Treaties Among the American Nations* (New York: Oxford University Press, 1924), p. 77 and *passim*.

[10] See Kalevi J. Holsti, *Peace and war: armed conflicts and international order 1648–1989* (Cambridge: Cambridge University Press, 1991).

on mediation of disputes by third parties; but Article 7 of the Convention stated that:

The acceptance of mediation cannot, in default of agreement to the contrary, have the effect of interrupting, delaying or hindering mobilization or other measures of preparation for war.

Again in 1907, the Powers had agreed 'not to have recourse to armed force for the recovery of contract debts claimed from the Government of one country by the Government of another country as being due to its nationals'.[11] That Convention effectively outlawed war as an instrument of debt collection, bringing an end to episodes such as the 1903 blockade of Venezuela by Britain, Germany, and Italy in order to compel it to pay the monies that it owed.[12] The provision did not, however, apply if the debtor State refused arbitration. But it was not until the conclusion of the League Covenant that there was a substantial move to limit the right of States to use force in their international relations.

Article 11 of the Covenant declared that 'Any war or threat of war, whether immediately affecting any of the Members of the League or not, is hereby declared a matter of concern to the whole League'; and Article 12 went on to stipulate that:

The Members of the League agree that, if there should arise between them any dispute likely to lead to a rupture they will submit the matter either to arbitration or judicial settlement or to enquiry by the Council, and they agree in no case to resort to war until three months after the award by the arbitrators or the judicial decision, or the report by the Council.

If a State failed to comply with this obligation, other Members of the League were committed to sever all trade or financial relations with it. The three-month cooling-off period was a start, supplemented soon afterwards by the more absolute terms of the 1928 Pact of Paris (the Kellogg-Briand Pact), in which the States Parties:

solemnly declare in the names of their respective peoples that they condemn recourse to war for the solution of international controversies, and renounce it, as an instrument of national policy in their relations with one another.[13]

---

[11] Convention respecting the Limitation of the Employment of Force for the Recovery of Contract Debts, 1907, Article 1.

[12] That crisis was ended by the reference of the claims against Venezuela to arbitration.

[13] <http://www.yale.edu/lawweb/avalon/imt/kbpact.htm>; 225 *Consolidated Treaty Series* 195; and in Franz Knipping, Hans von Mangoldt, and Volker Rittberger, *The United Nations System and its Predecessors* (Oxford: Oxford University Press, 1997), vol. II, p. 200.

Similar obligations were undertaken by States in the Americas in the 1933 Saavedra-Lamas Treaty.[14]

No-one should expect commitments of this kind to lead to an immediate and total change in State behaviour. As long as States have armed forces the temptation to use them against other States will remain, and occasionally prove irresistible. And States will always retain armed forces of some description because there is no clear difference between the kind of personnel and equipment needed to preserve internal law and order, and to cope with natural or man-made disasters, and for defensive purposes, and those needed to attack other States. What the Pact of Paris did do was signal an intention to change strategies and to prepare, through the development of diplomacy and processes for managing conflict, for the pursuit of national goals through means not involving the use of force. Sadly, even in this limited sense it was a failure. The 1930s saw the invasion of Manchuria by Japan in 1931 at what might be regarded as the start of a Pacific War that continued until 1945, and a more quixotic invasion of Abyssinia by Italy in 1935, as well as the invasions of Czechoslovakia and Poland by Germany. Japan, Italy, and Germany were all parties to the Pact of Paris. The League of Nations was powerless to prevent those episodes, or to force the withdrawal of the invaders.

8.3 THE CHARTER SYSTEM

After World War Two, no rational person could think either that the Covenant and the Pact of Paris had been successful, or that governments should simply give up the attempt to constrain international violence. The only sensible option was that advocated by Samuel Beckett: 'Try Again. Fail again. Fail better.' And try they did. And in the face of the failure of the provisions in the Covenant and the Pact, they aimed higher. There is much cynical criticism of the United Nations; but it should not be forgotten that the people who built it, and framed the provisions of the Charter, were people who not only knew what war was like—and were, indeed, drafting the Charter during the War—but also knew what failure and cynicism were. They had experienced at first hand the failure of League, but with a vision and determination that puts many in later generations to shame they built a global organization and an international order that has lasted for more than sixty years and, whatever its failings, has undoubtedly 'failed better' than anything that went before it.

---

[14] <http://www.yale.edu/lawweb/avalon/intdip/interam/intamo1.htm>.

The United Nations Charter contained a clear and absolute prohibition on the unilateral use of force, except in self-defence. Article 2(4) stipulates that:

All Members shall refrain in their international relations from the threat or use of force against the territorial integrity or political independence of any state, or in any other manner inconsistent with the Purposes of the United Nations.

Not only attacks on the territory of States but also attacks on manifestations of the State, such as its warships, military aircraft, and armed forces, fall within the prohibition. The rights and security of States were secured by two other provisions. One permitted the United Nations Security Council to authorize the use of force; and the other permitted States to take action to defend themselves in the period before the Security Council takes measures necessary to maintain international peace and security. The drafters of the Charter envisaged that the UN would have armed forces permanently at its disposal and that the fifteen-State Security Council (including the five veto-wielding Permanent Members—China, France, the UK, the USA, and the USSR) would decide upon their deployment if the use of armed force was considered to be necessary. Those UN forces never materialized. In the tense atmosphere of the Cold War, States were unwilling to relinquish control over any part of their armed forces or to add to their defence spending in order to establish an independent force which might be used against them, their allies, or their protégés.

8.4 USES OF FORCE AUTHORIZED BY THE UNITED NATIONS

The Charter structure remains as it was originally drafted, and the UN still has no armed forces permanently at its disposal. But within that framework it retains a very wide range of powers. Under Chapter VI of the Charter the Security Council may investigate any situation which might lead to international friction or give rise to a dispute; and any Member may take such a situation to the Council. The Council may make recommendations for the handling of the situation, and frequently does so. It sends missions to areas of crisis, collects and considers facts, and recommends ways to contain or resolve crises. If the Council determines that a situation constitutes a 'threat to the peace, breach of the peace, or act of aggression' it may exercise its powers under Chapter VII of the Charter. Under Article 41, it may decide to order measures not involving the use of armed force, such as the mandatory economic sanctions first imposed in 1966[15] in relation to the white minority Government in Rhodesia (now Zimbabwe) which unilaterally declared its independence of the United Kingdom. UN Member States are legally bound, under Article 25 of the Charter, to accept and carry out such decisions of the Council. And ultimately, under Article 42, it 'may take such action by air, sea, or land forces as may be necessary to maintain or restore international peace and security'.

The Council has found threats to the peace even in matters that may appear to be purely internal. For example, it determined that the failure to reinstate Jean-Bertrand Aristide, who had been elected as President of Haiti in a 1990 poll monitored by UN observers but was removed from power in 1991, amounted to such a breach, and over the following months the UN sent in a special representative of the Secretary-General, authorized a joint human rights mission with the Organization of American States, and imposed arms and oil embargoes on Haiti.

The Security Council has made extensive use of its powers under Chapters VI and VII of the Charter. It has established fact-finding or other missions, such as observer missions to monitor elections and peacekeeping missions to monitor truces. This may sound a weak and ineffectual move, but often it is not. A clear report, accepted by the UN, on a situation, which identifies the problems and those responsible for them and suggests an approach to the management of the crisis, can rapidly become the focus upon which the policies of States become aligned. The UN can thus help to form and articulate the policy that will be pursued by the international community. Decisions to use armed force have been much rarer. The first occurred in 1950 when the absence of the Soviet delegate from the Security Council made it possible to adopt a resolution recommending Member States to make 'forces and other assistance available to a unified command under the United States of America' in Korea. The ability of the United Nations to take 'measures necessary to maintain international peace and security' involving the use of force was impeded for many years during the Cold War by the actual or potential operation of the veto of the Permanent Members.[16] (The General Assembly asserted its residual right to act in this field in the 1950 'Uniting for Peace' resolution,[17] but it could only take initiatives such as the establishment of

---

[15] SC resolution 221 (1966); and see resolutions 216 (1965) and 217 (1965): <http://www.un.org/Docs/sc/unsc_resolutions.html>.

[16] Vetoes had been cast 261 times by early 2007, mostly by the USA and the USSR. The pattern is interesting. In the period 1945 to 1975 the veto was cast 113 times by the USSR, and 12 times by the USA. In the period 1976 to 2007 the figures are USSR/Russia 10 vetoes, USA 70.

[17] UNGA Resolution 377(V).

peacekeeping forces, which do not involve enforcement action.) Armed action was not authorized again until 1990 when, in resolution 678, the Council authorized 'Member States acting in co-operation with the Government of Kuwait' to use 'all necessary means' to secure the withdrawal of the Iraqi forces which had invaded Kuwait, and the restoration of international peace and security in the area.

Some people argued, and perhaps believed, that the invasion of Iraq by the 'coalition of the willing' led by the United States and the United Kingdom in 2003 was justified on the basis that the 1990 mandate was 'revived' when Iraq defied the international community by not admitting possession of, or allowing international inspectors to search for, the weapons of mass destruction which the United States and Britain wrongly insisted that it possessed. The argument, aptly described by Lord Steyn[18] as scraping the barrel, is fatuous: no-one could reasonably suppose that the 1990 Security Council resolutions lay dormant, like the seeds of exotic plants in the desert, until some State which happened to be a veteran of the 1990 Kuwait conflict might decide to water them back into bloom. The whole point of the UN system is that when the Security Council is seised of a problem it is the Council, and not individual Member States, that has the right to control matters. If the Security Council had intended that the United States, the United Kingdom and others should invade Iraq in 2003 with its blessing and its mandate, it would have said so. It did not.

The Security Council also has a prominent and distinctive role in international peacekeeping. Unlike the Korean and Kuwait operations, the forces involved in peacekeeping operations are not engaged in enforcement action. They have very limited mandates, and may not use force to impose solutions. The troops committed to these peacekeeping forces, familiar in many parts of the world from their blue helmets, operate with the consent of the State or States where they are based (and must leave if that consent is withdrawn) and attempt simply to maintain the peace by standing between opposing forces. They are accompanied by UN uniformed police and military observers and by civilian personnel. By 2007 the UN had established 61 peacekeeping operations of which 15 were still in existence, in places such as Cyprus (UNIFCYP), Kosovo (UNMIK), Lebanon (UNIFIL), and Sudan (UNMIS), the longest-serving being the United Nations Truce Supervision Organization (UNTSO) Middle East. Over 80,000 military and police personnel and over 10,000 civilian personnel were deployed on UN peacekeeping missions in 2007, with

---

[18] A distinguished retired Law Lord, and chairman of Justice, the civil rights group.

Pakistan, Bangladesh, and India the largest contributors of troops. This is almost ten times the number deployed in the 1980s, during the final years of the Cold War, and reflects the dramatic changes in international politics since 1990. Peacekeeping costs are shared among UN Members according to a scale roughly reflecting their wealth: among the top ten contributors China pays about 2%, Canada 3%, Japan 19%, the United States 27%, and six members of the European Union together pay 33%.

The study of the efforts of the Security Council, and of the General Assembly and the informal network of discussions in the UN cafeterias and Embassy reception rooms with which the work of the Security Council is intimately connected, gives a fascinating insight into the subtle complexity of politics as the art of the possible. To outsiders it may appear bewildering and unprincipled. Why does the UN act in some circumstances but not in others? Why does it not act sooner or more decisively to put a stop to blatant instances of aggression? Why do States sometimes choose to act outside the UN framework? There are answers to all of these questions, usually rooted in political considerations. In this field perhaps above all others, the UN, and in particular the Security Council, tends not to be very legalistic: it is more concerned to do what a working majority of Members considers to be right and desirable than to fit its actions within lawyers' categories. That said, it is constantly trying to streamline its internal structures and procedures, in so far as it can within the overall Charter framework. Strategic reviews of peacekeeping appeared in the Secretary-General's 1992 Report *Agenda for Peace*[19] and its more cautious 1995 *Supplement*,[20] written in the light of the UN experience in Somalia and the Former Yugoslavia. They show an acute awareness of the practical limitations on what the UN can do, as long as it has no forces committed to it by Member States and at its disposal.[21] And they advance a view— surely correct—of peacekeeping as only one aspect of a broader effort. Taking to heart Galgacus' criticism of the Romans, that they make a desert and call it peace,[22] the UN is clearly committed to the view that peace cannot be built only by dropping bombs. There is a need for preventive diplomacy, which seeks to avert armed conflict, and for long-term reconstruction

---

[19] <http://www.un.org/Docs/SG/agpeace.html>.

[20] <http://www.un.org/Docs/SG/agsupp.html>.

[21] The 1995 *Supplement* noted (in paragraph 43) that 'when in May 1994 the Security Council decided to expand the United Nations Assistance Mission for Rwanda (UNAMIR), not one of the 19 Governments that at that time had undertaken to have troops on stand-by agreed to contribute.'

[22] According to Tacitus, the words of the Caledonian chief Galgacus before his great battle with the Romans in 83 AD. Galgacus lost.

and post-conflict peace-building efforts, as the horrific consequences of the blundering invasion of Iraq in 2003 have made painfully clear.

8.5 SELF-DEFENCE

The Security Council will inevitably take time to respond to a crisis, and it cannot be supposed that States have no right to defend themselves in the meantime. The final Article in Chapter VII ('Action with respect to threats to the peace, breaches of the peace, and acts of aggression') is Article 51, which stipulates that:

Nothing in the present Charter shall impair the inherent right of individual or collective self-defence if an armed attack occurs against a Member of the United Nations, until the Security Council has taken measures necessary to maintain international peace and security. Measures taken by Members in the exercise of this right of self-defence shall be immediately reported to the Security Council and shall not in any way affect the authority and responsibility of the Security Council under the present Charter to take at any time such action as it deems necessary in order to maintain or restore international peace and security.

There has been a great deal of discussion about the precise limits of the right of self-defence, much of it the result of a combination of a near-theological reverence for the formulation of the right in the context of the 1837 *Caroline* episode and a suspension of common-sense. In the winter of 1837 a group of rebels against British rule in North America hired the steamboat *Caroline*, apparently intending to use it in a raid against Canada. The British militia seized it at its mooring on the Niagara River, set fire to it, and sent it over the Niagara Falls. An American, Amos Durfee, was killed. One of the militiamen, Alexander McLeod, later visited New York and bragged of his role in the episode. He was arrested and charged with murder. Britain had objected strongly to his arrest, asserting that those acting as part of the military forces of a government could not be prosecuted for their acts. It accepted responsibility for McLeod's actions while arguing that the action was justified as a matter of international law. Although Britain said that if McLeod were executed there would be war between the two States, the United States was powerless to act because the state of New York would not back down. McLeod was acquitted at his trial in 1841. The episode was brought to a close by the 1842 treaty concluded by the US Secretary of State Daniel Webster and the British Foreign Secretary Lord Ashburton;[23] but it is the heated

---

[23] <http://www.yale.edu/lawweb/avalon/diplomacy/britain/br-1842.htm>.

correspondence between the United States and Great Britain[24] for which the episode is chiefly remembered. Webster wrote that the British action would be justified only if Britain could show 'a necessity of self-defence, instant, overwhelming, leaving no choice of means, and no moment for deliberation', and also that it 'did nothing unreasonable or excessive, since the act justified by the necessity of self-defence, must be limited by that necessity and kept clearly within it'. While Britain and the United States differed over the question whether these criteria were met, they both accepted the essence of this definition of self-defence.

There are two critical elements in the *Caroline* formula: the lack of any alternative to the use of force, and the need for the force used in self-defence not to be excessive. Over-literal readings of the formula have led some commentators to suggest that a State must wait until an attack has actually been launched against it before it can respond, and that there is no right of anticipatory self-defence, such as Israel invoked in the Six-Day war. In the weeks before Israel's attack on its Arab neighbours Egypt had required the withdrawal of the UN peacekeeping force from the Sinai peninsula and ships carrying cargoes bound for the Israeli port of Eilat in the Red Sea had been blockaded. It is apparent that both Israel and its Arab neighbours were instructed by their respective protecting super-powers not to fire the first shot, so that when they did use the force for which they were so obviously preparing they could claim to be acting in self-defence. Israel moved first, and won a remarkable military victory.[25] That war illustrates perfectly the need for preventive diplomacy. Once the idea that an attack was imminent gained hold, each side was bound to pre-pare to repel an attack (or an anticipatory act of self-defence) from the other; and as preparations proceeded a point was bound to come at which one State would consider that it could wait no longer without serious risk that its military capacity and ability to defend itself would be destroyed. The right of self-defence cannot require a State to await an actual attack before lifting a finger to defend itself—though it certainly requires the most serious efforts to avert the use of force.

This much is clear. But the implications of it in a world of threats from sophisticated weapons launched at great distances from their targets and from terrorist cells hiding among civilian populations are significant and not wholly comfortable. Take, for example, the case of a group of people

---

[24] <http://www.yale.edu/lawweb/avalon/diplomacy/britain/br-1842d.htm>.

[25] Pyrrhic, perhaps. It is the territorial gains made by Israel in 1967 that are the fundamental cause of the continuing Middle East crisis over Palestine.

believed to have planned and about to execute a nerve gas attack on an underground transport system somewhere in Europe, and known to be meeting in a remote location in one State. The target might be London, Paris, Madrid, Moscow, or some other city. The United Kingdom, France, Spain, Russia, and others are all vulnerable, but each is more likely not to be the target. If the group is about to split up, one of them carrying the nerve gas to its target and the others going to other destinations, and if the State in whose territory they are meeting is unable or unwilling to act sufficiently quickly and decisively to track and detain them all, can no other State act? Must each of the potential targets wait, and hope that it can arrest them if and when they enter its territory?

A broad answer to that question is given in the United States' *National Security Strategy 2006*, where it is said that 'under long-standing principles of self defense, we do not rule out the use of force before attacks occur, even if uncertainty remains as to the time and place of the enemy's attack'.[26] This doctrine of pre-emption has been represented as a policy of dealing with threats before they become threats. The concern is not simply that it might be used as an excuse for specific uses of force that are shown in retrospect not to have been justified, but rather that the assertion of the right to take pre-emptive action is in effect an assertion of a permanent right to intervene with force in third States by the handful of States that have the technology and equipment to enable them to do so. Put crudely, it is seen as an arrogation to the United States of the powers of a world policeman, and it is feared as a manifesto for vigilante violence. These concerns were reflected in a remarkable analysis of the right of self-defence by the Attorney-General for England. Having quoted Article 51 of the Charter, he said that 'international law permits the use of force in self-defence against an imminent attack but does not authorise the use of force to mount a pre-emptive strike against a threat that is more remote'.[27] The statement was plainly intended to distance the United Kingdom from the United States' position on pre-emption, even though the British Prime Minister had advanced in his March 2004 Sedgefield speech an even wider doctrine permitting States—or at least the United Kingdom—to use force in the face of 'the risk of [the] new global terrorism and its interaction with states or organisations or individuals

---

[26] <http://www.whitehouse.gov/nsc/nss/2006/> at p. 23. The notion was first developed in the 2002 *National Security Strategy*, <http://www.whitehouse.gov/nsc/nss/2002/index.html>.

[27] Hansard, House of Lords Debates, 21 April 2004, col. 370; 75 *BYIL* 822, at 823 (2004).

proliferating [Weapons of Mass Destruction]', which he described as a risk that 'I simply am not prepared to run', adding that 'this is not a time to err on the side of caution.'[28] But the Attorney's more clear-thinking and precise speech identified common ground in the need for the development of concept of what constitutes an 'imminent' armed attack to meet new circumstances and new threats.[29] There is much to be said for interpreting the requirement of imminence to mean that action may be taken only at the last reasonable opportunity to take effective action to avert the threat, even if in some cases that opportunity arises a considerable time before the actual attack is expected to occur. That is, underneath the language, what the *Caroline* correspondence was actually getting at.

It is sometimes asked whether the right of self-defence exists in relation to attacks from 'non-State actors' such as terrorists. The question was fuelled by a passage in the Advisory Opinion of the International Court of Justice in the *Wall* case which stated that Article 51 of the Charter 'recognizes the existence of an inherent right of self-defence in the case of armed attack by one State against another State.'[30] The position cannot be seriously doubted. Self-defence is an inherent right; and the right exists whenever one is attacked, whether by a State army or by an individual terrorist. The question is, what action may be taken? No-one doubts that in September 2001 the United States would have been entitled to shoot down the aircraft flying towards the World Trade Centre, if that was the only way of stopping the suicidal terrorist attacks. Even if it were established that the attack had been planned and controlled from Al-Qaeda bases in Afghanistan, however, that right of self-defence would not have justified an attack on Afghanistan itself as a State. On the other hand, if further attacks emanating from Afghanistan were 'imminent'—as that requirement is now interpreted—and the government of Afghanistan was unable or unwilling to prevent them, the right of self-defence would justify an attack on those people and facilities in Afghanistan in order to prevent such attacks. The emphasis is on prevention: it is perfectly clear that international law does not permit the use of force in revenge, to punish, or to deter future attacks. The line between deterrence and prevention is difficult to draw: but the important point is that international law gives no warrant to States to use violence to terrify those whom it fears may be disposed to attack it in order to give them a taste of what they might expect if an attack is executed.

---

[28] <http://www.pm.gov.uk/output/Page5461.asp>.

[29] He added that 'It has never been the position of the Government that the military action against Iraq was legally justified on grounds of "pre-emptive self defence".'

[30] *ICJ Reports 2004*, p. 136, at paragraph 139.

The requirement of proportionality is similarly fundamental to the right of self-defence. Self-defence is the right to defend the State, not an opportunity for unrestrained violence against one's enemies. The scale of the 2006 Israeli attack on Lebanon and the widespread destruction that it caused, after the abduction of two Israeli soldiers and several years of suicide bomb attacks on Israeli targets, attracted considerable international criticism on this ground, even from those who were satisfied that Israel was justified in using force. But it is not easy to pin down what the requirement of proportionality entails. Is the degree force used to be calibrated against the scale of violence that would occur if the threat against which the State is defending itself were to be realized? Or is it to be measured against the force that is necessary to avert the attack? These two approaches (and others could be formulated) might yield very different results. One State may threaten the use of force against another but be unable to bring sufficient military power to bear to cause more than minor damage; but it might be so committed to the attack that it would take massive force to prevent or deter it: another State may threaten massive destruction from an attack, but be easily deterred by a symbolic display of force.

Self-defence may be exercised individually or collectively. Collective self-defence pacts are not uncommon. NATO, the North Atlantic Treaty Organization,[31] is probably the best-known and most developed organization. Article 5 of the 1949 NATO treaty stipulates that:

The Parties agree that an armed attack against one or more of them in Europe or North America shall be considered an attack against them all and consequently they agree that, if such an armed attack occurs, each of them, in exercise of the right of individual or collective self-defence recognised by Article 51 of the Charter of the United Nations, will assist the Party or Parties so attacked by taking forthwith, individually and in concert with the other Parties, such action as it deems necessary, including the use of armed force, to restore and maintain the security of the North Atlantic area.[32]

In eastern Europe the Warsaw Pact[33] was established in 1955 to balance NATO. In the Pacific, the ANZUS treaty was signed in 1951, establishing a collective self-defence agreement between Australia, New Zealand, and the United States.[34] Until 1985, when New Zealand distanced itself from ANZUS because of disagreements with the United States over nuclear weapons, that agreement overlapped with the 1971 Five Power Defence

[31] <http://www.nato.int/home.htm>.
[32] <http://www.nato.int/docu/basictxt/treaty.htm>.
[33] <http://www.php.isn.ethz.ch/>.
[34] See <http://australianpolitics.com/foreign/anzus/>.

Arrangements between the United Kingdom, Australia, New Zealand, Malaysia, and Singapore;[35] and it also overlapped with SEATO—the South East Asia Treaty Organization—to which Australia, France, New Zealand, Pakistan, the Philippines, Thailand, the United Kingdom, and the United States were Parties before its demise in 1977. Other similar groupings included CENTO, the Central Treaty Organization, which existed in the Middle East until 1979, and the 1947 Rio Pact[36] in the Americas, which still exists. There are many other formal and informal military agreements of a broadly similar kind. Some of these alliances have been invoked. For example, the United States invoked the Rio Pact after the 2001 terrorist attacks, and Australia invoked the ANZUS treaty after the 2002 Bali nightclub bombings. Above all, NATO has functioned as a real military alliance. The collective self-defence provision of Article 5 of the NATO Treaty was invoked in 2001 after the attacks on the United States.[37] Those invocations were true examples of collective self-defence, because all of the States concerned were in some measure under a common threat and they decided to act collectively in their efforts to defend themselves against it. Sometimes the matter is less clear. Judge Jennings observed, in a typically trenchant passage in his dissenting judgment in the *Nicaragua (Merits)* case, that the law does not authorize vicarious defence by States acting as authorized champions of victim States. 'The assisting State', he wrote, 'surely must, by going to the victim State's assistance, be also . . . in some measure defending itself.'[38] However sound that view may be as a matter of legal theory, the notion of the defence of a State's interests is now so broad that it is difficult to see circumstances where a court would strike down a use of force on the basis that although a victim State was being protected the protecting State was not itself under threat.

8.6 HUMANITARIAN INTERVENTION

In his celebrated (and well-balanced) legal advice dated 7 March 2003 on the legality of the use of force in Iraq,[39] the English Attorney-General stated that there are generally three possible bases for the use of force by States under international law. Two, UN authorization and self-defence,

---

[35] See <http://www.austlii.edu.au/au/other/dfat/treaties/1971/21.html>.

[36] <http://www.oas.org/juridico/english/Treaties/b-29.html>.

[37] <http://www.nato.int/docu/pr/2001/p01-159e.htm>.

[38] *ICJ Reports 1986*, p. 14 at p. 545.

[39] <http://www.ico.gov.uk/upload/documents/library/freedom_of_information/ notices/annex_a_-_attorney_general's_advice_070303.pdf>.

I have discussed. There is also a right to use force, he said, 'exceptionally, to avert overwhelming humanitarian catastrophe'. The UK claimed to be acting on the basis of this right when it used military force in Kosovo in 1999.[40] No such right was clearly established by State practice. States could give non-discriminatory humanitarian relief, dropping blankets and food parcels to those in need. States had also often acted to protect and rescue their own nationals abroad. But the very limited nature of the threat or use of force in those contexts is better viewed as being primarily a (defensible) infringement on the duty of non-intervention in the internal affairs of other States. Kosovo was different. It envisaged the use of massive military force (over 38,000 sorties were flown during the NATO bombing campaign) in a foreign State for the protection of the citizens of that State. Opinion on the legality of that intervention was divided.[41] Some pointed out that there is no hint of any right of humanitarian intervention in the UN Charter, and urged caution in slackening the constraints upon the unilateral use of force in international relations. Others took the view that if the United Nations was unable to act in the face of outrages such as the 1995 Srebrenica Massacre and the continuing 'ethnic cleansing' in the Balkans, there may come a point where moral imperatives eclipse the lack of any legal foundation for unilateral intervention—a point at which neighbouring States can no longer sit by and watch the calculated slaughter of thousands of civilians, but must act in the name of elementary imperatives of humanity. NATO States took the view that where there is an imminent humanitarian catastrophe which can be averted by the use of force and only by the use of force, and where there has been a prior determination by the Security Council of a grave crisis threatening international peace and security and an articulation by the Council of policies for the resolution of the crisis, States acting collectively through a body such as NATO are justified in intervening with the use of force even in the absence of Security Council authorization. An argument might be made out for the view that the law should leave matters as they are, and tolerate but not condone interventions of this kind, leaving them resting on a moral rather than a legal justification. It might be said that condoning such interventions will only encourage the unilateral use of force. Whatever one thinks of that consequentialist view, it would surely be a grave misunderstanding of the role and function of international law to assert that because the UN Charter gave States no legal

---

[40] See <http://www.kosovo.mod.uk/account/nato.htm> and <http://www.nato.int/kosovo/kosovo.htm>.

[41] See the discussion at 49 *ICLQ* 876–943 (2000).

right to act without United Nations' authorization in the face of a humanitarian catastrophe those States ought to have remained as inactive as the
United Nations itself.

8.7 THE LAW OF ARMED CONFLICT

International law does not forbid the use of armed force. Force may lawfully
be used with United Nations authorization, in self-defence, and perhaps in
exercises of humanitarian intervention. But even when there is an occasion on which force may lawfully be used, the law constrains the degree
and kind of force that may be used. These constraints are the concern of
the Law of Armed Conflict or *jus in bello*. There are two broad categories
of rules. One contains the rules relating to the means and manner of fighting; the other contains the rules relating to the rights and duties of States
which remain neutral and do not themselves participate in the hostilities.

There is a substantial body of detailed rules on the conduct of hostilities.
Such rules have existed for centuries. Prohibitions on the use of certain
weapons appear in the *Laws of Manu*, compiled around 1,800 years ago:
'When he fights with his foes in battle, let him not strike with weapons
concealed (in wood), nor with (such as are) barbed, poisoned, or the points
of which are blazing with fire.'[42] The laws of war were finely developed in the
medieval codes of chivalry.[43] But the modern rules are the product of a succession of codification efforts from the mid nineteenth century onwards,[44]
particularly those inspired by the work of Henry Dunant after he witnessed
the untended suffering of the huge number of casualties of the battle of
Solferino in 1859 and founded what became the International Committee of
the Red Cross. Though not the first,[45] the conventions produced by the
1899 Hague Peace Conference are probably the most important, because
they mark the beginning of attempts to set out a comprehensive, binding set
of rules of universal application in war. They are the lineal ancestors of the
1949 Geneva Conventions on the Laws of War which, together with their
1977 Additional Protocols, form the basis of the modern law of war.

War—armed conflict—has a radical legal effect. Combatants in States'
armed forces may kill and destroy property within the laws of war without

---

[42] Laws of Manu, chapter VII, line 90.
[43] See the studies by Theodor Meron, *Henry's Wars and Shakespeare's Laws* (Oxford:
Clarendon Press, 1993), and *Bloody Constraint: War and Chivalry in Shakespeare* (New York;
Oxford: Oxford University Press, 1998).
[44] See <http://www.yale.edu/lawweb/avalon/lawofwar/lawwar.htm>.
[45] See the 1856 Declaration of Paris, the 1863 Lieber Code, the 1864 Red Cross Convention,
and the 1868 Declaration of St Petersburg, all at <http://www.yale.edu/lawweb/avalon/
lawofwar/lawwar.htm>.

fear of facing trial for murder or criminal damage. That is the privilege that the law of war confers, and one reason why it is so important that in the debate on the so-called wars against terror or against drugs a clear eye is kept on the fact that they are not true wars but simply large-scale campaigns against very serious criminal conduct. Given the licence to kill that war confers, it is natural that the conduct of warfare should be the subject of close regulation. Many of the rules are technical, but most of them are based upon four fundamental principles. First there is the principle of military necessity. This is set out in the British *Manual on the Law of Armed Conflict* in the following terms:

> Military necessity permits a state engaged in an armed conflict to use only that degree and kind of force, not otherwise prohibited by the law of armed conflict, that is required in order to achieve the legitimate purpose of the conflict, namely the complete or partial submission of the enemy at the earliest possible moment with the minimum expenditure of life and resources.[46]

Second, there is the principle of humanity, which 'forbids the infliction of suffering, injury or destruction not actually necessary for the accomplishment of legitimate military objectives'.[47] Third is what is sometimes known as the principle of discrimination. That is to say, the principle that military operations are to be conducted only against the enemy's armed forces and military objectives, and that there must be a clear distinction between armed forces and civilians (between combatants and non-combatants), and between objects that are legitimate targets of attack and objects that are protected from attack.[48] Fourth is the principle of proportionality, which 'requires that losses resulting from a military action should not be excessive in relation to the expected military advantage'.[49] These principles are applicable in all situations of armed conflict.

A good example of their application is the pocket card issued to United States' forces during Operation Desert Storm, in which Iraqi forces were driven out of Kuwait in 1991. The card read as follows:

ALL ENEMY MILITARY PERSONNEL AND VEHICLES TRANSPORTING THE ENEMY OR THEIR SUPPLIES MAY BE ENGAGED SUBJECT TO THE FOLLOWING RESTRICTIONS:

A. Do not engage anyone who has surrendered, is out of battle due to sickness or wounds, is shipwrecked, or is an aircrew member descending by parachute from a disabled aircraft.

---

[46] UK Ministry of Defence, *Manual on the Law of Armed Conflict* (Oxford: Oxford University Press, 2004), paragraph 2.2.

[47] ibid., paragraph 2.4.

[48] ibid., paragraph 2.5.

[49] ibid., paragraph 2.6.

B. Avoid harming civilians unless necessary to save U.S. lives. Do not fire into civilian populated areas or buildings which are not defended or being used for military purposes.

C. Hospitals, churches, shrines, schools, museums, national monuments, and other historical or cultural sites will not be engaged except in self defense.

D. Hospitals will be given special protection. Do not engage hospitals unless the enemy uses the hospital to commit acts harmful to U.S. forces, and then only after giving a warning and allowing a reasonable time to expire before engaging, if the tactical situation permits.

E. Booby traps may be used to protect friendly positions or to impede the progress of enemy forces. They may not be used on civilian personal property. They will be recovered and destroyed when the military necessity for their use no longer exists.

F. Looting and the taking of war trophies are prohibited.

G. Avoid harming civilian property unless necessary to save U.S. lives. Do not attack traditional civilian objects, such as houses, unless they are being used by the enemy for military purposes and neutralization assists in mission accomplishment.

H. Treat all civilians and their property with respect and dignity. Before using privately owned property, check to see if publicly owned property can substitute. No requisitioning of civilian property, including vehicles, without permission of a company level commander and without giving a receipt. If an ordering officer can contract the property, then do not requisition it.

I. Treat all prisoners humanely and with respect and dignity.

J. ROE Annex to the OPLAN provides more detail. Conflicts between this card and the OPLAN should be resolved in favor of the OPLAN.

REMEMBER

1. FIGHT ONLY COMBATANTS.
2. ATTACK ONLY MILITARY TARGETS.
3. SPARE CIVILIAN PERSONS AND OBJECTS.
4. RESTRICT DESTRUCTION TO WHAT YOUR MISSION REQUIRES.[50]

The principles are implemented in much greater detail by the provisions of the four 1949 Geneva Conventions, ((I) on the Sick and Wounded in the Field; (II) on the Wounded, Sick and Shipwrecked at Sea; (III) on Prisoners of War; and (IV) on the Protection of Civilian Persons in Time of War) and their two 1977 Protocols (Protocol I on Victims of International

---

[50] (US) *Operational Law Handbook 2006*, <http://www.fas.org/irp/doddir/army/law0806.pdf>, p. 116. The 'ROE' are the Rules of Engagement and 'OPLAN' is the operational plan. The *Handbook* contains other examples of instructions issued to troops.

Armed Conflicts, and Protocol II on the Protection of Victims of Non-International[51] Armed Conflicts).[52]

The rules on the conduct of hostilities are widely observed as a matter of professional discipline and training. Certainly, States are obliged 'to respect and ensure respect' for the Geneva Conventions, and the inculcation of their principles is (or at least should be) a basic part of the training of all members of the armed forces. Breaches of the laws of war are serious offences, punishable by the soldier's own State, through courts martial or through the civilian courts. Serious breaches fall within the jurisdiction of the International Criminal Court,[53] which could in principle prosecute those offences if national courts of States Parties failed to do so.

The application of the principles and the rules that implement them is not a straightforward matter. The distinction between military and civilian targets is particularly problematic. Tractors may be designed to pull ploughshares, but they can also pull artillery. What if opposing troops set up a mortar emplacement next to, or even in, a school yard or hospital car park? What if opposing troops hide in densely packed civilian residential areas? What if, contrary to the laws of war, those engaged in an armed attack do not distinguish themselves from the civilian population by wearing uniforms, or consciously disguise themselves as civilians? These are not mere legal conundrums. They are practical problems facing members of the armed forces, and the answers are literally matters of life and death for them and for those who might be killed by their weapons. One might, indeed, ask whether the actual effect of the rules of the laws of war is in practice to minimize casualties—the kind of question that criminologists would answer in respect of criminal law; but, perhaps surprisingly, international law does not often engage in such empirical inquiries into its effects.

The treatment of suspected terrorists, in particular, has caused great difficulty. Some have been detained on battlefields in Afghanistan, but then denied the treatment required under the Geneva Conventions for prisoners of war. The detention of a large but unknown number of them by the United States in Guantanamo Bay has been a source of much criticism of the United States. There is some force in the observation that the Geneva Convention provisions on prisoners of war were aimed at regular uniformed troops, and not at fighters who are indistinguishable (at least to

---

[51] i.e., internal, civil wars.

[52] The texts are published at <http://www.icrc.org/eng>.

[53] And the International Criminal Tribunals for the Former Yugoslavia (ICTY) and for Rwanda (ICTR). For the ICC see <http://www.icc-cpi.int/home.html&l=en>.

western forces) from the civilian population. The classification by the United States of many of the detainees as 'unlawful combatants' tends to lead to them being denied both the rights of prisoners of war and also the rights of people detained under the criminal law. While most analysts accept that such fighters cannot be treated simply as regular combatants or as criminals, there is equally no doubt that, as human beings, they are entitled to a certain minimum level of treatment. Most lawyers take the view that rights set out in Article 75 of Additional Protocol I represent the irreducible minimum of rights that 'unlawful combatants' must be granted. Indeed, Article 75 says that its provisions apply to all persons 'who are in the power of a Party to a conflict and who do not benefit from more favourable treatment'. Those rights include freedom from murder, torture, outrages upon personal dignity, and collective punishment, as well as basic due process rights. It is sometimes said that the 1949 Geneva Conventions are outdated and cannot accommodate the harsh realities of the modern world. But before they are abandoned it is well to recall that they were drafted by men and women who knew very well—better than most modern politicians—what the harsh realities of war truly are.

The Geneva Conventions are by no means the only agreements relevant to the laws of war. There are treaties regulating the weapons that may be used: for example, the 1980 UN Convention on Conventional Weapons, which has protocols dealing with weapons which cause injury by fragments not detectable by x-ray, on mines and booby trap devices, on incendiary weapons, on blinding laser weapons, and on the removal of explosive remnants of war—the last addressing the grave problem of cluster bombs and other explosive devices which are left in war zones and continue to cause injury and death for many years after the cessation of hostilities.

Other treaties deal with biological and chemical weapons, nuclear weapons, and anti-personnel mines. There are, too, treaties that deal with the manner in which warfare is conducted. One, adopted in 1954, seeks to protect cultural property in the event of armed conflict.[54] Though widely ratified it appears to have been poorly applied during the 2003 invasion of Iraq. Another treaty prohibits environmental modification as a weapon of war.[55] Nuclear weapons have attracted particularly extensive regulation, relating to all stages of their production, testing, and deployment. The possession and use of nuclear material is overseen by the International

---

[54] The 1954 Hague Convention for the Protection of Cultural Property in the Event of Armed Conflict, published at <http://www.icomos.org/hague/>.
[55] The 1976 UN Convention on the Prohibition of Military or Any Other Hostile Use of Environmental Modification.

Atomic Energy Authority,[56] whose inspectors monitor national programmes to ensure that material is not diverted from civil nuclear energy programmes to military uses and thus supervise crucial aspects of the 1968 Non-Proliferation Treaty (NPT).[57] With its 188 States Parties the NPT is the most widely ratified of all disarmament treaties. In addition, there are treaties that have sought to diminish the risk of conflict by limiting the quantity of arms held by States—an approach that enjoyed much favour and little success in the early part of the twentieth century. The Strategic Arms Limitation Treaties, and the treaty on Conventional Armed Forces in Europe are among the best known examples.

The second body of rules of the Laws of War concern neutrality. In the past, States that have remained neutral in armed conflicts have benefited from certain rights, notably the right not to be targeted by the belligerents. In return neutrals were obliged to observe strict impartiality as regards the belligerents, and not to allow the use of their territory as bases for the commission of belligerent acts. The status of neutrals made sense at a time when States were legally entitled to resort to war, but it is doubtful how far they remain valid. If force may only be used lawfully with UN authorization, or in self-defence, and perhaps to avert humanitarian catastrophes, many would argue that there is no room for neutrality. Third States must follow the directions of the United Nations, or side with the State defending itself against aggression, or (surely) assist or at least not obstruct States taking humanitarian action. Nonetheless, States have in practice asserted their impartiality in respect of armed conflicts. The United Kingdom and United States, for example, claimed to be impartial during the Iran–Iraq war in the 1980s (although they seemed to give considerable assistance to Iraq and very little to Iran). Neutrality is perhaps not quite dead. It is thought that at least the basic principles of neutrality survive: neutral States must not allow their territory to be used by belligerents, and if they comply with that principle they must not be targeted by belligerents.[58]

8.8 WAR AND CRIME

Before leaving this topic, which I have surveyed in only the broadest of terms, there are two further points to be made.

The first is that we should be slow to abandon or blur the distinction between crime and war. In practice, that distinction is one that may have to

---

[56] <http://www.iaea.org/>

[57] <http://www.un.org/events/npt2005/npttreaty.html>.

[58] See UK Ministry of Defence, *Manual on the Law of Armed Conflict* (Oxford: Oxford University Press, 2004), paragraphs 1.42–1.43.

be drawn consciously and carefully, because it will not be evident from the facts. The invasion of one State by another is clearly a war; but internal conflicts usually start with protests and civil disobedience, rising to a scale of civil disorder and often involving acts characterized as 'terrorist', and then developing into a full-blown civil war. In the early stages third States are free to assist the legitimate government in suppressing the disorder. (Assisting the revolutionaries would amount to unlawful interference in the internal affairs of the State, as the International Court held in the *Nicaragua* case.)[59] But there comes a point, marked in traditional international law by the recognition of the revolutionaries as belligerents, at which third States were obliged to remain neutral in the conflict or to go to war alongside one or other party. The legal position is much less clear these days, partly as a result of the fact that the formation of policy in relation to such conflicts frequently rests with international or regional organizations, so that States consider that they have greater latitude to intervene because they are acting on behalf of the international community rather than purely unilaterally. But civil wars are armed conflicts, and the use of force in them is regulated by international law. The principles of the laws of war apply to them, albeit in modified form: that is the particular point of Additional Protocol II to the Geneva Conventions, which builds upon Article 3 common to the four 1949 Geneva Conventions and sets out the basic principles of humanitarian law applicable in non-international armed conflicts.[60]

From the internal viewpoint war and crime are even more starkly different conditions, and the shift from one to the other transforms the most basic social relations. In wartime, enemies are shot on sight, with impunity. They lose legal rights. Discrimination against them is not merely lawful but in many respects obligatory. Third States may be entitled to stand aside from the conflict and maintain their neutrality or impartiality in respect of it. In crime, on the other hand, even criminals are presumed innocent, and are entitled to a fair trial and to basic human rights. They retain their basic human rights, even in prison. And the rest of the world is expected to assist in the fight against crime and not remain neutral as between the criminal and the police. Blurring the distinction between crime and war carries a serious risk of transposing the cold harshness of wartime discrimination against The Enemy into everyday life; and that seems to some of us a path to social disaster.

---

[59] *ICJ Reports 1986*, p. 14.
[60] See also the decision of the ICTY in the *Tadić* case, *Prosecutor v Tadić (Jurisdiction)* (1995) 105 *ILR* 419, <http://www.un.org/icty/tadic/trialc2/decision-e/100895.htm> for a masterly survey of this area of international law.

The second point is that the international law on the use of force should not be seen in isolation. It is one body of rules among many which regulate relations between States. The avoidance of armed conflict between States is a goal in which the provisions of international economic law, human rights law, and many other areas of international co-operation, and the pragmatic political activity of the United Nations and regional international organizations, are every bit as important as the Laws of War.

9

Postscript

There is a tendency at present for international lawyers to write of the growth of NGOs and other non-State actors, and of the decline of the nation-State, with the gleeful enthusiasm of a cartoon character sawing off the tree branch on which he is sitting. Much of the enthusiasm derives, I suspect, from a wish to appropriate non-State actors and make them a part of international law, to keep the subject at the front of international concerns. My own view is slightly different.

It is undeniable that the influence of the individual nation-State is declining. Global interdependence is increasingly pervasive and obvious as improved communications and the lessening of trade barriers encourages businesses to obtain supplies, employees, and funds abroad. Transfers of powers to international and supranational organizations such as NAFTA, the WTO, and the EU entail a corresponding reduction in the powers of national governments. Within States, pressures for decentralization and the devolution of power also drain power from the central government. And decisions taken by large corporations have direct effects upon the daily lives of countless millions of people that are as important in their way as the taxes and legislation that emanate from their respective governments. It seems plain that the power of the State is in decline when it is measured in relation to the increasing power of other actors. The result, however, is not so much an expansion in the scope of international law so as to claim all these other actors as its own, but rather that the boundaries between international law and neighbouring legal subjects are breaking down. International lawyers share ground with others. And this trend will continue. But the most important point is that all of the ground occupied by international law is shared with others who are not lawyers of any description, but men and women in the vast range of other professions and businesses whose cumulative efforts shape the world. Lawyers have a contribution to make. They offer one way of going about resolving some of the most crucial problems that face the world. But it is only one way among many. There are many times when it is much better to call upon a politician, or a priest, or a doctor, or a plumber.

Index